THE SILK ROAD AND BEYOND

Narratives of
a Muslim Historian

THE SILK ROAD AND BEYOND

Narratives of
a Muslim Historian

IFTIKHAR H. MALIK

OXFORD
UNIVERSITY PRESS

OXFORD
UNIVERSITY PRESS

Oxford University Press is a department of the University of Oxford.
It furthers the University's objective of excellence in research, scholarship,
and education by publishing worldwide. Oxford is a registered trade mark of
Oxford University Press in the UK and in certain other countries

Published in Pakistan by
Oxford University Press
No. 38, Sector 15, Korangi Industrial Area,
PO Box 8214, Karachi-74900, Pakistan

ISBN 978-0-19-940596-1

Typeset in Adobe Garamond Pro
Printed on 80gsm Offset Paper

Printed by Mas Printers, Karachi

Acknowledgement
Cover image: Mir-i-Arab Madrasah (Miri Arab Madrasah) in Bukhara, Uzbekistan
© Andrii Lutsyk/Shutterstock

Contents

III   NESTLING IN THE WEST

Acknowledgements

Very much like the places of heritage visited and experienced in this volume, there are several friends and colleagues who deserve my gratitude for their hospitality, guidance, and a great mark of endurance in putting up with my endless queries. My youthful years in the United States spent in East Lansing, Skidmore, New York, and Berkeley, were preceded and followed by studying and teaching in Pakistan. The warmth of my teachers, class-fellows, and students helped me all through those decades of 'growing up'. Harold Marcus, Victor Howard, Thomas Hooker, Gordon Duff, Monica King, Donna Ellis, Douglass Miller, Surjit Singh Dulai, Fawzi Najjar, Ainslee Embree, and Thomas Metcalfe proved eminent torchbearers, whereas friends such as Rafique Afzal, Mukhtar Shah, Kabir Malik, and Masud Qaim never forsook their eccentric humour even during the dark days of General Zia's regressive regime. In Oxford, colleagues, libraries, and the common rooms at St. Antony's College, Wolfson College, and the Union helped me discover a wider and even more complex world of academia and ideas, while Bath Spa University kept me journeying for a quarter of century. In-between, exposure to the Silk Road and the other parts of a wider Islamicate and beyond continued to enrich my sensibilities, whereas days at the British Library and walks under the autumn trees in Bloomsbury kept an inquisitive spirit undeterred. I do miss the old Indian Institute Library in Oxford but have tried to compensate it by snoozing and musing in the History Faculty Library and at the Oriental Institute. Nick Allen, Tapan Raychaudhuri, Jim Hollifield, Elaine Chalus, and my colleagues and students at Bath Spa University: you all have been sources of enjoyment as well as enlightenment for this wandering historian. However, in most cases, it was the Union Society with its multiple libraries, unending debates, and certainly countless coffee sessions that kept reinvigorating my veins besides causing some naughty ideas which often took poetic forms. Friends in Konya, Tashkent, Samarkand, Lahore, Isfahan, Jerusalem, Bath, Helsinki, Tuscany, Sarajevo, Mostar, Pisa, London, Fes, Granada, Brussels, Islamabad, Patras, and Aligarh stood me in good stead every time I ventured to these places, and certainly it was owing to the respective history of the place and warmth of its people that I discovered Bukhara as the Muslim Oxbridge and Thessaloniki, a centrefold of Ottoman multiculturalism.

This volume took years and several incarnations to assume its present shape without becoming a familiar scholarly tome yet not losing its historical and academic underpinnings. Simultaneously, I did not wish to turn it into a how-to-do type of travel account. To what extent have I succeeded in staying on course between the above two strands is now left to my readers. However, words cannot suffice Nighat's support and encouragement though Imaan kept reminding me of the books in my study long waiting to be read. The keen interest shown by OUP Pakistan in publishing this work is owed to their commitment towards knowledge, quality debate, and printed word. Ghousia Ali's support remains unfailing and it has been joyous to work with her again on this volume. The two anonymous readers for Oxford University Press were generously comprehensive and constructive in their feedback that guided me to revise several portions of the manuscript more minutely before it took the present shape. However, the errors of judgment and of any technical types are my own and cannot be attributed to my referees and the Oxford University Press. I owe my sincere appreciation to them and in particular to Soha Khan and Fiza Kazmi in Karachi for their professional alacrity and help. Certainly, this account divided into three sections, often reverts to the author—which may be occasionally cumbersome—but I hope that by overlooking this lacunae, my readers will appreciate the intentions and efforts behind the entire work.

Oxford
November 23, 2019

Introduction[1]

Most studies on Muslims and Islam including those by Muslim authors tend to focus on geo-political conflicts, ethno-sectarian violence, civilizational contestations, gender imbalances, and identity issues in diaspora. Vital areas such as cultural and historical vitalities of the mainstream societies tend to remain absent from securitized, censorial, and state-centred accounts unless there is a need for some kind of statistical evidence to substantiate any given argument. Generally, Muslim youth in such narratives is posited as perpetrators, whereas Muslim women are caricatured as eternal victims whose own religiosity mingled with patriarchy may account for their disempowerment. Consequently, amidst a reenergized 'othering' of Muslims through discretionary discourses, many young Muslims have started to feel sceptical of their heritage, cultures, and communities, or in some cases, they may even turn towards an exclusive and even aggressive self-identification. A grave sense of indifference, apologia, and sheer antagonism underpins this cynicism which concurrently feeds into a pernicious form of individual introversion. It is no coincidence that numerous Muslims, especially in diaspora, complain about a pervasive exceptionalization that disconnects them from their own roots along with disallowing wider mutualities with the rest. Amidst this wider malaise, there is surely a need for a multidirectional 'reconnect' that literature, arts, and travel may engender by inducting a historical consciousness which goes a long way towards self-empowerment besides building bridges across multiple divides.

Historically and sociologically like the Silk Road before and since the arrival of Islam in Central Asia and Europe, Muslims and the rest should be ideally interconnected through historical trajectories where their religion, narratives, cultures, and heritage may work as enablers. Here and elsewhere in the Near East and North Africa, civic norms, hospitable values, and material cultures reflected through seminaries, tombs, Sufi shrines, gardens, recreational hubs, and literary edifices can surely help spawn this needed historical consciousness. These are the formidable pillar posts of traditional civil societies that anchored the communities through their adverse times. Going beyond scholarly works and reports by think tanks, often focusing on threat perceptions and tunnel views of Muslim groups, literary works, autobiographies, travel accounts, and culturelogues hold potential for reaching out to larger sections allowing greater participation.

Spanning over a period of more than four decades, my own travelling, teaching, and research experience across the continents has allowed me a learning curve where other than mundane adversities, I chanced to experience human excellence and spontaneity over and above all too familiar divides. These reinvigorating stories abound and have definitely enriched my own personal perceptions. For instance, in a farther corner of a traditional Pakistan, a woman undertakes to educate girls by pioneering a school where a matriarch and the mother of a national hero offers her moral support. Bridging over the division of 1947, a traditional hakim trained in Old Delhi carries on with his medical practice as a Unani physician. A literary meeting in London on Khwaja Shams-ud-Din Muhammad Hafiz Shirazi turns into an important intercultural session, whereas discussing history with the Tatar elders in Helsinki powerfully refutes some presumed Muslim unwillingness to integrate with the rest. A Moroccan family mistakes a South Asian academic for a fellow Berber outside Fes, whereas standing shoulder to shoulder with the descendants of the Moors in the Al-Karaouine University proves as uplifting as the meeting with an Urdu-speaking Uzbek outside Tamerlane's Tomb in Samarkand. Of course, Cordova, Seville, and Granada transmit powerful vibes connecting one with the once plural and equally vibrant Andalusia as do the converted mosques and seminaries in older Palermo or Thessaloniki. However, the bazaars in Isfahan and the vibrancy of Safavid architecture in that *Nisf Jahan* induce a deeper immersion in yesterday's Persianate, or what Shahab Ahmad called Bosnia to Bengal paradigm.[2] In a humorous vein, remembering Harold Marcus, a former teacher at my alma mater, brings back the memories of an open, kind, and sharp intellect, as do the reflections in Bukhara, once a preeminent city for the world's Muslims and a major destination on the Silk Road.

Its Minar-e-Kalyan amused Genghis Khan and survived that all too total destruction which descended upon Merv, Samarkand, Balkh, Baghdad, and so many other bright centres of Muslim learning and trade.

This historical sojourn allows an encounter with the Bukharan Jews, whose immersion in their rich past traditions amidst an overwhelming Muslim society points towards another reality in Khwarazm that gave us Imam Bukhari, Ibn Sina, Roudaki, Al-Biruni, Khwarizmi, Firdausi, and many other illustrious men of learning and wisdom. No wonder Bukhara was once the Oxbridge of the Muslim world, even if Ibn Battuta is not too enamoured of it; the Tangerine went there three centuries after its devastation. Imam Bukhari, as the name denotes, compiled the most authentic collection of Hadith (the Prophetic sayings), whose research was carried on by Imam Muslim, his student from Nishapur. Roudaki is officially viewed as the pioneer poet in Persian, whereas Firdausi became the chronicler of a glorious Persia through his masterpiece, *Shahnama*. Ibn Sina, a Bukharan and the disciple of al-Farabi, one of the earliest Muslim philosophers (originally from present-day Kazakhstan) is seen to be the most eminent Platonist and physician of an era which resounds as the Golden Age of Islam. His colleague and another Bukharan, Al-Biruni, wrote the pioneering sociological study of Hinduism and India, whereas a few generations later, Mir Alisher Navoi is officially acknowledged as the pioneer classicist of Chaghtai Turkish. This was the time and region that pioneered a 'forgotten Enlightenment' that Tamerlane and especially his grandson, Ulugh Beg, tried to revive in their own distinct ways. It was Beg who built the largest-ever telescope in Samarkand besides opening residential schools in Samarkand and Bukhara where the scholar-king himself taught philosophy and astronomy. Queen Gawhar Shad, his mother, like Fatima al-Fihri of Karaouine, became the first-ever woman to open schools for Central Asian girls which made Herat into a metropolitan city of seminaries, orphanages, and mosques.

Samarkand had amazed Alexander with its majesty and cultural vitality owing to its location in the heart of Sogdiana and for having taken over the trade and intellectual exchanges across the Silk Road. One of the cousins of the Prophet (PBUH) is buried here whose tomb survived the Mongol onslaught and remained the focal point for some of the most magnificent Muslim tombs. No wonder Shah-i-Zinda is one of the most historic and equally enduring necropolises in whose proximity lies one of the largest and oldest Jewish cemeteries. Bibi-Khanym Mosque and mausoleum in Samarkand, built in early Timurid style, foreran the three magnificent seminaries in the Registan Square, which over the past several centuries have been the prime symbols of Timurid architecture. In the same league of a graceful historicity are the Ulugh Beg Observatory and the Hazrat Khizr Mosque in that part of Samarkand that take us back to a time when this successor to Alexander's Marakanda and a hub on the Silk Road led the rest in Asia and beyond. In the ruins of old Marakanda, and not far from the Ulugh Beg Observatory and a Jewish cemetery, sits the 14-metre-long grave of Prophet Daniel, which has been visited by pilgrims, traders, travellers, and Sufis for a very long time including the atheist phase under the Soviets.

Tamerlane was in a hurry to build Samarkand as the new Merv, and perhaps the most splendid city on earth, and carried his dream with him while fighting the Chinese further east. Instead of his own town, Shakhrisabz, he was buried in Samarkand, neighboured by his sons, Sufi mentors, and Ulugh Beg. Any visit to this Silk Road city is incomplete without visiting the Amir's tomb as it is incomplete without appreciating the architecture of three grand madrassas in the Registan Square, Shah-i-Zinda, and Bibi-Khanym Mosque. Since 1991, there has been a vigorously renewed interest in Tamerlane as the father figure of this Silk Road nation as he sleeps in his impressive mausoleum with all kinds of stories about his exploits, physical prowess, and relations with the other regions in the empire. Alisher Navoi, Uzbekistan's poet laureate, was senior to Emperor Zahir Uddin Muhammad Babur by a generation; he took classical Turkish to its greatest height and is seen as its Chaucer. He opened schools and serais while patronizing literati, a tradition that was carried on by Tamerlane's daughter-in-law, Gawhar Shad, who made Herat into another Bukhara, Fes, or even Samarkand. Babur came from Fergana Valley and took pride in being Tamerlane's grandson; eventually this displaced prince and eloquent writer became the founder of the Mughal Empire in India. His foray into India took him on the same route that Al-Biruni had undertaken during the time of Mahmud of Ghazni. Babur, not too fond of India and its inhabitants, appreciated the beauty of the Salt Range—there stands a rock named after him at Kallar Kahar, about 15 miles from this author's birthplace.[3] Further down from Babur's hamlet are the ruins of the village that was visited by Alexander and was home to Pir Kattas, one of the ancient Hindu temples in the Indus regions.

As we know, all the three Abrahamic religions along with Zoroastrianism, Hinduism, and Buddhism travelled further 'East' on the Silk Road before they spread elsewhere and thus connected cities like Jerusalem, Damascus, Aleppo, Konya, Merv, Nishapur, Rey, Isfahan, Bukhara, Samarkand, Balkh, Herat, Taxila, Kashghar, Dunhuang, and Xian. Even today, Bukhara is a gem of a city, brimming with more than 350 historical monuments in its older parts and it is no wonder that it nourished scholars like Bukhari, Biruni, Avicenna, and Khwarizmi besides being the centre of Islamic mysticism. A city that outlived Merv, Balkh, and Nishapur surely owes much to its own literary, spiritual, and innovative attributes. In the same vein, Jerusalem's own tested histories and conflicts are rooted in that 'city upon hills' and are lived by its citizens who, in many cases, may be the descendants of Sufis, pilgrims, warriors, and traders from across the continents. East Jerusalem in particular is a journey through a rich but no less troubled history. Here Al-Aqsa Mosque and the Dome of Rock (Al-Quddus) sit next to the Western Wall while Caliph Omar's mosque faces the Sepulchre Church whose keys are maintained by a Muslim family since the Ottoman era. In between are the Roman arches, Christian monasteries, Jewish hospices, and numerous Sufi *Zawiyas*[4] including that of the thirteenth century Indian Sufi, Baba Fariduddin Ganjshakar, who spent 40 days in meditation here after the city was recaptured by Saladin from the Crusaders.[5] West Jerusalem, once the abode of affluent Arabs, looks less Middle Eastern and resembles an affluent Mediterranean suburb but has its own small historic corners reincarnated by Israelis as museums or parks.

While Jerusalem may leave a visitor with a lived experience of contested histories, Isfahan is a tribute to the great Safavid ambitions and efforts to create the most splendid city of its type. A visit even today takes one to that era of Persia's second glorious phase. More like Bukhara and also resembling Jerusalem, Samarkand, Lahore, and Fes, Isfahan is a gem where, in its covered bazaar, gardens, mosques, madrassas, and bridges, history seems to have come to a standstill. Further west, Konya is soothing and spiritually uplifting where some older seminaries built by the Seljuks remind one of Bukhara, Samarkand, and Khiva. The city of Shams and Rumi is a metropolis of historical eminence where

Seljuks, like the past Greek monarchs, built their capital and added to its munificence by making it into a city of learning. Closer to the terminus of the Silk Road, Aleppo, and Eastern Mediterranean, Konya was a prosperous metropolis and despite ravages by the Mongols and Crusaders never forsook its dynamism. A city of whirling dervishes and with a powerful spiritual aura, it also hosts the largest Turkish university, besides featuring well-planned boulevards overshadowed by millions of trees. Its mixed topography becomes further distinct due to its proximity with Cappadocia where once elaborate cave dwellings flourished during the Roman era. But of course Rumi remains the symbol of Muslim mysticism, classical Persian poetry, and is an embodiment of what is known as the Muslim Golden Age in arts and scholarship.[6] The piece on Rumi tracing his life all the way from Balkh, the Silk Road city, to this part of Anatolia and his total transformation owing to his encounter with Shams Tabrizi is meant to locate this splendid aspect of Persianate. Morocco may be a choicest destination for millions of tourists but its historic vitality, cultural diversity, and most of all cities such as Fes, Sale, and Kasbah retain a full-bodied medieval ambience that goes on without being disturbed by tourists, traders, and hikers across the Atlas lands. Home to the world's oldest university and an abode of Sufis, Fes is uniquely the largest living medieval metropolis in a country that amongst others produced Ibn Battuta, a traveller and chronicler of distant lands and cultures but no less an eminent Sufi himself. No wonder Tangier kept attracting pirates, artists, and painters, often not too enamoured with their own places of birth. Rabat and its old necropolis, Kasbah, and a slightly subdued Sale, alert a keen observer to a vibrant and transcultural heritage in Maghreb.

This book is an effort to capture history, literature, mobility, crafts, architectural traditions, and cultural vistas by focusing on diverse Muslim individuals, communities, cities, and their edifices. It also attempts to reconstruct deeper and munificent aspects of Muslim histories and lived experiences that either stay ignored by the writers and travellers or are bundled out as crowded, densely populated, and unsafe no-go areas. In some cases, some of these cities are routinely and lifelessly defined as tourist destinations where mechanical details deprive a reader of their cultural and historical richness. Written in an autobiographical genre, the volume aims at initiating readers of diverse interests into

encountering vibrant lives across the four continents where cultures
share commonalities beyond the narrowly defined premise of conflicts.
Experienced by a curious Muslim academic at different stages of his
life, these predominantly Muslim locales, along with frequent exposure
to representative Western sociocultural institutions, should help us see
and relish.

Notes

1. Each city, country, or continent mentioned in this narrative is endowed with an
   ever-increasing historiography of multidisciplinary composition. The present
   book is neither a world history nor a macro history of the Muslim world; instead
   it offers a personal journey across places and times, though certainly with an
   urban bias. Excluding some early chapters, the rest occasionally feature a few
   references, though from amongst a host of historical and critical works, one
   may highlight a few titles. The titles include: Tamim Ansary, *Destiny Disrupted:
   A History of the World through Islamic Eyes* (New York: Public Affairs, 2010); Ali
   A. Allawi, *The Crisis of Islamic Civilization* (New Haven: Yale University Press,
   2009); Reza Aslan, *No God, But God: The Origins, Evolution and the Future of
   Islam* (London: Arrow, 2011); Malise Ruthven, *Islam: A Very Short Introduction*
   (Oxford: Oxford University Press, 2012); James A. Millward, *The Silk Road: A
   Very Short Introduction* (Oxford: Oxford University Press, 2013); Rana Kabbani,
   Imperial Fictions: Europe's Myths of Orient (London: Saqi, 2008); and Timothy
   Mackintosh-Smith, *The Travels of Ibn Battutah* (London: Picador, 2003).
2. Shahab Ahmed, *What is Islam? The Importance of Being Islamic* (Princeton:
   Princeton University Press, 2015).
3. Zahir-ud-Din Muhammed Babur [Padshah Ghazi], *Tuzk-e-Baburi* or *Baburnama:
   A Memoir*, trans. Annette Susannah Beveridge (New Delhi: Rupa Publications,
   2017).
4. A house of mystics.
5. D. S. Adamson, 'Jerusalem's 800-year-old Indian hospice,' *BBC Magazine*,
   November 23, 2014.
6. Rozina Ali, 'The Erasure of Islam from Rumi's Poetry,' *The New Yorker*, January 5,
   2017.

I
MEMOIRS

1

Educating Girls in
Air Marshal Nur Khan's Town

I read about the demise of Malik Nur Khan on the day my better half
and our son were visiting his hometown, Tamman, along with my elder
sister, Bilqis Begum, to offer condolences to his sister and the family. Nur
Khan, also known as Air Marshal Sahib, was a hero in a country which
evolved in his youth, and has been destined to experience traumatic jolts
of varying and tantalizing nature. He was a role model in a land often
attached to a vibrant past, a confused present, and an unsure future.
Amongst a group of people with a strong bent of mind for idealizing
men of conquering nature, especially the kind that were transparent,
honest, and lead from the front, individuals like Nur Khan will never
have a shortage of followers. At the age of 88, Khan passed away on
December 15, 2011, and as per his will, was buried in his ancestral
Tamman, not far from his mother's resting place. A man of international
fame, a brave fighter, a competent commander, and a chief who inspired
love and adulation and not awe, Khan always desired better educational
facilities for the youth of his country. In addition, he pioneered Pakistan's
resplendent traditions in cricket, field hockey, and squash. The second
Commander-in-Chief of his country's young air force, he modernized its
fleet, professional capabilities, and technical facilities to the extent that it
triumphantly rose to the challenge by its much bigger counterpart from
across the border and defended the country in the Indo-Pakistani War of
1965. By the time the war ended, Pakistan had added to a pantheon of
its heroes, with Nur Khan commanding the highest pedestal. No wonder
when he passed away, the nation found itself both grieving and deeply
indebted to a man of honour, courage, and professional acumen.

Even before I met Bibi Sarwar Bano as a very young person almost half a century ago, I had conjured up the idea of a dynamic woman—more like my maternal grandmother—bubbling her hookah and issuing directions to a retinue of servants besides ensuring proper hospitality to an educated young visitor. That visitor happened to be my elder sister who had pioneered a school in this far-flung area of north-western Punjab, not too distant from the eastern bank of the old Indus. An arid landmass around Tamman represented the typical Potwar Plateau which came alive with mustard, shisham, and acacia blossoms during spring, while its dry ravines bubbled with water following monsoon showers. Most of the lands were owned by a few families who were referred to as Sardars—not as authoritarian as their counterparts in Sindh or Balochistan—who held their own local influence. Many of them had served during the great wars and had been ensured more land grants in canal colonies and thus held their heads with great pride over their horses, hounds, and falcons, and their descent from their Awan roots. More like late medieval aristocrats, they were an island of benevolence and conservatism that, following the formation of Pakistan and profusion of education, faced newer and more formidable challenges. Both lineage and land were crucial to them. They were believed to be the Perso-Arab descendants of the early Muslim conquerors of Hindustan whose ancestors had accompanied fortune seekers such as Mahmud of Ghazni (971–1030), Shahabuddin Ghauri (1149–1206), and Qutb-ud-din Aibak (1150–1210). They were not totally illiterate, uncouth, or repressive clusters since they often prided themselves on having inherited the literary traditions of Al-Biruni (973–1048) and other such medieval luminaries who had come along with the Turkic-Afghan adventurers in their escapades in upper India. A few of these Maliks sought fraternity with Tipu Sultan of Mysore who had put up strong resistance to the East India Company and was killed fighting in 1799. The stories of fighting the Austrians and Germans during the First World War had further added to their oral narratives, though they all continued to call themselves Qutb Shahi Awans, literally translating to the descendants of Qutb Shah, who was one of the generals in Mahmud's army and had settled on this side of the Indus along the Salt Range. As a consequence, the region came to be known as Awankari, with lands being parcelled off amongst clans over subsequent centuries until the British came up with the idea of martial races and began enlisting younger

Awans into their armed forces. Many of them were the veterans of wars in North Africa, Europe, Burma, Japan, and Malaysia, and often talked of their heroics with all kinds of nationalities thousands of miles away from their native Punjab.

Nur Khan was born in 1923 and his father, a retired captain from the British Indian Army, sent him off to Aitchison College in Lahore which was meant for the sons of chieftains, training them in academia and sports like horse riding and cricket. It was also known as the Chief's College, and unlike its older counterparts such as Foreman Christian College and Government College, Lahore, it was surely more elitist in a feudal sense. After his father's death, Khan's mother ran the household and lands, taking the role of a traditional matriarch; without shunning her chador, she ensured that her presence and discretion were felt far and wide. Bibi Sarwar Bano was not only the widow of an influential Malik, her authority and clout also stemmed from her being a scion of the Kalabagh family. Kalabagh, a princely state straddling the Indus at the northern end of the Salt Range, was a feudal estate personally owned by Nawab Amir Muhammad Khan, an Aitchison College graduate and subsequently the almighty Governor of West Pakistan under General Ayub Khan. He controlled this part of the country (present-day Pakistan) like his personal fiefdom, and the elite bureaucracy—especially the police—all stood beholden to this moustachioed man whose towering personality itself denoted aura as well as awe. In addition to regular police, his knowledge of and contacts with the rural 'influentials' allowed him to run the country through a parallel network of spies, tough men, and local lords. Amir Muhammad Khan, also known as the Nawab of Kalabagh, was certainly an age unto himself, and even Ayub Khan, Zulfikar Ali Bhutto, and other urban politicians and technocrats stood in awe of him. His personality and office not only allowed him a claim on the leadership of the Awan clans, but also bestowed a unique aura to Bibi Sarwar Bano. After all, he linked his roots to Qutb Shah, whose descendants had held on to this estate, *jagir*, for the past 900 years without being conquered by anyone. It is a different matter that eventually he met the tragic end of being murdered by his own son.

My elder sister, Bilqis, deeply valued women's education in this rural hinterland, given the fact that she herself had bravely confronted several taboos all through her school and tertiary years. Our parents were not cowed down by a social critique that abhorred women's education more than six decades back, and instead had ensured proper education for all their children, especially all five daughters. They became teachers, nurses, and health visitors at a time when for girls even going beyond primary education was viewed as being immodest by many in the extended kinship. After all, they had to be married off, and an educated maiden could put a possible suitor on the defensive. Female education as a means of earning was even more frowned upon because only men were supposed to be the breadwinners. Any earning woman was anathema to her parents and kinship during that time, and Bilqis, like her sisters, had withstood all the chagrin. She not only completed her education but also enviably stood first in her higher secondary examination across the four big districts of the Rawalpindi division, earning her special prizes and a stipend to pursue a teachers training degree near Lahore. Tamman was her second appointment as a freshly trained teacher and she knew that hers was an uphill challenge since the local influentials, the landed groups, as well as the clerics, were inherently against female education. Their resistance was rooted both in ignorance and self-interest as uneducated girls from poorer families provided almost free domestic labour in the houses of the landed families, whereas clerics saw in women's education a retort to their view of pristine Islamic traditions. In addition, many of them feared that their own madrassas would lose all these girls to this new primary school and lower their own clout and social esteem amongst a largely uneducated populace in this large village; incidentally, this village was served by only two buses per day from our own hometown. Many people in Tamman worked as tenants on lands owned by local landlords, while a few younger men toyed with the idea of joining the armed forces; the trend subsequently caught up with the outbreak of the Indo-Pakistan War of 1965.

Other than traditional Maliks including Nur Khan's family, another notable dweller of Tamman was Malik Muhammad Hayat Khan, who had earned a degree from the Aligarh Muslim University and spent most of his time in Lahore, serving as a cabinet minister in almost every regime. His huge house was located between a graveyard and the boys' school on the main unmetalled road that connected Tamman with Talagang and the rest of Pakistan. The same road further went up to Makhad, a town by the Indus known for a Sufi shrine then commandeered by Pir Safiud Din, an enigmatic and pampered soul. During the monsoon months, the buses could not ply on this road due to mud and also because the stream flowing by the village and the Soan River further up near Makhad would swell up. Needless to say, Muhammad Hayat Khan was acutely against women's education, though his own sons studied at Aitchison College, besides occasional coaching from my uncle, Malik Nur Muhammad, who had been teaching in Tamman for over 40 years. Hayat's wife was sympathetic towards women's education and her daughter spent some time with my sister even though her father was stubbornly against female education in Tamman, and ironically enough, did not encourage any development scheme in his native area. The road remained unmetalled; the stream went unbridged, and not a single industry or commercial project came this way despite the various schemes launched by the military regime in Pakistan. Hayat was an extremely reactionary person, more like those shrine-based spiritual demigods and big feudalists of the lower Indus Valley despite the fact that the nameplate next to his mansion's entrance announced his Bachelor of Law degree from the Aligarh Muslim University. In the afternoon, he, like his less influential Malik counterparts, held a kind of session where his tenants offered hookah to his 'courtiers' and the small talk went on until late.

Unlike Hayat, Bibi Sarwar Bano lived in the oldest part of Tamman and her house embodied a uniquely traditional and graceful architecture with its 200-year-old wooden ornate ceilings and specific cellars for storing grain. This must have been the oldest surviving neighbourhood where she commanded her authority over tenants and servants while ensuring a proper modern education for her son, Nur Khan, whose father had been long dead, leaving home and lands into the good care of his dynamic widow. Bano was ensured full respect and security by her more powerful brother, Amir Muhammad Khan, the moustachioed scion of Awan clan and de facto ruler of West Pakistan. My sister's several visits and helpful words from Uncle Nur Muhammad were successful in dissuading the Sardarni from discouraging women in her fold from attending the newly-opened school. Her support soon proved decisive as a few girls from the Malik families, always chaperoned by a train of female servants, began to venture into the school. These girls, belonging to varying age groups, often came from well-established families and were smart and confident and, unlike their less privileged counterparts, they showed keen interest in academia. These Malkanis, walking down the village lanes, encircled by older maidservants, attracted curious looks from men. There was no dearth of opposition from certain sections towards this innovation, and my sister's own credentials as a responsible and devoted teacher, in addition to the great esteem for Malik Nur Muhammad for his role in educating generations of these men, proved helpful. Soon the girls' school, itself located in three bare mud-baked rooms, needed bigger premises and more teachers. One of those rooms was my sister's dwelling where she prepared her registers, notes, and other paper work for school besides meeting her Malkani visitors who often came in during the night when I would shift to one of the classrooms with my own books to give them their privacy. Contrary to their fears, Bilqis was not a typical urban, self-righteous woman but instead was a serious-minded committed teacher who provided extra coaching to a motley of her pupils. In her free time, she read Urdu fiction, held on to books on English history, and adored Robinson Crusoe while often listening to a transistor radio to get the latest news from Rawalpindi on occasionally shy airwaves. Once in a while, she listened to early morning *Ceylon Urdu Service* that was known for playing semi-classical Urdu songs. Her efforts were bearing fruit, and following a move to a bigger private building donated by a kind person, the district government agreed to construct a purpose-built school on the site of an abandoned Hindu temple. I remember helping my sister and her caretaker, Auntie Gahran, plant trees, hedges, and seasonal plants which, thanks to all the gods and goddesses who had been worshipped on this site in the past, blossomed into full bloom and soon the school presented a lovely landscape. This school was in the town's centre at an easy distance for younger Malkanis. Besides, it added to Tamman's status in the hinterlands. Bilqis developed a close friendship with several local families of the bigger and minor landlords and was thus able to break the taboos and reservations against female education.

The Qazi family was a very interesting case since their men were supposed to be educated. They were often away working in Rawalpindi and Multan but their women, young and old, remained indoors; inducting a few of them into her school proved to be a trendsetter. They were and still are called Qazis either due to their ancestral name or because a few generations back the Mughal or Sikh rulers had appointed the clan's elder to the respectable status of a judge. Some of them had moved to Tamman from neighbouring villages and, while claiming social status, had become more conservative. A gentleman with a towering physique belonging from the Qazi family was known as Hakim *Sayyana* (the wise hakim). He originally came from the village of Sher Kot. With a bald head hidden under a white turban, Hakim Sahib sported a black handlebar moustache and retained an authoritative voice that resounded with both authority and compassion. Due to the lack of resources for medical check-ups or longer hospitalization in distant cities, Hakim Sher Koti was one of Tamman's messiahs and all and sundry flocked to his practice. Similarly, another Qazi hakim came from a very literary family since his father, Imam Ghazali, had been named after the known medieval Muslim jurist and used to lead prayers in the main mosque not far from Bibi Sarwar Bano's traditional haveli. Hakim Mahmudul Hasan conducted his practice in a solid, brick shop, which must have been owned by some Hindu seth in the past. Its heavy steel doors and strong window vaults witnessed an earlier version of hybrid, modern architecture that was very popular amongst the Hindu moneyed classes, locally known as Khatris. Hakim Hasan's brother, Ziaud Din, taught us Urdu with enthusiasm and often delivered impassioned speeches against illiteracy and feudal snobbery. He was certainly a handsome radical who carried his own charisma; if born in some Latin American country, he could have been Che Guevara's natural ally. These two brothers had inherited an impressive library of early Persian and Arabic manuscripts; they were conscious of their own lineage as independent scholars and professionals; and their father, Imam Ghazali, resolved local feuds and spoke with authority over Quranic subjects. People used to come from far and wide to his Friday sermons (this was the time before electricity and public address system reached our towns and villages). Imam Ghazali died on a very hot summer day just after the afternoon prayers. His death had been bereaved by the entire village. Its horizons turned dustier and, as per report from Auntie Gahran, the school's caretaker, even the jackals were heard howling during the day, mourning the death of a pious scholar.

I remember Bilqis' valiant efforts to persuade such families to send their girls to her school and she did succeed, largely because of Uncle Nur Muhammad's influence on the town's who's who. Bilqis, over some weekends, would venture into neighbouring villages donning her black, modern-looking burqa to seek out new students, and soon a trickle began to happen. Some of her own students and Auntie Gahran would accompany her during such forays which would become worthy excuses for wayside picnics, often curiously watched by peasants and shepherds along the way. They showed curiosity towards these 'city girls' donning flowery, colourful attires with their raw complexions glowing in the clear Potwari sun. This was not only my elder sister's way of reaching out to far-flung villages while advancing female education, but it also gave her and other colleagues an opportunity for social bonding besides undertaking some exercise. Once the rubicon had been crossed, the school became a centrefold for women's education, with some of them eventually moving on to bigger cities for higher education. With a clear immersion into consanguine marriages, soon the Qazi men were taking their educated spouses with them to the cities instead of keeping them at home, as was the case earlier on, and afterwards their next generation was competing for military jobs and foreign postings. It all began with the efforts of an untiring woman, whose own husband did not appreciate her devotion and diligence to this area and had moved in with another woman, leaving Bilqis with a young daughter who grew up near the new school in Tamman and herself became a university professor while senior women continued to call her 'our girl from Tamman' or 'the daughter of our teacher'. Malik Nur Muhammad had retired and soon passed away, leaving indelible memories in Tamman where he had educated generations of men, whereas Bilqis refused to retire and soon opened her own private school in another village, not too far from our home.

I am not sure whether Bibi Sarwar Bano ever got her daughter, Surrayya Khatoon, admitted in the school but I am positive that she must have had some personal coaching from my sister. My sister always talked of these two women with great respect and admiration and did not retain any rancour towards them. Even Muhammad Hayat's wife, who came from a landowning family near Attock, was supportive of Bilqis' efforts without ever being quite open about it. Her own daughter would venture into the girls' school once in a while chaperoned by maidservants and would stay only for a short while. Other than being worried about losing domestic servants because of women getting educated, especially ones from poorer families, these local influentials must have been trying to hold on to their patriarchal traditions. Despite Zulfikar Ali Bhutto's politicization of the Pakistani masses in areas like basic needs, his supporters from the landed elite refused to let girls' schools openly operate in some of their hinterlands. In one such meeting in the early 1970s, Hanif Ramay, an urban socialist and educationist, then holding the chief ministership under Bhutto in Punjab, was discouraged by Hayat from upgrading Tamman's girls' school to college status as the latter was worried about 'our women getting strange ideas and being misled by urban mischief mongers'. This encounter was related to me by a cousin who had served in the Royal and Pakistani navies and as an activist espoused universal education. Being the leader of Bhutto's Pakistan Peoples Party (PPP), Malik Muhammad Shafi was shocked to know how Hayat was fiercely opposed to the idea of upgrading the girls' schools in his own constituency. And it was even more shocking to both of us that the plaque by his main entrance in his Tamman's residence still announced his Bachelor's from Aligarh Muslim University, an institution founded by Sir Syed Ahmed Khan to further education and forward thinking amongst Indian Muslims. Hayat routinely held ministerial positions in various regimes and, after his death, the mantle was taken over by his son who carried on his father's tradition. Though he was educated at Aitchison and not at Aligarh, he still receives millions of rupees in annual rent from the urban property in Talagang, which originally belonged to the departed Khatris and which Hayat allegedly was capriciously able to obtain by manipulating the claims. On the other hand, Nur Khan's family did not have such a blemish added to their name, largely because of Bibi Sarwar Bano and her reluctance to use her kinship with the nawab to seek illegal property allotments that had tempted others.

Nur Khan's sister was eventually married to a distant cousin, Malik Mumtaz Khan, whose father and several close relatives had been mercilessly killed in a tit-for-tat attack. His father, Allah Yar Khan, was a close friend of my father and I remember dad returning home unexpectedly from the judicial courts one early morning very despondent and agitated. This was quite odd for him since he only came back in the afternoon after the courts had adjourned. I remember something to the effect that he said to my mother as soon as he entered home:

They have killed Sardar Allah Yar along with his entire family. These assassins came from another village and were seeking revenge for certain deaths that they had attributed to him. They knew their targets very well, and only an injured Mumtaz escaped somehow since he hid himself in the haystack near their stable. Hearing the shots in the middle of the night, the young man had hid himself but still received a shot in his thigh before the killers made it into the dark.

I never knew how my father had been so close to Allah Yar Khan as I was too young then, plus such killings were quite rare those days and shocked people who often shied away from discussing their lurid details.

Mumtaz Khan was not a studious young man. The shocking sight of so many murders before his eyes and then a huge inheritance kept him away from formal education, despite all the efforts of Nur Khan. The Maliks of Tamman were a strange, curious, and interesting lot. In retrospect, they may have appeared quixotic and eccentric but they were often serious-minded traditional men of charisma who were bound to their lands and families. The richer amongst them bred horses and hounds and often went on rabbit and deer hunting with falcons and eagles accompanying large shikar parties. Mumtaz devoted most of his youth to such events, and a retinue of servants and hangers-on ensured a proper upkeep of his hounds and falcons, while his evenings were spent in sessions where his friends, tenants, and visitors would assemble, sharing stories about the hunts and hunters across the Salt Range and Thar while inhaling smoke from ever bubbling hookahs. In one of those hunting rounds, one of Mumtaz's favourite hounds twisted his slim foot on a rock and began crying like a little child. It was a crisp spring day with a blue sky and mustard fields at their best when the party was stopped and Mumtaz tended to his hound whose pain was unstoppable until he asked one of the village minstrels to carry him along. After that, I stopped going to such events and often found myself in the company of a book, traversing the mustard fields and ravines that Tamman had in plenty.

Nur Khan, like his powerful nawab uncle, attended Aitchison College before moving to the Dehradun Military Academy following his enlistment in the Royal Air Force in the pre-1947 years. Both in studies as well as in his military pursuit, Nur Khan made his mark; the creation of Pakistan offered many new openings to this pilot whose experience on the

Burma front had testified both his daring and professional acumen. While working at the Public Records Office, now called The National Archives in Kew, I came across some references to Nur Khan, a young Pakistan Air Force (PAF) officer working at his country's embassy in Lowndes Square soon after Independence. Nur Khan headed the Pakistani flag carrier, Pakistan International Airlines (PIA), and fully ensured higher benchmarks in training, discipline, and service, earning plaudits for the airline. He never left PAF, which was headed by another capable and industrious commander, Asghar Khan, who had ensured modernization of its fleet and the force so as to make it into one of the smartest of its kind.

I remember Surrayya Bibi's marriage to Mumtaz Khan in Tamman which was attended by Nawab Amir Muhammad Khan with the retinue of police lining up the winding lanes in Tamman and its overawed residents talking in whispers about the arrival of the Governor Sahib whose authority, like his moustache, could never go unnoticed across the breadth of the Indus Valley. It was a hot summer day when the Nawab Sahib came to Tamman and the senior provincial and district officials housed themselves in this hamlet in full alert so as not to offend the powerful Indus ruler. The town, all of a sudden, was buzzing with police jeeps and flag-staff cars of the senior bureaucrats and ministers from Khyber to Karachi. Otherwise quite medieval and rural in its outlook and centuries away from modernity, Tamman elicited curious interest from everyone in the country due to its association with some of the most powerful men in the country and also because its Maliks, like Mumtaz Khan, Allah Yar Khan, and Mir Sahib, were known for their hunting parties, partridge fights, and connections with the Kalabagh Maliks. Nur Muhammad's high school, along with the girls' school run by Bilqis and its counterpart headed by Malik Maula Bakhsh, a kindly and alert soul, were especially white-washed, with flower pots lining the narrow dusty street that connected Bibi Sarwar Bano's haveli with the main road—which itself was unmetalled even though Hayat headed the railway ministry in the country back then.

I remember a big starched white turban on an imposing body walking majestically into the haveli with the vigilant police marksmen stationed on the rooftops that belonged to the neighbours including the Qazis, and atop the local Women's Health Centre which was run by a cousin, a pioneer in her field. Qamar Malik, always called Miss Qamar or Miss Sahiba, was a tall, sophisticated woman with an impressive physique resembling contemporary Bollywood actresses of black and white films. She was fond of classical music and, just like my sister, looked forward to those countryside picnics where women complaining of all kinds of ailments including bewitchment would swarm her. They all wanted to have a full supply of pills, which to them would cure them of diseases; some of them complained of getting pregnant often. This was the time when contraceptives were yet to make an entry in the Pakistani rural parlance and the World Health Organization (WHO) had not yet come up with the free distribution of any protective devices. When condoms finally arrived, many of them became balloons for the kids whose mothers had sought them to prevent pregnancies but had shied from offering them to their husbands. A white, transparent, filmy condom must have looked funny as well as curious to those women to whom smart city women advocating female education and contraception resembled creatures from Mars. Qamar Malik was married to a military officer who visited Tamman whenever he was on leave. Clean-shaven and wearing western clothes, he often went for brisk walks in the company of his tall and majestic wife. The couple raised envious and curious glances in this town which by now had more men moving out to far away cities.

Nur Khan, who rose to command the Pakistani national carrier without leaving his senior position of Air Commodore, ensured its expansion and excellent performance at various levels. Whenever he visited his native town, especially on Eid, the word would get around and people would talk about the arrival of Air Commodore Malik with pride as he was the illustrious native son. Unlike the visit by the nawab, Khan's visits were ordinary, with a single old Chevrolet parked in a lonely garage by the main road as it could not negotiate the narrow lane leading to the haveli. His was not the only car that would venture into Tamman, since another quiet, gentlemanly Malik, Shah Nawaz, also held on to his prized black sedan which was often parked in a specially built garage across Khan's facility. Shah Nawaz's Chevrolet, with its shining black steel and silver chrome, was kept spick and span. We hardly saw it on the road except when the Malik had to go to our hometown to pursue his litigation or had to drop his sons at their schools in Lahore. Hayat had a car which ferried his family and children to Lahore and Attock, and like

Shah Nawaz's automobile, his was often invisible within Tamman, since the town did not have proper metalled roads and only the old Bedford buses chugged along between Talagang and Makhad. Saifud Din, the Pir of Makhad, with a big following of disciples in Tamman, would appear in his jeep before the elections and often shared some rivalry over regional politics with Hayat. Most of these locals preferred horses and, given an almost free and ever-ready supply of servants, often peasants caring for their animals, they took great pride in riding them. On their individual shikar parties, a typical Tamman Malik would always don a starched turban. He led from the front with hounds, servants, and peasants following his ride and beating around the bushes for rabbits and boars while eagles would be kept on hand with their eyes covered by special blinds to stop them from flying off after pigeons and doves. Occasionally, the servants holding the eagles would offer them small pieces of meat which the latter would consume with nonchalance. The entire shikar was supposed to be a big phenomenon and perhaps had been reinvigorated during the colonial era when larger parties went on bigger hunts killing thousands of animals and birds across the subcontinent. In Tamman, shikar was a local affair, though other Maliks from neighbouring towns would often host such events with various teams and numerous beasts joining up to comb hills, ravines, and nullahs, looking for deer, boars, rabbits, and pheasants.

On July 23, 1965, Nur Khan came back from PIA to head the PAF, a force that had been turned into a small yet efficient fighting machine with excellent training and a deeper sense of discipline by his predecessor. By this time, the India-held Kashmir Valley had become restive largely because of the agitation against a stalemated control of this disputed region and also because the Pakistani government had started sending infiltrators to cause India nervousness. Generals like Ayub Khan, Muhammad Musa, Akhtar Ali Malik, and their colleagues had miscalculated the possible Indian reaction, assuming that the new Indian Prime Minister, Lal Bahadur Shastri, was a weaker substitute for a more seasoned Jawaharlal Nehru who had died a few months earlier after being heartbroken on India's defeat by the Chinese Liberation Army in Higher Himalayas. Pakistani generals believed that the Indian troops were utterly demoralized and would not be able to contain discontent in the valley and thus would be compelled to hold meaningful negotiations with Islamabad over Kashmir. Misled by such delusions and overconfidence in their own military invincibility, the generals, prodded by Zulfikar Ali Bhutto (then foreign minister), did not realize that a cornered India could even unleash an attack on any of the two wings of its neighbouring country. The generals had not informed their counterparts in the navy and air force of Pakistan's involvement in the valley, yet Nur Khan came to know of it and, amidst the triumphalist stories from within the valley, put PAF on a red alert. When the Indian troops crossed the international borders near Lahore on September 6, unlike the Pakistani Army, they found PAF in full preparedness and its fleet and installations escaped the fate of its Middle Eastern counterparts on the eve of Israeli-Arab War of 1967. Soon PAF, despite its obvious logistical and numerical constraints, especially its division into two separate wings, was able to defend the country's skies rather valiantly as people in cities like Lahore began to enjoy the spectacles of dogfights between PAF's Saber crafts and their Canberra counterparts. The Indian Air Force, despite its numerical strength and institutional and technical advantages, was not allowed to steal a march over PAF. Khan was often mentioned as personally leading sorties to defend air space. In fact, as affirmed by one of his colleagues, Air Commodore Sajjad Haider, even before the war, Khan had flown a C-130 to drop supplies over Lower Himalayas despite all the navigational hazards in an inhospitable weather. While army generals like Sarfaraz Khan and Muhammad Musa Khan often received public opprobrium over their miscalculations, Nur Khan's smart and alert air force gave the nation a whole train of heroes. He was furious when soon after assuming the command of PAF he was asked to facilitate supplies to Pakistani hatchet men in the valley, since he had not been taken into prior confidence by the generals who had designed 'Operation Gibraltar' of sending in infiltrators. He visited the army's General Headquarters (GHQ) to confront Musa Khan on this daredevil venture which threatened the security of the country and openly showed his displeasure to the army chief. Eventually, it was Nur Khan who was vindicated as his timely alertness and personal example as the competent commander all through the 17-day war stood him and PAF in good stead.

Ayub Khan had outlived his tenure and ideas, if he had any, and the country sought some proper and substantive democratic alternatives. Like Ayub Khan's other dictatorial contemporaries, he had crafted a system to suit his own prerogatives and—through a crowd of obliged politicians and self-servers and with due help from the nawab and his counterpart in East Pakistan, Monem Khan—got himself elected to the presidency. It was a small electorate of only 80,000 councillors who presumably elected him by 'defeating' Fatima Jinnah, one of the founders of the country. According to General Ayub Khan, the rest of the people had no right to vote as they were still not ready enough to practise and acquire a full-fledged democracy. One wondered if these millions of people had been so uncouth and uncultured then how were they able to create the fifth largest state in the world in 1947? The two strong governors and their henchmen had manoeuvred Fatima Jinnah's defeat which did not go well in the country. The grave sense of betrayal, following the 1965 War, led to Ayub Khan's decline, largely owing to a mass movement in both wings of the country. His exit in March 1969 was manipulated by his successor in the army, General Yahya Khan, who imposed his own military rule amidst wide dismay. He appointed Nur Khan as the Governor and Chief Martial Law Administrator of West Pakistan which shocked many of us amongst the youth who had been idealizing Nur Khan. It was out of sheer respect for this person that we warmly welcomed him to the Government College, Lahore, our alma mater, and were definitely relieved when he finally left the ruling junta. Khan had not only led PAF brilliantly, he had ensured Pakistan's global pre-eminence in squash, field hockey, and cricket, since he chaired their committees and strove hard to run them professionally and competitively.

Nur Khan came into public limelight again following the elections of 1985 when he was elected to the lower house from his ancestral constituency. People voted for him en masse as he promised to work in areas like education and rural development. People not only gave him their votes, they honoured him to their utmost by welcoming their prodigious son visiting all those hamlets across the Soan River. A system crafted by a pernicious General Ziaul Haq, more like Ayub Khan's, once again did not allow people like Nur Khan to work effectively; sitting in a party-less and even powerless house under a uniformed general was thoroughly a non-starter. Callously, a paid employee of the state who had taken oath to defend and serve it had been lording over it through a regime of coercion and selective Islamization. Ziaul Haq was naturally against any form of critical learning that would allow any debate or freedom of expression and used Islam and fellow Islamists to turn the country into a den of bigotry and intolerance. He especially singled out Islamabad's Quaid-i-Azam University for his wrath and abolished all its elected bodies besides unleashing his intelligence sleuths to harass some of those academics who protested not only against unilateral curbs but also critiqued his very martial law.

By that time Nur Khan had become a member of the lower house, a group of teachers sought to apprise him of the dismal situation in Pakistan's steadily deteriorating higher education sector, besides the brazen interference and harassment by the sleuths. It was in late 1985 when, on a cold day, a dozen or so teachers including myself reached Rawalpindi's Intercontinental Hotel where the retired Air Marshal retained a room. We were warmly received and the former pilot and now a parliamentarian heard us patiently and meticulously took down notes. Just before our departure, his personal assistant, who had known me from my younger days due to his friendship with my father, announced to our host rather suddenly and even a bit boastfully, 'This younger Malik is originally from your area, Air Marshal Sahib.' I naturally felt embarrassed as we had gone there to talk about a national malaise and not for some nepotistic fraternization. The Air Marshal came up to me and shook my hands very warmly and said, 'Well, I'm proud to know that.' I told him that I did not want to bring that personal element into it but was still thankful for his time and support to the cause of higher education. I guess that was the last time I saw him face-to-face.

In 1988, Ziaul Haq dismissed the parliament as well as the façade of a civilian government led by Mohammad Khan Junejo, a mild man who, on his return from a foreign visit, was told of this dismissal at the airport. Zia himself died soon after in an air crash near Bahawalpur following an act of sabotage since his long rule and pernicious policies had created serious fissures in the society and the army. Nur Khan came closer to Benazir Bhutto's party but, in the politics of musical chairs of the 1990s, he left it to his brother-in-law, Mumtaz Khan, to carry on. Mumtaz's only son had been killed in a criminal attack while studying in the United States; I heard of the tragedy at Oxford and could understand this former shikari turning into a reclusive puritan. It was on another cold, wet December day in 2011 when I heard of Nur Khan's passing away and his burial in Tamman. It brought back all the memories of that small town, its narrow, dusty streets, its first batch of female students, and the lifetime contributions of people like Malik Nur Muhammad and Bilqis Begum. On my next visit to Pakistan, I am certainly eager to visit Tamman to relive its past, a part of my own past, and then I plan to see Imran Khan's university at Namal, a village by the lake, and not far from Kalabagh where I had enjoyed a boat ride more than half a century ago. In the meantime, goodbye both to Malik Nur Khan and to an era!

2

Hakimji:
A Special Cousin in a Bygone Tradition

While we continued condemning the wanton killings in Iraq, Palestine, Afghanistan, Chechnya, and in London, the comparatively warm summer of 2005 quietly added to the tally of a growing list of obituaries of fellow academics. Losing three cousins within the month of June was itself sobering enough, despite all of them having enjoyed rather respectable if not long innings. The departure of four professors known to me only underlined the eventuality waiting in the wings. Hakim Muhammad Nawaz, generally known as 'Hakimji', was certainly the senior-most cousin who even during my childhood looked decades older than everyone else. More than his age, it was his forbearance that elicited deference while disallowing any frankness, especially when he was around. His presence or short home visits, to be exact, were always momentary yet they left everyone awestruck. To call him a bully or an autocrat would be unfair; he was a no-nonsense kind of a personality with little stomach for unnecessary details. Without being a scientist per se, he was mathematical in his words, timings, and dealings. His aura stemmed from the fact that he was a traditional physician who dispensed unsavoury potions—he gave several bitter tablets, did not often shirk from using a needle to inject some compound into an arm or a buttock, all without any hesitation or pep talk. His matter-of-factness was alien to a community that usually took time in expressing the actual point by preambling it with small talk. Certainly, Hakimji's towering structure, aloofness, mixed with a bit of authoritarianism, and most of all, a vast following of patients faithfully waiting long hours for their turns, made this cousin into a unique relative. Just like my other cousins, he was a tall man who always wore immaculate clothes in which a waistcoat was an integral item, always paired with black shiny shoes while his glasses never seemed to leave a clean-shaven and healthy countenance. In addition to a stethoscope, a chained watch hidden in the vest featured a highly disciplined life. He was always accompanied by his cycle which, despite its ripe maturity, never looked unattended. Like his brown leather handbag, it was an integral part of his personality and only experienced separation whenever he ventured out for some rare errand or had to undertake an unavoidable condolence visit amongst a large circle of relatives. He was a man of rigorous discipline where regular prayers, walks, diet, siesta, consultation, and gardening all happened at their right time. An individual of a few yet potent words, Hakimji was an upright fellow and even the nearest of his relatives did not dare disturb his schedule. For instance, no consultancy after he had gone home, especially when he had partaken his supper with the family, which included his second wife and two daughters.

A son from his wife's previous marriage was part and parcel of the Hakim family or Hakims, as they were locally known. This handsome young man was a quiet person who for years had been studying in Lahore, presumably encountering some difficulty in getting through his scholastic requirements. Eventually, on the insistence of the mother, who had been advised to the effect by a Pir Sahib, Muhammad Nisar became Muhammad Jawaid. The Pir had predicted that a name change would end the academic logjam of this shy man who wore stylish clothes and always walked a few inches behind Hakim Sahib—certainly out of deference. His curly hair and a loyal pair of rimmed glasses bestowed on him an academic appearance. For once, the Pir was right, for soon after the name change, Jawaid qualified the tests followed by a visit to Britain for an added specialization. Doctor Jawaid returned to Pakistan to initiate his practice in his native town, which was a bit odd as young men often dreamt of living in the glamorous West. Hakimji, feeling the strain of population, pressure, and the resultant enormity of patients, would recommend several complicated cases to Dr Jawaid, the 'Doctor Sahib'. Jawaid always wore well-pressed trousers and used a car unlike Hakimji whose faithful bike continued to weather an unending continuum of decades and dusty roads. Both Hakimji and Doctor Jawaid strictly avoided visiting patients at their homes; they had to be brought into the clinics or their medicines would be sent home through their relatives who always sat overawed listening to these matter-of-fact physicians.

Hakimji was certainly of authoritarian forbearance with his traditional attire and brief yet firm dispensation, whereas an aloof and soft-spoken Jawaid equally had no time and patience for small talk.

It will be unfair to talk of Hakimji without a few words about his dispenser who was also his namesake but knew his junior status quite well. While Hakimji sat in the front section of the dispensary with his table full of medicines and small paper slips, the patients occupied small wooden benches waiting for their turns quietly. Even the little children turned unusually quiet while gazing curiously at Hakimji's karakul cap and his chained silver pocket watch. Certainly, the syringes, red syrups, powdered aspirin, and a whole plethora of traditional and modern medicines were more than enough to scare both parents and young children who nervously looked at the passers-by in the busy little street. The street branched off the main bazaar which still had several old-style brick houses built by their Hindu and Sikh owners long before Partition. Well known, as well as immensely respected within the community, Hakimji always received salaams from almost everybody who negotiated through the lane. Hakimji's dispenser was a burly man of thick girth with his hair always dyed dark black, two piercings, and friendly brown eyes, quietly nodding at patients and pedestrians or cyclists. On occasion, he looked overawed by Hakimji's demeanour, but in the latter's absence, he appeared to regale in the occasional title of 'Chotay Doctor Sahib' by patients who had either mistimed their consultations or had been plainly too timid to ask Hakimji questions regarding their illness and its prognosis. Despite officiating as the viceroy, Nawaz, the compounder, never occupied the exalted wicker chair that was used only by Hakimji.

Hakimji usually felt the pulse of the patient, looked into their eyes and throats while conducting the usual rounds of an old leathery stethoscope on the torso and then muttered a few words about the symptoms. Patients mostly agreed to the diagnosis while some of them attempted to delve into narratives, which were often met by a firm interruption by Hakimji, who scribbled the prescription on a small slip and gave it to Chotay Hakim before moving on to the next patient. In between, Hakimji announced the fee, which included the cost of the medicines along with a few added directions on food and the next appointment. After receiving the chit with its own codes and abbreviated names of powders, pills, or syrup, the dispenser would disappear behind the curtain to seek them out from a wide array of jars. This routine continued until midday when Hakimji prepared to cycle home for a brief lunch, afternoon prayers, and a siesta. His homeward journey was rigorously timed and routed to an acute exactness and exemplified no sign of any alteration. However, on some rare occasions such as funerals, Hakimji might have been slightly delayed; in such cases Nawaz administered the routine cases, whereas the serious ones had to wait for Hakimji's afternoon consultation session. Given the tradition of periodic visits to the bereaved families which involved prayers with the rest, Hakimji, accompanied by Doctor Sahib, strictly preferred evening sessions as care was taken to minimize the impact on a daily routine devoted to surgery and an afternoon break.

Hakimji's wife must have been a good-looking lady in her youth and still ensured a sufficient supply of make-up under her glasses and hennaed hair. She was one of the earliest women from our town to have donned glasses besides a silky burqa, mostly made of special black, raw silk. She also undertook social visits in the evenings, mostly in the company of the two men who sat with the men while the Hakimni or Mrs Hakimji joined the rest of the women in the family quarters. Unlike some other bereaved women, she avoided wailing but often dried her tears for the departed soul with a handkerchief. She was my father's cousin and he showed her all the deference including a bowed head but like all other male relatives, the small talk never went beyond a few shy yet courteous words or some curious eyebrows. Hakimni, accompanied by her younger married sister and an elder daughter from her previous marriage, generated a certain amount of awe amongst the womenfolk who looked at her attire and demeanour with envy. Shaukat, the eldest daughter, like her mother, had been a divorcee and was now married to a transporter and her fashionable attire attracted due adoration. They were a sort of elite in the extended family and enjoyed higher social status and were certainly more prosperous than many other relatives. Hakimji, as well as the Hakimni, had a mysterious past and, despite occasional and rather meaningful gestures or naughty smiles, our parents and other relatives avoided gossiping about them. With the lapse of time, even those hasty references disappeared as some of the characters in the stories gradually passed away. However, it was inexplicably known to many of us that they both had children from their previous marriages and it was some kind of explosive romance that had brought them together, yet not without exacting cost.

As the rumours went, Hakimji had been married to a cousin who had given birth to two sons and the entire family lived with Hakimji's mother, Khala Mulkhan. This tough octogenarian was my mum's eldest sister and was indeed a domineering character. Sporting grey hair and thick eyebrows, Khala Mulkhan exuded awe and authority, and no wonder Hakimji had inherited her strong personality. Khala Mulkhan had arranged Hakimji's marriage to her sister's daughter who came from that branch of our family that manufactured soap in an abandoned Hindu house and was equally well known for breeding splendid cows of some specific breed. The Malik Soap Factory was a local landmark and happened to be right behind the famous *Joharan Di Marri* (The Johar Mansion). Just a few solitary visits to this factory during early childhood have bequeathed the impressions of a quiet place where several individuals tended to huge containers and, in place of talking to one another, simply nodded. Including three cousins, several labouring men seemed to be goading the mix in big cauldrons. The cousins were, by nature, quiet brothers and in their short breaks often tended to partridges that they kept in small knitted cages. While the partridges enjoyed frequent grooming, the cousins would turn talkative and sociable over their hookah, often accompanied by sugary tea served in glasses. The desi soap with the brand sign of a pair of scissors was widely used in homes across the land, whereas imported soaps such as Lux, Palmolive, or Rexona were reserved for special occasions. Desi soap was strictly light brown, thick, and round, while its imported counterpart was always white, oblong, curvy, and slim. People came from far to see the well-fed and immensely smart cows kept by the cousins who often covered their back with a big shawl so as to avoid evil eye. The three brothers, after working at the soap factory, spent hours massaging and combing their cows and took them out in the evenings for their usual stroll. On such occasions, people lined up the streets to see these 'spotty' agile beasts which never lost at the annual cattle festival. The cows, especially the calves, were a far cry from their docile counterparts in the town which spent long hours grazing the sparse clumps of grass in the sunburnt fields. Except for our *Naanaji's* (maternal grandfather) bull with five legs and an exceptionally aggressive cow, the rest of the bovine tribe always stoically tended to their own routine and turned slightly violent if bothered too closely during their grazing sessions. Another cousin called Dilshaad also manufactured soap in a part of his home and his output often came out in nicely-cut soap cakes; the ingredients, texture, and the complexion of these products from the New Malik Soap Factory were similar to those from the Malik Soap Factory. In hindsight, it appears as if both of them were competing with each other until mass produced and properly packaged brands from the cities damaged their local rivals and the latter eventually wound up. Dilshaad subsequently opened a cycle shop while the three cousins opened a factory producing *naswar* (brown snuff), besides selling other tobacco products, their penchant for prize cows never subsided. However, both these businesses went down the tube once their next generation took to the professions following their university degrees and a whole raft of traditions faced with modernity dissolved in thin air.

Khala Mulkhan, also known as Massi Mulkhan, was aghast at her only son's romance especially when Hakimji had already fathered two sons from his first marriage. Hakimni had been previously married to Hakimji's elder half-brother who was a police official and looked after his younger brother; both had the same father but two different mothers. It was rumoured that the younger brother, sporting handsome features and a debonair personality, fell for the Hakimni who had attractive features. However, it could not be authenticated whether the romance consummated into marriage after the death of the elder brother or earlier. Hakimji took a second wife and also adopted her two children, Nisar and Shaukat, from her previous marriage. His own two sons from the first marriage opted to stay with their mother and never bothered to relate with Hakimji. However, soon the couple had two girls who, along with their two senior siblings, lived in a nicely furnished house amply looked after by loyal servants. Hakimji's second marriage was the proverbial last straw that broke the camel's back. Massi and Hakimji fell apart forever as she never forgave him for abandoning his first wife and two sons. Hakimji had moved out while the rest stayed on with Massi, who somehow managed to shelter them while ensuring proper education for both her grandchildren. It is uncertain even now whether Hakimji had dissolved the first marriage or just managed to move on without undertaking a formal divorce. Massi was certainly helped by good harvests, but most of all, some nephews and cousins ensured the smooth running of the household to the extent that the eldest son not only graduated as a medical doctor but was also able to obtain a commissioned position in the army. Just a few months before the demise of his father, Doctor Zafar Malik, a genteel soul, had himself retired as a brigadier. However, the younger brother, Shabbir, was extremely uninterested in studies and spent his time catching quails and partridges. Both the brothers were extremely religious and loyal to their mother and Massi.

Some close relatives, including the mother and *Naanaji* tried to hammer out some reconciliation between Massi and Hakimji but to no avail. Both were of the same stubborn temperament and Massi, in a way, never forgave her only son for leaving his family in the lurch. Hakimji's own sons never visited or even held conversation with their father who, in the meantime, had built his own modern house besides fathering two daughters. Hakimni was from within the extended family but the marriage had polarized the entire clan while Hakimji was left to only rotate within the confines of her branch of the family. Everyone on both sides of the family kept quiet as well as distant while Nisar and Shaukat moved into the new house. Hakimji did visit Massi just before her death in her nineties but it was just a formality as she did not relent. Decades had passed and enough water had flowed underneath the bridge, hence the meeting happened but too late and to no avail. The sons lived their own lives, keeping a distance from their father while he seemed to be absorbed in his practice, disciplined life style, and a pre-eminent role in the town, augmented by a bent of acceptable authoritarianism. His aloofness, diligent life, and full devotion to his practice might have partly accrued from his own uneasy personal life but nobody ever dared to raise it with him. Hakimni must have been the real confidante as she was not only senior to him in age but was certainly an assertive person in her own right. Like all those men who appear strong and domineering in public life but are totally different behind the home walls, Hakimji must have submitted to this de facto force. Hakimji showered Hakimni's two children with everything all through his life but the entire family would never even venture into the street where Massi Mulkhan lived with her daughter-in-law and two grandsons. That house faced the place where cousin Dilshaad lived and ran his soap factory.

Hakimni's eldest daughter was a tall and beautiful woman who had been married to a distant cousin. Shaukat's looks, like her mother and brother, certainly exuded urbanity, sophistication, and an impressive degree of ease that comes with prosperity even in the rural families of Punjab. Her husband, Naseer, was a handsome, educated, and sophisticated man who, like many others of pre-1947 generation Indians, caught tuberculosis; the memory of an immensely fragile man lying on a cot with thick hair and piercing brown eyes under arched brows has remained imprinted in my consciousness. Naseer was a literary person, as I can imagine, and shared close friendship with Uncle Manzoor, himself a literary and romantic figure who happened to be my mother's youngest and perhaps most handsome brother, though sometimes she would reserve that epithet for Uncle Aziz, who had been killed in Sicily during the War. Naseer's father, a twice married retired revenue official, lived not far from Hakimji's house but it was rather strange to see that both the families had somehow abandoned Naseer. Naseer's cot ended up in the front room of *Naani*'s (maternal grandmother) house where, once in a while, his beautiful daughter sat holding her dad's thin hand. *Naani* looked after Naseer in his dying days while Uncle Manzoor spent hours with Naseer, often discussing Urdu poetry, journalism, and a bit of history and philosophy. Perhaps this was before antibiotics or a mere element of helplessness that Naseer passed away one quiet afternoon and within a few months Uncle Manzoor also came down with a debilitating fever. This young man, whose long brown hair parted in the middle over a towering height and a pair of greenish brown eyes, hid the anguish in the person that now awaited his final hour soon came to occupy Naseer's cot. Uncle Manzoor must have been inflicted with tuberculosis as well since his frame was thinning down with each passing day, though his eyes never forgot to share affection for us younger souls. Even in his bed, he would hold on to pen and paper or a newspaper since he used to write a weekly column in Urdu. Uncle Manzoor had abandoned his first wife and daughter, Tasleem, to marry another woman—the love of his life and a divorcee herself. They both had two daughters and a son but not a happy life and perhaps a grave sense of guilt kept agonizing my uncle, who began to consume increasing quantities of opium until a tall, swarthy, talented uncle took to the bed left by Naseer. My *Naani* and mother, along with my elder sisters, witnessed Uncle Manzoor wither before their eyes and I sat on his bed holding his hand when he passed away one summer afternoon. Mosques all around made announcements of the death of a youthful Malik.

Naseer's widow had stayed home and ventured out only on special occasions with Hakimni, while the relatives avoided talking about Naseer and his travails. A few years on, the news filtered in on her marrying the transporter from a neighbouring town. Malik Zammurud was certainly not a bachelor but a man of good reputation and wealth who wanted to marry an educated and sophisticated urbanite; the matchmakers sent to and fro by Hakimni finally registered a success. In the meantime, Hakimji, his two daughters, and the rest lived in the house which was known for its modern and rather prosperous appearance. Hakimji's house, despite being on a small plot, had two stories, a small compound, and a veranda, and its carved doors were topped by a balcony which had two sculpted swans on both sides of its rooftop. The seated swans held brown biscuits in their beaks which tempted young passers-by who, in several cases, considered them real. A few attempts to snatch these biscuits by flinging stones at them had miserably failed until the prevalent wisdom accepted their invincibility. The masons who built Hakimji's luxurious house took great pride in their achievement and were rumoured to have led a roaring business afterwards. Even though the two daughters had been educated and married off, the house appeared to be insufficient for the family. Jawaid, who had opened his practice in town, was already in his thirties much to the chagrin and shock of his relatives, all used to early marriages. However, Hakimni had her own plans as her emissaries were busy scouting for possible candidates for Jawaid from outside the immediate clan. One thing was sure, the Hakims were not going to seek a local girl, given their own estrangement with many in the extended family and, also given Jawaid's credentials, they sought a matching girl from somewhere else, essentially of a pedigreed family and, not a commoner. Whether it was due to their pride or simple aversion to marrying within the family at large has remained inexplicable. Khawar, the new bride did gel in the family and carried on living in our hometown, though her arrival hastened the construction of a modern, expansive, and well-designed villa by the main road leading towards Rawalpindi and Peshawar. Initially, womenfolk in the town showed curiosity and even some hostility to this 'outsider' who belonged to a landowning family from Gujrat, a good 130 miles further away. Khawar soon came to know everyone in the family and showed keen interest in relating with all, which won her praise even from her erstwhile critics. Hakimji and Hakimni continued to live on in their family home while their girls, following university degrees, took to cities and after their marriages eventually settled abroad. One early morning, Hakimni, by now in her nineties, took to the world hereafter and Hakimji moved into the new villa. Hakimji, in his new environment, turned quieter though he continued with his practice and busied himself with gardening in the evenings. His high-pitched voice and the traditional demure never withered away. Encountering Hakimji even in those years often appeared daunting, though one wondered about his agony due to his separation from his two sons. Even the daughters, now settled abroad, could not visit Hakimji that often so he tried to keep himself busy with Jawaid's daughters whenever they came back from the Convent School in Murree. Hakimji, in the company of Jawaid, visited relatives mostly early in the evenings but continued with his aloof lifestyle, imbued with a bit of authority. Even after decades, general deference towards this cousin was too visible to be missed. Other than his persona, it was his profession that created that enduring aura. Hakimji, as the name itself suggested, was no ordinary person; he was the wisest of all—the local *Aflatoon*—Plato!

It was in 1998 that a visit on a summer afternoon slightly disrupted Hakimji's gardening schedule though it was compensated with a journey into my own memory lane. His warmth was unmissable as we sat in the veranda in slightly modern wick chairs overlooking rows of roses, jasmine, and tulips, while a quiet but alert attendant served us tea and sandwiches, with Hakimji sipping on his own limewater. Here I sat before almost a century of experience, wisdom, knowledge, and kindness, and the sound level had not lost a single byte. A year earlier, I had spent a day in Old Delhi visiting the Jama Mosque and nearby residence of Mirza Asadullah Ghalib (1797–1869), the most famous Indian poet who wrote in Urdu and Persian. Right across from Ghalib's dilapidated house was Hakim Ajmal Khan's clinic and the school that had trained generations of physicians in traditional medicine. Hakim Khan had been active in Indian politics in the early quarter of the twentieth century but his reputation was anchored on his astuteness as a successful physician and tutor of traditional Greek and Indian medicines. Hakimji had been a student in this clinic long before Partition and long before my birth. I had just ventured in and, finding my way through stools, patients, and rows of jars, had met a senior hakim busy suggesting Unani medicines to men and women. His eloquent Urdu was not lost on me. I introduced myself simply as a Pakistani academic on a visit to Shahjahanabad eager to visit Ajmal Khan's *Dawakhana*. Ajmal Khan had been a front row leader in the Khilafat Movement that aimed at saving the Ottoman Caliphate in the teeth of Allied opposition and a cooked-up Arab revolt. These alert Indian Muslims were enthused by Pan-Islamism and, being mobile and professional, sought greater respect for the only remaining vestige of the Muslim past. Indian Muslims had sent doctors and volunteers to Constantinople to help injured soldiers and civilians who had been the victims of one more Balkan War.

Here I was in one of the oldest centres of traditional medicines called Unani or Greek, and where my senior cousin had been a student two generations back. That was my ticket for this liberty in reaching the hakim sahib in his *Dawakhana*, though obviously he would not know about Malik Muhammad Nawaz from a farther part of Punjab which was now a different country altogether. I was offered a special wicker chair and soon a cup of tea appeared with some local sweets while I tried to catch a glimpse of photos on the wall. In a short time and out of courtesy, I engaged in small talk with the hakim sahib while thinking of Hakimji, living hundreds of miles away in a different town and a different era!

While narrating the visit to his alma mater, I could see Hakimji enlivening for a moment yet the self-restraint soon struck back. Hakimji and Jawaid sat as two widowers, since Khawar had also passed away after a bout with cancer. Her treatment in London, despite a short recovery, had not cured her completely, though in her short visit to Oxford she, like Hakimji, still exhibited resilience. She wanted to live for these two men and for her daughters who were soon getting married in Lahore as extremely good grooms had been found for them. Khawar passed away in her adopted town and willed to be buried amongst many of those who had wondered about this 'outside' girl opting to live amongst them as a new member of the Hakim family.

Massi Mulkhan had already died and at her funeral Hakimji's sons kept their distance from their father. According to mother, Massi had forgiven Hakimji but both could not meet often partly because of their advanced age and largely because both the sons did not want their father's presence in their home. It is said that they did not participate in Hakimji's funeral either after he passed away one morning after his early prayers. According to Jawaid, Hakimji had offered his prayers and as always sat for a while in the chair to rest and gain the right posture as by now he had been quite weak and often needed to sit after some exertion. He had asked for his glass of milk that he drank every morning after prayers and just sat looking at the wall in the empty house. Soon his soul departed from his body; though Jawaid tried his best to revive Hakimji, he had already breathed his last. His end was dignified like his entire life which was governed by discipline, reserve, and a high degree of self-assurance. The lawn appeared to have been tended recently, in fact Hakimji had been busy the previous evening without failing his daily activity. The monsoon had brought the desired lush spring to the lawn and Hakimji had mowed the grass without any apparent sign of weakness or sudden exhaustion.

Once again, it was several months later that I visited the house to relive the eventful life of a late but senior cousin. The pictures, books, brown bag, stethoscope, prayer mat, and manicured lawn were all there but not Hakimji. The next day, I visited his grave, surrounded by all the bygones, certainly the graveyard brought back the memories of the departed souls, especially of Khawar, the outsider, now part of a bigger family and with Hakimji also ensconced in the vicinity. Massi Mulkhan was not too far from her son, whereas my mother rested nearby, close to my father and in the proximity of *Naanaji* and *Naani*. They were together in the world hereafter and quite certainly in peace.

3

Harold Marcus:
Remembering an Era in Michigan

I learnt of Professor Harold Marcus' demise on 13 January 2003 through an H-Asia email. A specialist on North-eastern Africa, Marcus, known to his students and colleagues as Harold, was a formidable, humorous, and enthusiastic historian. His academic tenure at Michigan State University (MSU) spanned several decades and continents. Of course, he will be missed by all of us who knew him and were taught by him. Driving a big Merc amongst numerous Chevrolets and Oldsmobiles in the 1970s, Harold sported thick glasses under a flowy lock of sandy hair. His sad demise rekindled the sweet memories of my graduate years at MSU and a pleasant interaction with its historians and other fellow academics. Our life in that era had been deeply impacted by events such as the Kent State killings, Watergate crisis, Yom Kippur War, the Arab Oil Embargo of 1973, and the mysterious murder of King Faisal of Saudi Arabia, amidst a serious disenchantment with the US policies in the developing world, especially at places like Vietnam and the Middle East. Led by a rather plain President Gerald Ford, a fellow Michigander, America searched for its destiny amidst growing scepticism. Ours was a small group of postgraduates seeking out solutions to the then Third World problems through the sages of the same, simultaneously attempting to bring about a change within the most powerful capitalist democracy. Our naivety led us to both overestimate and underrate America's potential to make or mar the world at large. Our hearts simmered with hope as we demonstrated for hundred and one causes besides working as janitors, cleaners, bus boys, waiters, or delivery boys. We felt secure in the sense that we were a vocal part of a trans-territorial Third World and the future Fanons, Cabrals, Eqbal Ahmads, and Chomskys. It looked so simple then. Our youth was nourished on Joan Baez and Bob Dylan's music; our souls had been inspired by a wise grey Old World and groomed by the well-meaning cosmopolitan elite of the West. Collectively, we believed in ridding the world of harrowing forces of poverty, racism, exploitation, and war. We all believed in a new Afro-Asian-Latino world which would offer humanity the best possible alternative. Most of all, we were an optimist bunch of students often pursuing our ideals in a Bohemian way, yet not short on kindred spirit.

***

It was a cold wintry morning of November 1987 when I walked into the corridor of the old Morrill Hall at MSU, East Lansing, my old alma mater. This was my first visit after completing my doctorate eight years earlier. As I wandered across, I realized that nothing seemed to have changed in this ancient building, 'Hi Iftikhar, you are back!' sounded a familiar voice. This was Harold emerging from his room with his usual smile and warm affection. While we both moved ahead for what was going to be a hug, the elevator door opened and out came Jim, a former class-fellow and the head of the African Studies programme at some East coast university. It was a wonderful and spontaneous surprise for the three of us; Harold's face, in particular, shone with a warm glow on seeing two of his former students from the East and the West standing in front of him with their grateful eyes fixed on their teacher, a guru.

Harold had taught me during the mid-1970s and rather launched several of my compatriots into Third World Studies. We read books on Africa, Afro-Asian unity, women and gay liberation movements, discussed David Kimche, Albert Lutuli, Jomo Kenyatta, Bernard Lewis, Kwame Nkrumah, W. E. B. Du Bois, Camara Laye, Frantz Fanon, Marcus Garvey, Martin Luther King, Malcolm X, Harry Magdoff, Aimé Césaire, and god knows how many more! His seminar series 893 and 894 was collegial, thought provoking, and usually ended before running full three hours which was a great relief especially when one worried about the long lonely four hours that were spent every night cleaning up the huge science blocks. One of my favourite places was a chemistry professor's office which kept an unending supply of *Playboys*. Another favourite recess stop was the TV studios where a producer kept all the 'juicy' calendars; the only nuisance would be a tipsy Mr Palmer, the senior supervisor making surprise checks on student labour at odd hours and always appearing unhappy, though no less drunk.

Harold was not the only one who engaged us, admonished us, and even gave us good grades; Thomas Hooker was the other Africanist whose seminars ended up in the bars on Grand River Avenue. Hooker tragically died in the Upper Peninsula while camping one summer when his tent caught fire. He had studied at London's School of Oriental and African Studies (SOAS) and had interacted with the African and Asian students. His cosmopolitanism went quite well with our romantic ideas of a growing Third World, away from the drudgeries of a polarized North. Mao, Castro, Che, Nehru, and Mandela shook us all, though Gandhi confused our youthful 'radicalism' in the heart of the American conservative Midwest. The Black Panthers, Black Muslims, Red *Moslems* (a contemporary Native American group), all made us look for a wider world all around us. Our liberalism was not merely confined to finishing off beer by pitchers; it stayed along to engage in a purposeful activism. Harry Goulet's classes mainly dealt with China, with each week convening at a different venue including once at my place where we experimented with chicken curry and split peas daal. The gallon of Red Rosé helped everyone gulp down the vagaries of spicy food cooked by a naïve 'native'. By the end of the seminar, more than Mao's Red, the red chillies and Red Rosé had already taken their toll upon several of us. That evening, we were reading *Don't Fall off the Mountains!* by Shirley MacLaine who was one of the six pioneer American women to have ventured into Mao's China. We reminisced about Hooker's death for several years to come as we missed him dearly and often talked about his fondness for a joint which had reportedly caused the fire in his tent.

Douglas T. Miller, apparently a shy and rather unassuming academic, always surprised us with his fantastic books in the realm of intellectual history. We literally devoured his *The Fifties: The Way We Really Were* in our sober moments to understand the vibes from the 1950s. Doug had written it with Marion Novak, his partner; both would periodically disappear to Nova Scotia during the summer breaks. A historian and a novelist working together and leading a combined weekly seminar warmed us up through the Michigan winter. Our idealism was further activated when we demonstrated a whole year for the release of

Sami Ismael, a Palestinian-American who had been interned in Israel while visiting his ailing father. Our rooms and digs were filled with revolutionary posters; my acquaintances duly warned me against such an activity as it might result in sleuths charging my premises. Our rallies made national news, and Sami's release was a no mean feat for all of us. We rushed to Lansing's Airport to welcome and kiss a smiling Sami. That picture will never leave my memory, no matter what happens in Israel or the United States.

It was in one of those classes of Harold's that, after having memorized Betty Friedan, Robin Morgan, and Eleanor Flexner, we sat meekly to hear a known woman liberationist deliver her monologue on male chauvinism. Nancy Friday was still not making any news though we were getting used to Gloria Steinem, Alice Kessler-Harris, and Germaine Greer. On a query, our guest speaker snubbed me: '… come off it, I know you all Muslim chauvinist pigs!' I was flabbergasted for a moment and would have reacted rather sternly if not for Harold's timely intervention. Anyway, I knew it was not out of any personal rancour against Muslims as such; it was a rather queer sense of humour. No doubt, the Oil Embargo, the Arab-Israeli wars, and the UN resolution on Zionism had begun to vitiate the communal atmosphere in the United States but Muslims were still far from being cumulatively denigrated as terrorists. Being an international student was still a privilege, sometimes exotic too. Though Linda Blandford's *Oil Sheikhs* or the various novels and movies had begun to transmit negative images of the Arabs in particular, the embryonic political Islam was still an academic monopoly.

The anti-Shah resentment was gathering momentum daily in contemporary America and elsewhere with several Iranian dissenting groups chanting together *Marg bar Shah!* (Death for the Shah). The stories about CIA's linkages with several Muslim rulers further fuelled our angst, though the greatest shock was its alleged connection with the great Gandhiite, Morarji Desai, whose confession of drinking his own urine gathered miles in the tabloid press. These revelations were still more puzzling at a time when Indira Gandhi had herself become so unpopular, especially after imposing Emergency in India. My knowledge of Persian helped me in translating leaflets and handouts on Shah's atrocities in Iran. I memorized the Sāzemān-e Ettelā'āt va Amniyat-e Keshvar's (SAVAK) list of crimes, including the political murders of anti-Shah activists. In my private moments, I still wonder about the destiny of Masoud, Afroz, Leyla, Suroosh, and many other Iranian friends who might have been killed during the long Iraq-Iran War. I could see these young Iranians turning more religious and seeking strong resistance in Shia traditions. On the other hand, there were several Iranians in the US whose academic sojourns never went beyond nightly parties and fun. The Shah had sent a whole generation of these people abroad under his modernizing project. The Saudis and other Gulf Arab students also made a visible presence on America's campuses and reflected this ideological divide (no wonder King Khalid's cabinet had more PhDs from Yale and Harvard than President Carter's). The funniest Saudi student colleague was Abdullah who was routinely carried by us a few nights a week from his car or from the dorm corridor to his bed since his stamina could not take in more than a few drinks. Before his departure back home on holidays, Abdullah would suddenly turn into a pious Muslim by growing a beard and starting to look more like a sober prince. On the other hand, my historian friend, Yusuf, endlessly dilated on the Egyptian Queen Nefertiti's escapades and Marcus' Jewish liberalism. A short man otherwise, Yusuf relished the longest cigars. We all enjoyed Ed Trusswell's drunken outbursts on Old Milwaukee when he would reiterate for the umpteenth time his resolve to take us home to his parents in Detroit where his mother would cook us the most sumptuous halal beef meal. Ironically, his ultimate desire in life was a beer-filled pool, and disgustingly enough, full of Old Milwaukee! Our more intellectual Oxonian-style Connecticut Yankee, Tom Sullivan, would have nothing to do with such wild maniacs, except for the fact that we were a 'different' bunch of warm-hearted crazies from the Old East. Variably, we would receive calls from his mother on his behalf with ready-made excuses of his immense academic engagements while Sullivan, suited like a tweedy English don, may be tutoring a young Midwestern maiden on sexual mores in England as depicted by Erica Jong in her *Fanny*.

Harold undertook a visit to India—a delayed 1960s style sojourn to the East. In fact, one of his former Afghan students held an important ministerial position in President Daud's government. He enjoyed a red carpet treatment and drove through the Khyber Pass into Pakistan to terminate his pleasure trip in India. He came back radiant and jubilant. 'Did you get a chance to see the British embankments and the tribal posts across the historic pass, Harold?' I asked innocuously. 'Oh yes, yes, we did—rough terrain though Iftikhar!' he answered. On my prodding on the Grand Trunk Road and journey through Kim's Lahore before reaching India, Harold gave out one of his big laughs, 'To tell you the truth, both K and I were so stoned after leaving Jalalabad that we do not remember anything from that 270 mile journey on the GT Road across Pakistan. We came back to some normalcy only somewhere near Amritsar, you know, that Holy Place!' Somehow, I knew he was not serious.

I could not say anything more to a man who was always in a hurry even while crossing countries. But I remember him and his other colleagues including the tough Warren Cohen, an affable Paul Varg, a verbose Duggan, a modest Surjeet Dulai, a knowledgeable Fauzi Najjar, an affectionate Victor Howard, and even a non-academic Mr Duff Sr. who always called me 'a terrible Turk' but was mindful of not saying it in front of a Greek or an Armenian. I hope Harold had a peaceful end and the closing days of his life were more like his smooth journey through the Khyber Pass.

4

Revisiting Michigan State University:
Lost for Words

Certainly Michigan State University (MSU) is an expansive, rather grand campus, spread over thousands of acres featuring miles of sidewalks and cycle paths while the Cedar River criss-crosses this Midwestern campus lying close to the capital city of Lansing that once was home to the Olds Brothers. The university, in its early incarnation during the mid-nineteenth century, was a land grant college and had been endowed with extensive lands. Despite an enormity of modern oblong or square structures which may not impress prying eyes from the 'Old' Europe, MSU still boasts of its share of lovely redbrick buildings, encircled by some magnificent trees. It was in fact the emotional aspect of going back to this alma mater that weighed heavily on my mind on that cold yet sunny March day in 2006 when spring had not yet set in, though winter had long lost its poignancy. In a usually snow-bound, wintry Michigan, prudence warns against any early spring as it can snow 'any minute' even in an otherwise balmy April. Still wandering by the river with a fewer number of pedestrians due to the spring term break, the number of bikes hitched at numerous stands certainly was rather encouraging compared to what it was three decades back. Some of the older bikes, predating the more slick and gadgetry reincarnations, reminded me of the rickety Raleigh that once carried me around a sprawling MSU. A much used two-wheeler, more akin to resting and rusting, it must have been confined to a history bin, unless some antique-loving soul had decided to reinvent the tottering denizen which, in its prime, had surely seen some greener pastures and youthful ventures.

Three decades later, all the familiar faces were long gone and it was only in the older buildings, residence halls, and less traversed winding pavements that one encountered glimpses of an unchanging MSU. The goods trains still passed by frequently blowing their whistles as the barriers closed at half a dozen crossings across the campus. Rows of trees of neighbouring residence halls such as Van Hoosen, Owen, and Holmes and also bordering the Cedar all the way to Hagedorn Road had remained thick and healthy, though the number of the ducks perching behind the library had turned smaller. The Cedar River was in flood, unlike a drought-like situation in contemporary England, and the library, in place of its erstwhile domination by books and bound journals, resembled an information repository equipped with an elaborate café. In fact, the section now featuring the café was once devoted to big reference tomes and used to be the favourite hideout for Bassam, who positioned himself behind the tall stacks while consulting huge dictionaries, occasionally turning his spectacled, scholarly face around to seek a quick overview of his immediate surroundings. The calculative and equally oversexed Bassam would often involve American girls in his brooding moments to seek out the native pronunciations of the words while keeping his pen and paper ready in case they ventured to share their phone numbers. Bassam's round face, adorned both by circular glasses and a jet-black moustache, never betrayed any predatory pretensions, though he judiciously avoided engaging male students in these pedagogical pursuits. The smart student from managerial sciences had no time and patience to waste on guys. A fleeting glance at a busy café only brought back the memories of an amorous friend, lost somewhere in the obsessive concrete jungle of a consumerist Gulf.

During this visit, I was determined to seek out my favourite washroom, John, in the library where I, like several others of my generation, had spent long interludes to decipher graffiti which, contrary to common misperceptions, was not always so crass. My favourite inscriptions on the two opposite walls, while vying with each other during that Cold War era, stated: 'Join US Marines and intervene in any country of your choice' and 'Visit USSR before USSR visits you'. These words of wisdom were long gone like the Cold War itself yet in the flurry of an extended interview and a rush to catch up with a friend from Kalamazoo, the cereal capital of the world, I could not update myself on the latest in the post-modern hieroglyphics.

One wonders how these apparently mute buildings and other similar landmarks at my old alma mater could invoke some of the fondest memories, especially when familiar names and faces were not easy to locate even by otherwise efficient secretaries, hired to succeed their bygone predecessors. The names of those long-retired academes, in most cases, got confused with some similar current names as the historian Douglas T. Miller invoked the addresses of some three retired Millers, of course with varying middle initials. These amused secretaries did not know how to react to a nostalgic and curious middle-aged man trying to be on his best behaviour yet they remained true to a courteous professionalism. They were polite and tried to be helpful and when they could not find answers, they looked at their colleagues and asked, 'Heard about Professor Russell Nye? He passed away about two decades back.' However, Victor Howard was confused with another Howard recruiting students in Cork along with his new girlfriend. Even a boisterous Harold Marcus, who died three years back, took some time in being identified in these corridors whose imposing, noisy, and thick doors once opened into the dens occupied by Cohen, Hooker, Varg, Reed, Gross, Nye, and a few others. Manning and Achebe sounded familiar in Morrill Hall which was now itself agonized with a constant hammering from next door where concrete slabs were going up by each passing minute to erect a car park. What a travesty to hem in this older MSU with the countless floors of gas-guzzlers! Mercifully, the Marshall Hall, another ancient monument, stood aloof and apparently unencumbered, though the Berkey was destined to go into purdah behind the emerging irreverent car park.

While hurrying out of the once-native Morrill Hall, a visitor might be dichotomically placed between a tourist with a prying camera and a father seeking out his erring son last seen lost in the classics. The graduate seminar rooms in the 'ancient' hall looked the same after having absorbed IT invasion, though the furniture somehow appeared familiar and even more indifferent. A seminar was to begin as I surreptitiously peeped in to reassure some startled faces by quipping that here once a woman liberationist, without any reason or rhyme, had blurted out an unenviable epithet for a young foreigner whose unruly, thick curly hair over a bushy moustache would elicit either friendliness or a total lack of interest. Then it was soon after the 1973 Middle Eastern War and the oil embargo that all us brown people with Muslim names and natural 'Afros' had become synonymous with the 'hated' Arabs who, as per prevalent stereotypes, drove luxury cars and lived in posh flats. The UN resolution in 1974 equating Zionism with racism had added further strains but the Americans in general were still friendly and chatty. Certainly, it was an era when being Muslim would not evince suspicions sending travellers into special cabins where reviews conducted by the American immigration officials and Homeland Security would go on endlessly, occasionally resulting in immediate deportations.

Our conference was in the International Center that had not changed a bit except for its name, though the cafeteria within had somehow reinforced the stereotypes of the usual American fast food joints which today characterize an increasing number of British campuses. While one might miss a continental-style café culture and the English pubs in small-town America, it is because of the emphasis on fast food, pizzas, the size of giant submarines, and unlimited refills of soft drinks that one starts yearning for healthier snacks in a more relaxed sociable ambience. This time around, the memorable sight was of a bearded student absorbed in a book while simultaneously sipping from a giant size Pepsi glass; he took off the moment his dual action came to an abrupt end. Of course, the Kellogg Conference Center is more like a luxury hotel now where students are occasionally spoiled by parents or Asian visitors congregate for conferences on automobiles and electronic gadgets. However, cafeterias in the Union and International Center were a world apart from their predecessors in the 1970s and seemed to embody a concept in quick catering and no socialization. The residence halls at MSU, locally called dormitories, have a certain element of self-sufficiency that reminded one of Oxbridge colleges, of course, without the luxury of butteries, scouts, common rooms, and high tables. Here at MSU, each floor in a residence hall features study lounges which can provide privacy to quickly draft a term paper besides catering to smaller parties or study groups and yoga sessions.

Detecting a large proportion of students at the conference's inaugural session, I thought of breaking the ice, owing to the luxury of extra time, since the other plenary speaker had been stranded at the Toronto Airport due to the vagaries of the weather.

'I first came to your lovely campus 32 years ago as a young and rather naïve student.' I could see the eyes squinting to detect an increasing number of wrinkles behind my glasses and a growing grey in a thinning crop of hair. 'I am as ancient as your Morrill Hall,' was my rejoinder, followed by a prompt defence: 'As an historian, where we normally talk of centuries and millennia, these 32 years surely do not count for much,' and I could see the smiles returning with an effort to grasp an accent that had lost its American veneer and, despite its British wherewithal, still somehow sounded 'Yankeeish'; or at least, the speaker with a rather very tall frame looked more like a Texan, lodged in donnish attire. Given the nature of my themes such as Islam, British Muslim youth, and the post-7/7 tensions, the audience might had been seeing in me a representation of British multiculturalism that itself has been bruised in a rhetorical see-saw. These issues again resurfaced in a discussion with the correspondent from the *State News*, where curiosity and interest in the societies across the Atlantic beamed through several questions. Just a day or two before the fourth anniversary of the invasion of Iraq, Donald Rumsfeld's *Old Europe* had predictably invoked probing interest through Asia and the Middle East; all sounded distant and equally ambiguous in the Midwest, itself more calculative and cautious in dealing with an academic who might have once spent several formative years of his youth here.

The Hagedorn Road, marking the eastern end of the MSU campus, now featured an entire row of churches, standing sentinel for young erring souls residing in some of the biggest halls such as Hubbard, Acres, and Holmes. While the MSU Sparrow Hospital and Marriott have spread across to the other side of this artery beyond the ever-busy railway tracks, I could not find some of those social hideouts which had once attracted sinners from amongst us. One of those places was reputed to hold dance competitions where participants were encouraged to flaunt their physical and artistic attributes on the tabletops. My own crude geographical skills identified a pizza parlour and a gym now displaying their neon signs over those bygone sites. Interestingly, the other end of the campus, bordered by the Harrison Road, sported an impressive Islamic centre, neighboured by a few old-time churches. Omar Al-Soubani, an old friend and a genteel soul, ran this complex, which in our time was a rather solitary green wooden structure. East Lansing had seen the disappearance of various familiar places, though the Bell's, Dairy Queen,

Little Caesar's, and Aztecito's still featured in the same neighbourhood, thanks to an undiminished presence of youth. An imposing hotel had sprung right in the heart of this university town and it took quite an effort to locate good old Linden Street where Al-Hillel now presided over the erstwhile rooming house that once used to be my pad. I flattered myself in assuming that the Rabbi might be using my old room as his office long after having anointed it against all its past accretions.

The woods next to the newly built health centre stood mute on my last morning at MSU and the trees held themselves aloft for a delayed spring, though the green patch leading to the entrance had been converted into a parking lot. It was here on that balmy morning in the autumn of 1974 that I had first sat to absorb Michigan's sun while thinking of years ahead at a university that initially overawed me with its size. It was certainly here that over a sandwich and a rather massive apple, an unending East-West journey had begun in earnest and which still continues inconclusively. In between, I was thinking of Anwar, my Pashtun friend who had been teaching engineering at the Gonzaga University for the past three decades, and other than working full time in his lab, would allow himself the luxury of playing soccer with some South American students. Anwar, a man of few words but a heart full of affection and kindness, had taken us all to a university in Brookings, South Dakota, to advise him on his new posting soon after his PhD; that busy Memorial Weekend journey itself turned out to be an indelible memory. Subsequently, I had visited Anwar in Spokane as I travelled across American northwest in the company of this agile fellow from Pakistan's northwest. Anwar also visited us in Oxford in 2005 and I took him to Bath which he liked for its hilly terrain, view card-like villages, and stone-built Georgian mansions. Though a teetotaller, Anwar enjoyed visiting English pubs to try his favourite beef and cucumber sandwiches though he avoided fish and chips. He preferred to eat daal at our home though once in a while he made *karahi* in Afridi style.

While sitting there, that brisk morning in 2006, I remembered Shams and Sofi, an Indian Muslim couple who held teaching fellowship in English and liked to discuss religion and politics enthusiastically. Shams, senior to most of us in age and experience, elicited well-deserved respect, and before his doctoral research on Virginia Woolf had been a Bollywood star. I knew about his passing away in the 1990s though I had lost touch with Sofi who most probably had moved to Canada where some of her relatives lived. Another friend, Zaki, had been at MSU slightly later than my session, though I had met up with him in 1987 during a short postdoctoral stay at MSU. Finishing his doctoral studies along with his wife, Khalida, herself a postgraduate student, Zaki was a look-alike of Tom Jones, the Welsh pop singer, and certainly enjoyed singing Punjabi folk songs. In the mentioned visit, while driving me around MSU, he had complained of pain in his fingertips and overall slowness in physique which had been initially diagnosed as chronic fatigue symptoms. However, he had some kidney disease which, combined with cardiac arrest, turned lethal and Zaki breathed his last. I visited his widow who took us to Mount Hope cemetery where I left flowers, both for Shams and Zaki, and spent some time reminiscing about time spent together with these genteel souls. During my time, I do not recall the existence of any Muslim graveyard in Lansing but now I could see quite a few resting places in the corner of this cemetery which had claimed some close friends in the past. It is not located far from the Spartan Village, the married housing for Spartans, and lies after a national park-cum-zoo where I often used to go to enjoy autumn colours besides saying hello to a caged bald eagle. The signboard outside its huge hermitage in the 1970s read something like this: 'This is perhaps the first and last bald eagle that you may see in your lifetime'. Worries about pollution and its cost on the animal kingdom had already turned into a major subject in the 1970s.

When the 72-year-old Chinese-American taxi driver started the journey back to the Lansing Airport, I was still quietly reliving my time at MSU while saying one more farewell to its familiar environs. An unstoppable conversationalist rumbling about his wife, health, and daily dosage of cod liver oil, the driver constantly tried to divert my reverie until we skirted around the Capitol to move further west. I wish I could have stopped in the Chestnut Street to take a look at the bohemian house where my friend, Monica, and her group lived and planned for a world revolution in ecology. Parallel to this road used to be a funeral home where Gordon, one of my class fellows, used to reside since he also worked as a caretaker in that multistorey building. He would regale us with the stories of his escapades in Vietnam, whereas Carol was more interested in wine tasting. Gordon subsequently moved to Cleveland with some other Carol without losing a bit of his verve. I wonder what happened to Marty who used to hold heated discussion with Gordon over Israel, being its unrestrained supporter though slightly in awe of Harold Marcus. Contrary to my musings, our taxi driver was more intent upon narrating his own monologue, soliciting my attention on and off.

At Lansing's airport, like all other passengers including a few disabled amongst them, I was thoroughly searched and had to take my shoes off before being let in. I remembered the parting words of Fred, the taxi driver, when he had cautiously alerted me about what was to come: 'Sir, you are a visitor. But don't mind the body search and the crude manners of the security personnel. They get only $7.50 per hour for their work and are an unhappy lot'. I could see how time changes us all and the United States had certainly changed quite a bit since 9/11.

5

An Evening with Hafiz Shirazi at the Nehru Gallery, London

Khwaja Sham-ud-Din Muhammad Hafiz (1320–89) of Shiraz, an ascetic poet, lover of beauty, both in its human and natural forms, surely the most preeminent ghazal poet of any time in any language, fuses the orthodox and the atheists together—something unique to this writer whose mother tongue, Persian, was once the lingua franca of almost half of the known world. A believer who had memorized the Quran by heart, all the 75,000 words, and had been tutored by some of the most eminent literary mentors, surprised both his predecessors and followers through his composition of lyrical poems which continue to defy restrictions of time, creed, class, and ethnicity. While Maulana Rumi (1207–73), through his *Masnavi* and generations of whirling dervishes, has given us, per Muhammad Iqbal (1875–1938), the second Quran in Persian;[1] Hafiz's romantic compositions escort lovers and worshippers to a different realm altogether. His uniquely selected words resound with some of the rarest similes and metaphors that even a modern, worldly person can relish with an equal sense of belonging and pristine transparency. His verses cajole, motivate, and enchant human aesthetics before turning into a serenade to human dignity. They uniquely bestow a superb elevation to devotional love for a paragon of beauty and sublimity in whose proximity even the angels may tread meekly. His beloved is not just a wholesome person; she remains unsurpassed by virtue of her apparent and inner distinctness. Her eyes are like those of a doe while the curved mihrabs in a mosque remind the besotted lover of her bow-like eyebrows shooting arrows straight into the latter's inner recesses. No wonder Hafiz remains the king of ghazal in all the languages between Bosnia and Bengal and his *Diwan*,[2] is a vital part of the traditional *Haft Seen* table that graces the Nowruz celebrations across the wider Persianate.

According to some narratives, Hafiz, who worked in a bakery, was in love with a contemporary beauty and embodied the desire and devotion for her nearness in his heart, however, he was stalled by his own humbleness or even by a kind of timidity that traditions or age, if not class, may impose in such situations. Like the proverbial blazing oven, he felt the depth and intensity of his love for that *pari chehreh* (fairy face) yet any thought of her nearness held him back for fear of being burnt like a *parvaneh* (moth). Hafiz, like Mirza Ghalib of Delhi and Muhammad Iqbal of Lahore, would have his own disciples and acolytes but did not lack in critics either, with some orthodox sheikhs leading them. A knowledgeable man, more like the Shakespeare of later centuries, he was fully apprised of delicate sensibilities as well as vulnerabilities which he combined with his own personal celebratory grief, reposing universal undertones. His knowledge of the sacred and secular allowed his disciples to put their own meanings to his words and ideas; however, they all agreed on the limitlessness of human feelings, devotion, and aesthetics that brokered no religious or racial distinctions and thus turned a lover into proverbial Farhad, an industrious, self-motivated, and committed individual who single-handedly triumphed in digging up the canal to reach Shireen, the coveted princess. However, where genuine love inculcates courage and endurance, it may equally unleash grief and even tragedy, either in the form of dejection or plain death. Farhad's beloved had been surreptitiously wedded to some other princeling and the former killed himself with the same *taishay* (axe) that he had used for years to dig up the canal to her father's palace, similar to Majnoon who loses his kingdom and even his self while looking for Lailah in the deserts of Arabia. Farhad symbolizes a perfect, hard-earned devotion, whereas Manjoon signifies *fana* (the terminal end) or lost in devotion. Thus, Hafiz's love is more than time-bound, youth-centred physical adoration. Instead, it turns into an Abrahamic or Muhammadan surrender, a form of prophetic tradition that elevates the lover to the highest status with the beloved somehow turning into an ultimate yet unattainable reality.

In a powerful way, Hafiz's poetry is beholden to physical attributes yet goes beyond that; it searches and celebrates inner endowments which makes his lover as *khusrow-i-shireen dehnaan* (the prince of those whose words usher sweetness and eloquence) and whose lashes break the hearts of the victorious warriors. Like any genius tested against the pedestrian yardstick of time, Hafiz was misunderstood and anguished by some of his contemporaries until a more intense form of austerity and reclusiveness took over his life. In one of his ghazals, Hafiz celebrated the attributes of his beloved in such a splendid way that even the most powerful and dreaded ruler of the time, Tamerlane, got incensed. Hafiz had simply recited:

Aggar aan Turk-i-Shirazi badast arad dil-i-maa raa
Bakhal-i-hinduish bakhsham Samarkando Bokhara raa.

If that Shirazi Turkish beloved takes care of my heart,
I am surely prepared even to give away both Samarkand
and Bokhara just for the sake of that one mole on her face.[3]

Tamerlane/Amir Timur (1370–1405), who had lost his leg and arm fighting for these Central Asian cities and for building up one of the largest empires in west Asia, read the verse to his chagrin at a time when he happened to be in Shiraz, the affluent city of knowledge, poets, and lovers. Understandably enraged, he summoned Hafiz to his court to admonish the otherworldly poet and said something to the effect: 'Don't you realize the struggle and sacrifices I've made to capture these two very beautiful cities whereas you, an ordinary poet, are ready to give them away for the sake of a woman's mole?' The austere Hafiz, in his own poetic renunciation, responded: 'Well, it is this very reckless nature of my generosity of giving away everything that has left nothing in worldly possessions except for this plain prayer mat where I sit day-long by the stream of Ruknabad'.[4] The conqueror was immensely amused by the wit, honesty, and the depth of poet's personality and let him go.

Hafiz was ostracized by the denizens of orthodoxy for his celebration of human physical attributes that he found in his generously endowed beloved. He often annoyed his critics by celebrating wine that, like Khayyam, was seen to be uplifting, or more recently like Ghalib, Faiz, and Faraz, who found it seductive. Reportedly, his funeral turned disputatious since those ulema refused to offer prayers for a 'worldly' person who mostly sang of women and wine, and the believers started to move away from the deceased until a thoughtful worldly soul counselled for reconsideration:

'I understand that Hafiz also wrote of divine love and we should not forget that he was a fellow Muslim. How can we abandon a believer's body just like that?' the wise man sought their indulgence.

'Then, how do we reconcile our own religious obligations given his mundane obsessions?' they retorted.

'Well, Hafiz wrote his couplets on scraps of papers and shards of ceramics before depositing them in his pitcher (*Surahee*). One of us may lower his hand into it and recite the first verse we find. If it is about divine love, we will go ahead with the funeral prayers, otherwise we move on.' His argument made some sense and a piece of paper was winched out to be read aloud before the crowd. It was a shocker: 'Don't withdraw from Hafiz's funeral; he may be a sinner, yet is heading straight towards heaven.'[5]

The verse had a dramatic effect on believers who began to perceive the erstwhile poet as a seer. Since then, Hafiz's tomb by the Ruknabad continues to attract millions of pilgrims, lovers, and picnickers to partake the bounties of his wit, eloquence, romance, and spirituality. Hafiz soon reached the lengths and breadths of Hindustan, Central Asia, and the Ottoman Empire. Subsequently upon the Europeanization of the world through a colonial hegemony and Orientalism; especially in the nineteenth century, he began to epitomize eastern wisdom, love, devotion, and mysticism. He inspired romantic poets like Tennyson, Shelley, and Byron, and a generation of translators including Edward Fitzgerald (1809–83), who introduced 'the old East' to the West. In North America, Ralph Waldo Emerson and Henry David Thoreau were greatly influenced by Sheikh Saadi (1210–92), Hafiz, and other classicists from this part of the world. Globalization of Hafiz continues despite the fact that fewer people are reading poetry and the knowledge of once-universal languages such as Persian, Sanskrit, and Latin is now confined to smaller groups of specialists. In this context, holding a short seminar on Hafiz, followed by musical renditions of some of his ghazals, was not an ordinary challenge that Ziauddin Shakeb and a few other colleagues undertook in London.

The Nehru Centre, run by the Indian government, is located in Mayfair. In its plush lecture theatre—about 70 Hafiz disciples, with a clear majority of seniors and some younger souls—an official of the centre welcomed us by amusingly mispronouncing several names involved.

Hafiz was announced as Hafee'z; Ziauddin Shakeb became Ziuddin Shakob and Ilmi Majlis turned into Hindi Majlis. Luckily, these atrocities were short-lived, however, they brazenly showed the current state of the once-celebrated Indo-Persian culture where Urdu, Persian, and Muslim names have now become a part of some distant, alien, obscure past. Listening to that welcome from the cultural and literary denizen representing the world's most plural country further brought home the need for holding this evening on these premises and not anywhere else. However, another travesty followed soon, though it was again short-lived; we were welcomed to the session by another speaker, herself a barrister who, after a tête-à-tête with Shakeb, disappeared from the hall altogether with an Anglo-Saxon soul following her out. Their exit was obvious and amusing yet in retrospect, it saved us from some more embarrassing moments as Shakeb, in his lucid Urdu, delivered us back to Hafiz.

To Shakeb, Hafiz was enthusiastically followed in India by all kinds of literary figures including Muhammad Qutb Shah, the first Urdu poet from the Deccan. Shakeb rightly introduced Hafiz as the greatest ghazal poet of any language who remains unsurpassed even amongst the contemporary poets. The Indian adoption of Persian for almost a thousand years enriched them both. It was under Emperor Aurangzeb that the first Persian dictionary was organized by Anand Ram Mukhlis though the Mughal emperors, their families, contemporary poets, official chroniclers, and religious scholars of all creeds invariably used Persian as the main medium of expression, irrespective of their ethnicity and gender. Shakeb, who belonged from Hyderabad, Deccan, and was a scholar of Urdu and Persian at the British Library, lamented the sundering of this superb, multidisciplinary Indo-Persian culture in the nineteenth century under the Raj. It left one wondering about the postulation that the language of Abul Fazl, Jahangir, Nur Jahan, Shah Jahan, Mumtaz Mahal, Dara Shikoh, Jahan Ara, Zebunnissa Makhfi, Shah Waliullah, Mirza Ghalib, Bahadur Shah Zafar, and Raja Ram Mohan Roy, which anchored a gelling culture in an immensely plural subcontinent, soon began to suffer from serious ruptures including the Hindi-Urdu and Hindu-Muslim disputations.

Bernard Lewisohn, an American scholar of medieval Persian thinkers such as Mahmud Shabistry (1288–1340) and an academic at Exeter University, viewed Hafiz as one of the greatest poets of Iran from amongst the Eleven Greats. While Shakeb had mentioned 25 translations of Hafiz, Lewisohn found interest in Hafiz, a major literary preoccupation of the nineteenth century poets and philosophers. Tennyson's Persian was claimed to be far superior to that of Fitzgerald whose translation of Omar Khayyam (1048–1131) is still viewed as the best. In 2010, the Fitzgerald Society completed the hundredth anniversary of its formation and the British Library convened a special exhibit on his decades-long immersion in Persian and Khayyam. This exhibit had followed an equally impressive display on Frederic Chopin (1810–49), the Polish nationalist poet-musician whose two-hundredth birth anniversary fell in the same year, though the artist never enjoyed good health and passed away even before the age of 40. To Lewisohn, the early translations of Hafiz's *Diwan*, which was undertaken by Colonel Wilberforce Clarke, suffered from some deficiencies; William Jones, Gertrude Bell, A. J. Arberry, and more recently, Peter Avery have offered more competent translations and commentaries of this Persian classic.

Khwaja Hafiz, according to Professor Lewisohn, was not an ordinary love poet as he had been a confluence of sophist and literary traditions inherited from Sheikh Saadi, Syed Shahabuddin Suhrawardy, and certainly from Shabistry. Ibn Battuta (1304–69) had found Shiraz resounding with Hafiz and 'some of the most beautiful women in the world'. Given Battuta's penchant for pedantry, as affirmed in our times by the travels and research undertaken by the Bristolean, Timothy Mackintosh-Smith, the Tangerine may be correct and, given his proneness to marry incessantly during his travels and then simply move on, the Moroccan Sufi must have amorously and minutely checked on female Shirazi Turkish presence. Shiraz, to our American scholar of Persian Sufi traditions, was ahead of any other metropolis of the time in terms of its creativity, affluence, tolerance, and higher excellence in scholarly and literary pursuits. It preceded Qum and Tabriz and certainly was the Paris of the East during the medieval period; no wonder Hafiz was its proud son as well as an illustrious emblem. During the nineteenth century, an Orientalist could dare his readers in the *Fraser's Magazine* by quizzing them about their information on Hafiz who was apparently a household name amongst the literary circles. Compared to our times, where only 8 per cent Britons share interest in poetry, contrasted with 20 per cent across the continent, a vast majority of British reading public in the nineteenth century knew about Hafiz and his poetic excellence. The 'spiritual eroticism' of Hafiz went quite well with the romantic Victorians; in the contemporary era, Louis Massingon has characterized it as 'the Quranization of culture' where sacred and secular converge, celebrating both human and divine attributes. To Lewisohn, there are 1,000 passages from the Quran which reverberate in Hafiz's *Diwan* and thus the great Persian mentor was not a heretic, as some of those sheikhs had wrongly assumed in his own time. In addition and equally in an emphatic way, Lewisohn found Hafiz to be a poet equally popular amongst the ecclesiasts, atheists, Brahmins, Sufis, Jews, Christians, and agnostics, which is certainly not an ordinary attainment.

After the speeches were completed, a recent edition of Hafiz's versed Urdu translation by Ehtishamuddin Haqqi of Delhi was unveiled amidst a genuine applause in which Persian and Urdu stand as equals without losing the originality, candour, and depth of both sides. They both are read in the same script and even sound similar yet pristinely retain their own respective distinctness—perhaps a living testimony of 'that' Indo-Persian culture. The crescendo of that evening awaited in the form of Persian-Urdu duets by Karuna and Surjeet Loomba who, through their immersion into classical ragas and intimacy with the Persian and Urdu nuances, sang us three ghazals from Hafiz's *Diwan* and their translations by Haqqi. Even with an overwhelming majority of the audience being retired diplomats, non-resident Indians (NRIs), with a small smattering of familiar literary figures in diaspora, the hall resounded with Hafiz's romantic eloquence and its penetrating rendition by two astute singers whose companions on tabla, guitar, and bass offered us a memorable nightcap:

Farsi:

> *Nokta'ee delkash be gooyam khaal e an mahroo be-been*
> *Aql-o-deen ra bas te'ye zanjeer-e-an geeso be-been.*

Urdu:

> *Nukt'ae-dilkash to sun, khaal-e-rukh-e-mehroo to deykh*
> *Aql-o-deen donon bandhey hain halq'ae gesoo to deykh.*

Listen to my heart warming point; but also witness the mole
on that moon-like face
See for yourself, how reason and faith both remain tied
together within her tangled, dark hair

Hafiz complains of the disappearance of lovers and friends though love remains there but wonders about the change in times when the world becomes even more selfish—something that we see all around us today.

The second rendition began with the following couplet:

Farsi:

> *Yaar andar kas ne-mee-be-neem yaaaran ra che shud*
> *Doostee'ee ke akhar amad doost da raan ra che shud.*

Urdu:

> *Kya hui yaari tumhari tum ko yaaron kya hua*
> *Dosti kyon mit gaee aye dost daaro kya hua.*

What happened to your friendship (love) and what happened
to you, oh friends (lovers)?
How come friendship has vanished, and oh friends what
happened to Love itself?

The third and the final ghazal began on the verse:

Farsi:

> *Dar namaazam kham-e-abroo-ye to bayaad aamad*
> *Haalati raft ke mehraab be faryaad aamad.*

Urdu:

> *Kham-e-abroo tera Masjid meain agar yaad aaye*
> *Aisee riqqat hoi ke mehraab se faryaad aaye.*

If I happen to remember the curve of your eyebrow
in the mosque,
I may begin to beseech so much that even the mihrab
might start crying[6]

Surely Hafiz, as a literary giant, deserves more sessions and extensive research, whereas his poetry needs to be read, heard, and sung more often with each occasion bestowing a newer, deeper, and more joyous experience. No wonder, Iqbal, Nehru, Faiz, Manto, and Faraz would be happier in their souls with this mentor—senior to them by six centuries—who achieved what every literary genius in any part of the world may strive to attain.

Hiding myself from a lashing rain and walking across an almost deserted Hyde Park, my soul felt replenished by the melodious creativity and sublime humanism of Hafiz Shirazi while a subdued and drenched body headed back towards the city of dreaming spires.

Notes

1. Vincent J. Cornell, *Voices of Islam* (Greenwood Publishing Group, 2006), 123.
2. Literary works of a poet.
3. Translated by the author with some minor modifications. For more details, see https://www.hafizonlove.com/divan/01/003.htm. On Hafiz's ever increasing popularity and following in his native Iran and abroad, see Robert Tait, 'Bigger than Elvis,' *The Guardian*, September 15, 2005. The Urdu versed translation of Hafiz was first published by Ehtishamuddin Haqqi of Delhi in AH 1358 (CE 1939). See Muhammad Ehtishamuddin Haqqi, *Mutaliaya Hafiz* (Delhi: Bombay J. B. Press, 1939).
4. There are several versions of this story; some even suggesting that Tamerlane in fact reached Shiraz long after Hafiz's death. However, parable of Tamerlane-Hafiz meeting in Shiraz is widely held in Iran, South Asia, and Central Asia, largely out of its poignancy or spiritual underpinnings.
5. Certainly there was a controversy soon after Hafiz's death, until his detractors were able to prevail and hold a proper funeral for the eminent poet. See Joobin Bekhrad, 'Iran's fascinating way to tell fortunes,' *BBC*, October 24, 2018.
6. For the various aspects of Hafiz's life and poetics, see Leonard Lewisohn, ed., *Hafiz and the Religion of Love in Classical Persian Poetry* (London: I. B. Tauris, 2010); also 'Hafez and His Poems' in https://www.irantravelingcenter.com/main/hafez_iran_poems_poet/.

II
TRAVERSING THE
SILK ROAD

6

Bukhara:
Amongst Scholars and Sufis

And, as the rooster crew, those who stood before
The Tavern shouted—'Open then the Door!
You know how little while we have to stay,
And, once departed, may return no more.'

Oh, come with old Khayyám, and leave the Wise
To talk; one thing is certain, that Life flies;
One thing is certain, and the Rest is Lies;
The Flower that once has blown forever dies.

Omar Khayyam[1]

A quarter of a century after the dissolution of the Soviet Union auguring independence for the various Central Asian and Baltic states, and almost half a century of hearing and reading about Bukhara Sharif, Imam Bukhari, Al-Biruni, and Ibn Sina/Avicenna (980–1037), I was finally here in the heart of the historic city. More sacred and sanctified than any other city after Makkah, Medina, and Jerusalem, Bukhara had the distinction of being a city of debate and scholarship which are uniquely attributed to the Golden Age of Muslims, and was certainly once the centre of enlightenment that preceded long before its Italian successor. Its intellectual traditions, both sacred and secular, flourished at a time when other major centres such as Damascus, Baghdad, Fes, and Cairo had been eclipsed either due to political factionalism or simply because of indolence. Turkic Bukhara, a city on the Old Silk Road and now a centre of international trade and mobility, emerged as the new threshold of Islamic Enlightenment, when both erstwhile Arab and Persian vitalities appeared to have radically declined with this region—very much like Muslim Iberia—evolving as the northern citadel of Muslim renaissance. The Perso-Turkic soldiers, Sufis, scholars, and merchants infused new ideas and a much-needed energy into the Islamicate, and with the Samanis, Seljuks, and Ghaznavids in command, Central Asia began to redefine a growing, plural Islamic civilization. Its interaction with Hinduism, Zoroastrianism, Buddhism, Judaism, and Christianity, and parleys with the Tibetans, Chinese, and Europeans in realms of political economy and social geography, the Transoxiana of the past Sogdians and latter-day Khwarazm Shahis, Timurids, and Shaybanis was destined to play a larger than life role. Enduring Central Asian forays into the South Asian subcontinent, Persia, the Caucasus, and Anatolia, largely because of demographic changes and also because of the Mongol invasions, helped Mawarannahr (Arabic for Transoxiana) attain a cosmopolitan outreach that, even after disastrous Mongol campaigns and subsequent post-eighteenth century squeeze by the Czars, failed to diminish nostalgia, respect, and pre-eminence of Central Asia across the Muslim world.

Bukharan scholars and traders once played a vanguard role in what used to be Poland-Lithuanian Commonwealth and replenished this part of north-eastern Europe with the infusion of ideas, skills, and artefacts that originated in Persia, India, and China. Helped by the Muslim Khanates of Kazan and Astrakhan, Bukharans were trading with the Vikings in Upper Volga regions, especially since the late fourteenth century, and survived the subsequent squeeze from Russification and Christianization forcefully augured by the Czars. The Bukharans, for a long time, had been operating as the main cultural bridgehead for Polish, Lithuanian, and Tatar Muslims all the way until the nineteenth century when these regions fell to the forces of monoethnicity, with Muslims, Jews, and Gypsies being further pushed to the margins. By that time, all various Muslim communities—through inter-marriages, shared Hanafi Islam, and faced by an ascendant Catholicism—had been subsumed under the larger definitional category of Tatars. During that era, they had steadily adopted Polish, Russian, Finnish, and Baltic languages, however, for religious literature, they still used Perso-Arabic script. Their trading and martial traditions kept them in good stead, though monoethnicity proved inimical to this historic pluralism, and by the late nineteenth century, Catholicism, Orthodoxy, and Lutheranism had turned these

Tatars into almost invisible communities. In the same vein, Jews who had flocked to Poland from Western Europe found themselves being squeezed into ghettoes despite proportionately retaining a higher ratio of the population than the Muslims. In the 1930s and 1940s, Jewish communities suffered the worst owing to the Holocaust, whereas Tatars, despite their military services to their respective nations, also faced purges and forced expulsions all through the Stalin-led Soviet Empire. During the Cold War, the West banked on the resilient Central Asian Muslims to tear apart the Soviet soft belly when the former would not shirk from even exaggerating the communist manhandling of the local ecology and traditions. In 1991, the end of the Soviet Empire, perhaps the last in the terrain of European colonialism, happened rather too promptly even for post-war Sovietologists and caused hasty and often alarmist propositions for this vast region all the way from Kazakhstan to Azerbaijan and further northwest. It is only in the recent era that, given the evolution of several independent nations in Eastern Europe and a growing interest in Islam, a curious 'rediscovery' of Islam in Upper Volga, the Baltic states, and in eastern Scandinavia has become noticeable.

Despite ethnic cleansing in Bosnia and Palestinian travails, the world's Muslims, during the 1990s, felt a greater sense of jubilation over the independence of several Central Asian states. However, their knowledge of Central Asian realities remained limited and quite past-bound. In the same vein, many policymakers and intellectuals, both Westerners and Muslims, expressed ambivalence over the role of 'the old guards' and the possibility of 'a million mutinies' owing to overlapping ethnic and religious trajectories. Of course there have been volatile incidents in the Fergana Valley, in Tajikistan's Badakhshan region, in addition to a constant rebellion in the Chinese Turkestan (Xinjiang), however, Central Asia has not exploded at all. Our lack of proper understanding of its historic, plural, and geopolitical dynamics continues to hamper our understanding of 'stans' which border Russia, China, Pakistan, Afghanistan, Iran, and the Caspian Sea, though the steadily increasing groups of travellers, cyclists, hikers, and cameleers have been on the move to discover the steppes of the ancient Silk Road. The hot and dry summer months contrasted with cold winters in otherwise vast land of rugged mountains, spacious deserts, and verdant valleys fail to thwart tough and curious souls and, like its past, the region keeps alluring steady streams of visitors.

Here the old conquerors like Tamerlane and Babur, and scholars such as Imam Bukhari, Ibn Sina, Al-Farabi and Khwarizmi, along with classical poets like Roudaki, Firdausi, and Navoi, and Sufis such as Bahauddin Naqshband, solidify a greater sense of history, rootedness, and pride. No wonder strongmen such as Islam Karimov, Nursultan Nazarbayev, Askar Akayev, Emomali Rahmon, and Gurbanguly Berdimuhamedow left no stone unturned in seeking out legitimacy from those past luminaries, especially the conquerors. Whatever one may say about governance, the gender equilibrium, civic probity, and most of all peace and tolerance permeate these societies where authoritarian systems ensure a status quo along with keeping dissent at bay. How long will they succeed in retaining this sorcery-like rope walking is anyone's guess. In the meantime, the old and the new mingle all across Uzbekistan in almost every city, in each mohalla, and in the lifestyle of its people where women wearing scarves comfortably walk along with their compatriots in skirts without anyone raising an eyebrow at this unique visibility of traditions and modernity and apparently, without any mutual rancour.

**

Emerging out of Bukhara's train station, located at a distance of 20 kilometres from the city centre, fills one with a sense of history, sanctity, and curiosity while looking across a crowd of taxi drivers, receiving hosts and mere onlookers reminding one of South Asia where the airports, bus, and train stations are always packed with jostling masses. Everyone ekes out some kind of existence from visitors, traders, pilgrims, wayfarers, customers, officials, and tourists—all looking slightly dazed in the morning sun. A vast sea of people exhibiting all kinds of complexions, costumes, and creeds meet a similar crowd, oozing out of the Russian juggernaut which contains no less than 14 long and sturdy carriages.

Our night train from Tashkent was on time, comfortable, and quiet, and had been whistling through the Uzbek heartland, chugging on the ancient Silk Road, passing through cities like Chinaz, Djizak, Samarkand, and Navoi—all located in green valleys and surrounded by brown deserts and formidable mountains defining the vivid contours of ancient Sogdiana long before Alexander ventured here. The train stations are often situated away from the older cities, and a traveller cannot grasp their historic features especially during the night when ensconced between sleep and half-awake; one awaits morning to raise the nocturnal curtain from humanity at large. Wrapped in clean sheets and buffeted by comfortable cotton pillows, we could never divorce ourselves from the realities of the cotton kingdom of the Soviet era when these valleys, irrigated by Amu Darya and Syr Darya, were made to concentrate on a single-crop economy. With the Soviets gone and the great rivers and the Aral Sea reduced to one-third capacity, and soil fatigued by chemicals, Uzbekistan has to seek out alternative resources which is not so easy, especially when it happens to be the most populous of all the stans.

Once aboard and 'in control' of our allotted berths in a rather spacious carriage, I was eager to reach out to the restaurant to assuage my craving for Uzbek cakes and tea—of course without milk as the old Pakistani and British habit of white tea had already dissolved into thin air somewhere near the statue of Amir Timur in Tashkent. Our carriage supervisor, to my Perso-Urdu query, simply told me to go towards the back of the train. Assuming it to be just a few carriages down, I began to walk that way. This was a rather interesting surprise since our carriage was towards the front end of the train while the restaurant happened to be the rear end and in between were long carriages where passengers as well as supervisors acknowledged my long strides with curious smiles. A very tall man with a dark complexion and some curls still left on his head was on some mission, trying to disarm curious eyes with a constant terrain of smiles. Finally, I got there to discover that the staff was asleep since it was well past midnight and was not really tea time, except if you were an uneasy soul on some Marco Poloesque adventure. My nosing around did awake a prostrate soul who rose to attention to serve me tea and cakes but, given the length of the train with several inter-carriage bridges to cross, he felt that this passenger would not be able to make it through all the doors and labyrinthine corridors. He volunteered to come along carrying my high tea while I, leading the way, ensured the opening of scores of heavy doors. We finally made it, though I was certainly imbued with a mixed sense of guilt and achievement. The gentleman left the tray on the side table and bowed out to walk back over the wooden floors and carpeted walkways through a mile of steely doors and an entire mass of humanity on the move. I was really pleased that after a joyous journey from Heathrow on the Uzbek national carrier, mostly filled with Indian

Punjabis and *Delhiwalas*, and a happy encounter with a green, quiet, and peaceful Tashkent, our effort to board the Bukhara Express had been successful through the numerous phases of finding the booking office, queuing, buying tickets, and then making it to the train itself later in the evening. And here we were finally in Bukhara—the ancient heritage town of noble souls and eminent buildings—that was once the Oxbridge of the Muslim world, and with its eclipse, we all went under! To me, it is here and in Khiva and Samarkand that the ancient story of Sogdiana had begun and I was fortunate to be undertaking this journey even in the hot August of 2015.

In its recent incarnation, Uzbekistan might have been a new name with younger boundaries yet it is a unique land of numerous historical epochs with layers upon layers of unknown history. Stalin might have devised his names and frontiers for these stans along with moving masses around so as to percolate a new and heavily Russified identity over and above religious and ethnic diversities, but perhaps he was unconsciously acknowledging the long-held plurality of these people. A country of 26 million, Uzbekistan is 88 per cent Muslim, with the rest following Christianity and Judaism, though all these religious identities, especially in post-Soviet years, mean differently to different people. For example, people of this region came to be called Uzbeks in the sixteenth century when the Shaybanis ruled them, though most spoke Turkish and Persian, they were akin to Tajiks and Turkmens to their east and south besides sharing commonalties with the Afghans, Kirghiz, Kazakhs, and Uighurs. Bukhara and Samarkand are still heavily Persianized, while Tashkent, other than its own Uzbek features, displays visible Russian and Kazakh commonalities. The Fergana region shares similarities with both the Tajik counterparts and fellow Uzbeks in Samarkand and beyond. Termez is yet another interesting city which resembles its neighbouring Afghan and Pakistani counterparts on this side of the Indus. The Fergana Valley— the land of Babur and his Mughal descendants in India—is green and fertile with a smattering of industries dating back to the Soviet period now mostly lying idle as elsewhere. Its cities like Namangan and Andijan were in the news during the 1990s for political upheavals and iron-hand clampdown by Islam Karimov. Cities west of Bukhara such as Urgench, Khiva, Beruni, and Nukus are the ancient Khwarizimstan which expands all the way into Karakalpakstan, and is drier and browner, though no less historic until one reaches the parched and saline soil that was once the Aral Sea and is now a mere wasteland. Khiva, more traditional than even Bukhara, is a city that takes a visitor into the early medieval era altogether as it existed during the lifetime of Al-Biruni.

Bukhara was called Vekara/Vekhara in Sanskrit and must have been influenced by Hinduism until it became a major Zoroastrian centre as it finds itself mentioned in the Avesta. Its people, syncretic traditions, and architecture have been influenced by these various phases in its past which began in the second millennium before the Common Era. By the time of Alexander's invasion in the fourth century BCE, this Sogdian region had already attained an international stature due to its location and commercial significance, similar to the Indus regions. Following the Achaemenid and Sogdian defeat by the Greeks, this region became part of a short-lived Seleucid Empire until Persian control was restored under the Parthian tutelage. Alexander had been surprised to encounter Greek-speaking compatriots in Samarkand and Bukhara, some of them even consuming Greek wine. The Macedonian conqueror married an Uzbek maiden, Roxanne/Rukhsana; like him, his spouse died quite young. The Parthians encouraged trade and business in the region and Jewish settlement in Bukhara, and that is where one of the oldest Jewish communities, Bukharans, came into existence. Before Alexander, during the sixth century BCE, Jews had been ordered to move to Palestine by Cyrus the Great, the Achaemenid emperor; however, the Greeks and Parthians allowed their return to Persia and Central Asia. The Sassanids posed some challenges for Bukharan Jews whose trade and presence had by then expanded to Samarkand, Tashkent, Kokand, and further east to Fergana Valley. Following several historical phases, including Chinese military campaigns in the region, the Silk Road witnessed persistent Jewish and Christian influences until the Arabs were able to capture this region in 709 for the Umayyad Caliphate based in Damascus. A few centuries later, Samani kings such as Ismail and subsequently the Seljuk sultan, Alp Arslan, while based in greater Khorasan and Anatolia respectively, helped the Abbasids by providing new strength to the Sunni caliphate in Baghdad. The Samanis, Karakhanids, and Seljuks often remained tolerant and protective of their subjects besides ensuring literary and scholastic patronage to eminent scholars such as Roudaki, Ibn Sina, Al-Biruni, Firdausi, Rumi, and others. As a consequence,

Khorasan (inclusive of Bukhara, Khiva, Herat, Merv, Nishapur) and Anatolia (with its capital in Konya), emerged as the two major centres of Muslim renaissance.

During the nineteenth century, a number of European Jews, tired of persecution in Europe, migrated to Central Asia and, to their surprise, encountered Bukharan co-religionists. The Jews remained a visible presence in Uzbek Soviet Republic and in fact their numbers swelled considerably during the Second World War. After the war, Israelis enticed many Bukharan Jews to their new country; even now there are estimates of about 30,000 Uzbek Jews in the country with a visible presence in Tashkent. People in general know about Sephardim and Ashkenazim but very little is known about the Bukharans, and it is only in recent times that Shlomo Sand and several traditional Jewish groups have begun to talk about the presence and prosperity of Bukharans in a Muslim heartland, avoiding pogroms or genocides which sadly happened in Europe so often. Subsequently, the Seljuks carried on their campaigns both in Central Asia and Asia Minor until the Mongols and Crusaders put an annihilative squeeze on Islam's glorious, forward looking, and creative genius. Sunni-Shia feuds and confrontations, such as between the Seljuks and Buyids and the Ghaznavids and Ismailis, exhausted the second phase in Muslim expansion, and it took several more centuries to revive some kind of past glory under the Ottomans, Safavids, Mughals, and Shaybanis in all these adjoining territories. Bukhara, Khiva, Samarkand, Balkh, Herat, Nishapur, and Merv were the bastions of this golden era until the Mongols heralded large-scale destruction, and it was only in the sixteenth century, after an insidious gap of four centuries, that Muslim dynastic polities were able to restore some kind of erstwhile political and cultural semblance; today Bukhara remains the most vivid witness of that. Tamerlane's conquests and campaign during the fourteenth century brought back glory, wealth, and prestige to this region, though elsewhere he only reignited the harrowing memories of Genghis Khan (1162–1227) and his descendants. Samarkand, Shakhrisabz, Bukhara, and Herat prospered under Tamerlane and especially under his grandson, Ulugh Beg (1394–1449), the scholar-king, but then Central Asia reverted to chaotic chasms until the Shaybanis augured another renaissance in art and architecture in the sixteenth century. In Islam's early golden age, cities like Bukhara, Merv, Rey, Balkh, Nishapur, Aleppo, Shiraz, Konya, Fes,

Cairo, and Baghdad played a vanguard role in spearheading knowledge and arts.

The most authentic sources on classical Islam are known as *Sahiain*, and these two earliest and most authentic collections of the Prophet's (PBUH) sayings (traditions) were compiled with dexterity and thorough extensive fieldwork by Imam Muhammad Ismail Bukhari (810–70) and Imam Muslim Ibn Al-Hajjaj (821–75), the latter being the former's student. Imam Muhammad Ismail was a native Bukharan who travelled extensively across the Muslim world, gathering 700,000 sayings of the Prophet (PBUH) and, following a very critical and rigorous research, compiled his select collection of 7,000 traditions. Imam Muslim, whose own collection shares 2,000 hadith with that of his mentor, carried on this painstaking research in Nishapur. The next most famous Bukharan in this early period and perhaps the most famous philosopher and expert on medicine was Ibn Sina, who was born in Afsana, a town 20 miles outside Bukhara. A polymath and genius like Imam Bukhari, he memorized the Quran, followed by an immersion in Aristotelian philosophy which he learnt through the exegesis by Al-Farabi (872–950), a native of present-day Kazakhstan who subsequently lived in the Arab Middle East and is buried in Damascus. Both Farabi and Ibn Sina are the two most prominent philosophers of the early Islamic era who revived classical Greek thoughts in addition to several other intellectual contributions. Ibn Sina was a polymath who wrote 450 books, out of which 250 remain, of which *The Book of Healing* (*Al-Shifa*) and *The Cannon of Medicine* (*Al-Kimiya*) served as classical texts on medicine for centuries. He was a very promising young man who received special patronage from Bukhara's Samani rulers as they made their well-endowed library in the Ark (fort) accessible to him. His discussions with Al-Biruni, an eminent scholar from Khwarizm/Khiva, focused on Aristotle and other philosophical classicists, with the former accompanying the Ghaznavids into India and Avicenna moving on to Hamadan and Rey. Biruni, who also benefited from Bukhara's educational institutions and consulted the royal library at the Ark, wrote his classic *Kitabul Hind* while based in the Salt Range of present-day Pakistan. It is a pioneering scientific study of the people of India, languages, and religions by a meticulous scholar who, like Ibn Sina, was a polymath. Other than his measuring of earth's circumference, Biruni's anthropological, linguistic, and religious study of Hindustan, following an immersion in Sanskrit, make him one of the pioneering scholars in these realms.

Abu Abdullah Jafar Rudaki/Roudaki (858–941), a literary genius in Persian poetry of this early classical era, was also attached to the Samani court in Bukhara. It is said that he turned blind at an early age but that did not deter him from assuming the status of a pioneer in Persian poetic traditions and is duly honoured in post-independence Tajikistan as the father of Persian literature though only 52 poems and quartets of his 130,000 verses remain today. Another Ghaznavid-era writer, and perhaps the most well-known chronicler-poet of ancient Persia known for his epic *Shahnameh*, Firdausi/Firdowsi (935–1025) was a contemporary of these luminaries who lived for a while in Bukhara. Firdausi felt a greater affinity with the prehistory of Persia and with a glorified versification of stories such as of Rostam and Sohrab, the well-known wrestlers, and of course, of the Sassanid kings and their successors; in a way, he proved to be the anchor of Persian identity. His Shia orientation further endeared him with post-1979 Iran, the way the early nationalists saw in him a chronicler of classical Persian 'exceptionalism'. However, there are all kinds of stories about his falling out with Mahmud of Ghazni, his patron, because of the king's stinginess and lack of due appreciation of what he had produced through his *Shahnameh*. Well, one could enumerate a large number of Sufi pioneers of the early Islamic era hailing from Bukhara and further west from Naqush and Khiva, yet it will be quite in order to say a few words about one of the rarest brains who has proven to be a permeating influence on algebra, astronomy, and geometry. Muhammad ibn Musa Al-Khwarizmi (780–850), who is eternalized through the Latinized term, Algorithm, a derivative of his name, was from western Uzbekistan. He studied in Bukhara before moving to Baghdad to teach at the Abbasid's House of Wisdom (*Baitul Hikma*) and other than geometry and algebra, he authored treatises on philosophy, geography, and astrology. For a long time, with his unique arithmetical equations and graphs (*jadool*), he was viewed to be the founder of geometry and a transmitter of eastern learning to the West during Islam's classical era. Of course, the political schisms within the caliphate, the growing spectre of sectarianism pushing Muslim intellectuals towards a kind of self-imposed consensus, and the Mongol invasions sealed the fate of this unique phase in Muslim history which, for many recent Muslim intellectuals—such as Jamal al-Din al-Afghani, Muhammad Iqbal, Muhammad Abduh, Ali Alawi, Atiya Fyzee, Farid al-Attash, and Khaled Abou El Fadl—is once again overdue.

***

Once a traveller moves out of Bukhara's station, spacious boulevards and some public housing interspersed with emerging shopping stores displaying English and Russian names accompany the traveller all the way to the Old City. Greenery, featuring orchards and irrigated fields, certainly gave us a constant reminder that we were in the valley. Vehicles of all types, including the small efficient Chevrolet cars and the huge Russian lorries, all moved steadily without any effort zigzagging the clearly laid out lanes and no noisy horns were heard either. We passed by a fair number of cyclists and a few horse-drawn carriages that felt safe on the roads, largely due to a more orderly traffic. The Bukhara that I was witnessing now appeared modern and resembled Konya and Tashkent, until following a crossroad, I began to detect light brown minarets, traditional edifices located near the road, and a growing number of pedestrians. We were on Bahauddin Naqshband Road, one of the main arteries in the Old City that connected to the Ark fort on the other side of the old town after circling several madrassas, old bazaars, and mosques. Our sleek van disgorged us just outside our hotel right behind the Lyab-i-Hauz, the main open water tank and the hub of sociocultural activities in the noble city. The Malika, a modern edifice built in traditional Central Asian style with ample but sensible use of stone and wood, was tucked beside an old serai and was abuzz with European tourists being chaperoned by their multilingual Uzbek guides. We were early but luckily obtained a spacious room within no time thanks to the maids who virtually ran this sleek facility including its kitchen, accommodation, and the bar while following every edict from Rustam, the food manager from Termez. His smile, short curly hair, and a quiet but very amiable demeanour reminded me of Anwar from Waziristan who was my session mate at Michigan State University, a fellow Spartan, and now a professor at the Gonzaga University in Spokane. From north-western Pakistan, our noble Wazir Pashtun had ended up in north-western United States without shunning his chukor hunting in winter. Rustam's resemblance to Anwar was a significant shock but it also reassured us that we were on a hospitable turf. Rustam soon took us to the dining hall where a wide variety of fruit, salads, breads, and other Uzbek dishes ensured a special welcome, though I was more eager to see the two minarets right behind our hotel.

The Malika, our compact and immensely charming accommodation, proved to be a judicious choice not just for its name but more for its location and now certainly for its services. We found out later that it was owned by an Iraqi-Austrian entrepreneur and drew a constant stream of visitors on packaged tours which kept Rustam and his kitchen ladies busy most of the time. Like their neat work on well-provided rooms and mouth-watering Uzbek dishes, its dining room was often bustling with multiple languages, with German seemingly holding a clear sway though a small smattering of Korean, Japanese, and odd Malay, along with some Swiss and Italian, ensuring cosmopolitanism in this little corner of the Silk Road. Breakfast and acquiring a spacious room might have been the initial imperatives for settling in Malika yet my soul was eager to get out of this 'comfort zone' to begin seeing some of those 140 rare monuments, each one laden with history. A full breakfast, interspersed with Rustam's smiles and fully provided by Hussein, his young assistant, did not deter me from venturing out, and in just a couple of minutes I found myself standing next to a well-maintained water tank neighboured by an old mosque with its two graceful minarets overlooking the beautiful square. Two mulberry trees faced each other on both sides of this *hauz*,[2] while the Khoja Gaukushan Mosque/Madrassa complex was itself locked as if it was not in use for quite some time, though its exterior, older entrance, and minarets all looked in a healthy state. Restoration work on this Shaybani complex had been impressive, though while peering through the minor cracks of an impressive wooden gate inside, I could detect some debris and unkempt growth of wild, brown grass. In fact, the Gaukushan complex was just behind our accommodation at the intersection of Bahauddin Naqshband Road and Jabar Street, and while sharing the bench with an elderly Uzbek by the water tank, I could even see my room just a few feet away. To my right and facing the main entrance to our accommodation was again an old multistorey building with its arched exterior that housed a photo gallery. While absorbing the first morning in a growingly warm Bukhara and sitting right in its heart, I kept looking at a stream of cyclists, who were passing by the *hauz* on their way to Lyab-i-Hauz, the popular focal point surrounded by some of the older madrassas, monasteries, and mosques besides its open air cafés. I was not in a hurry to cover those crucial hundred metres or so to get to Lyab-i-Hauz or even Minar-e-Kalyan or the Ark, since I first wanted to absorb the historicity of my own neighbourhood. Later, while looking at the old photographs of Bukhara both in our hotel and at other museums, it appeared to me that the Gaukushan Square was once the hub of religious and commercial activities with horse-drawn carts, turbaned and bearded shopkeepers, and customers congregating under the shop awnings, more like the usual ambience of a traditional South Asian bazaar. In a few other pictures, this complex and shops all around looked almost decimated following the Soviet invasion in 1924 and a revengeful punitive campaign led by General Mikhail Frunze. He had brought in fresh forces from Tashkent and Khiva to fight the rebels who had been putting up resistance against the Bolsheviks.

In fact, following the conquest of Tashkent in the 1860s, the Russians had tried to capture Samarkand and Bukhara from the local amirs belonging to the Mangat dynasty that had come into power in 1757 and was later confronted with what came to be called the Great Game. Before the Mangats, Nadir Shah Afshar (1688–1747) had destroyed these cities like his total destruction of Delhi, similar to Tamerlane's carnage in the city. These cities remained in his possession until shortly after his death when his successors fell into the familiar civil strife allowing an emirate to emerge in Bukhara. Samarkand was captured in 1868 by the Russian troops led by General Kaufmann who, following his defeat of Amir Muzaffar Khan, had begun to annex other regions on both sides of the old Silk Road. The British entanglement in the First Anglo-Afghan War in 1839–42 and its subsequent disastrous end for East India Company's troops did not lessen the British zeal to send in 'explorers' and 'spies' often looking like Tajiks and Pashtuns, including Charles Stoddart and Arthur Conolly. In fact, it was Conolly who had coined the term 'the Great Game' and, enthused by missionary spirit with a Victorian zeal for empire, had ended up in the Amir's prison, Zindaan/Zindon, located in a corner of the fort and palace complex. Earlier, Stoddart had visited Bukhara in 1838 to reassure Amir Nasrullah Khan that the British invasion of Afghanistan had no further expansive designs on his territory, yet his forbearance in the court was found to be quite rude, leading to his incarceration in a cell called the bug pit, locally known as *kanakkhana*. Stoddart's secret notes sent from his prison cell to India and England failed to provide any rescue mission and, as per some reports, he decided to convert to Islam and attained temporary proximity with the Amir. In the meantime, Conolly, the evangelist from Dublin, arrived at the city in 1841 to manoeuvre Stoddart's release but ended up in the same cell—infested with bugs with no entrance except for its ceiling which was at the ground level and amply fortified with steel bars—since the Amir suspected him of working with his opponent, Khans of Khiva and Kokand. Following disastrous retreat of the British from Afghanistan, an emboldened Amir decided to hold a public trial of the two British officials and executed them in 1842 in the Registan Square just outside the Ark. The British media carried extensive coverage of these executions and hysteria was created against the Amir though London and Calcutta soon after the disastrous Afghan venture decided against undertaking any punitive action. But Bukhara had become a household name, like Calcutta's Black Hole in Victorian Britain, and funds were raised to finance an emissary to the Central Asian city to seek all the details regarding the trial and executions. That is how an eccentric clergyman, Joseph Wolff, took off for Bukhara. His humour and elaborate Anglican costume came to his rescue and he was able to record all the details in his book, *Narratives of a Mission to Bokhara* (1845), which further fed into specific British images of the Bukharans.

Amir Alim Khan, the last ruler of Bukhara and also the last one to ascend the throne in the Ark, had refused to surrender to the Soviet troops in 1918 and, following an initial victory, was soon confronted with a massive and furious Soviet force. In several contemporary pictures before and after the invasion, one can see Bukhara taking a serious downturn. The Ark, numerous madrassas, the Kalyan Mosque, and Gaukushan Complex were reduced to rubble. The Kalyan Mosque, one of the largest in the city, rebuilt by the Shaybanis after the Mongol decimation of Bukhara, was turned into a Soviet storage, whereas a similar fate awaited the Amir's mosque within the Ark and also the Bolo Haouz Mosque across the Registan Square, itself an architectural rival of Chehel Sutoun Palace in Isfahan. The photographs of pre-1918 Bukhara taken by Sergey Prokudin-Gorsky (1863–1944) are rare visual archives of this city and the Amir before its eventual destruction by Frunze. Of course it was not a rich place and many of its monuments needed restorative care, yet it still symbolized a dignified Muslim past, and the physical destruction of most of the 325 institutions sent shivers amongst Central Asian Muslims. Furthermore, Russian influence had been quite visible here since the conquest of Tashkent and Samarkand by the Czars in the 1860s but the Bukharan Emirate had survived until the October Revolution when it began to attract all kinds of resistance groups. The Ottomans and other Turkestani Muslims, helped by the locals, raised the flag of rebellion which the Soviets derisively called Basmatchi or rebellion by miscreants and robbers. Most photographs in the photo gallery, Museum of Art, our accommodation, and at the Zindaan (now called Museum of Law and Legislation) show a different kind of Bukhara—traditional. Its people, their clothes, means of transportation, goods in the shops, and the exterior conditions of the three major bazaars and other shops in older mohallas were distinct witness of a long-gone era. Even a portly, bearded Amir Alam Khan with his turban, long bluish silky kameez with a *kumarband* (belt) and pointed shoes appears like a character from *Alaf Lailah*. (Please ignore if the historian in me sounds like a nostalgic romantic!)

The Amir's picture was taken in 1911 by Prokudin-Gorsky, the aristocrat-photographer who was exiled to France, and like his well-known picture of Leo Tolstoy taken in 1908, it remains a masterpiece.[3] In 1924, Bukhara was added to the newly created Uzbekistan Soviet Republic and for the next seven decades went through various phases of reforms and transformations. Independence in 1991 has inducted new vigour and challenges, though some people may still miss the assured safety net provided under the Soviet system, but Bukhara, like Khiva, Samarkand, Termez, and Shakhrisabz, might be at the cusp of history once again. 'Only Allah knows,' as the seers will say!

***

Irreverent of the hot sun and with some new vigour in my sinews, I decided to get lost in the alleys beyond the Gaukushan complex which is no longer a neighbour to any cluster of shops and customers with their horses and donkeys wading through the winter mud. It has well-paved lanes with a small stream flowing through the main street which at one stage must have fed into this and several other stone tanks across the old city. Only the *hauz* behind our room now remains in this neighbourhood though Lyab-i-Hauz, surrounded by some of the most magnificent madrassas and restored parts of the older city, has eclipsed the former. However, Bolo Haouz on the other side of Registan, reflecting all the wooden columns (*sutoon*) of the mosque in its water tank, somehow appealed to me the most. Partly, it reminded me of my other favourite city, Isfahan, and also because it did not have the usual touristic kind of atmosphere that seems to have overtaken the Lyab-i-Hauz. Walking through the streets and peering into the side lanes, I encountered cyclists, mothers carrying groceries, skirted girls hurrying to their college or places of work, and some elderly sitting by the wayside cafés sipping their brown tea. I passed by the (Soviet era) schools, a hospital, odd shops, and several older Ladas ferrying huge melons, gas cylinders, wooden panels, and some passengers. I also witnessed women operating shops while sharing smiles and pleasant greetings (salaam) without any pretention or hesitation while some were engaged in spraying water in the streets to curb the dust down. It is a brown land where water is not in abundance and the older neighbourhoods are congested though the sewerage system plus a great penchant for cleanliness keeps the older city neat. Near the old madrassas and mosques or by the palatial homes of older elites, several guesthouses, cafés, and even gyms have opened up and old Bukhara seems to be constantly redefining itself. Soon, I passed by the splendid Faizullah Khwaja's house which was built in 1891 by the father of this infamous Bukharan who had sided with the Bolsheviks in 1918 and, as a reward, was appointed to head Bukhara People's Republic. The house features wooden beams, older Turkic frescoes, and spacious rooms in customary Turkestani style and has duly benefited from recent restorative work. Built by a rich merchant, the house became a school in 1925 and now operates as a museum representing an uneasy turn in the city's contested, two generations old history.

Bypassing several sweeping maidens with no scarcity of smiles and curiosity for a tall, brown sojourner who leisurely kept getting lost in the warren of lanes, I kept detecting a resemblance with the interiors of Multan, Lahore, and even Fes, though here houses were not multistorey, and neighbourhoods did not reveal any sense of dense crowding. The life exhibited a slower pace, often interspersed by cars meandering through lanes and corner shops playing Uzbek and Persian (read: Tajik!) music but always in a rather low volume. Almost every shop was barricaded by heaps of green and yellow melons, baskets of green and maroon grapes, and round, thick naans. The streets were a world away from the boulevards and roads in Tashkent and, despite giving a dusty look, were neat without any polythene bags or rubbish heaps. It is to do with the strong element of civility besides a visible presence of an efficient cleaning force that includes a large percentage of women. Unlike South Asia, these women and men are not from 'menial' castes and classes, and instead are a fully paid urban force meant to keep the city clean and green. Bukharan women, like their compatriots elsewhere in Central Asia, display an astounding level of self-reliance, empowerment, education, and public profile. Elderly ladies definitely wear scarves while the rest vary in their choice of clothing; I did not see any women wearing a full niqab. Even in one family—and Uzbeks are surely family-bound—one comes across a wide variety of dressing choices amongst women though men mostly wear trousers, whereas the elderly amongst them will don the unique pill-box Uzbek cap on the head. Despite the hot sun and certainly cold winter, Bukharans are in general healthy people with a low crime rate, an organized life, a high rate of literacy, and active women involvement in the economy and social life. Because of their work ethics and often demanding physical labour, the populace does not seem to suffer from obesity that one comes across in the West and in the Gulf region. The traditional frugality inherited from Sufi traditions and Soviet regimentation on sports and hygiene have certainly played a vital role in keeping the society healthier. In addition, even in cities, the fast food joints are not a familiar sight. Except for bigger hotels, outdoor eating, like in the Mediterranean regions, is a social and relaxing event interspersed with smaller portions with more emphasis on soup and salads. Of course, as Rustam will reaffirm time and again, our food supply was a multilayered activity but still a larger share included greens, beans, soups, and fruits.

I was impressed by the humanity, spontaneity, and even the beauty of Uzbek women as talking to them following a *salamu alaykum* was not problematic at all largely due to my older age plus their traditional sense of respect for guests and visitors. My Persian and English, following the initial salaam, always caused friendly smiles and a dialogue which, despite its philological hiccups, would never let the smile disappear for a second. The endurance of Islamic traditions with a partake at modernity, despite their respective rigidity, were quite in evidence here where a male stranger like me soon began to feel like a native. This sense of ease of not being seen as a tourist rather 'one of us' soon allowed me to walk around not as a probing onlooker but rather as a familiar fellow with some 'interesting' characteristics. Never could I believe that a harmless salaam followed by a modest smile would prove so reaching, irrespective of age, gender, and place! I was overtaken by a number of women on their way to Lyab-i-Hauz, with some carrying their provisions while others were on their way to run those shops in bazaars which once made this city a major trading post and a cultural hub on the Silk Road. To me, more than silk and trade, this was the land of Sufis and scholars, long gone to dust but eternalized by their ideas, words, and deeds. So while looking at the houses, madrassas, narrow lanes, austere dwellings made of mud and wooden beams, and the inhabitants, I could not override my sense of history and immersion. I was like the Buddhist monks fresh from Gandhara to reach Sogdiana while the next moment I felt like the Jewish prophets seeking refuge amongst the hospitable people of these tough mountains. And at another level, I also envisioned myself to be a pained soul picking up pieces of my life after one more devastating invasion or an earthquake. Burying the dead and saving my own life while starting all anew was the sum total of my own history as, in my imagination, I would hurry to madrassa to listen to Ibn Sina or relish Firdausi serenading his choicest words to his glorified Persia.

Soon, I found myself next to Lyab-i-Hauz as if I had already completed my circular walk in one part of this majestic city. I did pass through the Taqi-Telpak Furushon Bazaar, currently a collection of orderly shops selling arts and antiques with a visible majority of shop owners being women. This is the hub of Old Bukhara as it is the centre of tourist presence and thus, like its past, it has its major share of hotels, pensions, and eateries, some of them inside newly restored mohallas while others surrounded Lyab-i-Hauz itself where younger trees stand next to some very senior colleagues, offering shade and fresh breeze. Lo and behold, here I came across my old-time favourite and always-elusive comedy character that I grew up hearing about some thousands of miles away further east.

**

I do not know whether it happens to other people as well when they venture into a place which they have cherished or have been mystified with for a long period of time that, as soon as they get there, they cannot have enough of it. Some of them may even get disappointed while faced with the objective realities but in my case—except for my most recent visit to Greece when Athens somehow appeared slightly bleak and too eager to make quick money—I have not been disappointed by my destinations. Lyab-i-Hauz on all its four sides has impressive edifices of mosques, madrassas, and a khankah, and faces the synagogue and Jewish school across the Bahauddin Naqshband Road. Soon after passing through the Taqi-Telpak Furushon Bazaar, one notices the Nadir Divan-begi Khanka located to the west of the Lyab-i-Hauz which was built by the finance minister of Amir Abdul Aziz Khan during the seventeenth century. Once a Sufi *Zawiya* used for public assemblies and prayers, it is now more like a museum housing paintings and photographs. However, it is the Nadir Divan-begi Madrassa, facing the khankah and east of the Lyab-i-Hauz, which is its more impressive counterpart. Like other Central Asian edifices often seen in Iran and South Asia, the entrance to madrassa is quite gigantic and decorated with intricate tiles, latticed jalis manifesting several pictorial renditions on the exterior. Its impressive exterior murals include a pair of phoenix-like peacocks with two attentive lambs underneath them, all crowned by the sun which, a bit like Minerva, has a human face. It is quite rare to come across human depictions on religious buildings across the Sunni Muslim world and this splendid madrassa appears to be a rare exception. The floral beautification on the multicoloured tiles, reaching all the way to the top of the entrance and enhancing the decorations over 12 twin-storey arches just by the main entrance, witness the amount of human labour invested in this unique building. The gorgeous entrance façade faces the *hauz* and is supported by six arches on both sides which replicate the floral patterns of the former, and with blue and green tiles, they offer a splendid contrast to a predominantly brown, solid, brick exterior. Inside the madrassa, double-storey arches mark entrances to several rooms, overlooking the square compound featuring grassy patches and floral beds which once housed visitors, merchants, and scholars. In the late sixteenth century, the madrassa began as a caravanserai but was converted into a mosque in 1622. More like a quadrangle and resembling Oxbridge counterparts,

it presently houses shops and cafés, and stores for rugs and artefacts. Its
structure remains intact though one may desire to see it in its original
form with the students and scholars debating intricate theological
and philosophical issues. Often in the evenings, they play live music
here to entertain a growing number of tourists and home crowds who
gather by the *hauz*. I was told to come back later in case I wanted to
enjoy some 'youthful' music with Uzbek, Persian, and English lyrics.
Compared to the quieter and more serene khankah, the madrassa is noisy
and commercial which may be hurtful to one's aesthetic and historical
sensitivities. I checked on some low-ceiling rooms and found them to be
in a healthy state, housing curious and glittery goods awaiting streams
of tourists. Crates of Uzbek beer sat outside as if one was not on the
premises of a once esteemed school but instead was visiting some rural
English pub after a busy weekend. While hiding my dismay, I slowly
moved out and faced the favourite character from my childhood who,
through his name and humour, connects central, southern, and western
parts of Asia—perhaps the only character of this type.

Khawaja/Hoja/Agha/Mullah Nasruddin is an international character
from the Medieval Muslim world whose innocuous sense of humour,
often bordering on lunacy or even satire, never fails to cause smiles on all
faces, irrespective of ethnicity, gender, and age. In Persia and South Asia,
he was called Mullah with all the funny connotations of his title, while in
the Turkic regions, his prefix varies between Khawaja and Khoja, and in
post-Ottoman Turkey, it is Hoja. Nobody knows where and when he was
born—if he was a real person as such—but every Muslim society claims
to have owned the Mullah whose name means 'helper of his religion'.
Stories about him abound in Persian, Turkish, and Urdu. People respected
him but in a curious way. Mullah's lampoon-like persona walking along
with an attentive donkey, his most faithful and loyal companion, would
certainly cause some mischievous smiles until he would come up with
some thoughtful wisecrack. His quips and actions would reverberate
simplicity as well as raw wisdom—both subsumed by a strong underlay of
humour. An example of this is the story about him praying in a mosque
at an odd hour, around 10 and 12 in the morning. The onlookers came
in to check on his mental state for praying outside the required time, to
which he observed:

Thieves stole my donkey last night. I was, of course, not riding the donkey; otherwise I would have been stolen as well. To that effect, I am offering my thanks to the Almighty.

The villagers felt the urgency to go out and locate the thieves who were caught red-handed. Mullah's donkey was brought back while he was still in the mosque. He patted his friend, thanked the villagers, and noted in his self-assured way:

See, prayers to Allah don't need any time or occasion. He understands your predicament in His own way and may come to your help.[4]

The villagers had no answer to this spiritual adulation.

On another occasion, thieves troubled Mullah Nasruddin in the middle of the night. He hid in a closet while the former looked all around his humble dwelling. Finding nothing worthwhile, they finally opened the closet and, to their shock, saw him hiding behind his old long, worn-out coat: 'How come, Nasruddin, you are hiding from us? Is it fear or something else?' He responded, 'I do not find anything worthwhile in my home even during the daylight, how could you find something valuable during the night! To save you from this frustration and mindful of my own inadequacy, I hid myself in this closet.' The thieves ended up sharing their own money with him, leaving some extra for his donkey.[5]

Just outside the Nadir Divan-begi Madrassa, slightly towards the left, stands the bronze sculpture of Mullah Nasruddin riding his donkey. Overshadowed by tall trees and wearing his peaked karakul and long overall with brooding mustachios, the Mullah, while holding the reins of his donkey, appeared to be saying salaam to onlookers. His donkey's longish ears look alert while his own head seems to be bowing to the people to the left. Mullah Nasruddin had ventured in from one of his forays into the country and, having completed his mission, looked quite confident on his ride. While surveying the Mullah and his donkey, I noticed the arrival of a group of children who were soon all over the sculpture including the donkey's neck and tail, with one sitting right behind the Mullah himself. I was glad that even so long after his demise, he was still entertaining multitudes through his statue. They were accompanied by their parents who, in their own ways, were remembering some of his parables. Stealthily, finding my own moment, I touched Mullah Nasruddin's extended hand, offered my salaam, and moved on to the open compound around the *hauz* to have my freshly made glass of Ayran, which back in South Asia is called lassi. While sitting there and gazing at parties of people venturing around, I noticed a kippah-clad Uzbek by one of the tuck shops sipping on a soft drink. He was one of the well-known and now disappearing Bukharan Jews who I was going to see on numerous occasions in the days ahead.

***

Rustam was present in our dining room with his full alacrity and was being duly assisted by his ever-present assistant, Hussein, and a couple of other hotel employees. The fruit, various forms of Uzbek breads, soup, and several other continental savouries might have monopolized a fair portion of my body, yet the eagerness to see Minar-e-Kalyan and two other magnificent monuments did not allow me to have a longer discussion with Rustam. This was his busiest time, with more tourist buses having arrived from Khiva during the night and their passengers anxious to see the city before their departure for Samarkand. Hussein was hurriedly taking away soiled crockery without forgetting his innocent smile and must have been wondering about the variety of tongues spoken around him. My Persian had already struck an element of cordiality with Malika's establishment and, mingled with English, it had allowed me to converse with a wide variety of people including our lady chefs who ensured a magnanimous supply of freshly cooked food, delicious baked breads, and cakes besides a steady supply of grapes and melons. Ayran was never in short supply and sausages, just like in Turkey, were of halal mutton, garnished with local herbs, however, one always had the choice of going beyond the usual egg dishes by asking for more indigenous Uzbek varieties. Despite its modern and fully efficient facilities with a sizeable traffic of European travellers, Malika's architecture, staff, cuisine, and ambience were strictly Central Asian which is what I liked the most about this place. It sat next to an old caravanserai with several rooms, stables, and storages completely restored, though not in use. But from Malika's terrace, other than fresh breeze and a clear view of Minar-e-Kalyan, I often peered into the deeper recesses of this serai, which in its heyday must have been busy with traders and a variety of goods that moved across the labyrinthine Silk Road. Old Bukhara is full of such serais, though several of them have been converted into rest houses and galleries including the one almost facing Mullah Nasruddin's sculpture where local craftspeople and artists run their work places and one could in fact witness carpet weaving, sketching, and active smithery. Other than providing jobs and enabling a proficient use of these historic buildings, they are already imparting hands-on skills to younger people, though Uzbekistan definitely needs a more diverse economy with enough wherewithal to reach out to its burgeoning younger population who in the post-Soviet decades face several mundane challenges. They in general feel that the tourists are prosperous westerners; in a persuasive way, they are right in assuming that. Even the hitchhikers and lone travellers using public transport on dusty roads have secure lives and jobs back home and despite apparent austerity can afford leisure and pleasure, which certainly portrays a 'fantastic' image of the West. Some of these young people have relatives in Dubai and other Gulf states where the society is being rapidly impacted by consumerism and mobility. Here people engaged in the service sector, especially in hospitality, are quite eager to study and work abroad which, to a great extent, would mean the European Union and North America, though older generation may have some mixed feelings about Moscow and other cities to the north. As per estimates, at least two million Uzbeks live and work in the Russian republic.

Between the Malika Hotel and the Lyab-i-Hauz, and quite close to Taqi-Telpak Furushon Bazaar, are the excavated ruins of older Bukhara that must have been some of the earliest residential neighbourhood with thick stonewalls, ample passageways, and well-delineated sanitary channels. Bahauddin Naqshband Road borders these ruins on two sides and a very old, unused mosque located in another corner. The Magok-i-Attari Mosque (the lower pit mosque) is not big and is built in the usual Central Asian style with a rising cupola, whereas windows and doors reveal hand-carved ornamentation and the brick walls retain symmetrical use of decorative tiles. Used as a carpet store, this is one of the earliest mosques in the city as it virtually sits amidst the excavated ruins of ancient Bukhara and, as the name denotes, it is very much below ground surface. Excavations have also revealed the existence of another mosque's foundation further down which might have been on the site of an earlier

Zoroastrian temple. However, the doors, ventilators, and jali work and its solid foundational work are evidence of its historicity; sitting next to the archaeological site, Magok-i-Attari Mosque must have been one of the earliest structures. In 943, the famous Bukharan historian, Abu Bakr Narshakhi, wrote about this neighbourhood:

> There was the bazaar in Bukhara, which was called Bazaar Mokh. Public sales were held there only one day twice a year. Every time idols were sold in this bazaar ... the inhabitants of Bukhara in antiquity were idolaters, and that time the idols used to be traded in this bazaar; this custom was preserved ... Later this place was the heathen temple of fire-worshipers; on the days designated for trade, people gathered here, all entered the heathen temple and worshiped the fire. This temple had existed before the establishment of Islam here, when Muslims, gaining strength, built on this site their mosque, and now it is one of the great mosques of Bukhara.[6]

Bukhara itself was called Vekara in Sanskrit whereas *Mukh*, in the same language means face, which in subsequent years turned into *Majoki*. In its Hindu past, this area must have held some trade dealing in idols and other temple-related artefacts until the Zoroastrians took over. Tracing the history of this mosque, one comes across accounts of Jews and Muslims praying together. As mentioned above, the Bukharan Jews were originally Persians who moved to this region and engaged themselves in trade and other urban enterprises. Their locality in fact is just to the south of the Lyab-i-Hauz where a synagogue and school still exist, whereas further down, there is a large Jewish cemetery as well. The Bukharan Jews spoke Persian like everybody else but often wrote it in the Hebrew script—this expression came to be known as Bukharan. They stayed here even during the early Soviet years as there were 10,000 Bukharan Jews in the city in 1948. But then migrations to Israel and the United States began to happen more often and, at present, a smaller community carries on. Reportedly, the Magok-i-Attari Mosque allowed Bukharan Jews to pray behind Muslims who either did not have their own synagogue or might have faced resistance from some Muslim quarters, disallowing them to build their own place of worship. However, there are several synagogues in town which in most cases are closed except for the one near the Lyab-i-Hauz, which is used both for worship and which also operates as a small museum preserving the history of Bukharan Jews.

Over the next few mornings, I sat here watching doves, pigeons, and parrots which, like me, were cherishing the early dawn hours before the bazaar and shops around the Lyab-i-Hauz became abuzz with shopkeepers and tourists. I also used to notice a steady stream of cyclists, mostly senior men, on their way to the markets in the modern/Russian parts of Bukhara to purchase groceries or sell their goods. I began to cherish these early Bukharan mornings and late evenings, given the coolness in the air plus greater solitude by the madrassas and mosques. People of Bukhara—despite their city's historic location on the great trading routes and penchant for world-renowned carpets, and its status as the world heritage city—appeared less pushy, though in the three bazaars and around some of them did try to sell their goods. In the Taqi-Zargaron Bazaar, my favourite haunt was a shop that had a unique collection of jewellery, coins, ceramics, and other small elements of the Silk Road, of which most were genuinely antiques. A few metres further down is the Museum of Carpets, right before one enters another domed bazaar with openings on all four sides, very similar to covered bazaars in Isfahan and Istanbul, but on a smaller scale. Within the Zargaron Bazaar, I made my way into a circular tomb-like structure which might have been a madrassa or even a tomb in the distant past. I could easily read Quranic verses and Persian couplets high above the walls and on the structure that now houses shops with extensive carpet collections. However, my favourite discovery was a very old mosque on Naqshband Road which might have been in use until a century ago but was now locked. Its wooden entrance, overseen by a gigantic but immensely charming arch, witnessed its historicity. I walked around it and saw the compound strewn with beams, fallen masonry, and wild growth. Its neighbourhood comprised of narrow lanes and even smaller houses, some double-storey with latticed windows; these houses were mostly built with mud and wooden beams. This kind of architecture in the Old City owes itself to the 'mohalla culture' inherited by generations; besides it is meant to survive earthquakes. In addition, like the British in India, Russians built their own cities away from older population centres and that is where one sees open boulevards, multifloored mansions, train stations, schools, and military institutions. Both the Czars and Soviets had their own tree-lined suburbia, whereas the 'natives' were left on their own with bare minimum facilities. Of course, within this new class structure and bureaucracy, the old neighbourhoods suffered from negligence, inferiority complex, but most importantly, the historic buildings decayed or were overruled by other administrative expediencies. Selective restorations did take place at a few madrassas and markets but most mosques, the Ark, or other shrines were left on their own or to the whims of their local caretakers. In a way, the national government has undertaken restorative work for both touristic as well as for politico-cultural reasons through which Uzbekistan's traditional cultural assets have, in most cases, regained better recognition and a longer life. Undoubtedly, given the enormity of the task and incurring costs, restoration of older neighbourhoods and all the monumental buildings is going to take numerous years, more money, and rigorous planning, but it is all worth it.

Notes

1. Omar Khayyam, *Rubáiyát of Omar Khayyám*, Volume 1, ed. Nathan Haskell Dole, trans. Edward FitzGerald (London: I. C. Page, 1898), 6 and 122.
2. A water reservoir usually in the centre of a city or a mosque.
3. 'Emir/Amir of Bukhara,' *World Digital Library*, https://www.wdl.org/en/item/5869/.
4. Rich Heffern, 'Nasruddin and his donkey: Tales of the holy fool,' *National Catholic Reporter*, February 9, 2011.
5. Ibid.
6. 'Magoki-Attari Mosque,' *Bukhara Hotels*, 2013–19.

7

Bukhara:
The Abode of Muslim Renaissance

I am deathless, I am the eternal Lord.
For I have spread the seed of the Word.

Firdausi[1]

The learned Bukharans keep reminding you of the Sanskrit origin of
their city's name, *Vihara/Vikara* (monastery), and proudly mention its
reference in Avesta, the Zoroastrian holy book. The city was founded
at least 13 centuries before the Christian era and must have seen the
migrations of its people to Iran, Afghanistan, and the Indus Valley where
they were called the Aryans. This is possibly one of the most well-known
migrations in Asian histories, followed by that of the Turkic people from
the eleventh century all the way until the colonial era. The builders of
Bukhara must have been exceptionally resolute people who never gave
up constructing splendid buildings for all the secular and sacred purposes
even if they frequently faced intermittent destruction at the hands of
perpetrators. Other than human marauders, plague and earthquakes
have often waylaid Bukhara, Khiva, Samarkand, and Tashkent but their
inhabitants never bowed out and outlived the Huns, Mongols, Nadir
Shah, and then the Russians. The Bukharan resilience, unique to several
other Afro-Asian societies, must have had endowed its people with a
greater self-confidence, much beyond the vagaries and legacies of colonial
and hegemonic West, the flag carrier of a pernicious Europeanization.
In post-Soviet years, Bukharans are once again trying to find a balancing
point between their long-time traditional mores and a seductive
modernization. While the monumental vestiges from the past engender
a sense of awe and respect, the exigencies for a respectable survival

equally lead one towards a greater share of modernity. Some people may still harbour nostalgia for the Soviet system, a major component of Europeanization, while others, tracing their rootedness in their Muslim and Asian identities, may try to recover a 'lost heritage' and thus the quest goes on. A dictatorial regime may be sitting on a powder keg holding back contrasts of this ideological and equally surreal crossroads, yet it may also be, by default, midwifing that needed a synthesis often not seen in many other Muslim polities. While walking around in Old Bukhara, these questions never left me alone as I searched for older cultures in the new city and modernity in the older town.

While walking down towards the Kalan/Kolon Square by passing through Taqi-Telpak Furushon Bazaar, I greeted the familiar faces of men and women selling a wide variety of handicrafts, clothes, rugs, samovars, ancient-looking coins, and curious jewellery from across Central Asia. I was heading towards the Taqi-Zargaron Dome, or the covered bazaar of goldsmiths. It is located towards the northern end of the Haqiqat Street and is foregrounded by an open space with more shops, museums, and cafés on both sides, whereas Taqi-Telpak Furushon Bazaar lies adjacent to the Malika. The open space between these two bazaars is occupied by resilient Bukharan women, eager to sell hats, jewellery, scarves, and tea sets to foreign-looking visitors; during long summer days, it is scorching hot here but these souls resolutely persist. The Taqi-Telpak Furushon Bazaar appears to have been a shrine in the past because there is a newly restored grave by its entrance in the Mukhtar Ambar Street. Behind this structure, characterized by high ceilings and several brown, semi-circular cupolas, lies an older mosque, Bazar-i-Khurd Mosque, already mentioned in the previous chapter, which was closed at the time, and was possibly undergoing some restoration. It seemed to have several residential quarters testifying its existence as a madrassa in the olden times. To its left and beyond, I came across narrow lanes and inhabited older houses, all built with mud or brown cement with artistically carved wooden beams laid across the breadth and length of the walls. These narrow and often twisting lanes appeared quite clean, though some dwellings seemed awaiting restoration and repairs. With mosques, madrassas, and markets abuzz with people, Old Bukhara had often peaceably negotiated its long existence during its multiple incarnations under Hindu, Zoroastrian, Buddhist, and Greek influences. Knowledge and international trade were its mainstay, though periodically, like metropolitan Samarkand, it received its share of destruction and rancour. Islam came to this part of the world in the early eighth century and since then has remained its most enduring reality along with impacting regions all around Central Asia.

As I was looking at the older and apparently frugal dwellings, I kept thinking about their past residents. Some of these houses, reached through narrow and often winding lanes that encircle religious and business places, would have once been the homes of Imam Bukhari, Ibn Sina, Firdausi, Al-Biruni, Khwarizmi, Bahauddin Naqshband, and more than 35 leading Sufi mentors in Islamic history. In Sufi Islam, this city has the unique privilege of producing one-third of leading Muslim spiritual mentors, and it is no wonder that it was often known as Bukhara Sharif or Noble Bukhara. Further to the west of Bukhara, Khiva also proved to be a comparatively smaller yet equally impressive centre of scholastic Islam and, despite all the vagaries of its past epochs, still retains its medieval ambience both in architecture and in its forbearance. It is in Old Bukhara, like in East Jerusalem and to some extent in the bazaar of Isfahan and narrow alleyways of Fes, that one is able to relive a unique past that came to a standstill. History is certainly a story of change and continuity, though we often focus mainly on victors and less on victims, it is the unsung heroes and heroines who defy the forces of annihilation and persist. Bukhara must have had an abundance of unsung heroes otherwise it would have been the recipient of more than a due share of destruction and transformations.

The Taqi-Sarrafon Bazaar is itself a warren of shops and workshops preceded by Tim Abdullah Khan to the right with Silk Road Spices facing it right across the Haqiqat Street. Here in this medieval section, the mixture of a high-ceiling bazaar, with its majestic brick structure, strikes one as the meeting point of old and new. Russian-speaking and often arty looking Uzbeks, while displaying their multilingual capabilities, attempt to define aesthetic and historical contexts of their artefacts, and one does not fail to notice this curious admixture of old and new which is neither aggressive nor indifferent. Not a typical connoisseur of shops and markets though cognisant of their value, I felt an urge to venture into the Silk Road Spices right behind a closed door and found it inexplicably quiet and even otherworldly. In a sense, it is a traditional place for Uzbek high tea and meals within the confines of a small museum of old and new handicrafts. Several kinds of tea, including a wide variety of herbs along with Uzbek and European delicacies, are minutely served by an all-women service, whereas the building looks more like an Andalusian home with its courtyard utilized as a serving area. It is both an accommodation and a catering facility which, like riads in Fes, may be more popular with international visitors. While sitting on an elevated platform, one could easily mistake it as just another shop. Its interior is certainly charming and quiet with the traditional Uzbek ambience displayed through furniture, carpets, wall hangings, wooden beams, verandas, old photographs, sketches, and some mini statues that make it a unique place to sit in and reflect.

Tea was a lateral follower to the silk in this area, though both came from China and were soon indigenized. Here in this Turkic part of Central Asia, soon the local inhabitants were growing silk worms along with operating their own looms and business outlets while using double-hump Balkhi camels to transport goods across Asia and beyond. In other words, the Silk Road was not just a one-commodity artery, instead it was the thoroughfare of ideas, faiths, ethnicities, languages, cuisines, skills, and provisions. Bukhara with its older and newer parts fully reflects diversity as well as antiquity despite all the past mishaps and political transformations in the wake.

Tea-ing and peering around charming collections of Uzbek arts, old and new, was a thrilling experience and perhaps a diversion from an increasingly hot sun that never seems to be threatened by clouds most of the year. These Uzbek women were not like the usual stewardesses that one comes across at tourist places; they appeared to be self-confident and elegantly dressed ladies whose features reflected plural origins. It appeared as if they were the partners in this joint hospitality venture that also worked as a window of their own rich cultures. But I wanted to move on to visit the Minar-e-Kalyan and the famous mosque with the same name and of course, the Mir-i-Arab Madrassa. Time must have flown by while I was trying out the various types of teas in blue floral Uzbek crockery and munching on numerous sweet accompaniments followed by more rounds of art specimens on the walls and in the windowsills as it was already rather late in the afternoon—the perfect time to visit the Kalan Square. Just before the entrance to the Taqi-Zargaron Bazaar, if instead of going straight, one takes a left turn, they enter a rather older and narrower street with a growing number of rest houses until they are almost right behind the Minar-e-Kalyan. Holding myself back from an immediate encounter with the minar, I tried to focus on an old madrassa just on my side of the minar; it was closed and looked like another museum that had seen its grand days and was now undergoing some restoration. To the right of its entrance stands the minaret, one of the oldest and the tallest structures in entire Asia which no less significantly escaped the unstoppable Mongol wrath. Instead, Genghis Khan, while destroying everything in 1219–20, somehow felt amused by this minaret that went up in a circular form and had been built with millions of small, even-sized pale brown bricks held strongly together by a thin cement of the same colour. The minaret had valiantly defied vagaries of invasions and earthquakes. It is now the unprecedented pre-Mongol specimen of a unique architecture with all kinds of myths attached to it.

Arsalan Khan, the Karakhanid ruler, had built this minaret in 1127, a century before the Mongol invasion, to be reached from within the Kalyan Mosque since it was meant as a higher pedestal for giving the call for prayer five times a day. It may resemble similar other contemporary minarets elsewhere, including the central Umayyad mosque in Seville which was subsequently converted into a cathedral whose Giralda Minaret/Tower still remains the tallest structure in the Andalusian city. While Minar-e-Kalyan is circular, Giralda's exterior is square and features a ramp so that the muezzin could ride his horse all the way to the top. The Kalyan Minaret is 47 metres high, featuring 105 stairs and is anchored on 10-metre-deep foundations which have allowed it to withstand tremors that are frequent in this part of Asia. This vertical structure is nine metres in diameter at its base whereas its top accounts for six metres. It retains a rotunda of 16 arches so as to afford a panoramic view of the city and beyond from within an elegant corniche. Some traditions link this most prominent symbol of the Kalan Square and of entire Bukhara to a Zoroastrian concept of a fire tower which was built by an architect called Baku. Its otherwise brown exterior, more like Bath stone, displays 14 ornamental bands, meant not only to strengthen its cylindrical structure but to equally enhance its aesthetic imprint. These decorative bands largely consist of bluish tiles, perhaps used for the first time here ever, that one otherwise notices on the façades and arches of other madrassas and mosques across Central Asia. Tamerlane was one of the earliest rulers to be fond of blue tile work on cupolas and minarets of his buildings and since then they have been the most familiar and impressive feature of buildings across the Silk Road, all the way to Herat and further down to Iran and the Indus Valley. In 1920, General Frunze's artillery deeply damaged the minar and through minute observation one can easily detect the subsequent restoration work. Like any other grand and historic monument, the Kalyan Minar does not lack in myths and stories attributed to its height and survival. One such familiar myth is about a maulvi who had been murdered by Arsalan Khan following a fight; the former began tormenting the ruler in his dreams until he lost his sleep owing to hallucinations. Reportedly, the maulvi told the king: 'You have killed me; oblige me by laying my head on a spot where nobody can tread'. As per this narrative, the sultan built the minaret and the maulvi's head was laid to rest over its top, which again is just a fable. However, the minaret's foundations, as checked later through scientific studies, reveal special arrangements to cushion the impact of tremors. Storks, for centuries, have continued inhabiting this vantage point and, as per speculation, might have even elicited a rare smile and a moment of remission from Genghis Khan.

The Kalyan Mosque, the biggest and perhaps the most beautiful mosque in Bukhara, sits next to the minaret and faces Mir-i-Arab Madrassa across the Kalan Square, locally known as *Po-i-Kalyan* or the Foot of the Great. This name may owe itself to the preeminent minaret, or even the Ark—the latter situated towards the north of this square. Like the Registan Square in Samarkand, with three of its uniquely built madrassas, the mosque and the minaret are the heart of the Noble Bukhara and the core of its historic majesty. All three buildings compete in beauty, grace, and grandeur, and even after so many centuries and tribulations, they remain in use. It is believed that the ancient town existed on the site of the Ark and might have housed the first mosque, even though at Kalan Square, there have been mosques since 713. In its earliest incarnation, the Kalyan Mosque was built by the Karakhanids but was destroyed by Genghis Khan a century later. It was in 1521 that the predecessor of today's mosque was built by the Shaybanis as the central place for prayers. It features 208 arches over 208 pillars on all the four sides of an expansive compound. A huge but immensely symmetrical blue dome tops the mihrab and the main prayer area. No wonder the

Kalyan Mosque equals Samarkand's Bibi-Khanym Mosque both in size and design which was built by Tamerlane in the fourteenth century for his favourite wife in his favourite city. Bibi-Khanym Mosque may be taller than Kalyan Mosque but, since it is located in a slightly lower area of Samarkand, it does not appear so. For a long time, the Bibi-Khanym Mosque has been characterized as the biggest mosque in the Muslim world though, in the last several decades, it has often suffered due to neglect or sheer denigration but it is now benefiting from a renewed interest.

The Kalyan Mosque, both in its compound and built areas, has the capacity for 10,000 worshippers, though during the 1920s, the Soviets used it as a warehouse until it reopened for prayers in 1991. On Fridays and Eids, the overflow fills up *Po-i-Kalyan*. The magnificent entrance to the mosque reminded me of the Badshahi Mosque in Lahore and Jama Mosque in Delhi—the two Mughal edifices which incorporate Central Asian and Persian architectural traditions. For the Mughal mosques, one has to climb dozens of evenly laid steps, since these monumental mosques are built on elevated platforms. On the other hand, the Kalyan Mosque is slightly lower than ground level, though not too low. Through a high and immensely majestic façade, one enters a covered structure of arches, corridors, and rooms which border a huge open compound on all the four sides. The main prayer area is also spacious and the ceilings are quite high and ornate, topped up by that grand blue dome. Just like the Mughal mosques, profusion of open spaces, corridors, and residential rooms on all the three sides complete the quadrangle which has a solitary mulberry tree—not too far from the main entrance and then further up a few graves on an elevated tomb. All the arches facing the compound from all the four sides display floral designs over bold blue and white tiles depicting Quranic calligraphy. Similar bold calligraphic inscriptions are displayed on the mosque's main entrance, a feature one notices all across the Muslim world. The mosque has its own distinct beauty, majesty, and spirituality. While standing near the mihrab and the main prayer vestibule, one can look back at the Kalyan Minar, the mosque's main entrance and the higher cupolas of Mir-i-Arab Madrassa across the square. If fully absorbed, the serenity, grace, and splendour of this skyline is certain to stay in one's memory forever. It is from this very point that I internalized an unforgettable sight in human aesthetics, spirituality, and devotion which owed itself to architectural acumen and sublime immersion. The view reminded me of standing inside the prayer area of the Badshahi Mosque in Lahore while looking back over its entrance and beyond towards the Lahore Fort—all retaining their own distinct identity but blending so majestically under a blue sky as if Mother Nature herself was offering her homage to god's divinity and human ingenuity. Of course Muhammad Iqbal's elegantly built tomb to the right of the Badshahi Mosque is a fervent reminder of 'the lost horizons' but combines intellectual with sacred and secular conventions while accommodating a subsequent Sikh monument in the neighbourhood. Spaciousness of these historic mosques, their simplicity, and a steady stream of worshippers walking humbly towards the mihrab underline the universality of Islamic ethos beyond the ethnic and linguistic pluralities. While the tourists were busy taking pictures of the compound, Minar-e-Kalyan, and of Mir-i-Arab Madrassa through an exceptionally symmetrical aggregation of brown minarets, blue cupolas, and magnificent entrances in the square, my spirituality took me to an adjacent section of the mosque. This was the area for prayers, secluded from the tourist humdrum. I joined fellow believers behind the imam who, with his turban and trimmed beard, could have been from any part of the Muslim world. Praying with fellow believers brought me closer to the Bukharans and I was no more an intrepid tourist; instead I was one of fellow believers spontaneously prostrating before a powerful deity while remembering the humanity of the Prophet (PBUH). I did not need any dictionary or encyclopaedia to connect with this world of which I was now an equal and, at the same time, an invisible member over and above race, age, and class differentiations. I stayed on in the prayer hall long after the worshippers had left and kept looking at the ornamented ceilings, Quranic calligraphy, artistic arches, elegant pillars, and a reaching simplicity of the ambience around me. I was thinking about the Samanis, Karakhanids, Seljuks, Mongols, Shaybanis, Astrakhanis, Mangats, and Russians who in their own ways had been here with all their awe and power but now live only in historical accounts thanks to fellow historians. Bukhara survived all the stampedes and so did the Kalyan Mosque which, following the destruction by Mongols, was adroitly rebuilt in the seventeenth century and regained its lost glory until the Soviets came in with vengeance and turned it into a store. Seven decades later, the mosque, as per its historical defiance, staged another comeback with its expansive compound full of worshippers, with Friday's overflow occupying even the Kalan Square outside the grand entrance. A multitude of turbans, square hats, karakuls, and handkerchiefs of various colours adorned those countless rows as the descendants of Bukhari and Ibn Sina stood facing towards Makkah and seeking divine forgiveness for the entire humanity as their ancestors did in the olden times.

My salaam and a rather more fluent Persian/Tajik by now had their due impact on the guards at the entrance to Mir-i-Arab Madrassa who quite generously allowed me to see the compound and the living quarters for the students and teachers as the school is in full use at present. However, the biggest and a rather very pleasant surprise awaited me when one of the guards allowed me to join a small group of some important visitors who were entering the big hall to our left. This is where Mir-i-Arab, the Yemeni Sheikh, is buried next to the Shaybani monarch, Ubaidullah Khan. The Yemeni scholar, a Naqshbandi Sufi, wielded great influence on the monarch who built one of the most beautiful seminaries in Central Asia featuring two blue domes overlooking the square surrounded by imposing brown rivals such as the Minar-e-Kalyan. Smaller than the magnificent dome of the Kalyan Mosque, these two domes stand like sentinels right behind the splendid entrance of the madrassa, which is decorated with both Quranic calligraphy and intricate tile work. Built on a slightly higher ground than the mosque, the madrassa appears to excel the former due to its façade and the immediate proximity of luminous domes. Built in the sixteenth century, it might have been inspired by the greater and exquisite use of blue tiles in Timurid buildings in Samarkand, Shakhrisabz, and Bukhara. In fact, Tamerlane's grandson, Ulugh Beg, ensured a more generous but no less charming use of blue tiles on arches, domes, façades, and minarets of his mosques and madrassas. Still Mir-i-Arab, with its enchanting exterior and undiminished internal beauty, is a captive piece in human devotion to aesthetics and could be characterized as one of the most beautiful buildings in the world which, despite its constant usage as a residential seminary, has maintained its originality and majesty. Of course, restorations have happened rather meticulously and the huge wooden gates and tile works have benefited from constant care, but one cannot help but admire the Bukharan fondness for education and beautiful edifices. The madrassa, like all its other counterparts here in Central Asia and further south and east, is multistorey and in a square shape featuring residential and scholastic facilities. The entrance is amply beautified by minute tile work with calligraphic inscriptions and is located right in the centre with two-storeys of several rooms on both sides featuring arched entrances. Each one of these arched entrances is decorated with Quranic verses on tiles of several soothing colours. The façade itself, like that of the mosque and other madrassas in Bukhara, is quite tall and neighboured by two blue-topped domes sitting on its left and right.

The lower section of each dome has a circular band featuring bold Quranic calligraphy on dark blue tiles with an even more complex and multicoloured tile work featured on the remaining lower body of the dome. The Mir-i-Arab Madrassa was in use up till the year 1920 when it was closed down under Soviet dictates and was not allowed to resume its teaching until 1944 when Stalin sanctioned its reopening so as to win over Uzbek Muslims. The main complex surrounding the compound is again a double-storey structure housing several rooms with arches crowning over their doors. The graves of Mir-i-Arab, the Naqshbandi saint, and of Amir Ubaidullah Khan in a room adjacent to the foyer reminded me of Rumi's resting place in Konya with green silken cloth covering the *turbat*s,[2] and the ceiling, other than its floral decorations, ensuring light from the outside. The high ceilings, domes, arched entrances, and open compounds were meant to supply sufficient light and cool air, especially during the dry, hot summer. My first encounter with Mir-i-Arab was unusually pleasant on two counts. Firstly, I was able to see its main entrance and domes just before sunset, which is supposed to be the best time to absorb the full glory of this architectural gem. Secondly, I was allowed to venture into the special room retaining the two graves and, other than offering *fateha*, I was able to see the entire length of one of the blue domes from within. By the time I came out of this madrassa, my mind and body both seemed to be out of sync with the mundane world and it took me some time to regain myself. Passing by a few vendors with their array of a wide variety of hats and caps, I began to move back to the Malika where Rustam was busy ensuring an ample supply of his cuisine to a big group of German tourists.

***

Even after a filling, multicourse, and scrumptious meal prepared by the Uzbek ladies, my sinews wanted to sit by the Lyab-i-Hauz to see old and new Bukhara promenading to the live music and indulging in local ice cream or even Lipton's iced tea. The live music which was mostly in Persian—Tajik to be exact—and Uzbek, with a few English renditions, was being played for customers at the busy restaurant. People milled around the Hauz, over the stairs and chairs in quite a relaxed manner, and scarfed seniors followed younger, skirt-clad maidens. We did detect some newlyweds in their formal Western attires, keenly followed by family and friends as if they had just returned from their receptions and extensive feasts and were bidding farewell to this heart of old and new Bukhara before taking off for honeymoon. Maybe they had come to seek blessings from Mullah Nasruddin who was still being kept busy with an army of irreverent youngsters. I pitied the donkey and its noble rider for not having been given a due respite even at this late hour. I did not venture into Nadir Divan-begi Madrassa as a late night bawdy music party at a former seminary would have deeply anguished me. Finding an open space, we joined Uzbek families on the stairs just outside the Nadir Divan-begi Khanaka and enjoyed the musical ensemble of the waltzing fountains in the Hauz that was lit with several colourful but not overpowering lights. In its middle, a small replica of the minar and a few other landmark monuments such as Char Minar, Mir-i-Arab Madrassa, and the Ark were now illumined as we tried to absorb a cool evening thinking of sages and saints of an erstwhile Bukhara before the Mongols struck here. As we slowly and rather reluctantly left this popular spot with all its diverse natives along with a small presence of tourists, we noticed a kippah-clad man talking to a group of men and women drinking milk shakes and tea by a tuck shop. I assumed him to be a descendant of the famous Bukharan Jews who had lived in this old, commercial city for centuries and in great numbers. Speaking Bukhari—a variant of Persian written in Hebrew scripts—and affiliated with several synagogues in the city, they are now a smaller community with most of them departed for Israel and the US over the past few decades; few stayed behind, and I was seeing some of them by the Hauz. Other than familiar Ashkenazi and Sephardic groups, Bukharans account for one of the oldest and least known Jewish communities who had prospered amongst Muslims since the eighth century. Their earlier escapades with the Achaemenids,

Seleucids, and Sassanids were often not too amiable except when the Parthians were in control, however, with the Arab conquest of Bukhara in 709, Jews experienced a greater sense of ease and moved on to either Samarkand, Tashkent, Osh, or Fergana. Except for his yarmulke, there was nothing else to distinguish him from people around. Before my return to the Malika, I ventured towards the Khoja Gaukushan Mosque and occupied a bench overlooking the Hauz. The lone mulberry tree, close to my room and facing the mosque, stood still under a full moon while a fountain in the Hauz pursued its chartered course. The entire square, once the limelight of commercial and scholarly activities, was now totally quiet as I tried to transpose myself to another gone era.

My itinerary for the next day included visits to some more known Bukharan madrassas and certainly a closer encounter with the Ismail Samani Mausoleum—the oldest of its kind in this area. After a hearty breakfast and some early morning Persian exchanges with Rustam and his younger assistant, I took to Taqi-Telpak Furushon and alerted my presence to the friendly shopkeepers who by now had become familiar with a lanky visitor loitering around assuredly flaunting his Farsi. I knew that this had originally been a covered bazaar of booksellers until changes took over and it now featured all kinds of hand-made crafts and antiques. I did stop to inspect a few more coins and jewellery pieces at a shop whose portly owner was never short on his vast knowledge of the archaeological sites where these artefacts had been excavated. Brooches, needles, silk ropes, beads, combs, cutlery, and vases were just a few items that his mini museum contained. It worried my heart that they would disappear in some private Western or Japanese collections. Brushing aside such concerns and moving ahead, I turned left on Khoja Nurabad Road and soon found myself between two grand madrassas. Two architectural masterpieces built by Ulugh Beg and Abdul Aziz Khan stood face to face inviting the onlookers to make their choice. I opted for Ulugh Beg first and ventured in after the usual exchange with the beautiful Uzbek lady who ran a shop in the foyer. More than the entry ticket, she was interested in selling her textiles, bed covers, shawls, or even a rug or two. Though I appreciated her collection, I wanted to move forward to see the madrassa itself, which I finally did. I had to promise her of my return with my spouse since she was a specialist on home decoration whereas I, as a typical male historian, was more enamoured with buildings, books, and people. I guess my humour cut some ice on her round face sporting joint brows, and she let me in.

Ulugh Beg was the grandson of Tamerlane and the oldest son of Mirza Shah Rukh (1377–1447), and his original name was Mirza Muhammad Tariq. His mother, Gawhar Shad (1377–1457), was a known scholar and a builder whose mosques, madrassas, and shrines in Herat and Mashhad showcased her fondness for these two illustrious pursuits. There are quite a few stories about this dynamic woman including her support for women's education, though her own end, like that of her son, typified a painful tradition of palatial intrigues and murders. Faced with intrigues, Shah Rukh had moved the capital of his vast empire from his father's Samarkand to Herat, while leaving Ulugh Beg behind to administer Samarkand, Bukhara, and other vast regions across the Oxus, also known as Amu Darya. Beg, by temperament, was not made for warfare and monarchical pursuits and spent his time and resources on scholarly and scientific pursuits. He built an observatory in Afrasiyab, just outside Samarkand, and built some of the most magnificent madrassas in Samarkand, Bukhara, and Gijduvan. He was born in Persia during one of his grandfather's campaigns and was destined to become the king of a vast empire which included Persia, Afghanistan, Turkmenistan, present-day Uzbekistan, Tajikistan, and southern Kazakhstan. Tamerlane of course controlled a huge empire all the way from the Black Sea to Mongolia and from southern Russia to India and Iraq, which had all been acquired by sword. Soon after his death, revolts began to threaten the very foundations of the Timurid Empire though Shah Rukh tried to hold it together and even moved his capital further south. Beg faced numerous revolts, including some from his own kith and kin, and might have had even committed violence in cities like Balkh, but he is still mainly known for his scholarly pursuits. His observatory was the biggest of its time, while his own astrological researches were adroitly committed to pen. Other than composing poetry, he authored a book on medicine and gathered known scholars and scientists to his court. Scholar-king Ulugh Beg met his tragic end while on hajj as apparently his own close descendants killed him. His remains were subsequently brought back to Samarkand and interned next to those of his grandfather. As I mentioned earlier, Queen Gawhar Shad, a promoter of poetry, philosophy, architecture, women's education, and science, was also killed when she was 80 years old and is buried in Herat—thus closing down this unique phase in the Timurid Empire that itself owed its existence to bloodshed and plunder, especially by Tamerlane. Her tomb resembles Tamerlane's own resting place in Samarkand as it is topped by a circular, ribbed blue dome with beautiful floral patterns—so distinctly unique to contemporary Central Asian architecture.

Ulugh Beg's madrassa in Bukhara, pioneer in its own way due to its age and style, allows entry through a gigantic but equally enticing entrance and features a quadrangle built around a square compound while its two-storeys contain numerous rooms and staircases, all preambled by fascinating arches. Similar to its entrance with floral decorations and Quranic calligraphies on the main arch and its other eight companions on both sides, the other end of the madrassa features the main prayer hall with a high ceiling topped by a magnificent blue ribbed dome, whereas two tall minarets built in the style of Minar-e-Kalyan stand like two sentinels guarding the very dome. The arched rooms located within the two-storey structure of the quadrangle had been designed specifically to ensure fresh breeze and enough light for scholars. It is certainly a meticulously patterned madrassa, the oldest in Central Asia in post-Mongol era. It was completed in 1417 and is a symbol of the unique Timurid architecture and the monarch's own interest in scholarly pursuits. The main dome is ribbed, unlike its Mir-i-Arab counterparts, and retains appealing floral and geometrical patterns. No wonder, despite all his failings, Beg was close to being an Aristotelian scholar-king. While sitting inside this seminary, I was trying to make sense of that period in Muslim history where fratricide was certainly frequent, but it did not deter rulers in Persia, India, West Asia, and Central Asia from building some of the most marvellous pieces of architecture. Perhaps their sense of mortality and uncertainty hurried them on this path to raise ever-lasting monuments. Like Alexander leaving almost a score of Alexandrias across his empire, all these kings and sultans wanted to outlive their mundane lives and legacies. Beg did face some opposition by some Bukhara-based Naqshbandi clerics who thought that these madrassas should be used only for religious learning and not for secular subjects. He sought the services of two contemporary leading architects, Najmuddin Bukhari and Ismael Isfahani, to build his madrassas in three cities. The prince had in fact begun his scholarly and architectural work while he was still in his teens, especially when his father had pushed the governorship of vast regions on him. The Abdulaziz Khan Madrassa faces and even competes with Beg's, though it was built slightly later in the sixteenth century and is awash with souvenir shops selling carpets, brass lamps, and textiles trying to hide the elegant tile works over the numerous arches and the ceiling of the main prayer hall. Whereas Beg's madrassa, other than its fewer handicraft outlets, houses a small museum of photography, especially of the period of before and after Soviet invasion; Abdullah Khan Madrassa retains a museum of woodcarvings. This museum is located right in the prayer hall whose ceiling features exceptionally beautiful stalactites, reminding one of some of the old Muslim buildings in Andalusia. Abdul Aziz Khan was a Shia minister and his madrassa was built to rival its older counterpart across the street. Bukhara must have been a tolerant place despite its own share of sectarian tensions, as allowing such a grand Shia madrassa right in the heart of this predominantly Sunni city speaks volumes about its tolerance for plurality.

These two illustrious madrassas and a walk-about the older part of the city further down Khoja Nurabad Road, and getting lost in the winding lanes claimed my entire day. The older parts of the town reminded me of my own childhood in similar streets and mohalla culture. Neat and quiet streets had tea places and corner shops at convenient distances, and at a couple of places, I saw people sitting together munching on extensive wedding feasts. Further down, I greeted a group of women who were sitting together as if offering their condolences to some bereaved family with several copies of the Quran. I passed by smaller mosques where congregational prayers were being held, though I could not hear the recitation out in the streets, given the official restrictions on amplification. The worshippers were often an interesting mix of several age groups, some donning turbans while others wearing traditional Uzbek pillbox hats. In my foray, I soon reached the end of the older town and began to comb down the Russian and more recent sections of this sprawling city. Here tree-lined boulevards with orderly traffic, air-conditioned offices, and shops selling all kinds of commodities along with bakeries and eateries brought me back to a different kind of Bukhara, though no less dynamic. These were mostly operated by smartly dressed women and one gathered a greater sense of hospitality and curiosity at these places which displayed a visible level of encroachment by Western capitalism. This new part of Bukhara appeared to be consumerist and vividly strong on the service sector and reminded me of similar localities in the Balkans and Southern Europe. My wanderings must have claimed a whole chunk of that day despite a couple of tea breaks on the way. Soon I found myself back at the Lyab-i-Hauz eager to devour an entire plate of kebabs and mixed grill along with steamy naans.

***

Fortified by an ample supply of fruit, yogurt, and bread, the following day I took off for the Ark, the Fort, which is viewed as the oldest habitation in Bukhara. Up until 1920, it combined as the royal palace, court, and the secretariat for Amir Alam Khan who, following the Soviet invasion, lived as an exile in Afghanistan. One can see the world-famous picture by Prokudin-Gorsky of this portly monarch all across the city in the museums and in the former prison, Zindaan/Zindon, which is presently defined as a museum. The Ark is on an elevated ground and is buffeted by massive brick walls and turrets, and is accessible only through the main entrance on a raised ramp and is guarded by two double-storey towers. According to several traditions, numerous layers of Old Bukhara, which is mostly in ruins since the Soviet occupation, lay underneath the present site. The palace, courts, mosque, parade grounds, and barracks for guards are features of this fort that has seen its good and bad days. In a way, it was a town within a town, though most of it lies in rubble, however, restoration work continues. Soon after the entrance, one sees the Friday Mosque, dating to the seventeenth century, and beyond it are the oldest parts of the ruined Ark which were once palaces that were air bombed in 1920. To the right, an archaeology museum is housed in what once used to be the prime ministerial residence, and further down are the royal stables and quarters holding musical instruments for parades. Several other museums and galleries are housed in former royal residences and embody past historical epochs in Bukharan history, especially from the Shaybani era. Towards the eastern corner are prison cells which, as mentioned above, are now designated as the Museum of Law and Legislation. Here, other than several early photos, thick legal statutes in Persian, mannequins of some of the past prisoners and their guards besides the handcuffs, and other such metallic implements are on public display. The small cells look very clean unlike their previous incarnations when they must have been dungeons reeking with smell, insects, and cries. Depending upon the then ruler, the subjects in the emirate could be convicted for not paying back loans or even missing out on religious practices, or for drinking and loitering. One particular dungeon dug deeper in the earth had held Charles Stoddart and Arthur Conolly, the two Britons who had ventured here during the First Anglo-Afghan War and were interned in this special cell called the bug pit. Stoddart had been suspected as a spy in 1839, while Conolly, who had reached Bukhara in 1841 to get Colonel Stoddart released, was seen to be rude in his encounter with the amir and got himself into trouble for it. They were hanged in 1842 and despite public demand, Victorian Britain refused to undertake a punitive campaign. A devastating retreat from Afghanistan must have been a deterrent. The narratives published by Joseph Wolff of the imprisonment, trial, and execution of these two Britons recorded their story. It made Bukhara a household and equally despicable name in Britain.

The area between the Zindaan and Mir-i-Arab Madrassa is definitely an older part of Bukhara but it has all the civic facilities, although the narrow, winding lanes and corner shops with occasional mosques and madrassas reveal continuity in historic traditions. Interestingly, here in Bukhara or elsewhere in Uzbekistan, one does not come across street urchins, flies, open rubbish bins, or such other civic abnormalities that characterize many other parts of our developing world. Between the Ark and Mir-i-Arab Madrassa, there is a covered bazaar in a reconfigured market that appears to be like an old serai. It is full of small shops hosting goldsmiths, craftsmen, clothiers, vegetable vendors, and small tuck shops mostly operated by women. There was a music shop towards the end of this market thronging with people where I froze on my feet. I heard an Urdu song being played on full blast. I soon recognized the singer and the lyrics. Atif Aslam, with his husky voice, was singing one of his hit songs, and hearing him so clearly and lucidly right in the heart of Old Bukhara was certainly not only a sweet awakening of some nostalgia but also a proof of this city's cosmopolitanism. I wonder how many people here could understand the lyrics except for common Persian words or maybe it was the tone and overall rendition of this favourite South Asian singer that had catapulted him into Uzbek homes and shops. I stopped and sat down by a small shop in the veranda facing the music outlet and resumed my journey only after the song had come to an end. Nobody noticed me, not even when I sat down almost between the two vendors. I kept going with Registan to my right and a hospital to my left. Soon I saw a double-hump camel ferrying two children around and I sat down again to observe. The cameleer reminded me of those western characters in American films—tough men of few words and quite close to their rides. After a few rides, he tied the camel by the tree and sat down to smoke while his wife looked at the departing tourist family. These are the camels that carried goods across mountains, deserts, and valleys for hundreds of miles through a history of thousands of years and, unlike their Baloch and Arab cousins, were smaller in size but no less sturdy. Their two humps made it easier for them to travel longer distances, whereas their hairy faces and necks ensured protection against harsh winters. Here in summer now, with most hair gone, this gentle fellow appeared even more reduced in height but not in beauty and genteelness. I always wondered why our Mullah Nasruddin would be shown with a donkey and not a cuddly camel. Perhaps a camel from South Asia or Arabia would be too tall for our Mullah to communicate with his joyful listeners, plus all our jokes happen to be about a poor donkey, whereas camels and horses are viewed with great respect and affection. No doubt, goats, foxes, cows, sheep, dogs, and jackals have their mixed shares of folk narratives which could vary from a compliment to sheer ridicule!

I crossed the bigger version of Bahauddin Naqshband Road here which, unlike its sections snaking through the older town, ran like a boulevard with several parks, big trees, and historic monuments located in its northern neighbourhood. After negotiating my way through the orchards and some modern looking offices, I finally reached the Abdullah Khan Madrassa which is certainly an impressive edifice, though needing some restorative work. Like other historic buildings, it is looked after by the state which charges a nominal entry free and is neighboured by Modari-Khan Madrassa. Once inside the Abdullah Khan Madrassa, I wandered through the medley of arched doors and low-ceiling accommodation which appeared to have been in use until recent past. This part of Bukhara, facing across the Ark and north of the boulevard, gives a more modern look but contains some of the older and equally preeminent buildings including this madrassa. The well within the compound reminded me of similar wells back in Pakistan which had been a familiar sight for drawing underground water through a roped bucket, long before the tube wells and hand pumps ventured in. Reliving my childhood, I soon engaged myself in that exercise and began watering a few solitary mulberry trees and hedges in the compound. Since it was a hot August day, I could certainly empathize with these plants and partook some of the cool fresh water besides sprinkling it over my head. The caretaker spoke fluent Persian and that allowed me to practise my limited proficiency with him. We discussed almost every topic on earth including the role of political Islam, merits and demerits of the Soviet rule, and most of all, the sanctified status of his city across the Muslim world for so long. He was proud of his city and wanted to see it regain its erstwhile status through a more vigorous plan in modern and traditional education. He allowed me to explore the living quarters of past scholars on the second floor and, taking it as a special privilege, I began climbing the slightly bruised stairs. Fighting the wasps away, soon I was reliving a bygone past where these students would share rooms; retain their Arabic and Persian books; a few pans and some limited provisions. I did notice several kitchen facilities, each allocated to a specific number of residents—very similar to an Oxbridge residence hall with communal kitchens. Certainly, the hall, topped by an impressively gigantic dome, in addition to facilities for prayer, featured places reserved for library, class work, and dining. Climbing through another stairwell and peering at small, thin bricks, the kind that one sees in Mughal buildings in India and their Safavid counterparts in Iran, I soon found myself over the roof displaying several smaller domes. I was in fact right above the prayer hall, and just behind the grand façade opening into the main courtyard and could see Minar-e-Kalyan, the Ark, and Modari-Khan Madrassa to my south and east. Behind the Abdullah Khan Madrassa, I could see a well-patterned park that would soon lead me to the earliest tomb in Bukhara.

Following a warm handshake with the kindly Uzbek official, I went around to check on the Modari-Khan Madrassa and then through a newly-built entrance to the neatly kept park, I headed towards the Ismail Samani Tomb—the oldest in Bukhara and even a trendsetter for such future shrines. Contrasted with the Abdullah Khan Madrassa, which lay deserted, here crowds of Uzbeks and visitors were heading towards a brown structure that stood in the middle of a compound and reminded me of Tughlaq tombs in Delhi. Featuring two-metre thick walls, the mausoleum rises to a great height, topped by a dome, though the lower structure is not circular; instead it is perpendicular and square. Four smaller brown domes top the four corner-ends of the mausoleum which display several geometrical patterns carved on slim brown bricks. Four smaller doors open onto a raised platform featuring graves lit in from all four sides through 40 symmetrically arched windows that are located towards the near top of the shrine. Built on an elevated ground, the architecture of this otherwise simple but sturdy and no less impressive shrine, according to some architects, resembles the old Zoroastrian towers. Its construction was completed in 905, making it the earliest Muslim monument in the city; it never needed any repairs except for some minor work on its spiked dome. It could possibly be the oldest surviving Muslim tomb in Central Asia. Luckily, it escaped the Mongol wrath and thus is an exceptional specimen of architecture and a living evidence of the earliest Muslim presence in Central Asia. The walls are built of terracotta bricks which are thin and geometrical but strong. Its pale brown shade keeps changing with the varying times of the day. The tomb was built for Ismail Samani, the founder of the Samani Dynasty of Persian origin who retained a great influence in the Sunni caliphate of the Abbasids in Baghdad and helped the latter fight their Shia rivals such as the Fatimids and Buyids. Eventually, Samanis became independent of Baghdad though retained a nominal allegiance to the caliph—a precedent followed by the Ghaznavids and Tughlaqs in subsequent centuries. Buried inside are Ismail Samani, his son, and grandson. Whereas tourists engage in touching the exterior walls while photographing one of the earliest Islamic buildings in this part of the world, the locals stand by the graves offering *fateha*, though I did not see anybody touching the gravestones. Partly overwhelmed by the ambience and historicity of the place and partly due to heat outside, I decided to linger on one of the benches studying the sturdy, simple, yet devotional architecture, and the streams of visitors all subdued by a greater sense of humility and respect. A few hundred yards behind the Samani Tomb are some older mosques and a few remaining portions of the city walls that the Shaybanis had built during their heyday. This area has now been converted into a vast park with tall trees and meticulously maintained flowerbeds which must have been a bustling habitation in earlier times.

Towards the western side of the Samani (Kirov) Park, Chashma-Ayub Mausoleum or the Spring of Ayyub is a preeminent monument of religio-historical significance. Named after Prophet Job, the spring is in fact the total sum of dwindling water levels in the areas including the ever-diminishing expanse and depth of the Aral Sea, which has happened just in the last 40 years or so. Its bed has simply turned into a saline desert with rusted remains of boats lying on sand both in Uzbekistan and Kazakhstan. We could not get into the room where the biblical Prophet Job is buried, yet we were able to encounter the traditional and contemporary perspectives on water in the small but immensely educational museum adjacent to the tomb. Maps and especially the shocking graphs of harrowing desertification are too obvious to ignore. Some people were drinking water, as one would see pilgrims at Kaaba in Makkah, Varanasi, or such other holy places, plus at all those streams flowing by legendry *Zinda Pir*s (Living Saints) across the Muslim world. Prophet Job had reportedly struck his staff here, causing the opening of soil with water gushing out, though the mausoleum itself was built in the twelfth century. Located next to this shrine-museum is Imam Ismail Bukhari Memorial with a glass exterior which is a tribute to the greatest collector of hadith (the Prophet's sayings) and a Bukharan who, like Ibn Sina, Roudaki, and several other luminaries, had turned the city into a sanctified place of scholarship. Imam Muhammad Ismail Bukhari was a native Bukharan who learnt his early Islamic instructions from his mother since his father had passed away quite early on. He had memorized the Quran during his childhood and went on to perform hajj with his mother and brother. His travels across various Muslim regions and parleys with leading narrators of the prophetic sayings led him to collect 700,000 hadith. Through his meticulous preening and authentication, he selected around 7,000 of them as the most reliable and thus provided, after the Quran, the second most vital classical source on Islam. His student in Nishapur, Imam Muslim, carried on his mentor's work and produced a similar collection, and thus both these hadith collections are called *Sahiain*—the authentic ones. Imam Bukhari died near Samarkand and is buried in Khartank where he had spent the last phase of his life. His grave was ignored during the Soviet era until Muslim dignitaries such as President Soekarno showed a keen interest in visiting the tomb of the most respected Muslim archivist of the early era. The Soviet authorities hurriedly restored the tomb and built a proper access passage but the fuller restoration with a duly designed compound was undertaken only after independence. However, in his native Bukhara, just to the left of Chashma-Ayub, the brown, modernist, circular structure with a rising tower in the centre holds the various editions of the religious texts besides other rare documents and portraits and is assuredly a due homage to the primacy of pen and paper.

One cannot help but admire the Uzbek efforts to develop green and open parks in urban spaces which allow family traditions to continue along with the traditional Turkic penchant for gardens since time immemorial. Babur and other Central Asian rulers in India and Persia missed shady places, ornate floral beds, fountains spewing waters, peacocks, nightingales, and parrots flying from a wide variety of trees whose bowers were the choicest places for lovers, courtiers, musicians, and poets. While walking across the Samani Park and its various sections, often reverberating with some soothing music, I could relate this continuity in aesthetics that Central Asians have retained despite all the havocs and transformations. In one day, I had an overwhelming amount of history and spirituality internalized after visiting madrassas and especially the Samani and Ayyub Mausoleums. Despite a deep desire to linger on and delve in the long-gone past of this special city, I slowly began walking in the direction of the Ark. Passing through orderly streets, newer houses surrounded by gardens and tall trees, and luckily without the fast food joints, I soon came upon an open restaurant in a charming garden. I was still on this side of Bahauddin Naqshband Boulevard and not too far from Bolo Haouz Mosque, which turned out to be a unique experience. I felt low on my dosage of black tea and was even tempted to try Uzbek samosas cooked in a traditional/modern oven. Samosas, lunch dishes, green salads, and evenly cut melon pieces were being prepared by women in a room while the oven was out in the open. The café's service included several young men and women, supervised by a slim, middle-aged, smiling Uzbek. He acknowledged our arrival with a nod and after hearing an *As-salamu alaykum* became even more cordial. Soon we were having our overdue supply of black tea while munching on samosas. In a yurt-like tent, we noticed some merry Uzbeks who were being entertained by a folk singer on his Rubab-like instrument. I could figure out some words, but the tones were immensely rhythmic and our neighbours were deeply immersed in renditions.

So while departing from the tea house, where some people were having rounds of local brew, I said to the charming owner of this garden café:

> *Uz jamkhana soay qaidkhana mee rawam*
> From the drinking hole I go to the ultimate hole

> *Uz Gulistan, sooay zindaan mee rawam*
> From your garden I move to the prison

I did not realize I would make them laugh. After a hearty *Khuda Hafiz* from our host, we walked a few feet down towards the Bolo Haouz Mosque, which proved to be a great enchanting experience. This being the afternoon prayer time, streams of worshippers were entering this exceptionally unique piece of architecture which was built in 1712 under the orders of the then contemporary queen. It was meant to be a dedication to the amir's mother, and he himself would offer his afternoon prayers here so as to meet up with his subjects. Of course, the amir had his own exclusive mosque within the Ark, across the Registan Square, but coming to Bolo Haouz Mosque allowed him to dress in his best to ride across the square and pray with his subjects. The Bolo Haouz Mosque is preceded by an *iwan*[3] featuring twenty 12-metre-high beautifully carved, slim wooden pillars made of elm, walnut, and poplar, and topped by an ornate wooden ceiling. These pillars are elegantly slim to the extent of looking delicate. They remind one of Chehel Sotoun Palace in Isfahan, which has 40 similar pillars supporting an equally beautiful ceiling that was used as a royal court by the Safavid emperors. The top ends of these Bukharan pillars have intricate woodwork, allowing them some thickness to support the ceiling. Unlike its Isfahani counterpart, Bolo Haouz Mosque has 20 pillars whose lucent shadows reflect in the *hauz* the entire day, making them 40 as well. In Uzbek, *Bolo* means children, which suggests that this *hauz* was often used by bathing youngsters. In Persian, this mosque is often mentioned as Bala Hauz Mosque which means 'mosque above the reservoir' since Bala means 'high' and 'above', and the mosque, like other historic buildings in Bukhara, is built on a raised platform, and in between lies an open compound that fills up with worshippers on Friday. In a subsequent era, a minaret was added to the mosque, located between the *hauz* and the *iwan*; it is a smaller version of Minar-e-Kalyan, with colourful circular patterns and an arched gallery near the top. The minaret which is of a medium height has not only added to the beauty of the complex but is also used to call for prayers. The mosque has been in constant use with Friday congregational prayers, overflowing beyond the *hauz* with worshippers converging on rows of red Bukharan rugs. However, during the 1920s, this mosque escaped significant damage from Soviet attack and was converted into a workers' club for some time.

My last day in Bukhara featured visits to Bahauddin Naqshband's mausoleum, which is in a suburban town not far from Bukhara's airport; it has modern housing, surrounded by fertile fields and orchards. A friendly and rather pious looking young Uzbek taxied us to the outskirts of Bukhara. He informed us of a growing number of Muslims from Turkey and Pakistan coming to Bukhara to pay their homage to its khankahs and madrassas, along with visiting the Naqshband shrine. Founder of the well-known Sufi Tariqa of quiet zikr, Bahauddin Naqshband (1318–89) was a Bukharan who received his spiritual training from some of his senior Muslim peers, and except for two pilgrimages to Hejaz, mostly stayed in his city. His influence reached far and wide to India, the Caucuses, and Cyprus. Instead of surrender or quietude, Naqshbandis, while faced with dire challenges against their creed and community, would put up resistance and have included noted thinkers and activists such as Shaikh Ahmad Sirhindi, Shah Waliullah Dehlawi, Imam Shamil, Abdullah Dagestani, Nazim Al-Haqqani, and several others. Here about 20 kilometres outside Bukhara, the entire complex covers a huge area including the grave of the famous Sufi surrounded by a medium height wall disallowing direct contact with the grave itself. The grave has a vast compound with a quadrangle sporting wooden beams on three sides while a charming mosque sits towards one end. Streams of pilgrims come in as joint families and groups and sit studiedly with covered heads on the benches in the corridor where an imam recites verses from the Quran. The Arabic recitation is followed by prayers with raised hands all around. The prayers are multilingual, mixing Arabic with Tajik, followed by pilgrims leaving the corridor in a single file, some offering charity to the imam. I noticed several such prayer sessions inside and outside the compound. Sometimes sweets are shared though cooking and qawwali parties are not allowed on the premises. The entry into this huge and recently renovated complex is through an arched entrance with Islam Karimov's picture and messages welcoming the visitors. Inside the older buildings, like the shrine itself, the mosque and nearby living quarters of early caretakers have been properly restored without any modernist eyesores. Outside the mosque is a fountain where Muslim pilgrims, local and international, are seen partaking the supply of water deemed as blessed. Across the fountain is a museum which itself is a due recognition of the past heritage of this eminent city and an equal reaffirmation of how the regime in Tashkent is sensitive to Uzbek nationalist sensitivities. It appears that the regime is aware of the tenacious power of Islam but is equally apprehensive of its political postulations which could prove threatening to its own autocratic dispensation, as it happened in Fergana during the 1990s.

By the shrine's museum, there in an open space where, on a raised structure, sits a huge *deg* (a big cauldron/wok) used for communal cooking of pulao, a practice very much alive in Pakistan even today. The shrines in Lahore, Multan, Pakpattan, Sehwan Sharif, Bhera, and all across the Indus lands have pilgrims coming in with their offerings, which are either in cash or through contributing a freshly cooked *deg* of pulao as *langar* (communal free food). Food is a social and spiritual form of charity in the Muslim world where informality and a sense of sharing helps people attain a greater sense of fraternity. In Uzbekistan, such activities are not encouraged at shrines though in homes, similar practices continue especially when events such as birth, circumcision of male children, marriages, deaths, and Eid festivals take place. The *deg* here is certainly smaller than its counterpart in Ajmer yet serves the same purpose and is a curious piece of history of mystical practices. Behind the mosque and museum is a large *hauz*, the size of Lyab-i-Hauz in Old Bukhara that served the same purpose of ablutions before visiting the shrine and praying in the mosque. Of course, these *hauz* are now tourist attractions but until the Soviet times they thrived with bathing children and worshippers undertaking ablutions. Deeming them to be a major cause of epidemics including the plague in the past, the authorities put a blanket ban on their use. At one time, there were scores of *hauz* in Bukhara, but now only a few remain and are a tourist attraction, besides allowing locals to gather in the evenings to enjoy the cool breeze. In addition, there were hamaams (communal baths) all across the town, though only a few remain and largely serve foreign tourists. A curious and rather amusing spectacle at Bahauddin Naqshband complex was watching the streams of men and women passing under an old fallen olive tree. The tree trunk had aged in time though its roots still held the ground keeping it alive and, being located in the proximity of the *hauz*, it still retained some branches and leaves. These Uzbek pilgrims believe in the special attributes attached to this tree, including fulfilling women's desire to have sons; it is not rare to see married women circling the site and then passing underneath its twisting, reclining trunk. I have seen similar rituals in Pakistan and India but seeing these Uzbeks—after all the education, Sovietization, and culture—one is definitely persuaded by the persistence of human beliefs in superhuman forces of saints and the phenomenon around their graves. I was tempted to pass underneath the tree just for the sake of experience but my height deterred me though I saw a fair number of elderly men and senior ladies also circumambulate the site and a few even passing underneath this otherwise low-lying tree trunk. The trunk seemed to be unwilling to go up straight and laid parallel with the soil, looking like a small bridge with a tiny open space underneath that was being negotiated by these visitors.

Of course, by then I was used to the brown of Bukhara both in its landscape and architecture, and its green fields, tree-lined boulevards in newer urban space and around the historic monument such as mosques and madrassas. After a week, I was assumed to be a part of the local landscape in every sense of the word and my Persian was proving to be both an icebreaker and a socializer. I moved and talked like a native or as 'a long-lost fellow' who had come back to his ancestral place trying to make sense of his life. To an Uzbek, I might have been a tourist but also not a typical one as my complexion and conversation sounded a bit indigenous and perhaps that could be the reason that the taxi drivers would not haggle for price or for exchanging so'm for dollars. Shopkeepers in town, both men and women, exuded genuine smiles and would not gawk at me and would instead often exchange greetings. They engaged in small talk with somebody who they assumed to be a fellow stani from somewhere Deep South where Muslims as well as the stories of Central Asian rulers and Sufis abounded and who, in many cases, sought affinity if not origins in these steppes. I did not want to leave Bukhara. Its sense of history, loss, and dignity had grown within me and I began to see a romantic historian growing within myself. This entire region with all its history and antiquity lay before me as an open book; its 350 or so monuments had become my archives. Many of them I had seen; several of them had taken me in; the others I had touched but I had not seen all of them. However, I could not leave Bukhara without visiting Char Minar—the beautiful and totally different kind of minarets right in the thick of Bukhara's populous neighbourhood, slightly away from the Hauz and Malika.

On my penultimate day in Bukhara, totally irreverent to the hot, bleaching sun, I began my walk on Khoja Nurabad Road. I passed the square lodged between the Ulugh Beg Madrassa and its rival Abdullah Khan Mosque and, shooing away some doves and pigeons and saying salaam to the charming lady selling her Bukharan rugs, I kept going. It somehow reminded me of Al-Baicin in old Granada where I used to walk when everyone else would be indoors enjoying a siesta. I would have Granada's narrow lanes and older neighbourhoods at my disposal and only occasionally be distracted by a passing car or motorbikes. Here in Old Bukhara, several lanes intersected this road which itself was twisting quite often and steadily narrowing though I kept going. A few shopkeepers, while peering from behind the walls of their gigantic melons, affirmed my sense of direction until I saw an assembly of women sitting in chairs or on divans in a semi-circle under an awning reached by intertwined grape vines. Uzbek naans, pastries, trays full of grapes, and melons sat before these ladies—many of whom sported colourful scarves—and I was tempted to join them but contented myself with an *As-salamu alaykum* and a bow. They all responded in almost one voice and reciprocated with spontaneous smiles. It must have been a social gathering though in fleeing moments, I could not afford to adduce its cause—possibly an engagement or even a death anniversary! My instinct impelled me to the right in a narrower lane, clean of any rubbish or urchins, and lo and behold, I was standing right behind the Char Minar. Its four circular, brown, and intricately carved minarets were topped by blue domes that guarded the familiar Uzbek dome capping the prayer hall underneath. Char Minar, as in Urdu and Persian, would mean four pillars, and in the subcontinent, these structures are called *Chauburji*—

again a Persian derivative. This is a very South Asian design that was popularized by the Mughals, especially during the early seventeenth century when Queen Nur Jahan built Jahangir's Tomb in Lahore and then Shah Jahan perfected it in Taj Mahal, further making the genre completely distinct.

The Char Minar is not huge and, despite having a compound in the front and on its two sides, is lodged in a dense neighbourhood. Inside there are arches and stairways all around the main hall that now sports a shop selling bridal dresses. The ceiling is decorated in late Shaybani style with tiles and floral patterns and displays meticulous Quranic calligraphy. The back wall and its smaller rooms are lived in by some families, as I could see children sitting behind the windowsills. I also noticed two bold Persian verses on the exterior of the back wall. The encroachment by the neighbourhood on the site of the monument was also evident. The front garden has apple and apricot trees along with some flowerbeds and there are some living quarters just to the left of the main structure itself. A shrine, a mosque, or a school, it appears to have combined Indian and Central Asian architectural traditions and skills. I decided to sit on the footsteps of a couple of shops facing the minar. Seeing my presence, the shops raised the volume of their music, which deeply amused me; assuming that the ladies inside might have underestimated my age, I took it as a compliment. Naturally, I could not buy their special textiles, scarves, rugs, or pieces of furniture but I bought some sweets and bottled water and sat down on the wooden shop front to examine the Char Minar. Four round minarets made of brown and slim bricks were trying to reach the blue sky. Just beneath their greenish blue domes were some floral patterns with bordered squares, though like the minarets, they looked slightly in need of restoration. It is a sturdy piece of architecture and I could detect a few turret-like openings on all the four minarets allowing light and fresh air to the people using the stairwells. The main entrance has two arches with the smaller one immediately over the carved wooden entrance and between the two was a square window featuring blue and white pieces of tiles. The geometrized window must be for air and light though its presence on an otherwise brown façade appears quite enhancive and, like blue cupolas, very distinct from an overwhelming brown. Sitting there, listening to soothing music and watching an intermingling of Central and Southern

Asian architecture, I was reminiscing about my youthful years spent at Lahore's *Chauburji*, which in fact was once a vast Mughal garden around the graves of some known Mughal nobility, though unfortunately, urban encroachments, pollution, and civic irreverence have taken a toll on that once great monument. Char Minar, though having lost gardens all around, especially towards the back, still looks afresh, vigorous, and less tragic than its counterpart in Lahore but it is certainly a place with a major difference and distinction even in a sublime Bukhara. Perhaps Char Minar is the right place to say *Khuda Hafiz* to this city of prophets, scholars, Sufis, saints, *sarafa* (jewellery, coinage), and of course Nasruddin and Rustam!

Notes

1. Abolqasem Ferdowsi, *Shahnameh: The Persian Book of Kings*, trans. Dick Davis (Harmondsworth: Penguin Publishing Group, 2016).
2. A tomb, often of a holy person.
3. A rectangular and vaulted space.

8

Samarkand:
Tamerlane's City on the Silk Road

O, Navoiy with sweetest wine enjoy that manhood into thee
For, where a cup of joy appears, a woe never tries there to come

Alisher Navoi[1]

Amir Taimur or Tamerlane is one of the most revered and concurrently despised conquerors in human history but amongst Uzbek, Tajik, and South Asian Muslims, his atrocities are conveniently overlooked since he is perceived as a proverbial deliverer on the white horse. He is the father figure for Uzbek national identity followed by Zaheer-ud-Din Muhammad Babur (1485–1530) and Alisher Navoi (1441–1501). His statues adore major crossroads across Uzbekistan where he is simply and fondly known as Amir—the Leader. Following the demise of communism in Central Asia, the Amir has been radically rehabilitated more quickly than those erstwhile aliens from the north—Lenin and Stalin. 'The New Guards' in all the former Soviet possessions have tried to posit themselves as father figures, combining old and new in their persona and by embodying a kind of tribal orientation based on benevolent authoritarianism. Their hold on power all the way from Mongolia to Azerbaijan, Armenia, Belorussia, and Ukraine reflects a curious continuity of those traditions despite the fact that women seem to be more visible and educated in all these places and retain due credentials and ambitions to play leading roles. The civil societies in all these states remain weak since the state is certainly the most powerful medium and source of authority, resource distribution, and change. It is not just Islam Karimov (1938–2016) who revived and romanticized the personality and exploits of Turkic heroes like Taimur and Babur, but even the common Uzbeks look up to them as the founders and precursors of their nationhood. Mongolia concurrently idealizes Genghis Khan as a de facto father figure, and same is the case with several other younger nations where such heroes are needed or even created to give a semblance of some golden past with promises of security and prosperity in the years ahead. Samarkand has every reason to celebrate its world-known Amir but this is not the only cause of celebration that the historic city is dependent upon. Real Samarkand is old, rather ancient, and no less vital because the crossroads of history and civilizations and its older and newer incarnations have their own distinctions, often unparalleled. When Alexander attacked it in 329 BCE, the city was known as Markand/Markanda and had already been thriving with a mixed population of the Sogdians, Persians, and Greeks. He liked the place and reportedly observed: 'Everything I have heard about Marakanda is true, except that it's more beautiful than I ever imagined'.[2]

Located on the Silk Road at the intersection of caravan routes to the north and south, Samarkand had already developed its own silk industry rather than only being the conduit of silk products, and as an imperial capital of the Sogdians, following the downfall of the Persian and Greek empires, had retained its focal position as the main hub of cosmopolitan cultures and communities. In fact, the Silk Road began in China though its major starting point in older times was Xian, the former capital. Moving through the 600-mile-long Gansu Corridor, it would reach Dunhuang, and circumventing the Taklimakan Desert, it would divide itself into two routes—northern and southern—until they connected in Samarkand after covering a distance of two thousand miles. The Gansu Corridor was neighboured to the north by the Gobi Desert whereas to its south rose the Qinghai Mountains which stretched to the point where the Silk Road connected Dunhuang, the city now known for caves and their historic artefacts. The southern route would pass through Kashghar and modern-day Kyrgyzstan and Tajikistan before reaching Samarkand, whereas the northern route traversed through Kazakh territories into Sogdiana. Thanks to Sogdian entrepreneurs, there was busy traffic and trade on this 2000 mile stretch of the Silk Road which connected itself with Balkh, Peshawar, and Merv. Zhang Qian (d. 113 BCE), an early traveller to Sogdiana and Afghanistan, found Chinese goods being sold in these regions, whereas Dunhuang caves have revealed Persian and Hebrew texts written on used paper in Chinese script.[3] However, Baron Ferdinand von Richthofen, a German cartographer, not only gave this artery a unique name but also drew a detailed map delineating its various sections and subsidiaries, and more significantly coined the term *SeidenStrafen* (The Silk Roads) in 1877.[4]

Fed by Amu Darya and featuring fertile valleys, Samarkand's brown parameters featuring rugged mountains did not pose any hurdle to its favourite pursuits of trade, scholarship, arts, and intensive agriculture which allowed it to flourish despite all the upheavals and invasions. Alexander was deeply impressed by its grandeur and, unlike the Mongols, avoided decimating it to the Stone Age. It was the capital of the northern possessions of the Achaemenid Empire, mostly run by native Sogdians who owed their allegiance to the Persian emperor in Persepolis. The Scythians/Sakas, who were succeeded by the Kushans and Huns, followed the Greek interlude under Alexander and the Seleucids, however, in the meantime, Hinduism, Zoroastrianism, and Buddhism made their entry into the region from further south. All these three religions have had strong Aryan connections and their migrations into Afghanistan, India, and Persia had allowed a unique intermixing of languages and beliefs. Evidently, Aryans dealt a serious blow to the indigenous people of Persia and South Asia but like the Mongols, these early conquerors gradually acculturated to the host languages and belief systems. Sanskrit, like ancient Pahlavi, was able to unite this part of Central Asia with the Indus regions until Persian replaced this major mainstream of Indo-European languages. As mentioned earlier, the Aryans were followed by waves of Scythian, Kushan, Hun, and other Turkic conquerors whose future successors were the Samanis, Seljuks, Ghaznavids, Tughlaqs, Khaljis, Ottomans, Mughals, Shaybanis, and the Safavids until the Russians and the British established their enduring legacies. The Hindu, Zoroastrian, and Buddhist influences added to ethno-cultural pluralism of this metropolis until the Arabs captured it in 711, followed by many Turkic tribes becoming Muslims. In 751, the Arabs, helped by local Muslims from Fergana, decisively defeated the Chinese at Talas in present-day Kazakhstan, and Islamic influences reached further north and east all the way to Mongolia. The newly-established Abbasid Caliphate led by Abul Abbas Saffah defeated the Tang forces by the River Talas and stopped the Chinese march into Turkestan. In the next few centuries, Islam became the dominant religion from Xinjiang—Eastern Turkestan—to present-day Azerbaijan. This expansion and the concurrent Muslim control of the Indus Valley greatly helped Persian become the lingua franca though religious scholars still preferred Arabic for their treatises. Samarkand witnessed and harnessed these historical movements and processes, hence it is no wonder that it is a world heritage town with several novels, movies, and even a small planet named after it. Like Bukhara, Balkh, Khiva, Nishapur, and Merv, it was the focal point of early Muslim renaissance and, despite ravages by the Mongols, it revived itself under the Timurids and Shaybanis.[5] Its classical heritage laid dormant in the colonial past when newer suburbia, modern infrastructure, and an energized agro-industry attempted to bypass the Old City whose heritage places were left to rot as the vestiges of a feudal and an almost lost past. One may find several faults with the post-1991 regime but its restorative efforts and uplift of civic facilities at public places are certainly noteworthy. Of course, Tashkent, by virtue of becoming a colonial metropolis, received more official attention and was prioritized over its other 'medieval' counterparts, but in reality, it is cities like Samarkand which bestow majesty and grace not just to Uzbekistan but also to the entire Central Asia. It is here—even more than Bukhara—that one experiences the powerful presence of tradition and modernity, and they are not often conflictive either.

***

Leaving Bukhara, after a week that had left me feeling almost 'nativized', was not an easy proposition as I stood by all the old pictures of Bukhara under the Mangat amirs including the one of Gaukushan Mosque Madrassa complex just behind our accommodation and facing the Museum of Art. I had already bid farewell to Rustam and his assistant, Hussein, following a sumptuous breakfast, fully supervised by our food manager. Rustam was to leave later that afternoon for Termez on his periodic visit to his wife and daughter, which was rather consoling as over the past several days we both had developed a greater sense of friendship through our Persian and Urdu exchanges. Before the arrival of our taxi, I took a quick exit to bid farewell to the Gaukushan Square and its two mulberry trees besides glancing at the Old City beyond the complex. Soon we were on our way, passing by Kukeldash Madrassa,

Nadir Divan-begi Khanaka and Madrassa, Mullah Nasruddin on his donkey between the Kukeldash Madrassa and the Hauz, and the synagogue and Jewish museum beyond Bahauddin Naqshband Road, almost behind the Carpet Museum. The Jewish caretaker that I had often said shalom to by the Hauz in the evenings must have been dusting off his premises, readying them for a steady stream of visitors. His pictures with Karimov and Hillary Clinton, along with the curious memorabilia of the past Bukharan Jews, a fairly old and graceful Torah, and several older samples of traditional Jewish costumes in their eastern regalia were certainly preserved in my memory. I could not see the Minar-e-Kalyan but thinking of Arsalan Khan and the Maulvi allowed me a nostalgic smile as I thanked Genghis Khan for constructing this rare and tallest piece of unique architecture in this Muslim Oxbridge city. As the taxi rolled towards the train station, I tried to locate Char Minar on my left but did not succeed as the old and new of Bukhara blocked my view. I finally bade farewell to Bukhara on behalf of Pir Bukhari, buried near my birthplace and where my late mother used to go every morning after her prayers and recite the Quran besides checking on Syed ladies—the 'Bibis'. They lived behind those two massive berry trees that I have been fond of ever since my childhood. In those early years, I had often accompanied mother to offer *fateha*, sometimes we also went there on the tenth of Muharram as well when a Shia cousin, who was a poet, used to recite his elegiac poems before the mourners. Their procession would begin here, led by banners, a decorated horse called *Zuljinnah*, named after Imam Husain's horse in Karbala in 680 CE; besides Muharram, this shrine is a quiet place for prayers and reflections. Our whole locality is still called Pir Bukhari Mohalla and even now while walking through the street, I habitually slow down for a few seconds, reliving my childhood as it allows me to remember mother and all those who are long gone. We grew up internalizing that this Sufi Syed came to our hamlet a long, long time back and was a refugee from a distant but quite respectable city called Bukhara. So naturally, a special *Khuda Hafiz* on behalf of Pir Bukhari to his native soil! Both of us had our own ways of connecting with this city.

The train left on time and we shared the compartment with two other passengers: the young lady, Ameena, appeared to be an Anglo-Saxon, on her way to Tashkent to attend her university, whereas the gentleman, like us, was en route to Samarkand and then Shakhrisabz,

Taimur's birthplace. Ameena conversed with us about her courses, family, and life in a very modern city such as Tashkent and had no recollections of the Soviet times since she had been born after independence. We shared our cakes and biscuits with hers while sipping on black tea served by the uniformed train staff who were immensely polite and turned even friendlier when Ameena told them about our place of origin. The Uzbeks fully realize the high esteem their cities like Bukhara and Samarkand enjoy amongst the world's Muslims, especially across the Hindu Kush. I would often tease them by preferring Babur to Taimur. I would refer to Babur's sense of poetry, love for gardens, and openness rarely found amongst rulers, though like Taimur, he too built minarets of human skulls of his enemies. Babur was an astute and high-calibre author and not a mere conqueror, while Taimur was in a hurry to build his native Samarkand and Shakhrisabz, irrespective of the expense. Our prearranged stay in Samarkand was in a family-run house, quite close to Registan, the heart of Taimur's city. We were looking forward to living in the Old City though reportedly, the Russian sections were equally green and amiable. Coming out of the train station, we ran into the owner of the Malika, who had been on the same train and generously volunteered to pick up a piece of our luggage. His chauffeured car was waiting and soon we were lodged in a limousine passing through tree-lined neighbourhoods built by the Soviets and since. The generosity of the proprietor, himself an Iraqi-Austrian and now an entrepreneur in Uzbekistan, was quite overwhelming as we were dropped right outside our intended B & B. He appreciated the fact that, instead of a luxury hotel, we had decided to live in the older parts of the city with an Uzbek family to allow ourselves a real flavour of Uzbek family traditions. Through an open door, like back home and not too far from Registan, was our B & B. We barged in at a time when other guests were still waking up and trays of grapes and freshly cut red and pale melons waited on a divan, inviting a steady stream of wasps that one does not see in Europe. They are the preserve of Central and South Asia and, given a childhood spent in their proximity during scorching summers, I remember their single-minded search for water. If disturbed persistently, they would attack you, and it was not a minor attack, given the pain and rapid swelling. Unlike wasps in Britain (those could be meaner and very territorial), these wasps, along with flies, mosquitoes, lizards, snakes, scorpions, and a whole lot of creepers, learned their hostility from us children, even though the elders kept warning us to stay away from these marauders. I gulped down a few pieces of juicy melon often interspersed with red, lush grapes. Soon teapots with blue floral patterns—by now a familiar Uzbek crockery—appeared with an ample supply of biscuits. Tea here, as noted earlier, defied its South Asian affinity since milk never accompanied it, though sugar cubes did come along. I did not miss milk by then and instead compensated it with an ample supply of Ayran that one could buy fresh or in cartons all the way from Western Thrace to Xinjiang.

Somehow, despite the enormity of the Bukhara *feelpa* (elephant foot design), rugs, and grape vines shadowing over the compound, and a constant movement of visitors on motorbikes and even some cycles, the place did not impress us although it was towards the eastern corner of the extensive park built around the Registan Square. The sensible owner asked us to accompany him to his other B & B run by an older brother and just a few more streets down towards the old Jewish quarters and close to the Koroboy Oksokol Mosque. Negotiating through well-paved but narrow lanes, we were finally ushered into a double-storey home with a spacious balcony offering vintage views of the historic monuments and we settled for it. Soon another generous supply of naans, grapes, and melons appeared on the long table meant for dining, bordered by two divans occupied by some Europeans lost in their iPads. The family quarters were downstairs in one portion of this rather big house, whereas the adjacent newer area and its second floor, including the balcony and a kitchen, were for guests. The place reminded me of old South Asian neighbourhoods—mohallas—only cleaner and less populous here. Irreverent of the hot sun, I took off for Registan although it was quite clear that due to some construction work for a forthcoming major fair, the three madrassas in the Square were closed and would only open for a few hours the next day. This did not deter me from exploring the park and its older neighbourhoods on the two sides that must have been the Old City before the Russians arrived here in the 1860s. I decided to wander off into the northern side of the Square and, after traversing for some time, found myself in a mosque with the familiar *hauz* in its compound, though now mostly serving ornamental imperatives since water for ablutions was available through regular pipes in a separate section. Featuring slender and artistically carved wooden pillars like those of the Bolo Haouz Mosque and its counterpart inside Bukhara's Ark, the ceilings of both the balcony and the main inner section displayed beautiful patterns with Quranic ayahs on the front wall. I sat down and began to study the inscriptions besides ensuring a sufficient supply of cool air even though the air conditioning was off since the worshippers, having finished their afternoon prayers, had already left. Undisturbed, I sat there for a bit until it was time to resume my reconnaissance. Emerging from the Old City, I found myself on one of the main boulevards going east from the Square with green lawns, hedges, and tall poplars with two rows of modern shops, restaurants, and offices on both sides. This was the Tashkent Avenue heading towards the Bibi-Khanym Mosque and the Bibi-Khanym Mausoleum. This new development must have cut through the old town since it exists on both sides beyond the parameters of these new stores and offices. Bibi-Khanym Mosque, once the biggest in the Muslim world, was built under Tamerlane's orders for his favourite wife who was reportedly of Chinese origin. She herself sleeps in an impressive mausoleum across the road, which is topped by a Timurid blue dome. While deciding to see the mosque the following day, I ventured into the brick tomb and was warmly welcomed by the guards who, on knowing my Pakistani identity plus intimacy with Persian, did not charge me an entry fee. I did not want to go back without offering *fateha* at the queen's grave, which is further below in the basement chamber and not on ground level. The queen's sarcophagus, along with those of her mother and two other ladies, is covered with a silk chador, and is located in a beautifully restored brick vault. Though the tomb itself rises to a suitable height, it is still smaller than the mosque and is topped by a single, blue cupola. The entrance to the mausoleum is through a square *iwan* with Quranic calligraphy and floral patterns displayed on geometrically designed tiles. Inside is a big hall with arched vaults displaying a honeycomb pattern. Built in the fifteenth century, this simple, majestic but solid structure certainly became the trendsetter for future Mughal and Safavid buildings. Like other historical monuments, it suffered from negligence but was fully restored in 2007. The interior floral patterns retain charming mosaics including a depiction of heaven.

The evening at our B & B was abuzz with several guests exchanging their views about Samarkand, Shakhrisabz, and around. We were sitting in the open balcony on the upper floor and could see the three famous madrassas in the Registan Square topped by several blue domes, while to our right were the domes crowning Bibi-Khanym Mosque and her Mausoleum. An Italian couple with another companion were in a mood to visit the Russian parts of Samarkand for supper and we agreed to accompany them. Soon we were walking amongst orderly crowds of Uzbeks strolling and picnicking at various sections of the Registan Square. The area facing the three madrassas, the heart of Registan, and emblem of Samarkand was barricaded since rehearsals for a big parade and concerts were underway. Following various pauses, we kept going west until we passed by Taimur's tomb which faced an old mosque, and then following a short climb, we entered the Alisher Navoi Park. On our way, we passed by various attractive colonial-style buildings, housing, offices, and university departments. The park itself was immensely delightful and, on a cooler summer evening like this, it was as full of children as it was with flowers and birds, all being looked over by a beautifully carved sculpture of the famous classical Turkic poet, Alisher Navoi, who, like Muhammad Iqbal in the case of Pakistan, has been appropriated solely by Uzbekistan.

Born and buried in Herat, Navoi spent several years in Samarkand and was recalled to the former to serve his friend and patron, Sultan Husayn Bayqara (1438–1506). Navoi restored several schools, tekkes, and mosques all over Khorasan and built a splendid tomb over Omar Khayyam's grave in Nishapur. Navoi, other than his ministerial duties, wrote some classics in Turkish (Uzbek) and Persian, accounting for 6,000 verses, often dilating on romantic and mystical themes such as Leyla-Majnoon and Shireen-Farhad. He upheld Saadi, Khayyam, and Hafiz as his literary mentors and composed poetry in their styles with due acknowledgement. In fact, Navoi was his Turkish-Uzbek literary name while for his Persian poetry he called himself *fana*. His prose and poetic works, consisting of 20 volumes, have been published in Moscow and Tashkent, and an entire province, a city, and several institutions have been named after this preeminent intellectual. The national government revived interest in Navoi by constructing a museum-cum-library devoted to him in Samarkand quite close to the university and in proximity of Gur-i-Amir. His father had been quite close to Shah Rukh Mirza, Tamerlane's son and Ulugh Beg's father who, along with his queen, Gawhar Shad Begum, pioneered an intellectual and artistic renaissance in Herat. In fact, the contemporary Herat, thanks to the efforts of Shah Rukh, Gawhar Shad Begum, Ulugh Beg, Alisher Navoi, and Sultan Bayqara was the Florence of Asia and augured what many scholars believe as the third Muslim renaissance in Southwest Asia. Other than his several works in Persian, he mainly used Turkish for his literary and philosophical works, and has been characterized by Bernard Lewis as the Chaucer of this language at a time when Persian was the dominant official and literary expression.[6] To some of his students and followers in Uzbekistan today, he viewed Turkish as superior to Persian, although the claim could be contested. Navoi, followed by Babur, amongst many more such scholars, ensured literary salience of the Turkish language which flourished both in Central Asia and the Ottoman lands without completely displacing Persian. Tamerlane's other eminent grandson, Mirza Iskander Sultan (1384–1415), the son of Mirza Umar Shaikh, ruled Fars province and, for a time, Tamerlane even thought of appointing him as his successor. The Amir changed his mind due to his grandson's rebellious disposition, although even in his short reign, the prince took Astrology to its highest level of development. Like his cousin, Ulugh Beg, Iskander Sultan was fond of books, decorative miniatures, and promoted Astrology and Astronomy to their new heights, despite being in power only for a short while. A complete zodiac horoscope decorated with an ornate miniature and brocaded in silk was prepared for him in Shiraz by a master artist, Mahmud al-Kashi in 1411. It is the only complete and illuminated Timurid horoscope that survived and is now kept at the Wellcome Institute in London and was on display at Oxford's Ashmolean Museum during 2016–7. This special exhibit called 'Power and Protection: Islamic Art and Supernatural' was devoted to horoscopes, charms, and such other artefacts and practices prevalent amongst several Muslim communities all the way from Nigeria to China and Indonesia. Consisting of one hundred spectacular objects, this first-ever exhibition of this nature highlighted practices such as reading zodiac signs, predicting omens, and deciphering dreams besides ensuring special inscriptions on banners and armour to protect against evil forces or opponents in battlefields. Other than horoscopes, the exhibition showcased *alams,* (flag), swords, daggers, and metallic productions of a hand attributed to the Battle of Karbala (680 CE), which were quite popular amongst the Shia rulers in Awadh, Deccan, and Persia. It was a symbol of the hand of Abbas, the half-brother of Imam Hussain who was killed by Umayyads in present-day Iraq. In addition, there was a special Ottoman shirt displaying Quranic verses and Prophetic sayings which was reportedly worn by Caliph Sultan Suleiman the Magnificent who was persuaded by his chief consort, Hurrem Sultan, to wear this tunic while leading his troops.

Our Italian team leader, Marco, would often consult his map that somehow made us cross several roads, skirt numerous buildings, and markets until we did not know where we were. A property dealer from Milan was lost in modern Samarkand looking for an older restaurant in a posh area of the city, while Christine, his wife, kept apologizing to us for her spouse's geographical inadequacies. They had advertised this Great Silk Road Travel in Italy to form a viable group but, despite early queries, most people had dropped out except for a librarian from Rome. The trio had been travelling together but Dana was most probably resigned to Marco's escapades and thus was often quiet, unless you made some persistent efforts to strike a conversation. In a row of quite modern shops, we tried all the shopkeepers one by one, seeking direction for our elusive restaurant and ended up confusing our hosts even more until somebody started speaking in Urdu with me: *Aap Ko Samarkand pasand ayaa hai?*[7] Shaheen, an Iranian lady, had studied medicine in India and, after meeting an Azeri husband and a short stint in Dubai, had decided to live and work in Samarkand. Her Urdu and my Persian confused Marco, Christine, and Dana even more and they thought that we had finally met a real match in this city who would lead us to the sought eatery. Unfortunately, Shaheen had not heard of the restaurant and, following our sixth sense, we kept going until a kindly soul pointed to a rather exclusive edifice hidden behind poplars and rose bushes. More than the food, we enjoyed the live music at this spacious place, which retained a whole army of smartly dressed Uzbeks to serve us, however, each table got only a single copy of the menu but with Russian, Uzbek, and English versions. I guess our success in locating the elusive restaurant was itself a great achievement so we did not bother about what was on the plate or how the bill was divided. Marco was not totally crestfallen and Christine and Dana had begun talking to each other. Our journey back to the old town was no less hilarious, given the fact that we could have easily followed the straight road to a sign-posted Registan and then should have slid into the older town by passing by a shop run by a mother and son who took turns but were never short on courtesy and smiles.

***

The next morning led me to Bibi-Khanym Mosque and, instead of taking the newly built Tashkent Boulevard route, I decided to walk through the old town, especially its Jewish quarters. I would have missed the synagogue altogether if not for a kindly soul who took me all the way to the place while showing some square houses through winding lanes that once belonged to Samarkandi Jews. According to Nauroz, very few were left now since most of them had migrated to the United States and Israel. The expatriates helped the dwindling population and ensured the upkeep of a sprawling Jewish cemetery next to a Muslim graveyard towards east Samarkand which in fact was the old Afrasiyab or Markand of Alexander's era. Areas around the Bibi-Khanym Mosque, Jewish quarters, Registan, and Tamerlane's resting place date from Tamerlane's era. The older town must have been destroyed by the Mongols a century earlier, although the grave of the Prophet's (PBUH) cousin, Kusam ibn Abbas, escaped the Mongol wrath. Over subsequent centuries, several other members of royal families and Sufi saints were buried here and the area came to be known as Shah-i-Zinda or Eternally Living Monarch. The name refers to the Prophet's cousin as a holy presence and is partially related with the Hazrat Khizr Mosque which is just across the Muslim graveyard and overlooks the Bibi-Khanym Mosque and Mausoleum.

There are several hypotheses about Bibi-Khanym and her ethnic origins and thus numerous views about the mosque named after this Timurid queen—which until recent times happened to be the largest in the entire Muslim world. To most observers including the Spanish Ambassador, Ruy González de Clavijo, who was based here from 1403 to 1406, the mosque was built in memory of Tamerlane's late mother-in-law, though the conqueror constantly found faults with its structure. Under his daily supervision, often quite authoritarian, its designs kept changing which led to some corrosion in the near future.[8] To a few others, Bibi-Khanym was a Chinese beauty and Tamerlane's favourite wife. She wanted to surprise her warrior-husband with an exceptionally splendid mosque on his return from his invasion of India that happened during the 1390s. The invasion cost millions of Turkic, Afghan, and Indian lives, and exhausted the conqueror, but it also helped him gain a huge booty in gold, silver, and diamonds besides a large number of Indian artisans, scholars, and of course elephants. Reportedly, Tamerlane was happy to be home, laden with his treasures from Hindustan to reunite with his partner, but he was an ailing man and his early injuries that had caused a fracture of his right arm and leg were now adding to his pain.

Another view purports the premise that the queen built this mosque as homage to her own mother; this might be partly true since 'Bibi-Khanym' is itself a title and not a name. It literally means respectable spouse of the Khan, a rather double-barrelled title, very familiar across the former Persianate. A folk tale, making rounds in travel books and without any historical evidence, posits the Chinese queen to be of such exceptional beauty that it turned the mosque's chief architect into her love-smitten fan. As the parable goes, the queen was in a hurry to get her project completed before Tamerlane's return from his long campaign, whereas the architect had his own designs and began to drag his feet to blackmail her. His completion of the work was conditional on the queen allowing him a kiss on her cheek, to which she reluctantly agreed. However, that one-time kiss proved to be fatal as somehow it left a permanent mark on her soft skin. She confided in her husband who, to cover up the entire episode, reportedly made face covering mandatory for all women in his empire. The story is sheer exotica as, given Tamerlane's temperament, one would not expect the queen to survive her husband's wrath even if he was bedridden. According to another account, the mosque was Tamerlane's own idea and he supervised its design and construction. Temperamentally, he changed its design quite often and would never relent in his urgings to speed up the construction to his labour force even if it meant sheer drudgery. There are even more exaggerated stories about how the workforce was given meals while they worked in trenches or above the scaffoldings. However, it is true that Tamerlane desired to make it into an unparalleled structure and his architects, designers, labourers, and certainly the elephants ensured its completion just before his demise. The mere height of the four *iwan*s of this square structure, with the covered area facing the mihrab being topped by his favourite azure cupolas, posed serious risks of erosion and cracks, especially in view of frequent earthquakes. The residential quarters for scholars and all the interior walls are decorated with a multiplicity of tile work and Quranic calligraphy. The massive entrance of this splendid mosque, now fully restored, only makes a visitor aware of the smallness of human height. It must be one of the tallest of its kind in the entire Muslim world, even though the mosque is not located on a hill and is instead constructed in a slightly low-lying area. Right under several double and even triple roofs allowing an unparalleled height in a pioneering Central Asian art design, the main façade is square with arches reaching down all the way to the wooden gate which itself looks tiny under such a huge magnificent edifice. Floral patterns on meticulously designed tiles on the exterior are refreshingly inviting and one walks through the gate to see a green courtyard where a sculpted book—meant to be a replica of the Quran with its *rehl* (reading stand)—allows one to study the vastness of the place. While one may see Uzbek women walking underneath the stand seeking divine assistance for fertility, it is in fact the four splendid *iwan*s facing one another on all the four sides that transmit a sense of Tamerlane's unlimited prowess to achieve his objective. It must have taken years of diligent work, strenuous devotion, and a large-scale labour force to build and then maintain this gigantic mosque-cum-school complex.

Tamerlane had initially devoted most of his energy and attention to building mosques, palaces, and madrassas, and even a tomb for himself in his native town, Shakhrisabz, but subsequently decided on Samarkand to be his metropolis. In Samarkand, Bibi-Khanym Mosque, her mausoleum, and Tamerlane's own tomb, Gur-i-Amir, became the trendsetters for a powerful architectural tradition set to augur a new genre in Herat, Agra, Isfahan, Delhi, Meshed, Bursa, and Lahore. Tamerlane built a wall around his capital city of 150,000 people, with a circumference of five miles, further protected by a specially dug moat all around its parameters. Given his own lifelong pursuits of invasions and large-scale killings, Tamerlane was apprehensive of retributive attacks on his city. His city would include areas beginning from Gur-i-Amir, all the way to the eastern end in Afrasiyab where his grandson, Ulugh Beg, built his observatory. With the Russian city to the west and parks and roads often hiding the old town, Timurid Samarkand is a proud gem in itself. The areas beyond Shah-i-Zinda and the Jewish cemetery, all the way to the Ulugh Beg Observatory, were part of ancient Marakanda with River Siob flowing through its middle. Even before Tamerlane, this city was a prosperous and populous metropolis with canals irrigating numerous gardens and most houses retaining orchards. Houses, mosques, bazaars, and tombs, all reflected Islamic features. Persian carpets were used lavishly in private and public places. The aforementioned is the reason why Yelu Chucai, a close friend of Genghis Khan, in 1218, described Samarkand as the most beautiful city he ever visited.[9] Tamerlane was not only reconstructing a preeminent metropolis, he wanted to ensure his own stamp on the city as well. His preference for melon-like domes and cupolas, often ribbed on the exterior, might have been consciously patterned on Mongol yurts, given his own partial links with that ancestry. He preferred blue tiles to top these domes so as to offer a soothing contrast to overwhelmingly brown edifices, besides seeking some kind of spiritual solace in deep blue.

I had been witnessing not only the capital of the Timurid Empire and its architectural monuments but also the mainspring of the three successive empires further across the region in the Islamic world. The way Bukhara became the trendsetter for scholarship, Samarkand, following its past Sogdian traditions, proved to be the imperial centre of this unique tradition in arts with architecture being its most pronounced component. Since Tamerlane wanted all the cupolas crowning the main minarets as well as on the main prayer area to be of the utmost height, the idea of double and even triple roofs evolved, even though they are not visible from the outside and blue cupolas appear to be the natural culmination points of the city's earliest skyline. As mentioned earlier, the main entrance of the Bibi-Khanym Mosque, the biggest *iwan* of its kind in Central Asia, faces the Tashkent Avenue which has duly benefited from modern landscaping, though this has hidden some older mohallas behind the newer façades. While Tamerlane wanted to make Samarkand into a city unrivalled on earth—another Merv—Islam Karimov, in post-1991 era, ensured his own writ on this country's old and new.

On the mosque's right side, there is a hotel-cum-modern open air café and to its left is the open air fruit and vegetable market. The former is a popular point to try some brown tea amongst the foreign tourists, while the latter is abuzz with Uzbek men and women and is closer to the feel of a bazaar yet quite neat and orderly. I walked around the Bibi-Khanym Mosque and ventured into the older town situated adjacent to the mosque's outer wall behind its several domes and cupolas which, before this modern restorative work and development on both sides of the

Tashkent Avenue, must have been connected with the older parts behind the mausoleum, synagogue, and beyond, all the way to Shah-i-Zinda. Now a dual carriage cuts through this part dividing Shah-i-Zinda and Afrasiyab on one side while leaving Timurid Samarkand on the other.

The visit to the mosque, despite an ambiguous temptation to pass underneath the stand, is a joyous experience but no less strenuous as it requires quite a bit of devoted study, reflection, and some physical exercise. Tamerlane's own energy, his eventual exhaustion, and then an unstinted masquerade to build a nadir, when tallied against the lateral decay of this monument owing to earthquakes and lack of care from authorities over the centuries, leave one with a sense of melancholy. A visitor first feels subdued by its sanctity and is overawed by its size, arches, cupolas, and tile work, and then is saddened with what it went through. Tamerlane had destroyed numerous countries, cities, and communities to build his Samarkand and such monuments, and had even sardonically named mohallas after those devastated cities, yet he could not save his masterwork from its own tragic decline. His own health deteriorated but he refused to budge and carried on fighting in China. He reportedly willed to be buried in Shakhrisabz but fate had its own plans. He apparently died of pneumonia in Kazakhstan in 1405 and was rushed for a burial in Samarkand as the passes between his capital and Shakhrisabz were snowbound. Tamerlane's sisters and other Timurid elite are buried in Shah-i-Zinda but he found his resting place in Gur-i-Amir, which had been originally built in 1404 for his favourite grandson, Shah Muhammad Sultan. Ulugh Beg, Tamerlane's other and more illustrious grandson, lies buried next to him in that tomb, while here in his grandmother's mosque, the Quran stand which the scholar-sultan built stands true to his devotion to pen and paper. Nadir Shah Afshar (1698–1747), the eighteenth century Persian invader, repeated history in reverse by robbing Samarkand of its numerous valuables, including the doors of the mosque and the large jade slab from Tamerlane's own tomb, and faced his own travails.

Picking up some water and fruit to brave a more daring sun, I skirted the big food market, the Sion Bazaar, and crossed that newly-built dual carriageway which signals the end of lived Samarkand, as beyond it are located some of the most memorable markers which now lay as quiet witness to a bygone history. This vast area, characterized by Muslim and Jewish cemeteries, Shah-i-Zinda, Hazrat Khizr Mosque, Afrasiyab Museum, Prophet Daniel's Tomb, and Ulugh Beg Observatory must have been the Sogdian Markand, a bustling place where Alexander came pursuing his Persian rival. Brown plateau must be the old urban heartland with the River Siob flowing through its midst. Except for a small village towards the other end, it is a vast area that belongs to the dead and is certainly a memorial to Samarkand's ancient and sacred attributes. Khawaja Khizr, as per Sufi Muslim beliefs, is an invisible Prophet who is always green clad and guides lost travellers. Immortal forever, he has been sighted only by a select few in an ephemeral way. The Hazrat Khizr Mosque, built on a hill overlooking Tamerlane's Samarkand and marking the western end of the old Afrasiyab, dates back to the eighth century and remains the earliest of its type. It was razed to the ground by Genghis Khan and remained in ruins due to Tamerlane's preoccupation with Bibi-Khanym and other edifices slightly west of its location. The Hazrat Khizr Mosque was finally rebuilt in 1854 and a complete restorative work in the 1990s, financed by an affluent Bukharan, turned it into the most beautiful mosque in the city. It is not big but the *iwan* and the inner side of the cupola represent a dexterous work in Islamic calligraphy. Joining a group of Uzbek men and women, I entered its main prayer area where a younger cleric recited Quranic verses followed by prayers for all. While the group left the room, I stayed on for a small meditation session. Before the arrival of the next batch of his visitors, the cleric found time to join me in a conversation that was held in Persian. He had easily figured out my Pakistani origin and we talked about several epochs that this historic mosque had witnessed since the beginning of the Islamic presence in Central Asia. These clerics, like ordinary Uzbeks, avoid talking about prevailing political situation in their country and around, either out of some official fear or largely because they do not want to be seen offering opinion on rather controversial subjects. When it comes to politics, their counterparts in Afghanistan and Pakistan are certainly a different community altogether.

On a hot summer day, I found myself crossing the road towards a magnificent entrance to the graveyard which, despite being populous, was well-maintained as I could see several men and women clearing bushes and watering shady trees. The newer graves displayed the names of their male and female occupants inscribed on black and white marble headstones next to their pictures and some Quranic verses. Right in the middle of the graveyard runs a well-maintained pathway that goes on to merge with the complex of the tombs and graves collectively called Shah-i-Zinda and which, after three madrassas in Registan, has become the most impressive emblem of this majestic city.

Kusam ibn Abbas, the Prophet's (PBUH) cousin, who travelled to Central Asia to spread Islam during the early seventh century is buried here—not far from the Hazrat Khizr Mosque. His grave escaped the Mongol wrath and over the centuries, it became the focal point of a growing cemetery all around it. Located on this end of Afrasiyab, this site became the favourite choice for Timurid burials and that is how this whole necropolis emerged with impressively designed tombs rising over several graves with a well-maintained passage running in the middle. These tall, symmetrical brick tombs topped by blue cupolas account for perhaps the most impressive cemetery in the entire Muslim world, even more impressive than Registan's madrassas. Here one is automatically soaked in a spontaneous sentiment of humility and mortality with Muslim visitors giving way to the guided Western, Korean, Chinese, and Japanese tourists. The Japanese are visibly careful to the extent of being restrained in using their cameras and other gadgets, and a kind of serenity and quietude permeates. I visited almost every tomb in this necropolis reflecting on tiles, terracotta, calligraphy, and the biographical details of the people buried in those historic graves. These were certainly the imperial and religious elite of the medieval era including Tamerlane's own siblings who were buried in the proximity of Kusam ibn Abbas' resting place. Ibn Abbas' own tomb is further to the left towards the end of an L-shaped corridor, topped by domes and neighboured by a mosque. It is certainly the busiest part as the Living Royal is himself buried here. Of course, he was not a king but his kinship with the Prophet (PBUH) and his own devotion and travels allocated him a spiritual status much higher than the kings. The Prophet's descendants, his cousins, and his companions are the most revered Muslims whose names and deeds reverberate in Muslim narratives and prayers and like Abu Ayyub Ansari in Istanbul, Shah-i-Zinda remains the fulcrum of spirituality and history in Central Asia. Men, women, and children queue up to stand by the jali of the chamber and are often led to prayers by a cleric who receives groups of pilgrims, the descendants of those early Muslims who would have been converted to Islam by Kusam ibn Abbas, and future Sufis. I was lucky to find a small space next to the cleric on a bench and joined him and many more groups in prayers. These visitors, with the occasional presence of foreign tourists, often bestowed a curious smile in my direction by virtue of seeing a mundane person sitting next to a robed mullah and raising his hands with everyone else while whispering Quranic verses.

If not for shortage of space, I could have stayed on even longer as I could see all kinds of complexions and ethnicities filing in here with a sublime sense of devotion. I saw several young Uzbek women, none of them wore skirts and each female visitor would quickly don a head covering. It was a place of immense sanctity and humility, and with men and women being so close in proximity, it reminded me of the Kaaba, the only difference here was that men wore trousers and square Uzbek caps while women wore shalwar-like long trousers and colourful tunics with their hair covered under beautiful scarves or shawls, often failing to cover their unique eyebrows. However, this was not a place to focus on physical attributes. I soon exited towards the mosque while enjoying its cool air and artistically carved wooden pillars. As it was not time for prayer yet, only two or three worshippers filtered in for some Quranic recitation, I had the entire place to myself. I visited other tombs and sat on the steps of some of them trying to absorb what I had been seeing while smiling at the steady streams of visitors. Each tomb has its own unique feature and grace but the most enchanting one was the Shodi Mulk Oko Mausoleum, which is home to Tamerlane's sister and a niece, and is situated on the right just before the long flight of stairs that leads towards the main entrance to Shah-i-Zinda. This tomb of intricate brickwork, restored terracotta, and an ornate dome dates back to 1372, the heyday of the Timurid Empire. Recent restorations are certainly visible but the very survival of all these tombs and their upkeep over the past so many centuries is nevertheless a monumental achievement. I spent quite some time in this unparalleled Muslim preserve and kept thinking about the Makli Graveyard in Sindh. Many of the tombs and mausoleum in that biggest necropolis in the world are Central Asian in their styles and forms, and are built of small bricks or yellow sandstone with those of the elite often topped by decorated domed superstructures. Of course, those graves have survived but Pakistan may need more resources and better skills to turn that graveyard into a befitting sojourn through unique historical vistas. The survival of the largest necropolis in the world from the periodic ravages of the Indus has owed itself to its location on the hills.

I had seen every tomb in the vicinity of Kusam ibn Abbas' grave and spent some time at its main entrance, almost facing the old Jewish neighbourhood across the dual carriageway and later decided to walk back to my accommodation. The twisting streets, often floored by asphalt and occasional mosques and pomegranate trees, looked quite familiar and Bukhara-like. Even the people here resembled those back in Pakistan, Morocco, Anatolia, or the Iranian hinterland. *As-salamu alaykum* to both men and women would elicit spontaneous and very affectionate smiles. In the midst of getting lost in these thoughts, I realized I had lost my way since I could not locate the Gumbaz Synagogue. I had already passed by Karboy Mosque and had lost my way near the Mubarak Mosque, which was not far from my accommodation. I requested a slim, middle-aged man for help as he spoke to his friend in a corner shop. Initially, he explained some directions but, detecting a bit of confusion and exasperation, he volunteered to lead me all the way to my destination. We chatted on the way, with him often greeting his acquaintances in between. He also showed me some solidly built houses once owned by Samarkand's Jews. These were Bukharan Jews who traded in Samarkand and beyond, and had built their synagogue which has been recently transformed into a museum open to public. According to some Israeli websites liable to exaggeration, there were 17 synagogues just in Samarkand in 1917, and subsequent Stalinist purges and population transfers added to restrictions and anxieties. Most Uzbek Jews had connections with Bukhara and it is from here that they spread to other Central Asian cities including Samarkand and Tashkent until the European Jewry began swelling their ranks besides looking down upon their Asian/Persian roots. Jews have been present in Bukhara and around since the pre-Christian era though the Achaemenids pushed them to the Holy Land but the Parthians encouraged their return. However, following the Sassanid takeover in the third century, Jews once again faced severe restrictions which were relieved only with the arrival of the Muslims in 709. The Mongols initially destroyed Jewish synagogues and businesses until a century later when Tamerlane encouraged Persian and Arab Jews to settle in Bukhara and Samarkand. The development of a syncretic culture had shocked some Ashkenazi visitors to Central Asia who reposed a sense of great self-importance. A terrible earthquake hit Samarkand in 1720 that caused a Jewish exodus to Bukhara. During the nineteenth century, many European Jews, exasperated with Anti-Semitism and pogroms, sought safety and business opportunities in Central Asia, and cities like Tashkent and Bukhara received new enthusiasts. The Gumbaz Synagogue has a tablet fitted in the outer brick wall while inside it has an open courtyard overlooked by a veranda and an inner sanctum featuring a domed ceiling and a pentagon-like room which retains an old Torah and Menorah and several black and white photographs of Bukharan Jews. It reminded me of its resemblance with its Bukharan counterpart though this part of Samarkand definitely lacked Lyab-i-Hauz as its social hub. It is interesting to note that Bukharan Jews remained unknown to their fellow co-religionists for quite some time and it was in the nineteenth century that many European Jews began to filter into this part of the world. The presence of a historic Jewish community right in the heart of a Muslim land was a major surprise as they found the former deeply assimilated in a larger Perso-Islamic culture. By that time, Persia was itself predominantly Shia, whereas Central Asia followed Sunni jurisprudence; Bukharans shared affinity with their fellow Sunni neighbours, all speaking Persian, locally called Tajiki. The Jews, in many cases, wrote their own religious correspondence in Hebrew script but were familiar with its Arabic script as well. However, the migrations of European Jewry focused on Tashkent, the capital city under the Czars, whereas a sizeable number remained in Bukhara until the end of the Second World War. According to several Israeli websites, there were about 200,000 Jews in Uzbekistan soon after the Second World War and most of them lived in Bukhara, Samarkand, and Tashkent.[10] Israel and the United States soon became the choicest destinations for Uzbek Jews though Bukhara still accounts for a few thousand of them, whereas just a few hundred remain in Samarkand.

Notes

1. Dinara Sultanova, trans., 'Selected Gazels of Navoiy,' *Internet Archive*, 2015.
2. Sophie Ibbotson, *Uzbekistan* (Globe Pequot Pr, 2016).
3. For details, see Valerie Hansen, *Silk Road: A New History* (Oxford: Oxford University Press, 2015).

4. Andrew Forbes, et al. *Insight Guides: The Silk Road* (London: Insight, 2012); Jonathan Tucker, *The Ancient Silk Road: An Illustrated Map Featuring the Ancient Network of Routes between China and Europe* (Hong Kong: Odyssey Publications, 2013).

5. S. Frederick Starr, *Lost Enlightenment: Central Asia's Golden Age from the Arab Conquest to Tamerlane* (Princeton: Princeton University Press, 2015).

6. Quoted in Barry Hoberman, 'Chaucer of the Turks,' *Aramco World*, January/ February 1985, http://archive.aramcoworld.com/issue/198501/chaucer.of.the. turks.htm.

7. Do you like Samarkand?

8. Ruy González de Clavijo, *Embassy to Tamerlane 1403–1406*, trans. Guy le Strange (Routledge & Sons, 1928).

9. Xinru Liu, *The Silk Road in World History* (Oxford University Press, 2010).

10. *Encyclopedia Judaica: Bukhara*, Uzbekistan, Jewish Virtual Library, https://www. jewishvirtuallibrary.org/bukhara. Also see Andrew Higgins, 'In Bukhara, 10,000 Jewish Graves but just 150 Jew,' *The New York Times*, April 7, 2018 and Mark Edele et. al., *Shelter from the Holocaust: Rethinking Jewish Survival in the Soviet Union* (Detroit: Wayne State University Press, 2017).

9

Samarkand to Tashkent:
In Search of Navoi and Babur

And 'tis not me who's to be blamed for heavy rains pour'd from sore eyes,
As they were not tears, but blood of mine that night tears fail'd to come.

Alisher Navoi[1]

Returning from Shah-i-Zinda, inebriated with the spiritual experience
at Bibi-Khanym and Hazrat Khizr Mosque and following a bird's eye
view of the Gumbaz Synagogue, it was time for me to sit in the balcony
looking towards Registan's blue and brown skyline. Grapes, melons,
and pieces of thick brown naan for breakfast never tasted so good and
well-deserved. To my right were the cylindrical domes of the mosque
and mausoleum, while right in front of me, over the roofs in the old
town, I could see the minarets and blue cupolas of the three madrassas
that form the heart of legendry Registan Square. In between stood the
corrugated iron rooftops often bordered by grape vines and some poplar
trees but none disturbing the sumptuous view of the blues against
the blue. The sun was heading further west and the summer heat was
tempered by a fresh breeze from over Afrasiyab and beyond—possibly
even from Tamerlane's Shakhrisabz. Similar to the subcontinent, this
breeze was doused in the fragrance of jasmine, citrus fruit, and roses. In
that moment, I felt a natural concurrence with Emperor Babur's innate
love for gardens from his native lands, contrasted with the congested and
often brown landscape of South Asia. He missed his native Fergana and
Samarkand, especially their gardens, fruits, and well-designed residences
that he did not find in India. He blamed it on the lack of aesthetics
amongst the Indians as they were endowed with enough money and
other resources. Babur, the conqueror, was derisive of the Indian will to

fight, although some scenic spots like Kallar Kahar in the Salt Range did impress him quite a bit and found a place in his memoir.

I share childhood memories of Kallar Kahar, a hamlet quite close to my birthplace that Babur immortalized in his *Tuzk-i-Baburi*. He sat here on a rock overlooking a vast expanse of a lake surrounded by green, low-lying hills of the Salt Range. The rock had fallen off the hill and provided a vantage point to enjoy the natural landscape. Babur used the point to its maximum and since then it has come to be known as *Takht-e-Baburi* or Babur's throne. Thus, the rock has an additional historical and even recreational attraction for thousands of tourists to this hamlet which is looked over by a saint's tomb, who himself had been a refugee from Central Asia. Located only 15 miles from my hometown, Babur's Rock allowed me several enthronements during my childhood, though with age, I became more discreet for its conservation. Surrounded by a once lovely garden of mulberry and loquat trees, with rose and jasmine bushes all around, the peace of the place is often broken by the flights or singsong of peacocks who dwell by the saint's tomb. Even though locals may sometimes pluck their ornate feathers for decorative purposes or to even to sell them off surreptitiously in the cities, they try not to hurt these birds due to their long proximity with the Sufi saint. Climbing up the hill to reach the tomb, one still encounters these beautiful birds sleeping in the bushes while keeping a safe distance from urchins. However, as tradition goes, they are never to be hurt, killed, or bothered and no wonder they have survived like Babur's Rock, even though the lake has shrunk and big signs of Pepsi and Coca Cola block the view of the vistas. The construction of a busy motorway in the neighbourhood and a few cement factories have equally raised the noise, pollution, and traffic in the area. I often wonder about the usual dusty horizons sweeping out our dwindling green valleys in Potwar.

It is just a few miles east from Kallar Kahar that the great Indian plains begin and from there they extend all the way into Bangladesh. On this side, the Salt Range is the entry point for the Himalayas, Hindu Kush, Pamirs, and Karakorams, with Potwar Plateau spread all along as an open museum of stupas, monasteries, temples, shrines, havelis, and *bawalies*,[2] with an occasional presence of banyan tree. It is the land between the Indus and Jhelum that saw Aryans, Greeks, Huns, Turks, Mongols, and Afghans, all stampeding into India and surely there were saints, Sufis, and scholars who ventured into these valleys of our Hindustan. Herodotus alerted his Greek compatriots about the fighting men living around Taxila whereas Katas Raj flourished under the Hindu Shahis until Mahmud of Ghazni began his intermittent series of invasions. My grandfather took great pride in being a descendant of Qutb Shah who came here with his clan to fight alongside Mahmud, and that is how we Awans, the helpers, became the dominant presence across the Salt Range, all the way from Kalabagh to Jhelum. I was not much taken in by these ancestral heroics but did enjoy Potwar the most in spring with miles of mustard fields in bloom, even envied by our often-blue sky. Though I am not sure about our Qutb Shahi forefathers venturing into the upper Indus Valley, Gandhara, I am certain that all those Central Asian scholars such as Al-Biruni, Ali Hujwiri (1009–72), Khwaja Mueenuddin Chishti (1141–1236), and several others went further east through this route. Bukhara's Al-Biruni was based a few miles south of Kallar Kahar and close to Pir Katas in order to complete his study of the circumference of the earth besides penning down his classic, *Kitabul Hind*.[3] Katas Raj was a Pandavan temple from an early era that was catering to Hindu Khathris of our region, all the way until 1947. My mother's friends would walk or ride camels to this hamlet nestling in the hills, served by a stream—itself viewed as the tears of Shiva—and would return tired but happier for having completed the pilgrimage. Bhaun, another village near Katas and Kallar Kahar, is an ancient hamlet with several Hindu temples and homes that have survived the test of time. Near the hamlet lies the historic village of Dulmial, which has the largest number of senior military officers in the Pakistani Army, a tradition handed down since the Raj when several cherished awards including the Victoria Cross and George Cross were bagged by the forefathers of some of these senior officials.[4] A local museum highlights this recent military history, though one may like to focus on civic and educational uplift more than military prowess. While Bhaun was the home of the late Professor Amir A. Hussein Malik (d. 2002),[5] a known economist and friend who had spent a lifetime in Bonn studying and teaching, Pari Darwaza, not far from Biruni's Tilla Jogian, is the locale of *What the Body Remembers*. Shauna Singh Baldwin, a Canadian Sikh novelist based in Milwaukee, wrote this novel about her grandmother who married an educated and affluent Sikh from Rawalpindi long before 1947.[6] This work of fiction is in fact a true story of a landed Sikh family in this part of Potwar, not far from Jhelum, and how it got intertwined with Partition.

***

Registan, the heartland of Samarkand, with its three illustrious madrassas dating from the Timurid and Shaybani periods, is the focal point of contrasting strands of modernity and tradition. It is a meeting place between old Samarkand and its Russian section. While old Samarkand has to be lived in order to experience it, Registan and the Russian sections are open, well-patterned, and surrounded by social hubs. As an old mosque adjacent to the Sher Dor Madrassa was being repaired to resume its role as a museum, I hurried to buy the entry ticket, given the restrictive hours due to preparations of the forecourt for some grand musical ceremony to celebrate the country's national day. Skirting around the usual gift shops, I went into the first madrassa to the right which in fact is the middle one, with the Ulugh Beg Madarasa and Sher Dor Madarasa to its right and left, respectively. Tilla Kari Madrassa, as the name denotes, has a beautiful courtyard looked over by arched and staired rooms that were earlier used by scholars-in-residence. Like its two other counterparts, it received major restoration efforts from the Soviets and since then is certainly an emblem of Timurid-Shaybani architecture. Towards the left from the main *iwan* is the mosque, with its walls, arches, mihrab, and dome, all decorated with gold leaf. The patterns are floral and reflect minute work that must have claimed years for its completion. Aimed at showing the wealth of Samarkand to all, the mosque is a unique and rather extravagant work of art and is always full of prying eyes. According to some observers, the ceiling over the main prayer area is not domed, however, its decoration and ornamentation leave that impression. Underneath the mosque are opulent galleries displaying Uzbek arts and a picture gallery which builds up the historicity and uniqueness of this entire region. Looking at the ornate ceilings and walls of the mosque, one is certainly reminded of its post-Mongol history since Genghis Khan had destroyed everything in the area. All three mosques-cum-madrassas in the Registan Square may be smaller than the Bibi-Khanym Mosque—about a mile further towards east—yet together they form an unprecedented ensemble in history, arts, and aesthetics. More like the Maidan in Isfahan, this is the heart of that glorious Samarkand which made it into a city of desire, maybe even more than Istanbul which could have been a lateral entry.

I did not want to leave the Tilla Kari Madrassa and especially its luminous mosque but my keenness to see a prized and perhaps the earliest educational complex in the city took me out to the right where I joined a queue. I was standing outside the Ulugh Beg Madrassa complex where the philosopher-king himself used to teach. Beg was the grandson of Tamerlane but more than soldiery and conquests, he was devoted to scholarship. The completion of his madrassa happened after thorough work in 1420; Beg himself taught arithmetic, astronomy, and philosophy here. So while roaming through its classrooms and former lodges of the students, I could not brush aside the dignity of this scholar-king who built two more similar madrassas. Finally, here I was in the rooms where he must have lectured and deliberated upon delicate intellectual and scientific issues. His madrassas became the trendsetters for such future edifices and anchored an almost forgotten renaissance that made Central Asia so unique in Muslim consciousness. The Tilla Kari Madrassa and Sher Dor are both patterned on the Ulugh Beg Madrassa-cum-mosque complex and collectively they must have catered to several generations of scholars and students. Many of the dormitories of these madrassas are now art galleries and antique shops and, instead of enticing scholars, are eager for wealthy shoppers. I climbed up to the second floor of the Ulugh Beg Madrassa in order to be away from the tourists who wandered around those rooms that once were abuzz with wit and intellect. Restoration work goes on and one has to climb up through the narrow staircases, reminding one of some of those secret exits in the Lahore Fort. Bricks used here are the same size and style as those in South Asia and Iran. Thin bricks were widely used in Seljuk and Ottoman buildings across Turkey, and even at the Acropolis near Hadrian's Library, I discovered an old mosque built of thin reddish bricks. At present, it is used as an art gallery but we should not forget the fact that Athens for a long time was not a metropolis and it is only after independence that it gained its ever-growing size and significance. Further north in Thessalonica Saloniki, mosques and their Roman predecessors were all built of thin red bricks and this second largest city in Greece, for a long time, kept overshadowing Athens. Mosques in Thessaloniki, if not falling apart, are also used as covered markets or art galleries. One particular mosque facing my hotel during my stay in 2015 had been used as a cinema and was right in the heart of this Ottoman city that was once a Jewish majority town. The Ottomans, following their expulsion from Spain, had brought most of these Jews here; they retained their Spanish names and customs until the Nazis came and took them to extermination camps. Earlier, the Ottomans had ensured their safety. Located at a strategic point, Thessaloniki was a natural link between the Balkans and the Middle East.[7] Mustafa Kemal Ataturk (1881–1938) was himself born in Thessaloniki, not far from the ancient Roman arch, the Arch of Galerius, and within walking distance of the old walls of medieval Thessaloniki. The Friday Mosque next to Galerius is now called Rotunda and, as per locals, has been converted to its pre-Islamic incarnation, though one can still witness remnants of the Quranic calligraphy on its arches. Like the Cordova Mosque, the Juma Mosque in Seville, and the main mosque in Palermo, the Mediterranean world abounds in such transformed histories or changed demographics.

The Ulugh Beg Madrassa retains a mosque within the complex, as was the tradition, and it is a pattern that one sees in older Oxbridge colleges. This magnificent mosque is neighboured by a lecture hall, whereas the other classrooms are located beneath the domed corners. In a rather limited space, there are several rooms with their doors opening towards the compound that boasts of several green trees and flower beds. It seems that all these madrassas were self-contained with religious and residential amenities along with sections reserved for teaching and libraries. Across the complex stands the Sher Dor Madrassa which was built by the Shaybani Sultan, Amir Yalangtush, and had taken 17 years to complete in 1636. The designs of tigers/lions on the top of its main *iwan* above the entrance, though not found so often on Islamic buildings, gave the name to this complex that follows the familiar pattern of Timurid architecture. The exteriors of all three complexes have been restored to their past glory, whereas some internal conservation still continues as it is a minute labour needing the utmost care. The courtyard of the Sher Dor Madrassa is often used for Uzbek marriages, though the compound facing all the three grand buildings is the choicest place for official grand events, with one going through its endless rehearsals during our stay in Samarkand that summer of 2015. However, during my February 2016 visit, the entire compound was open to public and the number of visitors did not seem to have diminished. The imposing *iwan* of Sher Dor, with its lions overlooking a minute medley of tile work across its surface, is a tribute to its two senior neighbours. Collectively, all three of them could mean hundreds of students and scholars partaking in a competitive academia. But what stopped them from becoming Oxford or Harvard for Muslims? This is a question that every genuine visitor may raise. I was certainly impressed by the majesty and beauty of these edifices but could not reconcile to their standing there as sentinels of history or quiet onlookers of passing events. Perhaps their builders shared lofty and no less noble dreams but their successors lacked the will and motivation to transform them into high-calibre places of learning as some of them had been in Bukhara and Khiva a few centuries earlier.

I went back to the Ulugh Beg Madrassa and sat there in the courtyard just gazing at classrooms, alcoves, and what once would have been the student residences. I started imagining Beg as a mild fellow, without a sword or helmet or any martial wherewithal, but rather immersed in subjects such as astronomy, theology, and philosophy. No wonder they killed him while he was on the way to Makkah on pilgrimage. As the narrative goes, his father, who had selected Herat as his capital and thus had moved south from Samarkand, had appointed him Governor of Transoxiana. Queen Gawhar Shad built schools and mosques in Herat and made it into another Samarkand like her father-in-law, Tamerlane. Following the death of Shah Rukh, Beg ascended the throne amidst a fratricidal war of succession. He headed towards Herat to defeat his rebellious nephew who had declared himself as the new king. He, though not made for warfare, was able to defeat the rebel prince and subsequently returned to Balkh. According to some reports, he wreaked a vengeful campaign in Herat, though given his temperament this may not be totally true. In Balkh, his own son rebelled against him and eventually caused his beheading while on his way to pilgrimage. It was after his death that one of his other nephews rehabilitated the prestige and fame of Ulugh Beg. Beg had been born in Persia during one of Tamerlane's campaigns and had been to Anatolia and India before becoming the ruler of Transoxiana. He, in a rather short reign, built several schools and revived education and architecture following the Mongol devastation. In Afrasiyab, he built Asia's largest observatory equalling three stories, with the sextant reaching a radius of 118 feet; his generation did not have access to a telescope. His astronomical studies highlighted several anomalies in the contemporary planetary measurements. The sextant, partially restored, had walls covered in marble and was named Gurkhani Zij; it was bigger than its close counterpart in Constantinople. Beg was an astronomer and mathematician in the esteemed traditions of Khwarizmi and Al-Biruni, his Central Asian peers. One of the greatest astronomers and mathematicians of the Muslim world, he was even celebrated by the former Soviet Union, which in 1987 issued a special postal stamp depicting Beg's portrait and observatory. Even though I had been postponing my visit, I knew that I needed to visit his resting place soon. Maybe I was only postponing because I was not enamoured of Tamerlane buried next to Beg.

Gur-i-Amir or Amir Taimur's tomb is less than a mile to the west of Registan and is curiously the entry point to the Russian parts of Samarkand. The Ulugh Beg Observatory, on the contrary, is about three kilometres to the east above a hill overlooking Afrasiyab. Registan had consumed me and especially the agonizing thought that Beg's own son had killed a rare brain. I decided to slip away to an open café, canopied by tall, graceful trees almost facing the three madrassas. A hot afternoon and crowds of local and international visitors had led me to this modernist spot affording a beautiful view of the entrance to the Ulugh Beg Madrassa. I was thirsty and, despite having consumed quite a supply of water, decided to have an Uzbek ice cream that tasted doubly scrumptious and soon I was queuing up for another serving. Never in my life have I had two ice cream servings one after the other but perhaps my body, like my soul, was thirsting for some cool nourishment. The manicured and immensely green lawns of Registan, with lines of cypress and Christmas trees and rose bushes often being sprayed by fountains, certainly had their impact on my disposition yet provided no answers to my abounding questions such as: What had gone wrong with us Muslims? Did we build edifices to let them decay or get destroyed by others while we engaged in our own petty internecine wars? Have we learnt any lessons from our history? Not really, as the news from Syria, Libya, Egypt, Pakistan, Yemen, and Afghanistan kept reminding me of the cheapness of human life.

***

Samarkand had gone deep into my body, and its history, glory, and pre-eminence both inspired and dispirited me. I was relishing my encounters of discovering layers of history, while the romantic historian within kept egging me on. But thinking about the sordid events of the past and a continued collective drift in the present kept sapping my enthusiasm. Samarkand's history began to appear symptomatic of what has been unique about Islam and what has been so pathetic about us Muslims. We adore our past and dream of recreating it yet we are far from preparing ourselves for this gigantic work. In the same vein, we keep overlooking what was wrong and non-salubrious in our past and tend to avoid talking about it. Like Tamerlane, we assume that building up a huge empire, no matter the amount of blood and misery, we will build up edifices and that will secure our place in history. I guess the efforts should be towards maintaining institutions in a qualitative way and not by just building monuments to leave to routine irreverence by posterity.

My next morning was earmarked for old Afrasiyab to visit the observatory and Prophet Daniel's resting place. Having fed myself boiled eggs, black tea, yogurt, and melons, I embarked through the old Jewish quarters saying salaam to shopkeepers and looking like a determined man on a holy mission. The lady shopkeeper to the left had been piling up green melons outside her shop while a gentleman across the Mubarak Mosque was busy discussing the latest news with his friends, including the kind soul who had accompanied me to the synagogue. Passing between the Bibi-Khanym Mosque and Mausoleum, I was waiting with some other pedestrians to cross the dual carriageway which appeared busier due to school time. Passing by the Hazrat Khizr Mosque up the hill, I again resumed my walk on the Tashkent Avenue. On both sides, behind the pomegranate trees and flowerbeds, were the boundary walls of the cemetery that I had visited two days back to reach Shah-i-Zinda. There were two gardeners ensuring a steady supply of water to the rose bushes and marigolds which ran parallel to the pavement until I reached the main entrance to the Jewish cemetery. The gate was open which tempted me to venture in. Like the Muslim graveyard next door, the recent graves displayed portraits of their occupants and there was an overall greater sense of neatness about the place. It appeared that, other than the authorities, the community members in Samarkand, helped by the Bukharan Jews in Israel and the United States, had been ensuring the proper upkeep of the second largest Jewish graveyard in Central Asia. Of course, Bukhara's is the largest and perhaps the oldest in this part of the continent.

There was another visitor on the premises who acknowledged my presence as I stood in a corner reciting *fateha*, the first chapter of the Quran, as I often do whenever I visit any cemetery. My paternal grandfather had inculcated this wonderful habit in me during my childhood when I often sought to accompany this retired policeman on his religious and mundane engagements. Each time he passed by a cemetery, he uttered the Arabic salutation: 'Peace be upon you, oh dwellers of these graves. You are gone; we'll follow you soon. May God bless you, but do remember us in your prayers'. Then he stood still, fixed his white turban, and raised his hands to recite *fateha*. His prayers were not reserved for only Muslim graveyards; he had been doing it for all and perhaps he had learnt this from his father, Malik Ahmad Khan. I had always heard about that dynamic great grandfather who, like my maternal grandfather, was a landowner heading a big family with five daughters and two sons, with my paternal grandfather being the eldest. My maternal grandfather, Malik Nawab Khan, had more lands, sons, and daughters, and was a centurion; his presence always caused awe and respect amongst everyone. His horses, bulls, cows, and donkeys were the best in town and sadly it was one of his cows which threw him aside when he was very old and frail and wanted to help her newborn calf. Animals can misunderstand and that is what I witnessed when he was thrown over and broke both his legs but never his determination. His home was just a few metres away from Pir Bukhari's resting place but *Naanaji* would never sleep on the roof even during the summer nights, simply out of respect for a buried Syed saint in his mohalla who had been sheltered by his ancestors a long time back.

Beyond the boundary wall of the Jewish graveyard are empty spaces on both sides, this is where the Markand once had its presence, as the artefacts in the Afrasiyab Museum reveal through some of their rare ancient Sogdian murals. Outside, the sculptures of a few camels with merchants remind one of the old Silk Road and, except for the modern road and the Museum's building, the landscape does not seem to have changed over the millennia. My body was feeling the summer heat and after crossing River Siob, I started looking for a shop to buy some water.

Next to a friendly cobbler was a small shop with minimum amount of provisions run by an elderly gentleman who gave me generous smiles but could not understand my desire to have a cup of tea. I contented myself with a big bottle of water and moved ahead until, passing by some newer dwellings and shops, I could see a modernist structure. I was close to the observatory, and in its foreground was the sculpture of Ulugh Beg welcoming his visitors and followers. The remains of his observatory were excavated a century ago as they had been buried under soil following earthquakes and other urban transformations. The remains of a curved 30 metre astrolabe are now open to visitors and are perhaps the only major sections of the observatory left for posterity. The walls on both sides of this curvy astrolabe were once covered in marble though not anymore, however, the restoration of this finely designed instrument, originally completed in the 1420s, was worth that long walk in the August heat. I stood amongst a group of international and Uzbek visitors and spent some time looking at the astrolabe before going into the museum which is basically a heritage collection of different epochs of this nation-state. The earliest hand written collections of poetry by Alisher Navoi sat next to Babur's *Tuzk*. The older pieces of ceramics excavated by archaeologists, bead works, and samples of works by Al-Biruni, Muhammad Khwarizmi, and poems by Abul Qasim Firdausi and Nur Ud Din Jami (1414–92), all sat in this museum displaying the diversity as well as the wealth of this nation's past. Beg's own seated massive sculpture appeared to be welcoming curious visitors. The museum's rich Persian, Turkish, and archaeological collections are housed in an air-conditioned, modern purpose-built facility. I was quite happy to see a large number of women and children observing their heritage with due interest and respect. The quest for knowledge in a predominantly literate society is too obvious to be missed. Once outside, I walked around the site which is on top of a hill and offers a vantage view of the old Samarkand.

The ice cream shop did not offer tea which was rather shocking so I had to go a few yards further down the street where people were sipping tea in blue and white Uzbek crockery. After a salaam, I just politely settled myself in a chair while smiling at the men sitting around. The shop was an extension of a bigger room where several more men were sitting and some more arrived after every few minutes; everyone then raised their hands to pray. I realized that the place was having its session of condolence over someone's passing away so I joined the assembly when hands were raised for *fateha*. It happened quite a few times until I discovered a small tray with blue Uzbek crockery of a teapot and small, round teacups and their saucers sitting on a stool in front of me. Next to them sat a cup full of sweet almonds and dried raisins. I was double-minded about making myself a cup until I saw a few others helping themselves to the beverage. With tea settling in my inner recesses, I tried to probe some people sitting next to me who were both impressed by my Persian as well as by my participation in the *fateha* instead of being a heedless tourist. There had been a death in the family a few days back and men were congregating here in the usual Muslim way of praying for the departed soul. When I prepared to leave, everyone stood up, including the elderly imam, and offered me a handshake which I took as a rare privilege and slowly moved away from the premises. Soon I was back where the friendly cobbler mended old shoes and greeted him. He motioned me to cross the road and go further down in the direction opposite his shop. Initially, I did not understand what he was trying to suggest but then it occurred to me in a flash. He was giving me the direction to Prophet Daniel's tomb further down by the river, a few hundred metres away. I guess I had almost forgotten about it. The heat, Ulugh Beg Observatory, and then an unexpected condolence session had deeply tested my memory and I had nearly forgotten that I had planned to visit the tomb. I could not thank him enough. The elderly shopkeeper kept smiling without realizing that a few hours earlier I had been hankering for tea in his little shop. These descendants of Ulugh Beg were proud and kind people and I had been experiencing it to the fullest. All right, I could forgive Tamerlane ...

Passing by a few homes and following a rather neat and narrow river, I crossed over to the other side. These were low-lying sandy hills with some bushes and trees reminding me of my own native Salt Range or the landscape that I had seen near Sale in Morocco. There was a steady stream of people going up the stairs towards a longish, low-lying building with five brown domes riding its roof. This was the tomb of Prophet Daniel, who passed away in Susa about five centuries before Christ. Inside, a green silken sheet with embroidered Quranic calligraphy covers the 18-metre-long sarcophagus, serving as a reminder of Shah Shams Tabrizi's resting place in Konya, though in the latter's case, on a smaller (normal) scale. According to some versions, the prophetic remains were brought to Samarkand by Tamerlane from Persia and buried here. The common belief has been that Daniel's body grows by half an inch every year and thus the grave keeps growing in length.[8] Well, anything could have been expected from Tamerlane. He killed millions of people in India and Persia, brought back all the wealth he could accumulate, and fetched artists and artisans from these places as well as a large number of elephants which were used to build some of his monuments in Samarkand and Shakhrisabz. Inside it is a narrow room with some space on the side of the grave itself where one can stand, observe, reflect, and then leave. I thought of offering *fateha* and lingered on while Uzbek families kept coming and leaving. Subsequently, they sat in a separate veranda where a cleric led the prayers in Sufi tradition with both men and women joining him. Similar to South Asia and North Africa, people here may not be necessarily seeking any special favour but rather only feeling more spiritual due to the body buried there. Prophet Daniel's burial place overlooks the river valley and is not in a populous area, though a small stream flows by the shrine, giving currency to all kinds of hypotheses. Right behind the shrine are some old trees which due to their age may hold a special status for some visitors; at Bahauddin Naqshband's shrine in Bukhara, I saw people walking under a twisted tree trunk that must have lain there for ages. People attribute special powers to such manifestations which for a logical observer or a literalist may appear irrational or irreligious, but their existence certainly is owed to folk narratives and practices. I have heard about such extra-long graves in Pakistan since my childhood including *Naugazi*, which would literally mean a nine-yard-long *turbat*. In the same vein, there are stories of prophets living for hundreds of years, which is a devotional matter and possibly not acceptable to skeptical quarters. It is like the belief in seven skies, seven seas, and certainly the seven lives of a cat.

I sat in this small uphill corner of one of the world's busiest and most cosmopolitan cities wondering how it could afford such isolated, quiet, and vitally sacred spaces. Perhaps modernization in the recent past, including the cleaning and banking of the river, in addition to the construction of kiosks, roads, and parking spaces, had made it into what I was seeing. I could imagine huts of shopkeepers in the narrow lanes, old-style serais, and certainly armies of holy men lodged in the neighbourhood, similar to Sehwan Sharif in Sindh or tombs in Lahore,

Multan, and Old Delhi. Here the Soviet and post-Soviet regimes had 'cleansed' the place of all kinds of those vestiges, and pilgrims would now come in groups, offer prayers, munch on ice cream, and then depart as quietly as they came in. I am sure that just like in South Asia, this place must have once been a bustling centre of folk activities with the occasional arrival of Jewish and Christian visitors. In the meantime, Prophet Daniel's sarcophagus in his other life has kept growing, more like Tamerlane's legacy as the father of this young nation-state. I thought Amir Taimur's tomb deserved a visit; visiting Ulugh Beg's observatory had slightly changed my mind and had force stopped my procrastination. It was for the sake of Beg that I would venture into the tomb but on some other day as the heat and exertion had exhausted me, or perhaps there was a sense of satisfaction at having visited Afrasiyab. I walked back waving at the sculptures of the camels and merchants outside the Afrasiyab Museum who, like the Sogdian patriarchs and monarchs on the artefacts housed within, quietly stood witnessing another chapter in the history of their tumultuous land. Given the time of the day and the heat, there was not a single soul on the road. How could the heart of Alexander's favourite Markand be so quiet and deserted! Those poplar and pomegranate trees offered me respite while I looked at the running water channel with envy. In fact, heat had generated some naughty thoughts of having a dip in the river itself but better sense prevailed. I could not do that with Prophet Daniel's remains looking over me from above their abode, nor could I shock the steady stream of pilgrims in their colourful dresses. Across the Hazrat Khizr Mosque, I slowed down to pick up some fruit. Grapes and melons never looked so tempting and I bought a few of them after amusing the Uzbek saleswomen with my Farsi/Tajiki. I also bought naans from the other one who sat quietly by her goods with a rare smile on her charming face. I was stealing an impish look at her Frida Kahlo-like eyebrows under a colourful scarf as she packed my bread in a brown bag which itself was unusually subdued before its majestic handler.

Our accommodation facility was unusually full with small dusty cars and their equally brown European drivers who had been on a trans-Asian car rally of smaller cars sponsored by their manufacturers. A couple of Americans and British felt energized sitting lazily on divans while talking about Turkmenistan and the drive from Khiva. They had lost some of their colleagues on the way due to mechanical issues but the rest appeared fully focused on reaching Beijing within the next few days. However, a couple from York had taken a break from their cycle marathon destined for Indonesia since they did not have any deadline to meet except for some visa requirement to get into Tajikistan. Besides, the gentleman, a doctoral student and part-time copy-editor, had a bad back necessitating a forced rest. Their journey from Bukhara had been mostly on public transport since he could not cycle and, despite the need for urgent rest, their Uzbek visa was expiring in a couple of days. Nevertheless, stories of their experiences in the Balkans, Georgia, and Azerbaijan were quite captivating, though worries about the challenging nature of the next leg of journey through the hilly terrains of Tajikistan did pose some issues. Their conversation with us also proved a needed diversion for the gentleman from his back pain, even though most of it was conducted by the lady who reminded us of one of our own friends back in Oxford. Soon, I was on my feet to visit the corner shop run by the mother-and-son team as we planned on cooking vegetables and rice. The naturalness of greens was an additional temptation, though we ended up cooking a rather generous quantity which was shared by the new arrivals who were not in a mood or position to venture out.

***

Skirting around Registan before the rush hour and glancing at the lovely café in the park with its ice cream extravaganza, I kept heading towards the Russian part of the town. Gur-i-Amir or Amir's Tomb sits between the older and newer sections of Samarkand. Surrounded by expansive lawns and walkways, the tomb is in the familiar Central Asian mausoleum surrounded by green compounds and flowerbeds on all its three sides. Once inside the grand *iwan*, archway entrance, and through the lawn, one ventures into the main resting areas where Tamerlane, his two sons, and grandsons are buried along with two spiritual mentors—the Syeds. Taimur wanted to be buried in his native town, Shakhrisabz, and had specified some plain crypts at his resting place. His present tomb was originally built in 1404 for his favourite grandson and prospective heir, Muhammad Sultan, who had passed away in 1403. In 1405, Taimur was on his last military campaign against the Chinese in Kazakh regions, Mughalistan, when he passed away after catching pneumonia. His body was brought back to his capital city but, since the passes to Shakhrisabz were snowbound, he was buried next to Muhammad Sultan. Ulugh Beg's grave is to the left of Taimur's while Sultan's is towards the front; to Taimur's right is the resting place of Mir Syed Baraka, one of his favourite teachers. The resting places of his sons, Miran Shah and Shah Rukh, are located towards the back of Taimur's grave. Sheikh Sayed Umar's grave is situated behind these two graves and honours another one of Taimur's favourite teachers. The gravestones are plain marble slabs though the resting places are further down in the usual Muslim chambers. Taimur's grave is covered in lozenges black jade slab which was rumoured to have once belonged to the Chinese emperors and was supposedly the biggest of its kind in the world. The ornate mausoleum rises above these graves featuring impressive ornamentation all over the walls, arches, and ceilings decorated with Quranic calligraphy in gold letters in the middle. The signal blue flute-like ribbed dome that one sees in his other buildings and those of Shaybanis, tops the entire edifice. This dome has impressive geometrical designs on an azure background. I was struck by the resemblance between this azure dome, and its counterpart over Maulana Rumi's tomb in Konya. Rumi's flute has ribbed patterns but is slender in size and precedes these more circular and bigger domes of Central Asia. The graves of Rumi, his father, son, and other Khorasanis are all on raised platforms adjacent to one another. Here in Gur-i-Amir, they are fewer and more slender without any silk sheet covering any of them.

It is reported that Nadir Shah Afshar, the Persian invader of India and Transoxiana, robbed Samarkand of many of its possessions, similar to his devastation of Delhi, and took his loot to Isfahan. Shah was from Khorasan and while exploiting the instability in the later Safavid Empire, this former Qizilbash shepherd captured vast tracts of land in Persia, Afghanistan, and India, and pursuing his role models, Genghis Khan and Tamerlane, killed thousands of people at all those places. His possessions from Samarkand, amongst other expensive commodities such as the doors of Bibi-Khanym Mosque, included the jade slab covering Tamerlane's grave which, as per Sufi traditions, caused several moral and health issues for the Afshar king. His son and future heir fell seriously ill until he asked some sages for comfort who advised him to return the mentioned slab back to Taimur's grave, which he did. In the process, the

long slab broke but it was restored to its original place and reportedly
Shah's son recovered. Maybe it is true or it could be just one of those
mystical parables which flourished in older times to inculcate a more
honest and moralist behaviour. What happened to his son subsequently
is itself a story of the suspicion and paranoia that Shah had developed
about everyone around him, leading to the murder of his close ones.
Suspicious of his son's involvement in some palatial plot, Shah ordered
that his own son be blinded.

There is yet another and more recent story about Gur-i-Amir
and Soviet research on his remains. Mikhail Gerasimov, the Soviet
anthropologist and archaeologist, curious about Tamerlane's height and
body structure, opened the crypts in 1941 and found his stature to be
1.7 metres long with signs of fractures on his right arm and leg.[9] These
findings affirmed the stories about Taimur *Lung* (Tamerlane, the Lame!)
though some spice is added to this historical evidence which relates to the
discovery of an inscription on his grave. As per rumours, it warned against
opening up his grave or otherwise a more powerful enemy would defeat
the perpetrators. Gerasimov had opened the crypt on June 21, 1941 and
a day later Hitler mounted his attack on the Soviet Union. Historical
coincidence, a true prediction, or just a touristic fable?

Everyone inside the mausoleum appeared overawed both out of respect
and perhaps due to the aura and fear that Tamerlane has engendered over
the past seven centuries. Visitors from faraway places in Uzbekistan filed
in as groups and families and then sat on benches until the sheikh began
his recitation followed by prayers. Men and women both joined in the
ceremony with raised hands and subdued eyes looking at the plain slabs
while reading *fateha* until it was time to stand up and leave. Party after
party filled in, though there was no sense of crowdedness and the place
was eerily quiet. I had been sitting on the far end side of the tomb and,
while focused on the graves or reading the Quranic verses on the walls
and ceiling, kept raising my hands with every praying group. The sheikh
had gotten used to me and the guards seemed friendlier. Tourists had
kept venturing in and were lectured by their guides in German, Japanese,
Korean, Chinese, and English; Tamerlane, even after his death, is global.
Of course, we Muslims forgive the dying or dead, all their sins and even
crimes, though historians keep seeking out heroes and villains amongst
them. We feel sorry for evildoers but then leave their retribution to God;

however, in some cases, like Yazid and other assassins of the Prophet's family, we do carry on with our own condemnation and commiseration in our own unique denominational ways.

Tamerlane is fascinating for historians despite all his horrors; and for Uzbeks, he is the father figure and with Lenin, Stalin, and other such newer demigods vanished, he proves invincible. In his life, sheikhs and officials imposed his writ by force on reluctant subjects, and now in his other existence, there are 'other' reasons and forces ensuring homage to this great savage and triumphant conqueror in world history. I thought of his grandson, Ulugh Beg, whom I had been following through his madrassas and observatory, and who himself had been beheaded on the orders of his own son, and is now lying next to his tyrant grandfather. His own father did not have a smooth sailing; being overlooked by Amir Taimur and then faced with revolts. Shah Rukh chose Herat to keep a stronghold on his Indian, Persian, Afghan, and Anatolian possessions, while Balkh, Bukhara, and Samarkand proved untenable. I missed Gawhar Shad here the most—a dynamic woman in the tradition of Bibi-Khanym—but made of a different matter. Like Khadija, the Prophet's first wife, and like Fatima Al-Fihri, the founder of the first university in Fes, she was made in a different mould and must have inspired Babur's daughter, Gulbadan Begum (1523–1603) and Queen Nur Jahan (1577–1645). After all, these Mughal royals traced their origins to Babur and Tamerlane and some of them carried on scholarly pursuits and institution building in succeeding centuries. Sitting there and lost in the past, I did not notice a charming young student taking down her notes in Russian, still the compulsory language in Turkestani republics. She was drawing some graphic sketches on her gadget as she looked at those graves so intently. Both of us were lost in our own separate worlds while I was trying to overcome a keen desire to talk to her. A teacher within me was itchy but having finished her assignment she was soon gone. I lingered on in the compound absorbing the minarets and domes of this entire edifice which for centuries would have resonated with Quranic verses and exegesis. Like older mosques, notable Muslim shrines often had residential madrassas built adjacent to them to make these places more wholesome along with seeking blessings for the buried notables.

Across Tamerlane's Tomb is the Ruhabad Mausoleum, built in 1380, which might be the oldest in the city following the Mongol devastations, though erstwhile classrooms and residential facilities in this quadrangle now operate as crafts shops. This is the tomb of a famous Sufi, Syed Burhannuddin Sagarji, who led Islamic missions into India and during the 1340s, even met Ibn Battuta, the intrepid Moroccan traveller. Sagarji was the father of Mir Syed, one of Taimur's tutors who is buried next to him. In fact, Taimur supervised the construction of this mausoleum, which as per narratives also had a hair of Holy Prophet (PBUH) in a casket buried next to the body of the Sufi Sagarji. *Rukhabad*, or to be exact *Ruhabad*, literally means abode of the spirit/soul though the Tajik word here in Uzbekistan is often pronounced is *Rukhubod*. *Rukhabad* in Persian would mean something that makes one's face flourish. I was eager to seek some café or even an ice cream parlour to sit in and absorb its ambience but was confronted with more mundane realities all around me. All-brown walls, domes, and arches stood mute as enduring observers of human power plays, routinely ending in more tragedies with a capricious nature often joining in through a medley of periodic earthquakes. A wall surrounds this park and the two mausoleums and separates the older parts of the city from the south where Ak Saray Mausoleum, with its restored frescoes and glazed mosaic sand calligraphy in gold leaf, offers another chapter in the turbulent and ever-changing history of Transoxiana. Ak Saray (white palace) was in fact built in 1470. It is the final abode of Abdel Latif, the son and assassin of Ulugh Beg, whose own headless body was subsequently affirmed by archaeologists.

Soon I heard a rather muffled adhan. It was the afternoon prayer time and the mosque lodged between the three mausoleums had begun to attract a steady stream of worshippers from amongst the shop owners, visitors, and neighbours. It was a diverse assembly of men which grew to a rather large size and the inside chamber was soon filled up. The air conditioners had been turned on and the outside midday heat was thwarted. A raised wooden ceiling displaying calligraphy and a veranda featuring several slim, wooden pillars reminded me of Bukhara's Bolo Haouz Mosque, though this mosque did not have a water tank in front of it. Many of these mosques had been closed down during the Soviet era and their water tanks were decommissioned for fear that they had been spreading epidemics such as the plague and cholera.

Samarkand, unlike Bukhara, lacks in old water tanks, which in the latter's case are places of antiquity, beauty, and sociability. The city has its own preoccupations, and even though its Registan Square, Shah-i-Zinda, and certainly the Gur-i-Amir are comparatively more busy with visitors and pilgrims, I still missed Lyab-i-Hauz and its cosmopolitan atmosphere, especially the younger people who served me tea in blue crockery, often preceded by a cool glass of Ayran. Following prayers and nourishing myself with several glasses of water from a modern fountain, I slowly sought my way out until I picked up some salutation in Urdu. Eqbal was a student of Islamic studies in Samarkand whose Russian teachers had been tutoring him Urdu. My eagerness to speak Persian was tempered down by his determination to try Urdu on me and I was bowled over. It was quite polite, literary, and formal as Urdu in old cities of Lahore, Lucknow, Delhi, and Hyderabad would have been a long time back. He had figured out my South Asian appearance from amongst a hundred or so worshippers and we were now discussing education, politics, religion, and of course, Bukhara. Pakistan, 'Englistan', and Uzbekistan kept coming back in our conversation, and here in Beg's proximity, I felt even more at home. Neither a conqueror nor a scholar of the stature buried a few hundred metres away from us, I stood as an eternal seeker or even a lost soul before this Uzbek young man whose own journey seemed to be going in an opposite direction to mine. He had been planning on going east and south while I had ventured into the east from the far west making sense of history or at least of my own existence in an ever-changing world.

***

We were missing kebabs and naan and took off for a recommended place that afforded us a quiet and rather distant view of Registan. I would have preferred some local joint but was advised to visit this place that was unique due to its location where the food was both Western and Eastern. Two Dutch visitors who had quite a few stories to tell had in fact suggested the place. My favourite one was about their very first evening in Samarkand, when walking beside a modern hotel, they saw men in black tie and women dressed to their best. Obviously, it was a real Uzbek wedding, famous for extravaganza in food and music. Dust ridden and tanned, the Dutch were eyeing the Uzbek men and women when two men invited them in. Initially, they thought they were being accosted or some cruel joke was being played on them yet the hosts were persistent. Once inside, they were regaled with piles of meat dishes, salads, fruits, and desserts to the tune of live music with dozens of couples busy dancing. They first polished up the food which was mostly barbeque and several types of pulao until they could not eat anymore. Rather than taking a quick exit, they joined the dance floor that went on endlessly. Before leaving for Shakhrisabz, they had recommended this second floor restaurant while keeping our eyes open for any possible wedding!

The State University of Uzbekistan is located just to the left of the Timurid Mausoleum complex and I wanted to visit their history faculty. Traversing tree-lined boulevards in the Russian part of the city and passing by the Alisher Navoi Museum and Centre, we started seeing an increasing number of youngsters until we came upon a guide. A quiet young lady asked us to follow her and took us to the entrance of a large building where, following some exchange with the porters, we were taken to an office. A neat, majestic, and well-kept building housed the faculty where most of the secretaries greeted us with smiles. We wanted to meet some historians but they were either away or teaching. As I soon learnt, without prior appointment and 'intermediaries', striking acquaintance with Uzbek colleagues is not often possible. One cannot go beyond smiles, a Soviet era legacy. However, a doctoral student with some smattering of English soon came to our rescue and took us on a tour of the building and its charming gardens in the back. Then he led us to the museum where a senior Russian curator gave us a generous tour of her collections on the prehistory and medieval era of central Uzbekistan. She had spent her lifetime conducting fieldwork and teaching and knew the various phases of the collections which included stone implements, ceramics, jewellery, weaponry, and other paraphernalia. We then entered a literate period with an even more diverse representation all the way from the Aryan, Sogdian, Persian, Greek to Arab phases in the history of Central Asia. Our questions about the dwindling of the Aral Sea, tempering of soil with a view to have a bumper cotton production, and now the post-industrial era in an independent nation-state elicited scholarly and measured responses. Indeed, several Russians had left for the mainland especially with Putin's nationalist rhetoric but there were people like her who had been here for a few generations without any intent to leave.

***

I would have loved to stay on in Samarkand, however, our visa was valid only for specific weeks and, in addition, I wanted to visit Hast Imam in Tashkent. We decided to share a taxi ride with two other passengers for the sake of experiencing a popular form of Uzbek travel. Our taxi was a rather new American Chevrolet whose minor versions we had already experienced in Tashkent and Bukhara. An early start from near the Ulugh Beg Observatory afforded me an opportunity to say my farewell and soon we were travelling through the industrial hub of the city. A modern dual carriageway, surrounded by green fields and separated from us by poplar and pomegranate trees, led us through the most fertile lands of central Uzbekistan. Of course, brown hills in the distance were never too far away but we were definitely seeing greenery at its best like in South Asia where monsoon rains, despite an unremitting heat, turn out to be our actual spring. We passed by several towns and villages, driving by piles of brown and green melons often being sold by women. A few check-posts did not bother our driver, who stopped only once to get some water, otherwise we carried on for the next three hours. Almost halfway through, we drove past brown terrain but soon another green expanse engulfed us as we neared Tashkent. We bade farewell to the kind driver and the two other passengers before boarding our taxi which soon began zigzagging through the busy streets of southern Tashkent. This greenery owed itself to Syr Darya, Amu Darya's northern counterpart; the city looked quite orderly with modern mansions, green parks, and steady rows of tall trees. Like our early impressions of Tashkent, the capital city's suburbs were also opulent and green and did not give any evidence of being crowded or rundown. Our hotel happened to be a tall mansion located near the presidency, subway stop, museums and, best of all, it looked over the Taimur Square. We could see Tamerlane on his ride with a well-designed park all around in attendance. Our hotel turned out to be quite cosmopolitan as we could hear Chinese, English, Hindi, Turkish, and even Urdu, especially at meal time. Evening walks in the park brought us nearer to the father of the nation as Uzbek couples and families strolled around or filled in the cafés in the post-independence centre of their country's political and cultural munificence. We enjoyed walking across Tashkent while checking on its parks and broad pavements with occasional open cafés during this last leg of our stay. Our favourite restaurant, owned by a spectacled Turk, did not fail our expectations as we sat down for our evening meal close to the Kukeldash Madrassa, the city's most beautiful complex from the olden times. In its neighbourhood, other than the main Friday Mosque and Chorsu Bazaar, are the tombs of some early Mughals, including that of Yunas Khan, Emperor Babur's grandfather.

My familiarity with Tashkent's subway system proved useful as equipped with my passport like other Uzbeks, I set off on my long-awaited visit to Hast Imam complex—the most venerated section of the Old City. Our hotel concierge, a portly man with many decades of experience, had insisted on the Kukeldash Madrassa being the repository of one of the earliest Quranic scripts and, in his forgetfulness, seemed to confuse it with Hast Imam. Not too good at reading maps, I just counted on my own sense of direction and entered the main courtyard of the Kukeldash Madrassa which, unlike many of its counterparts in Bukhara and Samarkand, was abuzz with students and tutors. They encircled this lanky visitor who spoke a kind of literary Persian and claimed to be not only a Pakistani by origin but also a historian by profession. This impromptu jamboree was heart-warming and I left following several bear hugs with the advice to take a taxi to Hast Imam which was just a couple of kilometres further up the road. No sooner had I stood by the main road with Chorsu Bazaar in the back that a small American car driven by a woman stopped by my side asking me to jump in. Another young Uzbek lady sat in front and both of them operated this taxi for tourists. Our discussion continued in Persian and English and, after saying salaam to several traffic wardens and skirting through traffic jams, I was offloaded outside the complex with offers for future chauffeur-driven rides in the city. Unlike their charming appearance and amiable manners, I had not been too enamoured by their sense of direction and felt a great sense of relief as they disembarked me outside the Hast Imam Mosque. Perhaps this chance encounter with two Muslim women taxi drivers—a first ever experience—slightly unnerved me.

The Hast Imam Mosque is a renovated as well as an expansive complex with towering minarets. It is definitely a testimonial to the powerful and continued presence of Islam and is a showcase of unique architectural design that has become specific to Central Asia. However, it is a kind of Islam that most Muslim states including Uzbekistan like to show to their people and the outside world. It is often seen as a kind of 'high Islam' that may be miles away from the grassroots practices and beliefs even in confessional states such as Saudi Arabia and Iran. The official apprehensions about a populist appeal of Islam always unnerves the rulers who, through information, education, and economy, would jealously prefer to retain a hold on public and private phases of their Muslim societies as any trajectory in the name of Islam could unleash nervousness. The official co-optation of Muslim clerical groups acting as intermediaries is pursued by almost every state that has a visible Muslim presence in its society. Given the political nature of Islam, like several other similar cases including Judaism in Israel, Hinduism in India, and Buddhism in Southeast Asia, official hierarchies try to control or contain religious elements. Political Islam at state level is quite different and even staid compared to the versions of political Islam appropriated and followed by several Muslim groups—both Salafis and Sufis. Unless we see some kind of synthesis and consensus reached through honest and genuine dialogue, these parallels will keep feeding into schisms and disorder. The Mushaf-i-Quran or the Quranic script attributed to the Prophet's companion and the third caliph, Hazrat Osman (RA), is securely kept in a purposeful facility right in the middle of the vast compound of the Hast Imam complex. The cubic building, an archival repository, has Hast Imam Mosque and Imam Bukhari Institute in its proximity and is accessible following thorough security checks. The script itself is showcased in a glass cabin on a raised platform displaying two folios from its middle portion. Dating from 640 CE, the rare script was brought to Samarkand by Tamerlane from Basra in the fourteenth century and was whisked away by the Russians in the 1860s following their conquest. It was returned to Tashkent in the 1920s and is definitely a splendid and equally historical volume inscribed in Kufic style on buckskin. In 1905, the Russians made 50 copies of this rare volume with a few on public display in this repository which also holds some of the earliest Persian and Arabic manuscripts. It was a wonderful experience to see this copy authenticated by the United Nations Educational, Scientific and Cultural Organization (UNESCO) and the Central Asian Muslim Board. I also noticed a visible sense of spontaneous respect and humility amongst both Uzbeks and other visitors. As mentioned above, the Quran is safely cased and one cannot check on the reported blood spots attributed to Osman on some of its folios. The caliph was killed while reciting it. This copy must be the contemporary of the Quranic folios 'discovered' at the University of Birmingham's Library in 2015. There is a similar copy in Kufic script at Topkapi Palace Museum in Istanbul that also claims to have belonged to Osman. Both Turks and Uzbeks have their own claims of the historicity of their respective copies that could belong to the same caliphal era. I spent quite some time in the side rooms where collections of Hadith as well as some of the early Quranic exegetes are kept. Arabic, Persian, and Chagatai Turkish, all in Arabic script, feature in all these masterpieces from the early Islamic era. On a piece of paper, I kept jotting down the titles and features of some of these classics which in case of poetry displayed some miniatures, while in a few cases, graphs and scales accompanied the prose. I positioned myself on a side bench facing the *Mushif*.[10] Reflecting on my presence amongst Islam's rare manuscripts, I had kept venturing into the side rooms to ascertain 'one' more look at those books that once underwrote Islamic renaissance. While leaving the building, subdued and humbled, the historian in me had banished the tourist of a roving temperament and the former, having taken command, took me to Imam Bukhari's Institute where I spent the rest of the afternoon talking to students about their curriculum. I decided to walk back to the Kukeldash Madrassa and on the way took a left turn to visit another historic complex where Emperor Babur's grandfather, Yunas Khan, and some other known personalities of the past are buried.

I was subdued more than being exasperated by a piercing sun. So much of the past had unfolded before me that I was shaken out of my own bliss with some familiar Urdu words as I noticed a group of Indian visitors boarding their conveyance. They had just come back after visiting Hast Imam and were now on their way to Tashkent's most beautiful building, the Kukeldash Madrassa. We exchanged smiles and moved on until I caught them again when they emerged out of the seminary and got lost in the crowd of worshippers and shoppers heading towards the nearby Chorsu Bazaar. While I was climbing up the steps, an elderly

Uzbek gentleman came up to me and gave me a bear hug the moment he came to know that I was a 'wandering historian' from the other side of the Hindu Kush! I knew this was both a welcome and farewell from the land of Avicenna, Al-Biruni, Imam Bukhari, Firdausi, Tamerlane, Ulugh Beg, and of course Babur!

Notes

1. Dinara Sultanova, trans., 'Selected Gazels of Navoiy,' *Internet Archive*, 2015.
2. A covered underground well having steps down to the water.
3. Abu-'r-Raihān Muḥammad Ibn-Aḥmad al-Bīrūnī, *Alberuni's Indica: (a Record of the Cultural History of South Asia about A.D. 1030)*, ed. Ahmad H. Dani (Islamabad: University of Islamabad Press, 1973).
4. For the famous gun since the WWI and the local museum, see 'Dhulmial gun,' *Flickr*, https://www.flickr.com/photos/tango48/3379221125/.
5. For more on the professor, see a note by his daughter, 'Remembering Dr Hussein Mullick,' Haider Ali Hussein Mullick and Mushaal Hussein Mullick, *The News*, August 12, 2008, http://watandost.blogspot.co.uk/2008/08/remembering-drhussein-mullick.html.
6. Shauna Singh Baldwin is an author of several historical novels, essays, and short stories published in North America and India. See *What the Body Remembers* (Delhi: Rupa & Co., 2011).
7. For more information, see Mark Mazower, *Salonica: City of Ghosts* (London: Harper, 2005).
8. Rustam Qobil, 'Uzbekistan: Land of a thousand shrines,' *BBC*, September 16, 2018; 'Tomb of Daniel at Samarkand: 18m long sarcophagus of a constantly growing dead prophet,' *Atlas Obscura*, https://www.atlasobscura.com/places/tomb-daniel-samarkand.
9. Christine D. Baker, *Gale Researcher Guide for: Tamerlane and the Timurid Empire* (Ann Arbor: Gale, Cengage Learning, 2018).
10. A manuscript or a primary source-material.

10

Jerusalem:
A Journey Across Contested Histories

'I do not understand a word you say but I'm not so bad in guessing. I guess you are asking me about the buses; I only know about No. 18 that connects my part of Jerusalem with the Old City and even takes you to Yad Vashem and beyond,' a young Israeli girl figured out right away that I was neither a Yemeni Jew nor a North African immigrant; instead I was some Asian visitor who did not speak Hebrew, though could still be passed off as a possible non-white Jew. This happened near the King David Hotel and was just one in a series of such encounters within a few days of my reaching Jerusalem. While passing by a newly-built synagogue in the Gonen area, a young cyclist had approached me to inquire about some address in Hebrew, assuming that I knew the language. When I gave my seat to an elderly couple on No. 18, my polite English elicited some curiosity and friendly smiles all around as it appeared to have had disclosed a 'foreigner amongst us'. When I narrated these encounters to Astor during a meal at a restaurant, she was happily amused since she had forewarned me about possible rude behaviour from some unexpected places, given the fact that I did not speak any Hebrew which could mean that I was a non-Jewish stranger. I walked and bussed myself all over Jerusalem and made special efforts to talk to all kinds of people, irrespective of their creed or age. Astor had equally hinted on the 'advantages' of being an English speaker in a country where both Israelis and Palestinians desired to attain excellence in this language. Of course, my own polite and often general conversations with people, especially Jews, were meant to seek out their reaction about the presence of a British Muslim of Pakistani origin; perhaps my age and profession proved quite helpful here.

My visit to Jerusalem came about largely because of an academic-friend who had volunteered her apartment back home while pursuing her own research at the Sackler Library in Oxford. Her children, Astor and Sam, offered to chaperon me around on some specific occasions. Equipped with a place to live and useful contacts and information on bus routes and a guidebook in my backpack, again lent by a senior historian-friend, I found myself at Luton's airport one bright early September morning. The alert Israeli security staff was certainly amused at my keenness to visit the historic city but did have questions about my place of birth and the duration of my residence in Britain. My British passport changed several hands and hush-hush observations between the staff, and supervisor ensued until I remembered the letter from Professor G. that confirmed my identity and academic interest in visiting Israel and East Jerusalem. Beautifully handwritten, this letter was in fact my de facto visa to embark on the journey to Israel and a source of great reassurance during my longer walks, bus journeys, and forays into all the holy places appropriated and jealously guarded by the devotees of all three faiths.

***

The plane bound for the Holy Land had mostly Caucasian passengers with one or two exceptions like me, and from beverages to food, it was a kosher affair, fully orientating me for my destination ahead. I was curious about how the Orthodox Jews were faring in terms of food since their rules are stricter than those of an average Muslim; Jews often bring along their own edibles. However, not finding any in my sight, I continued reading the tourist guide on Jerusalem. Flying time from Luton to Tel Aviv was half of what Pakistani or Indian destinations from London would incur, though slightly more than what it takes to get to Istanbul. I knew that soon after touching the Lebanese horizons that we had started our descent. Lebanon was my earliest encounter with the Middle East in 1974, and its pluralism and cultural openness had stayed with me as had the nostalgic reminisces of Khalil Gibran. Professor Fauzi Najjar, my teacher at MSU, and several Arab friends had certainly built up some kind of special relationship with this small country that often appeared to be an island of peace in a sea of turbulence. In the 1980s, when Lebanon exploded at all its various fault lines, I was no less shocked the way a decade later Yugoslavia shocked everyone who had essentialized the longevity of an operative secularism and stable pluralism. Israel, Syria, USA, France, Iran, and several other regional and global players had turned this beautiful country into a cauldron like it was for a while during the Crusades. The falling apart of Lebanon, and especially the urban mayhem in a cosmopolitan Beirut, forewarned similar scenarios in Kabul, Sarajevo, Mostar, Karachi, Baghdad, Libya, Yemen, and then in Syria—a kind of dominoes causing each other to fall in a rather systematic but no less painful way. The professor's handwritten letter was quite effective in hastening a visa stamp on my British passport, and I was soon waiting for a Nesher taxi to ferry me to the 'city upon the hills'. If not for his Hebrew or accented English, the driver could have been an Arab or a Baloch. He was possibly a Yemeni or Moroccan or Arab Jew who was a bit curious about a lanky passenger who carried a scribbled address in the 'newer' part of Jerusalem not far from its metropolitan buildings. The Ben Gurion Airport serves both Tel Aviv and Jerusalem; a motorway going east is the main artery connecting it with an ever-growing, diverse, and perhaps the most historic and no less contentious city in the world. If not for signs in Hebrew, the road and buildings on either sides or extensive farmlands could pass for a region in Southern Italy or Spain, given a similar Mediterranean climate and the nature of the terrain. I could well imagine the generations of people who had lived, tilled, and toiled here before it became the heartland of a new country with multitudes of refugees and immigrants filtering in from the ghettoes and kibbutzim across Europe. A major part of the Europeanization of the world, the Holy Land experienced migrations, colonization, and cultural conflicts between the newcomers and the indigenous people until the European leaders, for their own reasons, sought various solutions to what they called 'the Jewish problem'. Anti-Semitism, the Holocaust, and the imperial prerogatives converged to create a new state that had been germinated as a utopia in the heady days of nationalism in Europe. Zionism was both a romantic and a colonizing ideology which appropriated history, religion, and some kind of racial exceptionalism to push for a state anchored on primordial pretensions. This state had survived its early challenges and, in the process, had instigated another wave of Jewish migrants from Afro-Asian lands, though power and privileges remained in the hands of their Caucasian 'senior' counterparts. More recently, Russian Jews came in huge numbers to fashion this state into their own unique vision without any reverence or interest in the native realities of this historic land. The Jewish influx, at the behest of the state and Zionist propounders, has been recently attracting Ethiopians, Indians, and Latin Americans who are racially adjudged to qualify as the lost tribes of Jews. These groups benefit from quick citizenship whereas the Palestinians, for generations, continue to wither as refugees in the turbulent lands all around their original home.

***

Dropping other passengers on the way and encircling several hillside residences peering from behind the tall trees in a cool September evening, the van finally disgorged me outside an apartment block. Astor waited for me at the right point with the keys to the apartment while I got off the van with the driver asking her, 'Is this gentleman your visitor?' Feeling reassured, he took off while we climbed up a few stairs to the second floor. Ensconced amidst rows of books and overlooking green lawns of a school with some American students having a late evening cookout, I soon felt at home and let Astor return to her own flat. I had already memorized the locations of the nearest shopping centre, the bus stop to board the bus for East Jerusalem, and had a hazy idea of where the Museum of Islamic Arts happened to be. Of course, I wanted to visit all those places right away but it being a rather late hour, I opted to make myself some tea remembering the tea mat on my desk in Bath: 'When nothing seems to work, there is still tea and cake'.

For a pilgrim or a casual tourist, Jerusalem, especially its eastern part, the Old City, is overwhelming and, even for a detached historian, it is an exceptional place where cultures, creeds, classes, complexions, and contestations dare a probing eye. It is a city where the 'notorious' Huntingtonian clash of cultures finds its affirmation as well as its negation. The Haredi Jews can be seen here daily, hurrying towards the Western Wall, reading the Torah prayers and carefully treading busy streets while passing by the robed Orthodox bishops and elderly Arab sheikhs donning their keffiyeh. Along with these followers of the Abrahamic religions, 'the city upon hills' receives a steady stream of visitors, pilgrims, spies, and media pundits. It is certainly awash with watchful and armed security guards representing the young and ambitious State of Israel and those from the Palestinian Authority, whose 'authority' is strictly ceremonial. It is certainly a geopolitical front and quite prone to periodic volatility where parallel territorial claims, rival theological carousing, respective historical discourses, and competitive nationalist ethos have refused to subside. With all its tensions and dissensions, it is a unique city that grows on a visitor, combining in itself Makkah with Rome and Bethlehem with Benares (Varanasi). Long after the morning prayers have been offered at Al-Aqsa, Omar Mosque, and several others, groups of uniformed children begin their daily yatras to their schools, eyeing sweet shops lining narrow lanes, housing some of the oldest Sufi hospices overlooked by Roman arches. On Friday, the Old City is jam-packed with streams of Palestinians on their way to congregational prayers at Al-Aqsa and the Haram al-Sharif—the Dome of Rock—the third holiest Muslim site in the world. The Jerusalem of the past few decades has become an epitome of claims and counter-claims signalling as if the Medieval Crusades have never been away from its urban ethos, and the comparatively peaceful realms of the Mamluks and the Ottomans are a distant dream.

Amidst throngs of pilgrims and visitors, passing by hospices, souvenir shops, and bakeries, one may walk up to Church of the Holy Sepulchre where Jesus was crucified. A grave within this historic and immensely majestic edifice is also a reminder of a parallel narrative on the man who at the prime of his youth had been tried and shackled by the Romans. The trial itself took place further down towards the Muslim part of the city, not too far from the famous Damascus Gate and close to a Naqshbandia hospice which still retains some of the antique slabs and earthenware. The subdued pilgrims walk across Via Dolorosa to reach this former Roman court which is now a church sporting a small garden within its sanctuary. Despite an ever-dwindling number of Palestinian Christians, this city retains all its denominations and respective churches whose evolution is owed to various contestations which certainly fill the annals of the most historicized city on earth. The Western Wall is situated adjacent to the Harmain Sharif (Al-Aqsa and the Dome) and in between lies a small covered bazaar which, in addition to chai places, houses an old madrassa. Hemmed in between the Aqsa and the Wall, this tunnel-like market—a reminder of the great bazaars of Istanbul and Isfahan—is quite symbolic as it highlights the proximity of two preeminent places claimed by two Abrahamic faiths, who otherwise, until the past century, did not experience many flashpoints. This uneasy neighbourhood could have become the beacon of a cerebral coexistence that for centuries had featured in Muslim-Jewish relations across the three continents, however, it now stands as an evidence of the delicate and even banal nature of the city's volatile politics. Observing chess playing Palestinian elders sipping their tea or vending their goods and Jews praying just a few yards away on the other side may let one forget that it is a rather tenuous peace that pervades precariously in this sanctified neighbourhood.

The Western Wall has separate sections for men and women to pray. Both groups are supposed to cover their heads which underlines the fact that gender relations and body coverings are not only limited to Islam but are instead shared by all religions with almost similar intensity. I spent quite some time facing the Western Wall while keeping a safe distance from the women's enclosure until some Indian Jews, who visit Israel every year since half of their family is settled in West Jerusalem, offered me a kippah. I had been hearing familiar Hindi-Urdu words and, despite the dwindling Jewish community in India, this family was devotedly Indian.[1] In fact, I had met them outside Yad Vashem the previous day where, overwhelmed by human cruelty and caprice displayed during the Holocaust, I had taken refuge in a solitary corner staring at countless pairs of shoes belonging to the victims in Poland. After salaam and shalom, our discussion had centred on some common acquaintances including Nissim Ezekiel (1924–2004), whom I had the privilege of meeting in Lahore at a literary session in 1985. My surprise knew no bounds when I was told that within this small group of Jews from Cochin, one of the ladies happened to be the niece of the famous man of letters.

When I visited Al-Aqsa for the second time on a quiet late morning, I was allowed to go inside the main building. I was only allowed in after my recitation of certain Quranic passages certifying my Muslim credentials as there is always a genuine concern of some hothead getting into the holy sanctum with the intention of committing mischief. I could not believe that I was at a place which during the Prophetic era was the first Muslim Qiblah before Makkah assumed that status though the Holy Land was conquered by the Muslims in 638 CE during the reign of Caliph Omar—just six years after the death of the Prophet (PBUH). The ceremonial handing over of the city's keys from its Christian patriarchs to the new rulers had happened on a Friday, right in front of the Church of the Holy Sepulchre—an open site which houses the Omar Mosque now. The simple structure of the Al-Aqsa Mosque, its ornate work on the wooden ceilings and piles of Quran and Islamic literature by the marble pillars reminded me of the dominant Ottoman imprints on what were the original Umayyad architectural features; although they had been seriously damaged in the enduring series of the Crusades. The Dome of Rock was built seven decades after the death of the Prophet (PBUH) during the caliphal reign of Abdul Malik whose son, Walid, is accredited with the concurrent conquests of Spain, Central Asia, and the Indus Valley—all happening between 711–2. By that time, Islamic polity had transformed itself into a monarchical order as these Umayyad caliphs were deeply influenced by Byzantine statecraft and focused on Jerusalem while shying away from Makkah. In reality, the people of Makkah and Medina, known as Hejazis, often raised questions about their legitimacy to the caliphate which to them was a rather spiritual assignment and not a grand entitlement. The latter had internalized a less mundane form of the caliphate and, given the Umayyad hostility towards the Prophet's descendants, the new rulers concentrated on Jerusalem, Aleppo, and Damascus as their metropolitan favourites.[2] In 750, the Umayyads, were overthrown by another dynasty from Makkah, the Abbasids, whose support mainly came from Persia and beyond, generally known as Khorasan, the adjacent regions in present-day Iran, Afghanistan, and Pakistan. The Abbasids ruled these regions until Mongol invasions in the thirteenth century. They maintained a kind of equilibrium between the three spiritual centres of Makkah, Jerusalem, and Medina though their own capital was Baghdad, known for scholarly pursuits and thronged by philosophers, jurists, scientists, historians, and poets from across the various religious traditions. The Abbasids were deeply influenced by the Persian (Sassanid) monarchical traditions and in several cases their caliphs came close to the classical Greek ideal of a philosopher-king. While the Abbasid caliphate faced numerous doctrinal and sectarian issues emanating from an increasingly plural Muslim world, Muslim Spain on the contrary was more at ease with its own ethno-religious plurality until the events of Reconquista and Inquisition. Many Spanish Muslim notables such as Ibn Arabi (1165–1240) and Ibn Jubayr (1145–1217) visited these holy places and have left copious accounts which are quite revealing for any student of theology and history. Both of them were philosophers followed by eminent scholars such as Maimonides (1132–1204), Ibn Rushd/Averroes (1126–98), Ibn Tufail (1105–85), and Ibn Khaldun (1332–1406) who in their own realms were Renaissance men for Judaism and Islam, respectively.

The early Crusaders have left ebullient accounts of their conquest of the Holy Land in 1099 and this triumphalism does not shirk from offering the gory details of massacres of Muslims and Jews in the Old City.[3] These residents were asked to gather at Al-Aqsa and were mercilessly slaughtered with the mosque's compound drowned in knee-deep blood, as recorded in contemporary accounts. The ideology of holy war was internalized by both Christians and Muslims with a greater emphasis on martyrdom. A century later, when Salah ad-Din/Saladin (1137–93) recaptured Jerusalem after defeating the forces of Richard the Lion Heart (1157–98) and his allies in 1191, he declared the holy city equally accessible for all three communities.[4] King Richard, a native Oxonian, was born at Beaumont Palace and amidst a tortuous warfare also shared a major claim in chivalry with Saladin.[5] Saladin's chronicler, Baha ud-Din ibn Shaddad (1145–1234), has left us detailed accounts of how the Kurdish Muslim Sultan[6] sent his own horse as a gift to Richard when the latter lost his mount. The story about his physician treating the English king is also recorded in those chronicles.[7] Jerusalem was defended from the Mongols by the Mamluks, especially Sultan Baibars (1260–72), who was in fact a former Circassian Muslim slave. He ensured the reconstruction of the walls, Al-Aqsa Mosque, and hospices in the Old City. His imprints in the city are still visible like their earlier Roman counterparts.

Following Ottoman victory over Egyptian Mamluks in 1517, Jerusalem like Makkah, Medina, and Baghdad was administered by the Osmanlis who added outer walls, refurbished older buildings, redecorated the main entrances, and ensured proper management of Jewish and Christian holy places. In fact, the upkeep and keys of the Church of Holy Sepulchre had been given to a Muslim Palestinian family following an enduring dissension amongst the feuding Christian sects. The Ottomans had wrested Constantinople from the Byzantines in 1453 but retained the Archbishop of Greek Orthodox Church within the city. Their proper upkeep of Jerusalem, to a great extent, meant pacification of the Orthodox, Copts, Armenians, Catholics, and Lutherans who, in many cases, made a major section of their subjects and were defined as a millet. The Ottoman Empire included an overwhelming population of Christians in the Balkans, Greece, Armenia, and Georgia, along with Arab Christians and certainly the Sephardic Jews. In fact, Constantinople was a Muslim minority city until the exiles from the Balkans during the last quarter of the nineteenth century radically changed its demography. All the way up to 1917—the time of the Balfour Declaration by the British and secret Sykes-Picot Pact of 1916 between the British and the French for the imperial division of a post-Ottoman Middle East—the Holy Land did not witness any major volatility amongst the followers of the three faiths. Interestingly, hundreds of thousands of Spanish Jews had been saved by the Ottomans during the Inquisition and Expulsions and they were encouraged to settle in Constantinople, Salonica, Sarajevo, and across North Africa. It is revealing to know that Salonica, modern day Thessaloniki in Greece, had been the only Jewish majority city until the 1940s when 40,000 of its inhabitants lost their lives in the Holocaust.[8]

During my recent visit to Bosnia, a few years after the war and the publication of my book on the same, I was pleasantly surprised to see a meticulous restoration of the Jewish cemetery on Mount Igman overlooking Sarajevo. During the war in the 1990s, the cemetery had been totally desecrated by Serb snipers who used its vantage position to bomb Sarajevo while imposing the longest-ever siege in recent European history. This restoration and proper preservation of Europe's largest Jewish cemetery by the small vulnerable Muslim state of Bosnia deeply inspired me at a time when hypothesis about cultural clashes are so ascendant. The Jewish Museum in Sarajevo also escaped shelling as a Jama Mosque and a Catholic Cathedral protected it on two sides. It is not out of place to suggest that some of the founders of Israel, such as David Ben-Gurion, once held military positions in the Ottoman troops but subsequently opted to support Britain in its war with the Sublime Porte, since the former's victory would duly help the Zionist objectives.[9] When colonial-Orientalists such as T. E. Lawrence, Henry McMahon, Gertrude Bell, and Louis Massignon were promising monarchical inducements to some Arab chieftains to rebel against the Ottomans, the War Office was worried about the sensitivities of South Asian Muslim troops within the British forces. On the eve of General Allenby's entry into Jerusalem in 1917, following the Ottoman defeat, an advisory was sent around to the press advising against highlighting Crusading symbolism so as not to warrant any Muslim antagonism since India was already astir with a pro-Khilafat movement.[10] In fact, other than an 800-year-old Indian hospice in the Old City, there are graves of several Indian Muslim pilgrims near Al-Aqsa and the Omar Mosque.[11] The first-ever Muslim graduate from Oxford's Lincoln College, Maulana Mohammad Ali Jauhar (1878–1931) was in fact the leader of this Khilafat Movement, and it was during one of his visits to the United Kingdom for political negotiations that he passed away.[12] He had willed to be buried in Jerusalem instead of a 'colonized India'. Hailing from Rampur and having studied at Aligarh, Jauhar had established the pioneer Asian student society at Oxford University, the Majlis. Although, for most of his life he had been addressing political rallies, or like his colleague, Mahatma Gandhi (1869–1948), the Pan-Islamist remained incarcerated.[13] Another notable Indian Muslim buried in Jerusalem is Begum Ghaffar Khan, who hailed from the Frontier and died in the Omar Mosque after having suffered a concussion from a fall. She was the wife of the legendry 'Frontier Gandhi' Khan, Abdul Ghaffar Khan (1890–1988), the Pashtun leader who followed non-violence and had begun political defiance even before Gandhi landed back in India.[14]

In general, a routine curiosity of Jerusalem's on-going political realities pushes one back into a labyrinth of an unending spectrum of eventful epochs which continue to feed into its present. Like its bustling streets, watchful arches, fragrant food stalls, streams of worshippers, and visitors, all minutely watched by Israeli police and security agents, the Old City, like Old Fes is still medieval and even ancient. It is certainly a city of parallel histories which bestow upon it an unparalleled uniqueness with the three Abrahamic faiths not only vigilantly watching over one another but also trying to endure a medley of conflicts which have rather become its perennial attributes. The city is overlooked by rows of white settlements and apartment blocks along with several new buildings rising within the old quarters. It is also surrounded by a 22-metre-high parameter wall which makes it the only city divided on the basis of religion and ethnicity, and that too at a time when pundits never tire of talking of globalization. Here, one group of people, even if they happen to be recent immigrants, have become citizens whereas another section of its populace is downgraded from citizens to residents. Depending upon one's own discretionary choice of the term, Israeli occupation or unification of Jerusalem has resulted in a radical transformation of the city, where new hierarchies and selective rights of citizenship, property, and mobility have been inducted with its past being left at the mercy of unilateral modernism. This transformation first began in West Jerusalem where, amidst apartment blocks, prosperous bungalows, buzzing restaurants, and official buildings, it is still not uncommon to come across places which originally belonged to the Arabs in the pre-1948 era. For instance, one of my favourite places in that area was the Museum of Islamic Arts which sits in the bygone affluent Arab neighbourhood. The museum houses some rare collections donated by the rich friends of Israel while its basement holds a unique collection of watches and clocks which have their own interesting history. I was living in a flat owned by a senior academic friend and was often welcomed by friendly cats of the neighbourhood. This part of West Jerusalem could have been a familiar place in Berkeley, Nice, or Bristol. My neighbours in the block were all of Caucasian origin with seniors amongst them being looked after by Sri Lankan and Filipino nurses who often took the wheelchair-bound pensioners on their early evening outings. I often used a volley of shaloms to my kippah-clad neighbours who might have had wondered about my complexion, creed, or the country of my origin as I could easily pass for a Yemeni, Somali, Sudanese, Ethiopian, and in some cases a South Asian but certainly not a Euro-American Jew. My familiarity with the buses, streets, and restaurants quenched my curiosity to walk in and around the entire city in addition to a visit to the Dead Sea which on a hot day I was trying to dive into while wrestling with salt on my body. Sleek roads circling the island-like Arab areas and especially the Bedouin settlements overlooked by craggy hill crops took me back to the Biblical times with the historian within me kowtowing to an archaeologist.

Despite it being September, the daylight had its own share of heat; tall trees and parks in a highly modern West Jerusalem were a distant world from the Old City itself. In the evenings, under some of these tall trees, I could hear visiting American students discussing their academic and extracurricular activities until late, while in the morning, kites, crows, and parrots came alive. A superstore next to a synagogue, located within a covered shopping centre, was my daily haunt for shopping and grabbing a cup of coffee while reading a book before taking off for the Old City. I marvelled at those fresh, succulent vegetables and wide varieties of breads and olives and wondered about their histories and soil. This shopping centre could have been anywhere in the West; initially, as with everyone else, the security guard would shuffle through my bag but eventually began to spare me which I thought was quite generous. The daughter of my academic friend called me every evening to check on my welfare and to ensure that I had not been discomfited by any rude behaviour. Astor thought my height and English would keep me in good stead. I once went to a kind of kibbutzim to attend a marriage party of her extended family where an immense amount of warmth and affection competed with a generous amount of Mediterranean and East European food. The fact that I was accompanied by an Israeli female allowed the armed guards on the external security parameters to relax though their guns in the holsters reminded me of the frontier nature of this society where, other than Hebrew, Polish and Yiddish both reverberated in the air. On the way out of West Jerusalem, we had driven through a natural reserve of mainly pinewoods that resembled a section of Yosemite Park.

Astor's brother, a television producer, drove me around to see the older and newer parts of his city including a visit to the Hebrew University where, other than a splendid lunch with an eminent academic, I saw some Palestinian female students. A curious encounter took place at the library's entrance when a Persian Jew was overjoyed to hear me speak his mother tongue and quickly invited over a colleague to shake hands with me: 'Iftikhar, this is Moshe, a Kurdish chap and does understand a bit of Farsi'. I was certainly overwhelmed by this appropriation of old and new by the '*Muslim*' Jews, though for some reason they are often collectively called Arab Jews. By the entrance to this lovely campus of the university overlooking the Harmain Sharif and the Wall, neighboured by separate Christian and Jewish cemeteries, I saw Palestinian children selling olive branches as souvenirs from the Holy Land, while a couple of Bedouin saddled their camels for some expected tourists. Contrasts between the university populace and these Arabs would never leave me alone; I felt embarrassed since a few shekels or a passing smile were not what these people deserved. Once I was inside the campus and walking across the well-tended lawns, jasmine bushes, and olive groves, an Israeli academic took me to a higher point of the university right behind the teaching block named after an American benefactor and showed me the cement wall separating Palestinians from Jewish areas. It was a curvy structure that tried to mingle in the dusty horizons yet could not hide the contrast on both its sides. 'Iftikhar! This wall is not to keep the suicide bombers away from us but is in fact erected to guard us against prying on the sordid life on the other side.'

My favourite spots for picnicking after walking across the Old City were just outside the Damascus Gate where I would buy Palestinian bread and sweets to munch on by the great Ottoman Wall surrounding the Old City. I often consumed tomatoes, cucumbers, and humus before sauntering into one of the cafés which reminded me of *chaikhana*s (tea house) across rural and tribal Pakistan. I sometime took the Sultan Suleiman Street to walk across to Salah ad-Din Street into Arab areas just outside the Damascus Gate before getting lost in streets named after Abu Bakr Siddique, Ali ibn Taleb, Khaled bin Walid, Ibn Battuta, Avicenna, and other eminent Muslims of the past until my walk ended at the American Colony Hotel. This part of the city has its own issues because here tensions occur quite often due to settlers trying to take over properties with all kinds of legal lacuna in their favour. I was often grieved to see quite a few Palestinian youths aimlessly milling around empty corners, given a very high rate of unemployment and a deepening sense of loss. Very few industrial and business opportunities exist for them unlike their privileged counterparts in West Jerusalem and in the rest of Israel for those who belong to a different class and community altogether. Even within one city like Jerusalem, there are two or even more cities where forces of contested histories, rivalling nationalisms, competitive religions, hierarchical classes, and varied complexions pervade. The aforementioned issues generally underpin conflicts where matters like individual rights, multiculturalism, self-determination, or a possible two-state solution with a shared metropolis appear simply chimerical. Jerusalem, a city of several histories and peoples, appears intent upon wiping out this plurality in favour of a single narrative which does not really bode well for its old and new inhabitants.

'The Jerusalem Syndrome' may inflict visitors to the city with its own paranoia and dilemma but its inhabitants certainly share a sense of antiquity, majesty, and melancholy. While the State of Israel, as per Zionism, has been steadily encroaching upon the Arab properties, which the latter call a regimented form of dispossession or *Nakba*, its own claims on the entire land, Ertz Israel, are based on religious specificity and racial particularism. Even many secular and atheist Jews subscribe to this sense of nativity despite the fact that most Israelis are not indigenous per se which, as posited by Ari Shavit, makes Israel 'a nation in doubt'.[15] For some Israeli academics such as Shlomo Sand, Jewish claims of belonging to one single root emanating from the Holy Land may not be sufficiently persuasive as Jews have a wide variety of ethnic origins. To him, a substantial conversion to Judaism happened under the auspices of the medieval Khazar Kingdom that was located in the Caucasus.[16] Accordingly, conversions to Judaism and Islam were happening concurrently. On the contrary, narratives by Paul Johnson and Simon Schama keep reminding us of the pre-Christian historicity of the Jewish people with their roots strictly in the Holy Land.[17] While Ben-Gurion and ultra-Zionists may view Palestinians as completely non-existent or as people who had moved into the regions latterly, the Palestinian national discourse posits them as indigenous people seeking their origins from Abraham through his son, Ishmael. The Palestinians, both in the refugee camps and in the Occupied Territories, resist becoming 'American Indians' on their own lands and nor do they accept a status which disallows them equal citizenship, the right of return, and equal claims on the city. It is certainly quite unfair to expect millions of Palestinians to forego their roots and history and, in the same way, it is unfair to overlook the pangs and pains of Jewish history all through the pogroms and Holocaust.[18] Israel's uniformist attitude to become an exclusive Jewish state only for Jews may have an understandable rationale in their painful history in Europe but certainly the Palestinians had no part in it until the dissensions in recent times began to underwrite mutual hostilities. The 1.5 million Arabs within Israel and those living as citizens of a future sovereign state can certainly reconstruct the centuries-old tradition of interdependence amongst the three communities with a shared administration of Jerusalem. Certainly, token measures,[19] within the context of denial and dispossession, do not augur well for a society which itself suffered heinous acts for so long and is thus expected to be more sensitive to the Palestinian plight than anybody else. The majority vote in the European Parliament on 17 December 2014 supporting an independent state of Palestine and the convention of 126 nations in Geneva in the same week, urging Israel to respect Palestinian rights besides withdrawing from the Occupied Territories, show that Israel needs to be proactive and forthcoming.[20] Its periodic invasions of Gaza and keeping its own people in a permanent state of fear and hostility only showcases a bleak sense of expediency amongst its leaders. Meanwhile, the liberal and critical opinion groups in Israel are weaker than ever and are silenced by being denounced as self-haters. In the same vein, voices critiquing Israeli policies are contemptuously dismissed as anti-Semitism which is not helpful to this nation and its well-wishers. Instead of exceling in rejection and animosity, the leaders must build bridges with the Palestinians and Muslims at large who are themselves tired of intra-state and inter-state violence, nor are they realistically waiting for the Jews to be pushed into the Mediterranean. After all, Noam Chomsky, Avi Shlaim, Ilan Pappé, and several other scholars and the former citizens of Israel with years of service in the Israel Defense Forces (IDF) are not just verbose peaceniks. These people desire a self-respecting and peaceful Middle East where Israel emerges as a power engine for peace and democracy, with Arabs as equal stakeholders in its stability and prosperity.

Notes

1. Edna Fernandes, *The Last Jews of Kerala* (London: Portbello, 2009).
2. Jerusalem like Makkah never became a centre of philosophers as that status was reserved for other imperial cities all the way from Damascus to Cairo and Baghdad to Istanbul and Delhi. I am indebted to Ziauddin Sardar for this point. See his exhaustive history of the Muslim holy city, *Mecca: The Sacred City* (London: Bloomsbury, 2014).
3. An Englishman wrote from Jerusalem in the 1090s about a fellow Crusader: 'He was not afraid to die for Christ. At long last crushed rather than conquered by spears, stones and lances, he sank to the ground and joyfully passed to heaven with the martyr's crown, triumphant'. Furthermore: 'Death is sweet when the victor lies encircled by the impious people he has slain with his victorious right hand. Such a great number of Turks had rushed in to attack ... In fact, rumour has it that one person was moved with more fervour than the rest. He cut off the man's genitals, and kept them safe for begetting children so that even when dead the man's member—if such a thing were possible—would produce an heir with courage as great as his'. Quoted in Christopher Tyerman, *The Crusades: A Very Short Introduction* (Oxford: Oxford University Press, 2005), 1–2.

4. There are several research works on the Crusades from contemporary Muslim viewpoint other than the chronicles of Baha ad-Din ibn Shaddad. See Amin Maalouf, *The Crusades Through Arab Eyes*, trans. J. Rothschild (London: Saqi Books, 1984).

5. Historiography on Crusades is quite extensive and even ever-expansive. See Thomas Asbridge, *The Crusades: The Authoritative History of War for the Holy Land* (London: Ecco, 2011); Steve Runciman, *A History of the Crusades*, 3 volumes, (Harmondsworth: Penguin Books, 1965).

6. For a biography of Saladin, see Geoffrey Hindley, *Saladin: The Hero of Islam* (London: Pen & Sword Military, 2010).

7. Eulogies were often accompanied by selective heroism as well where Richard is shown winning over Muslims. For instance, in Ladybird's series dating from the 1960s, the English king is presented as a very tall personality with a cross on his garb who is killing a whole bunch of short 'Saracens'; or Richard could even break iron with his sword, whereas Saladin's sharp sword would only cut a silk handkerchief into two.

8. For more details, see Mazower, *Salonica*.

9. For efforts by Theodore Herzl and others in seeking a firman to establish a Jewish state in Palestine and their rejection by Ottoman Caliph Abdul Hamid, see Philip Mansel, *Constantinople: City of World's Desire, 1453–1924* (London: John Murray, 1995).

10. The secret message noted: 'The attention of the press is again drawn to the undesirability of publishing any article, paragraph or picture suggesting that military operations against Turkey are in any sense a Holy War; a modern Crusade, or have anything whatever to do with religious questions. The British Empire is said to contain a hundred million Muhammadan subjects of the King and it is obviously mischievous to suggest that our quarrel with Turkey [the Ottomans] is one between Christianity and Islam'. Quoted in James E. Kitchen, *The British Imperial Army in the Middle East* (London: Bloomsbury, 2014), 72.

11. The hospice was established in commemoration of the 40-day meditation by Baba Fariduddin Ganjshakar (1173–1262), a Muslim Sufi buried in Punjab, Pakistan. This founder of Chishti Sufi order visited Jerusalem soon after its reconquest by Saladin.

12. For more on the Khilafat Movement and the Indo-Ottoman relations in a Pan-Islamic spirit, see M. Naeem Qureshi, *Pan-Islam in British Indian Politics: A Study of the Khilafat Movement, 1918–1924* (Leiden: Brill, 1999).

13. Mohammad Ali Jauhar's autobiography, *My Life*, was written while he was in jail and does not dwell on his studies at Oxford. For more on this connection, see Iftikhar H. Malik, *Islam, Nationalism, and the West: Issues of Identity in Pakistan* (Oxford: St. Antony's-Palgrave Series, 1999).

14. Khan Abdul Ghaffar Khan, *My Life and Struggle: Autobiography of Badshah Khan* (Delhi: Hind Pocket Books, 1969) and Khan Abdul Wali Khan, *Facts are Facts: the untold story of India's partition* (Delhi: Vikas, 1984).

15. Ari Shavit, *My Promised Land: the triumph and tragedy of Israel* (New York: Spiegel & Grau, 2013), xiv.
16. Shlomo Sand, *The Invention of the Jewish People* (London: Verso, 2009).
17. Paul Johnson, *A History of the Jews* (London: Harper, 2004) and Simon Schama, *The Story of the Jews: Finding the Words 1000 BCE–1492* (London: Vintage, 2014).
18. Andrew Roberts, 'From an Era of Refugee Millions, Only Palestinians Remain,' *International Herald Tribune,* November 21, 2014. In this piece, the British historian is surprised at Palestinian refugees for not having disconnected with the place of their origins. One wonders whether he would have recommended the same to anyone else!
19. Eetta Prince-Gibson, 'Jerusalem's Train to Nowhere,' *The International New York Times*, November 22, 2014.
20. Peter Beaumont, 'EU parliament backs Palestinian state "in principle",' *The Guardian*, December 18, 2014.

11

Maulana Rumi's Konya in Whirling Times: A Bridge So Far

> Why do you stay in prison?
> When the door is so wide open?
>
> Rumi[1]

'He is perhaps the most well-known Afghan for all times.' With this statement, I definitely shocked a few Turkish friends gathered by the entrance to the *rauza* (mausoleum) of Jalaluddin Rumi, known as the Maulana/Mevlana of Konya—the preeminent Sufi mentor and founder of the Mevlevi order. Rumi and Anatolia have become rightly intertwined in the same way as Shams Tabrizi and Rumi—the illustrious duo of the tutor and the taught—are inseparable. Balkh—once a city of great political, economic, intellectual, and cultural significance by virtue of its location on the Silk Road—like Merv, lay waste before the Mongol hordes who had come down from their steppes to destroy the contemporary kingdoms and empires in China, Central Asia, subcontinent, and West Asia.[2] With the Abbasid caliphate already on its deathbed and Maghreb and Spain under their own separate and weakened monarchies thanks to internecine warfare, the invasions by the Mongols and the Crusaders put Muslims in a precarious nutcracker. While Crusaders and the Great Khan might have caused and benefited from their unified followings, Muslims, like today's drift, awaited angelic deliverers to steer them out of internal chaos and external threats. For the second time since the death of the Prophet (PBUH), Islam, as per W. C. Smith, was in the throes of a global crisis threatening its extinction, though the Seljuks in Anatolia, and Shams ud-Din Iltutmish and Ghiyas ud din Balban in India, Yusuf ibn Tashfin in Spain, and Saladin in the Levant tried to stem these invasions in their own respective domains.[3] But a common, united, and spirited front could not evolve owning to sectarian chasms and ethno-regional rivalries with Assassins in their own pursuit of targeted killings of Muslim notables. Merv, the Seljuk capital and the biggest medieval city of 500,000 souls, celebrated by contemporary visitors due to its opulence, was destroyed in 1222 by Oulu Khan, the son of Genghis Khan who killed 700,000 people in the Seljuk heartland. The city, now in Turkmenistan, never recovered.

Bahauddin Walad (d. 1232), Rumi's father, like numerous other Muslim nobles, took to exile and reached Shiraz while passing through decimated regions of Khorasan. Walad was in fact a well-known mystic and jurist whose writings were subsequently compiled as *Ma'arif*. The Mongol assault was unrelenting and, in its wake, these Afghan and other Khorasani Muslims of influence and affluence moved further west and, after visiting Baghdad and Damascus in 1228, they chose to settle in Konya, the capital of Western Seljuk sultanate.[4] This was the heart of the Anatolian basin which had been formed by alluvial plains, low-lying hills, and conical pinnacles owing to volcanic eruptions in the past. Hemmed in by the sea and mountains, and featuring salt lakes and lush valleys, Anatolia became the abode of some of the earliest human communities. Like the Indus Valley, Anatolia developed its agrarian cultures until the Egyptians, Hittites, Persians, Greeks, and Romans ventured in at different times. It became the centrefold of Aryan and Greco-Roman mythologies which were institutionalized under various Persian, Greek, and Roman dynasties. That is why Turkey has the unique privilege of retaining the largest number of ancient monuments. Soon the Middle Eastern religions like Zoroastrianism, Judaism, and Christianity took their roots here as they had been adopted by respective dynasts, though not so smoothly. For instance, the Byzantine Emperor, Constantine, popularized Christianity and founded the city of Constantinople but also fervently held on to Greek mythologies of powerful gods such as Zeus and Apollo, exactly the way Macedonian Alexander had emerged as a synthesizer a millennium earlier.

The Seljuks[5] were from amongst the waves of Central Asian/Turkic tribes who, following the Arabs, Berbers, and Persians, inducted fresh energy and optimism into the Muslim world. The others being exhausted and in retreat, India and Anatolia emerged as the new centres of Muslim political salience soon to be joined by a reinvigorated Persia. The four early modern empires of the Muslim world—the Ottomans, Safavids, Shaybanis, and the Mughals—were Turkic and steadied the world of Islam for a time. However, their squabbles over Sunni-Shia issues, territorial wrangles, lack of a clear principle of succession, and irreverence towards the changing times and challenges sealed their fate until European powers with better organizational acumen and efficient navies were able to colonize vast swathes of Muslim territories.[6] Only Afghanistan, the birthplace of Rumi, remained nominally independent as the British and Russians could not fully subdue it and settled on a buffer status for this fiercely independent and traditional society. The Seljuks (written as Selcuks in modern Turkish), following a decisive victory at Manzikert in 1076 in eastern Anatolia, had moved further west, capturing extensive tracts. Sultan Suleiman ibn Qutulmush chose Konya (old name: Iconium), the Byzantine town in central Anatolia, as his capital largely because of its location in the middle which strategically tucked it away from any major threats that could have bedevilled this new sultanate. Konya and the treeless land around it reminded these Turks of their ancestral, rugged Central Asian steppes but, like the Mughals in India, Asia Minor, *Arz-i-Rum*, was now their home. This powerful state engaged in trade, arts, education, and despite various attacks by neighbouring tribes—the Assassins, Crusaders, and the Mongols—the Seljuks persisted until the Ottomans—Osmanlis—eventually took over.

Having been an integral part of the Roman and Byzantine empires, Anatolia was called Rum and that is how Jalaluddin Rumi acquired his *nisbeti* (geneological linkages) and literary name. One of the illustrious Seljuk kings, Sultan Alaeddin Keykubad, had eagerly invited scholars, artists, architects, administrators, and theologians to his kingdom to run madrassas that were to transform his empire into a land of preeminent institutions. He was the host to these Afghan and Khorasani émigrés who helped Persian language flourish while offering a synthesis amongst Greek, Persian, Arab, and Roman scholarly and philological traditions. The Seljuks were proud, acculturative, and tolerant Muslims, and their protection and patronage of the Greeks helped both ways. The erstwhile Christian communities ensconced in cave dwellings in Cappadocia and further west were won over through mutual coexistence and by avoiding any forcible conversions. So while Rumi's family had to suffer due to dislocation, personal losses, and an arduous journey to *Arz-i-Rum*, their acculturation in the Perso-Muslim culture of Konya happened smoothly and, like the Christian and Jewish residents, these exiles were promptly indigenized and even assumed elite positions. No wonder very few people realize that Rumi was in fact a Bactrian but became the undisputed symbol of Anatolian, Turkish, and Sufi identities. Since his translations during the nineteenth century, this most illustrious spiritual poet has become the embodiment of universal humanism. Within the theological domain, both Shams and Rumi bring in *Ajam*,[7] and Arab together by congregating Shias, Sunnis, Sufi, and secularists on a broad platform. Undoubtedly, very few individuals can claim such a status in world history.

It will be unfair to discredit Rumi's immersion in contemporary Christian theology and asceticism which, other than his philosophical and mystical thoughts, is evident from the top minaret of his *rauza*. Anatolia had been the centrefold of Perso-Greek conflicts extended over centuries. This rivalry was inherited by the Sassanids and Byzantines—the successive empires to the Achaemenid and Hellenic legacies. Certainly Alexander in the early fourth century BCE was not out to conquer the entire world; instead he was determined to put an end to Persian control of Anatolia, Egypt, Mesopotamia, Afghanistan, Sogdiana, present-day Pakistan, and Persia proper. The Anatolians welcomed this 20-year-old Macedonian who symbolically combined Zeus with Pharaoh, and quite shrewdly sought collaboration from Anatolians and Egyptians who desired an end to Persian hegemony.[8] Alexander founded several Alexandrias, temples, and other such institutions to ensure his empire. He passed away when he was only 34, with his final battles having been waged against the Pashtuns in Swat and Punjabis by River Jhelum.[9] Hard life, adventurism, and alcohol caused the early death of a man who often became synonymous with Dhul-Qarnayn for some early Muslims. His empire was divided amongst his generals but the most powerful legacy of this disciple of Herodotus and student of Aristotle augured the Hellenistic age.

Greek (Orthodox) influences reflect in the circular domes of Turkish mosques, madrassas, and shrines. While Greek philosophy reverberated in debates between the purists and syncretists, Persian statecraft proved popular with the Seljuk Sultans and their counterparts across Asia. Vizier Nizam al-Mulk Tusi (1018–92), a Khorasani like Firdausi, had contributed to *Siyasat-Nama*, a treatise on political philosophy and governance with its enduring impact on Seljuk governance.[10] The green fluted dome, the most illustrious symbol of Konya, rises above Rumi's sarcophagus and is surrounded by several domes whereas other Seljuk tombs all around the old city centre and near Alâeddin Palace and mosque have spire-like conical structures rising above the respective graves. These shrines, built of stone blocks or thin bricks and plastered by tiles depicting Quranic calligraphy, had a mosque and a madrassa in their proximity. For instance, the tomb of Syed Tacul-Vezir, built in 1238, has a pointing spire that resembles volcanic chimney-like structures in Cappadocia which were once home to major Christian communities all the way until 1923 when, under the Treaty of Lausanne, Turkey and Greece agreed upon an exchange of population. England's St. George in fact was a Cappadocian from Goreme while St. Basil was from Uchisar, the town known for its chimney-like volcanic dwellings which reverberate in Maulana Rumi's rising green fluted dome, on Tacul-Vezir's tomb and on Ince Minaret Madrassa.

The Seljuk sultanate was a centre of classical and Islamic learning and attracted scholars from far and wide, reintroducing Europe to its erstwhile Greek philosophical heritage which had been banished due to clerical opposition for obvious reasons. West Europeans were familiarized with Plato, Socrates, Aristotle, and many other luminaries through their Arabic and Persian translations undertaken in Baghdad, Damascus, Palmyra, Aleppo, and Konya through the efforts of pioneering intermediaries such as Adelard of Bath (Latin: Adelardus Bathensis). Adelard (1080–1152), who had come into contact with Muslim learning in France after a sojourn in Sicily, spent nine years in Aleppo studying with Muslim scholars. On his return to England, he translated Euclid, al-Khwarizmi, and several others into Latin for a wider audience of British and European scholars. There is a strong possibility that it was Adelard, who translated al-Khwarizmi's major work, *Kitab al-Jabr* (The Compendious Book on Calculation by Completion and Balancing), commonly known as Algorithm, which inducted Arab numerals and zero into English usage by gradually replacing their Roman counterparts. This was not a minor achievement, given the fact that both the ancient Greeks and Romans were not familiar with zero and had their own formulas of arithmetical measurements.[11] Jalaluddin Rumi too spent some time in Aleppo with some contemporary eminent scholars. In the recent civil war, this world heritage city appears to have suffered immeasurably.

Shams and Rumi

Bahauddin Walad's academic and religious pursuits during the thirteenth century were carried on by his son and heir, Jalaluddin Rumi, until on a fateful day of November 1244, right in the heart of Seljuk city—area called Alaaddin—he met Shah Shamsuddin *Parinda* (bird), a wandering fakir from Tabriz. This eclectic encounter transformed Rumi as well as the theocratic history of mysticism and Persian literature for all the centuries to come.[12] Reportedly, Rumi, the illustrious son of an eminent scholar and an aristocrat, was riding his horse followed by a retinue of his students when this ascetic stopped him in the middle of his path posing some difficult questions for the 37-year-old tutor. According to Annemarie Schimmel (1922–2003), the eminent authority on Rumi and Islamic Mysticism, Shams Tabrizi changed Rumi's thinking and lifestyle altogether.[13] Rumi used to hold tutorials in the nearby Iplikci Mosque and like his name and his persona once exuded academic authority and scholarly awe. Shams stayed in Konya, mostly ensconced with his new disciple for days on end which irritated many members of Rumi's family and some other people who thought that this *qalandar* (ascetic) had waylaid Rumi. There were all kinds of hushed questions being raised about their mutual relationship that to some was too intimate and was at an expense of Rumi ignoring his family and students.[14] Shams-Rumi parleys, amongst other numerous studies, have been fictionalized quite lucidly in Elif Shafak's novel, *The Forty Rules of Love*.[15] As per traditions, Shams took off one day, leaving Rumi in a quandary, until the news came that the poet-mystic was in Damascus. Rumi sent his son, Sultan Walad, to bring him back.

Shams stayed in Konya for four years and spent most of his time with Rumi, often engaged in debates and discussions causing prolonged absences. He was married off to a young lady who worked as a help in

Rumi's household. On the night of 5 December 1248, both Shams and Rumi were holding their deliberations together when the former took off through a back door never to reappear. There are various interpretations of what happened to Shams; to some he was murdered while to others, true to his literary name *Parinda*, Shams departed for other lands, leaving Rumi in even more distress which led to his writing poems and eventually turning towards *Sama'a* (sky).[16] After some time, Rumi came quite close to one of his students, Salah ud-Din-e Zarkub, the goldsmith, but this friendship did not fill the gap left by Shams. After Zarkub's death, Rumi would recite his poetry to another student, Husam Chulabi, who recorded the six volumes of his *Masnavi* during the last decade of Rumi's life; he is also buried in his close proximity under the same dome. Rumi used to recite his verses while circling around which led to the well-known tariqa of 'whirling' dervishes. Rumi's *Diwan* consists of 40,000 verses often induced by a trance-like state. In addition, it also includes 1,600 quatrains whereas *Masnavi*, his seminal masterpiece, has 25,000 verses divided into six books.

Rumi's verses mix worldly themes with spiritual deliberations often narrated through parables and rendered in classical Persian; they became the mainstay of his Sufi order, the Mevlevi. In a typical *Sama'a* session, following the recitations from the Quran and led by a murshid, Sufis may start moving in circles while singing verses from the *Masnavi*. Raising one hand towards the sky, wearing robes, and cone-like topis made of coarse rug, these Sufis seek ascension or spiritual trance and thus came to be called Whirling Dervishes. In fact, many of their rituals and costumes (*kharqas*) were developed by Rumi's son, Sultan Walad, following his father's death, and then were further choreographed by the Turkish authorities in the mid-twentieth century, though Mustafa Kemal Ataturk had banned these clerical organizations and Sufi tekkes. Ataturk in fact was apprehensive of the influence of Mevlevi tariqa and of Rumi's successors on Constantinople and wanted to circumscribe their legacies across Anatolia. Undoubtedly, Sufi orders had often enjoyed a preeminent status within the Ottoman Empire, given their links with the grassroots along with their role in the local politics. Other than ideological reservations, Ataturk was apprehensive of the outreach that the Sufi orders had, both on the traditional power elite and the grassroots, and thus viewed them as a major roadblock to his dictum of modernization.[17] The Kemalists, for two generations, retained their statist control of Sufi tekkes though, by the 1960s, military regimes began to acknowledge the cultural significance of the Dervishes especially outside Turkey, and they soon became a soft trajectory of public diplomacy. The state was not going to relent its policies towards ulema, khankahs, hijab, Arabic script, and such other 'vestiges' of the Ottoman past, so instead, it used secularism in a more regimented way—similar to what one notices in case of French Laïcité system. It is only in the last two decades that the polity has begun to relax over these matters and certainly not without protestations and apprehensions at numerous levels. Movements and parties established by Saeed Nursi (1877–1960), Fethullah Gulen (b. 1941), Necmettin Erbakan (1926–2011), and Recep Tayyip Erdogan (b. 1954), with their predominantly Anatolian roots, backed by a vocal Turkish middle class, have played a significant role in moderating secularist ethos along with bringing back the Ottoman past and Islamic practices into public consciousness. Such a major transformation has taken place amidst a growing affluence, political stability, and a retort from the European Union over joining the European club. These processes are not yet complete and consensual and in their wake have engendered various questions and even concerns about the 'old order' seeking a back door entry.

Rumi, in his poetry and Sufi precepts, did not renounce the world. He instead reinterpreted it in a 'soulistic' way where philosophy, moralism, spirituality, and mundaneness coalesce in an existence where earthly necessities, cares, and urges turn fallacious until humanity discovers a sublime context and contact with the Ultimate Truth, the Almighty, who is both the lover and the beloved. For Shams and Rumi, on the way to that ascension, worldly love amongst humans, irrespective of gender, age, or class assumes a divine embodiment of becoming one and the same thing:

> Why should I seek? I am the same as he.
> His essence speaks through me.
> I have been looking for myself![18]

In the above verses, Rumi is rather underlining the mystical philosophy of 'know thyself' which is the focal point in Attar's *The Confluence of the Birds*. Or in a more transcendental way:

> When you are with everyone but me,
> you're with no one.
> When you are with no one but me,
> you're with everyone.
> Instead of being so bound up *with* everyone,
> *be* everyone.
> When you become that many, you're nothing.
> Empty.[19]

Devotion to the lover is an unrestrained journey as guided by the murshid until *fana* (the terminal end), rather than becoming the end, presents itself as a *baqa'a* (eternal living). Rumi's Sufi order, Mevlevi, continues to thrive especially through the dervishes who, following a rigorous regime of training and immersion in Rumi's poetry and practices, whirl with a murshid in attendance. Rumi's *Diwan* is named after his mentor, Shams, whereas *Masnavi* is certainly an unsurpassable classic in Persian literature whose calibre impelled Allama Muhammad Iqbal to liken it to 'a Quran in Farsi'.[20] It is the personality, teachings, philosophical thoughts, spiritual searchlight, and devotional practices through his order of whirling dervishes which have continued to soothe troubled souls for almost a millennium. No wonder Rumi remains one of the most quoted references for a wide variety of creeds and classes where sects, complexions, ethnicities, and genders become irrelevant. Like his arduous times, Rumi even becomes a permeable guide to humans in agony and thus his poetry or meditation at his *rauza* is often seen as a journey towards self-discovery with deeper esteem for humanity:

> In your light I learn how to love.
> In your beauty, how to make poems.
>
> You dance inside my chest,
> where no one sees you,

but sometimes I do,
and that sight becomes this art.[21]

As a student of classical master writers such as Hafiz, Saadi, Rumi,
Attar, Khayyam and, in recent times, being an avid reader of Mirza
Asadullah Ghalib, Muhammad Iqbal, and Faiz Ahmed Faiz (1911–84),
my desire of visiting Konya never diminished over the decades. Like a
visit to Nizamuddin in Delhi, an attendance at Lahore's Data Durbar,
deliberations at Moulay Idriss' *Zawiya* in Fes, a meditation session at
the shrine of Bahauddin Naqshband in Bukhara, and some solitary but
nostalgic moments spent in Cordova, Toledo, Palermo, Mostar, and
Granada became integral parts of my consciousness, so did a visit to the
Maulana. It is even more gratifying that I wrote a portion of this piece
dealing with a meeting between the Maulana and Shams in the proximity
of the old Seljuk town where old and new cohere to form the heart of
the third largest city in the country. Surrounded by well-patterned and
minutely designed gardens sits Alâeddin Mosque and the tombs of eight
Seljuk Sultans which crown this hill in an otherwise flat terrain. On the
hilltop stands Alâeddin's Jamia (Cemii), which might be the oldest of
its type built by Kayqubad who is buried in its compound with seven
other dynasts. The old gigantic entrance to the mosque and the tomb
still retains some early remnants of the walls and interiors and is built of
huge stone blocks inscribed with bold Quranic calligraphy. The Persian
poem on the entrance to the tomb was composed by an earlier Sufi, Abu
Said abi al-Khair, and is attributed to Rumi. It exhorts pilgrims to think
and reflect:

Come, come, whoever you are.
Wanderer, worshipper, lover of leaving.
It doesn't matter.
Ours is not a caravan of despair.
Come, come, even if you have broken your vow a thousand times.
Come, come yet again, come!

Inside, following a courtyard and the remains of what once might
have been a well, one sees two parallel Central Asian tabular structures,
one totally bare while the other houses the adjacent graves of Seljuk

Sultans. The solid but bare graves retain a Quranic verse inscribed on blue tiles—the predecessors of their Iznik counterparts. The mosque, like the Cordova Mosque, was extended at different times as the community grew and is anchored on some of those early massive pillars which one finds in ancient Ionian and Roman buildings heralding Hellenistic influences. The area around the Alâeddin Mosque and *turbat* was once the oldest part of the Seljuk town and housed a castle and a royal palace but only a portion of that palace remains covered by a more recent protective arch. This hill now features landscaped gardens, popular with families and young lovers, but is surrounded by a gyratory road that ironically cuts across the hill and other Seljuk mosques and madrassas.

Rumi's Konya Today

While walking down from the hill towards the Maulana on Alaaddin Road, I passed by the small memorial which is shown as the meeting point between Shams and Rumi on that memorable November day in 1244. Further down to the right is the Iplikci Mosque and almost facing it is another impressive piece of architecture called the Serafettin Mosque, built in the sixteenth century. Just a few hundred feet across the main entrance to this mosque and right in the middle of a shady and often busy garden sits the small mosque housing Shams' grave. It is visited by thousands of Anatolians and Rumi's followers. Wrapped in a green silky chador with Quranic inscriptions in golden thread, the sarcophagus is topped by the familiar Ottoman headstone and a green turban, unique to Sufis and sheikhs across the Muslim world even today. On the other side of the hill are two madrassas, the Karatay and the Ince Minar, the unique paragons of Seljuk architecture and home to some of the rare pieces of Seljuk arts and crafts. The Karatay Madrassa, whose round ceiling is decorated with several small, specially baked blue tiles, reminds a visitor of pre-Mughal Central Asian architecture in South Asia found in Rawat and Rohtas. The madrassa complex also houses the grave of Vizier Celaleddin Karatay with a turban fastened over the familiar Turkish headstone. This minister had served the Seljuks for 40 years and was viewed as an immensely accomplished personality who also oversaw the construction of a capital city by the lake just outside Konya. The Ince

Minar Madrassa was in use until a century ago when its circular minaret was hit by lightning and partially damaged. With restoration work almost complete, it consists of a main hall with a *hauz* in the middle and, like Karatay Madrassa, it consists of several side rooms dedicated to teaching, cooking, and living. Originally, it was meant to be the teacher's residence characterized by opulence but was instead used for instruction, and now it is the museum displaying Seljuk arts. While the Karatay Madrassa exhibits blue tiles covering the interiors of its magnificent dome, Ince Minar's domes are bare but no less attractive with successive rows of thin red bricks that one finds in Mughal monuments or in Isfahan's mosques and minarets. In fact, both the madrassas resemble Safavid buildings in Isfahan, though the latter claim more area and opulence since they were built later with more resources at the disposal of Shah Abbas and Shah Ismail. The entrance to the Ince Madrassa is quite magnificent with Surah Al-Kursi carved on its patterned designs.

Rumi's resting place consists of a well-kept garden with remnants of some early structures that once neighboured his *rauza* which is approached through a quadrangle featuring several rooms now converted into a museum. These rooms once accommodated Sufi masters and trainees, and offered teaching, dining, and residential facilities but presently house ancient Persian and Turkish (Osmanli) manuscripts, firmans, musical instruments such as rubaab and flutes, along with early Sufi turbans and *kharqa*s. In addition, they are home to manuals on Sufi practices and lifestyles which characterized the Mevlevi order and allowed a kind of communal, austere but very demanding lifestyle. As per traditions, the dervishes had to undergo strenuous training so that their feet and body could move in a prescribed rhythmic order, and fresh disciples were often asked to move their toes around metallic nails so as to attain full control of their body movement. The new disciples were expected to meditate for three days before embarking on a rigorous training extended over 1,001 days. Here, teaching included a variety of disciplines including the Quran and Hanafi interpretations besides a rigorous training for *Sama'a*. Inside the tomb, the Rumi's sarcophagus is the highest of all the 65 bodies interned and displays two turbans on his traditional headstone. The carpet dates back to an early period whereas the silk chador bedecking the grave is green with Quranic verses embroidered on it. Visitors are not allowed to get too close to the sarcophagus that is located in the corner of a big Seljuk structure. Interestingly, turbaned and perpendicular headstones are not found upon Seljuk graves which are built more in accordance to Central and South Asian styles. In fact, like the madrassas described above, those graves remind one of the Makli graveyard in Sindh which is viewed as the largest necropolis in the world.[22] The Bosnian graves of men are also in Osmanli style and, in spite of thousands of hastily built graves during the siege and ethnic cleansings by the Serbs and Croats, the former continued to reflect a permeating Ottoman influence.[23]

Across the road from Rumi's *rauza* and Sultan Selim Mosque lies an expansive, rather congested, but a well-maintained graveyard. A walk beside it takes one to some military barracks and further down to a gigantic multistorey Mevlana Complex. These facilities have been built by the *Baladiyya* (local government) which has ensured a planned growth of this neatly patterned city. Every Saturday evening is devoted to a performance by Whirling Dervishes with all its different components of recitations, instrumental music, appearance of the robed dervishes led by a murshid and his assistant, and then their immersion in the whirling dances. The entire session, watched by the Turks, Kurds, and international visitors, is a unique experience and people of all ethnicities, classes, genders, and age groups sit next to one another in this state-of-the-art amphitheatre. Konya, unlike common perception, is not a forlorn town in the hinterland but a cosmopolitan—a sprawling city with its high-rise apartment complexes, shopping malls and, most of all, boulevards edged by millions of green trees, hedges, and rose bushes. Of course, some of those historic buildings stand surrounded or are even peripheralized by modern roads, high-rises, and open cafés, yet the city itself is quite green. Also because of occasional rainfall, rigorous civic facilities, and a responsible populace, it is a pleasant place for walking, exploring, and stopping for an unlimited supply of tea—always accompanied by sugar cubes. The Konyans are quite proud of their Seljuk heritage; respectful of their world-known Christian sites in Cappadocia and self-assured of their identities as Muslim Turks, though the civil wars next door in Iraq and Syria evoke concerns as well.

Rumi's city is more plural than ever with a steady stream of visitors at the Mevlana along with a growing number of entrepreneurs in the region's agro-based economy and certainly a large presence of students since

Konya, amongst others, is home to the Seljuk University. The sprawling campus hosts 100,000 students, making it the country's largest institution of higher education. But in addition, there are refugees, both Arab and Kurd, who have moved in from across the Syrian-Turkish borders. At open air restaurants, it is not unusual to eavesdrop on people discussing politics in Arabic. I remember venturing into a kiosk on a hot summer day—not too far from the tallest tower in new Konya—and asking for some chilled water. The owner queried about my place of birth and when I mentioned Pakistan, he immediately called in his young daughter to come and say salaam 'to a Muslim Uncle from Pakistan' and only reluctantly accepted my money. Our parleys had brought in a few more Syrian refugees who were quite pleased to meet a fellow Muslim from another troubled land. Turks carry some special warmth for Pakistanis as I experienced time and again and for which one can conjecture several reasons. However, it was again during a short hike across the dunes and canyons in Cappadocia that I encountered a Turkish peasant keen on knowing my nationality. His enthusiasm was unprecedented when I told him about my place of birth followed by his spontaneous outbursts: 'Zulfikar Bhutto, Benazir Bhutto, Ziaul Haq ... CIA,' he said loudly by making a circle around his throat as if their murders had something to do with the CIA. He offered me dried apricots, water, and tea at his modest abode. We communicated through signs, in addition to a mixture of easily understood Urdu, Arabic, and Turkish words. This conversation happened right in the heart of Anatolia, overlooked by chimney-like geological structures; our dialogue went on for quite some length until it was time to leave. Of course amidst these whirling times, Rumi, the refugee from Balkh, was once again the major link, and here he must have the final say:

> There is a community of the spirit.
> Join it, and feel the delight
> of walking in the noisy street
> and *being* the noise.

> Drink all your passion and be a disgrace.
> Close both eyes to see with the other eye.
> Open your hands if you want to be held.

Consider what you have been doing.
Why do you stay with such a mean-spirited and dangerous partner?

For the security of having food. Admit it.
Here is a better arrangement.
Give up this life, and get a hundred new lives.

Sit down in this circle.

Quit acting like a wolf,
and feel the shepherd's love filling you.

At night, your beloved wanders.
Do not take painkillers.

Tonight, no consolations.
And do not eat.

Close your mouth against food.
Taste the lover's mouth in yours.

You moan, but she left me. He left me.
Twenty more will come.

Be empty of worrying.
Think of who created thought.

Why do you stay in prison
when the door is so wide open?

Move outside the tangle of fear-thinking.
Live in silence.

Flow down and down
in always widening rings of being.[24]

Notes

1. Rumi's translations by Reynold Nicholson and A. J. Arberry have been popular for quite some time, whereas for a quick selection of his ghazals and other poems, one could refer to Coleman Barks. See Coleman Barks, *The Essential Rumi* (New York: HarperCollins, 1995).

2. John Man, *Genghis Khan: Life, Death, and Resurrection* (London: Bantam, 2005); Morris Rossabi, *The Mongols: A Very Short Introduction* (Oxford: Oxford University Press, 2012).

3. Wilfred Cantwell Smith, *Islam in Modern History* (New York: New American Library, 1959).

4. Feyzi Halici, *Konya* (Konya: Konya Turizm Dernegi, 1982).

5. A. C. S. Peacock and Sara Nur Yildiz, *The Seljuks of Anatolia: Court and Society in the Medieval Middle East* (London: I. B. Tauris, 2012).

6. Some historians believe that Tamerlane was the first 'modern' empire builder and certainly his possessions included vast areas and diverse communities. See John Darwin, *The Empire Project: The Rise and Fall of the British World-System, 1830–1970* (Cambridge: Cambridge University Press, 2011).

7. An obsolete term for Persia used by the past Arabs.

8. Jill Dudley, *Holy Smoke!: Travels in Turkey and Egypt* (Orpington: Orpington Publishers, 2007), 72–3.

9. Though the doyen of historians, Herodotus (484 BCE–425 BCE), himself an Anatolian, never visited eastern Persia or the Indus lands yet his knowledge of the tribes living in present-day eastern Afghanistan and northwestern Pakistan was quite impressive, and Alexander would often read him by candle light. See Herodotus, *The Histories*, ed. Carolyn Dewald, trans. Robin Waterfield (Cambridge: Cambridge University Press, 2006) and Alice Albinia, *Empires of the Indus: The Story of a River* (London: John Murray, 2012).

10. Nizam al-Mulk, *The Book of Government, Or, Rules for Kings: The Siyar Al-Muluk, Or, Siyasat-nama of Nizam Al-Mulk*, trans. Hubert Darke (London: Routledge, 2002).

11. There are only a couple of works on Adelard, who mostly lived in Bath and Wells, and pioneered Islamic learning in England. On the other hand, one may find more entries on Abelard, the French philosopher. There is a bit of controversy about his first name being Peter or not. See Iftikhar H. Malik, 'Peter Adelard and Islam: Bridging the Medieval Worlds,' *Bath History*, December 2012. Also see Charles Burnett, *Adelard of Bath, Conversations with His Nephew: On the Same and the Different, Questions on Natural Science, and On Birds* (Cambridge: Cambridge University Press, 1998).

12. Afzal Iqbal, *The Life and Work of Maulana Muhammad Jalal-ud-Din Rumi* (Karachi: Oxford University Press, 1999) and William C. Chittick, *The Sufi Path of Love: The Spiritual Teachings of Rumi* (Albany: State University of New York Press, 1983).

13. Annemarie Schimmel, *Rumi World: The Work of the Great Sufi Poet* (Denver: Shambhala Press, 2002). According to her, Plato once lived on these plains as well.

14. Man-to-man relationship, often seen in Persia and further north, might have proved offensive in a culture which since the Arabo-Islamic era was deemed to be either a taboo or remained confined to a strictly private domain. A few academics that I met in Konya, who have spent their lifetime studying Persian literature besides contributing research on Rumi and Shams, have raised questions about Rumi's rather bold and often assumptive claims on the eminence of the *Masnavi* which did not sit well with some traditional religious circles. For the sake of their protection, I would rather keep their identities undisclosed but would not undervalue the calibre of their knowledge. One interview in particular, conducted in Konya on September 16, 2014, was quite instructive, given the senior scholar's extensive research on some leading twentieth century Muslim scholars besides his command over Persian.

15. Elif Shafak, *The Forty Rules of Love* (London: Penguin, 2015).

16. According to some reports, Shams was killed by Aleddin, Rumi's son, who had accused the former of having killed his own wife. For more details, see William C. Chittick, *Me & Rumi: The Autobiography of Shams-i Tabriz* (Louisville: Fons Vitae, 2004).

17. Norman Stone, while dilating on the various aspects of Turkish history, has mentioned several books including some of his own. His interview also sums up his personal experiences in an ever-changing Turkey, see 'The best books on Turkish History recommended by Norman Stone,' *Fivebooks*, http://fivebooks.com/interviews/norman-stone-on-turkish-history. See Feroz Ahmad, *The Making of Modern Turkey* (London: Routledge, 2015); Philip Mansel, *Constantinople: City of World's Desire, 1453–1926* (London: John Murray, 2006); and Hale Yilmaz, *Becoming Turkish: Nationalist Reforms and Cultural Negotiations in Early Republican Turkey* (Syracuse: Syracuse University Press, 2012).

18. Coleman Barks, *Rumi: The Book of Love: Poems of Ecstasy and Longing* (New York: HarperCollins, 2009).

19. Barks, *The Essential Rumi*, 28.

20. Most of Muhammad Iqbal's poetry is in Persian as he wanted to reach a wider Muslim audience, though his Urdu collections remain easily accessible to readers and poetry lovers in South Asia. His English lectures delivered at the Madras University witness his philosophical thoughts on Muslim history and politics and were published as *The Reconstruction of Religious Thought in Islam* (Oxford: Oxford University Press, 1934). Iqbal had studied in Lahore, Cambridge, and Heidelberg, and his *Payam-e-Mashriq* is a philosophical response to Jung, Nietzsche, and Bergson, whereas other Persian collections such as *Asrar-e-Khudi* and *Ramuz-e-Bekhudi*, besides *Zaboor-e-Ajam*, dilate on multiple subjects including self-awareness, socialism, transcendent humanism, prophetic love,

and responses to European colonialism. *Zarb-e-Kaleem*, his final collection, is divided between Urdu and Persian. Iqbal's relevance in its multidisciplinary way has proven enduring though he was uncomfortable with the regimented forms of Islam as manifested in clerical and mystical circles, but his love for Rumi and Shams remained a lifelong commitment. Iqbal viewed Rumi as his teacher (*ustaad*) and often used the term of *Pir-i-Rum*, which means the spiritual doyen from Anatolia. The quoted verse here reads as such: *Mathnawi-i-Molvi-i-Maanavi—Hast Quran dar zaban-i-Pehlawi*. Iqbal's immersion in Rumi synchronizes with the Sufi's own unabashed self-celebration of his poetic masterpiece. See Nazir Qaiser, *Rumi's Impact on Iqbal's Religious Thought* (Lahore: Iqbal Academy, 2004).

21. Barks, *The Essential Rumi*, 122.
22. The Makli graveyard is built over a hilltop since the land in this lower part of the Indus Valley has been flat and often vulnerable to floods. Thus, with the arrival of Arab, Persian, and Central Asian Muslims, this hilltop became the focal burial place. Across miles and miles of this landscape, one sees Afghan, Turkic, and Persian traditions besides mosques built in pre-Mughal Central Asian style—much similar to the Ince Minar and Karatay Madrassa in Konya. On Makli, see Annemarie Schimmel, *Makli Hill: A Center of Islamic Culture in Sindh* (Karachi: Institute of Central and West Asian Studies, 1983); Ihsan Nadiem, *Makli: The Necropolis of Thatta* (Lahore: Sang-e-Meel Publications, 2001); Iftikhar H. Malik, *Culture and Customs of Pakistan* (Westport: Greenwood Press, 2006), 92–8; and 'The City Of Silence "Makli Graveyard",' *INCPAK*, February 10, 2013. For images, see Syed Kumail Hasan, 'In pictures: Makli, one of the world's largest graveyards,' *Dawn*, June 27, 2016.
23. Amir Pasic, *Islamic Architecture in Bosnia and Hercegovina (Studies on the History and Culture of Bosnia and Hercegovina)*, trans. Midhat Ridjanović (Istanbul: Research Centre for Islamic History, Art and Culture, 1994). Pasic's works on restoration since the war and especially on the Mostar Bridge are noteworthy.
24. Coleman Barks, *Rumi: The Big Red Book: The Great Masterpiece Celebrating Mystical Love and Friendship* (New York: HarperCollins, 2011).

12

Isfahan:
Half the World or the Heart of Another
Misunderstood Land!

The angels knocked at the tavern-door last night,
with man's clay, they kneaded the cup outright.

The dwellers of God's heavenly abode,
drank wine with me—a beggar of the road.

Heaven could not bear this wonderful trust,
that to a madman this honour was thrust.

Disputes of religions is but a false pretence,
having not seen the Truth, they speak nonsense.

Thank God! There is peace between Him and me.
So dancing mystics took their cups with glee.

What makes the candle laughing isn't a flame.
The fire that burned the butterfly is my aim.

No one can display thoughts as Hafiz can,
no such words are written by the pen of man.

Shams-ud-Din Muhammad Hafiz[1]

Surrounded by these tall, green, and majestic trees waving like African dancers in a cool breeze, I am reminded of a ghazal by Khwaja Shams-ud-Din Muhammad Hafiz where the Persian classicist celebrates the height of his beloved who is blessed with an exceptional beauty and a melodious voice. I am overwhelmed by the history and arts that I have been trying to grasp in this Palace of Forty Columns (Chehel Sutoun), with 'forty' holding a special significance in the Muslim imagination. For the last two days, I have been trying to absorb the history, gentility, and beauty of the famed city of Isfahan, always complimented as *Nisf Jahan* or half the world! On my left in this well-patterned garden, sit three elderly Iranians on a divan while several tables, covered with traditional Persian rug pieces, are strewn around. Two lovers sit across from me, and in between their frolicking, they have been trying to determine my nationality. Both my computer and complexion are sufficient enough to confuse any simple soul that comes to this heartland of the Perso-Islamic heritage, seeking solitude, beauty, and refinement. The young maiden is covered in a traditional black chador and her arched eyebrows move with the romantic phrases she hears from her companion who seems determined to make an impression on her. Even an otherwise teacher in me is eager to listen to some Khayyam or Khaqani from a whispering lover as this is the place and time for making his mark. The Iranian traffic, despite its notoriety for anarchy, is beyond the medieval parameters of this jewel of an ornamented architecture where, in 1543, the proud Safavid monarch, Tahmasp I (1524–76), had received Humayun (1508–56), the ousted Mughal emperor of India. Here the Uzbek and Turcoman rulers from the north and emissaries from the rival Ottomans witnessed Safavid splendour at its zenith. Monarchs such as Shah Ismail I, Shah Tahmasp I, and Shah Abbas I—Safavid rulers during the sixteenth and seventeenth centuries—made sure that their guests and visitors were fully dazzled by their power and aesthetes. The dynasty, seeking its roots from a fourteenth century Shia Sufi order of Ardebil, had initially chosen Tabriz as their first capital before they moved it to Qazvin, whereas Shah Abbas I finally decided on Isfahan. They had selected this city as the capital and hence ensured its uniqueness through some of the most beautiful mosques, madrassas, palaces, bridges, bazaars, and gardens that would certainly inspire the Mughals and the Ottomans to follow suit in Agra and Constantinople. The Fatimids had built their Cairo to rival the Abbasid Baghdad which itself was meant to rival the Umayyad's Damascus. One wonders about these kings who always thought of ensuring their place in history through winning wars and building grand monuments. Ibn Battuta, the fourteenth century Moroccan traveller, marvelled at the Hall of One Thousand Pillars in Delhi built by Muhammad bin Tughlaq, the eccentric Delhi Sultan. A few centuries earlier, Caliph Abd al-Rahman

III had built an elaborate new capital city, Madinatal Zahra, three miles outside Cordova—the capital city known for the grand mosque and dozens of libraries. Like Tughlaq's city, Daulatabad, in the Indian south, the new Spanish metropolis was soon abandoned, and for the next several centuries it lay vulnerable to the vagaries of vandals. Even Alhambra in Granada had been turned into a jail and then allowed to rot; if not for Washington Irving's efforts, that jewel of the medieval cities would have become another Tughlaqabad, Sikri, Merv, or Rey.

The Chehel Sotoun in Isfahan, resplendent in its impressively carved pillars, proportioned hallways, and palatial rooms decorated with the works of the contemporary world-famous calligraphers and miniature artistes, certainly impressed past visitors the way they amaze any traveller today. Persia, like India, was the land of literature, arts, and statecraft, and the rival Timurid dynasties, both to the east and west, were in awe of the Safavid power and grandeur. The Uzbek Shaybanis in the north were always an eyesore for the Shia monarchs of Persia as they were for the Mughals. Interestingly, all these four contemporary dynasties were the heirs of legacies left behind by the Mongols and Tamerlane. The Mongols, after their decimation of Muslim urban and political centres, were gradually acculturated within Islamic traditions, especially during the reign of the Ilkhanid dynasty. In the same vein, other Central Asian Turkic dynasties including the Timurids repeated the patterns and, following Tamerlane's devastating campaigns, became the new stakeholders in India, Persia, Central Asia, and the Near East. The world of Islam was reenergized by the Turks who, in most cases, quickly adopted Persian as the literary and court language while assimilating Persian statecraft as the guiding ideology. However, the Turkic Safavids, unlike their Sunni counterparts across the Ottoman lands and the subcontinent, had begun to champion the cause of Shi'ism. Shi'ism, occasionally imposed with some coercion, gave the Persian heartland a form of unity as well as political salience, although the border regions inhabited by the Kurds, Baloch, and Central Asians remained Sunni. The close intermingling of religion and politics, while adding uniquely to the architectural splendour of Safavid Persia, also banished Zoroastrian and Persian Sunni elite to a more tolerant and affluent India or further west towards an expansive Ottoman empire. Thus, when Humayun sought help from King Tahmasp I against his Afghan rival, Sher Shah, his hosts not only helped him militarily but also sent in the contingent of their troops to help restore a friendly, and possibly, a Shia regime in Delhi. Even after centuries, many descendants of those Persian émigrés have remained a vanguard section of a vibrant, mobile, and creative genius that not only added immensely to the Indo-Islamic culture but also, in cases such as Lucknow, spread Shia theology, ensuring a proper upkeep of holy places in Najaf, Karbala, and Mashhad. Thus, Isfahan was not merely a centre of a powerful dynasty or a cultural metropolis; it also operated as the power engine of the Safavid public diplomacy and springboard for Shia theology before being taken over by Najaf and then Qom. One wonders about the conflicting tastes of the four rival Timurid dynasties of the Mughals, Safavids, Uzbeks, and the Ottomans who brought a long-awaited renaissance to Islamic art and ensured the universalization of Persian as the lingua franca of a vibrant Muslim world, all the way from the Mediterranean to the Pacific. Of course, it was also the language of Muslims in Eastern Turkestan, now largely in China, which other than hajj, kept that distant community in touch with their coreligionists in the Muslim heartlands.

Back at a café in the meticulous garden of the Chehel Sotoun, a cleric sermonized on the topic of piety on the radio that accompanied us through tiny speakers hidden in flowerpots hanging by the outer walls of this traditional *chaikhana*. I could make out a few words of praise for Ahl-e-Bait, the family of the Holy Prophet (PBUH), and could follow some of Allama Khomeini's sayings yet did not detect any lyrics from Hafiz or Saadi in his utterances. I was more interested in the Chehel Sotoun and the beatitude of Isfahan that certainly never failed to move any heart, whether of a lover, invader, or even British visitors such as Sir Robert Shirley (1581–1628) and Thomas Coryate (1577–1617). The Shirleys converted to Islam and were appointed official emissaries to their native England by Shah Abbas I, who sought Britain's help against his Ottoman rivals. Coryate was the historian-traveller from Somerset who walked to India at the time when the East India Company was opening up its operations in the Mughal lands. The son of a vicar from Ham Hill near Glastonbury, Coryate wrote books about his travels across Europe and reported on India, and is credited to have introduced the umbrella and the fork from Italy into British homes. Eager to meet Mughal emperor Jahangir, he had walked through Arabia and Persia before travelling to

Agra but sadly passed away near Surat after falling ill. Shirley, from an aristocratic family of Sussex, had helped modernize the royal Persian army and also met up with a rather eccentric Coryate in Isfahan. The Safavids, like Mughals, had ignored building up naval defences and in the process lost out to Portugal, a small emerging Iberian nation which captured Hormuz while the former fought their neighbours to the north and west. It is such a travesty to know that all these land-based empires, despite their potentials and pretensions, lost out to smaller seafaring states on their own home soil. Like these Muslim empires, the Chinese and Native American dynasts succumbed before European encroachments which is even before industrialization had set in.

A caged parrot that is more eager to narrate its song, especially to the absorbed lovers, is obstinately interrupting the mullah's sermon on the radio. Symbolically, there is a contest going on between religion and romance! Inside the café, there are pictures of the emperors, queens, and charming Turkmen girls with conjoined eyebrows moving with their traditional trays, balancing wine goblets strategically placed around some exquisitely carved pitchers. Their arched eyes and dancing poses were certainly meant to move the lovers and cajole the poets imagining their next flourish of romantic similes and metaphors. The originals of some of these paintings were pioneered under the Qajar dynasty in more recent centuries, whose commissioned portraits on large canvases embody bejewelled kings resplendent in their royal costumes and sporting thick long black beards. Inside the *chaikhana*, on the wall facing the main entrance, sits Imam Khomeini with his piercing eyes fully assured of his Iranian-ness but a bit uneasy with this ongoing romance, due to which nobody seems to be interested in listening to his sermon, not even the rude parrot with its sonorous rebuke. The three elderly Iranians enjoying their hookah seem oblivious of the amorous goings-on and are engrossed in some deeper conversation of a worldly type. The late Imam's portrait is neighboured by Khamenei's in a corner of the café, though the contemporary president of the Islamic Republic is not visible. Soon the mullah is overruled and a ghazal from Hafiz finds its way on the radio; even the parrot turns quiet! Today, no Iranian has asked me about my denominational identity partly because they are too busy in their own world or I look like any other tourist in the city. For them, I am one of many who come around full of curiosity, with probing eyes and dangling cameras, before their restive legs take them somewhere else. To many of them, I might be an Iranian Baloch, given my darker complexion and accented Persian. Anyway, this is the historic district of Isfahan where, other than this luminous palace, several unique monuments are located and, given a temperate weather, scores of people are on the move with only a few of them interested in observing any foreign-looking soul.

Isfahan or Esfahan has been a historic town in central Iran but, like Agra, Bukhara, Merv, Fes, and Cordova, it obtained its unparalleled prominence as the centre of arts, scholarship, and culture when the Safavids made it into their capital in the early 1500s. In particular, under Shah Abbas I, also called Abbas the Great—similar to his contemporary Akbar the Great and Suleiman the Magnificent—Isfahan's excellence in arts reached its pinnacle. He came to power in 1588 and ambitiously extended his rule in all directions and earnestly engaged to make his capital city into an unrivalled metropolis until in the late seventeenth century, when following the Afghan invasions, the capital shifted to Shiraz and subsequently to Tehran. Abbas was the fifth Safavid king who decided to shift the capital from Qazvin to Isfahan and is credited to have wrested the Caucasus and eastern Anatolia from the Ottomans until they were lost again by his successors. He also annexed Mughal and Uzbek territories to his empire and pushed the Portuguese further east of Hormuz. He invited Circassians and Armenians to run businesses in his empire besides building some historic monuments in the kingdom. It was under Abbas I that the Chahar Bagh Abbasi Street, the main thoroughfare across the historic Safavid metropolis, was built as a grand boulevard with palaces, tall trees, and gardens lining up on both sides of this bustling artery. The Safavid thoroughfare, built in 1597, is five-kilometres-long and is known as Chahar Bagh because of the four main gardens situated in its proximity. Even now, most of the museums, galleries, madrassas, palaces, shops, and gardens happen to be between the Takhti Square in the north and the river to the south, although the boulevard stays on its straight course beyond the river until one reaches Jolfa, the Armenian quarters. Following this historic road, the river is crossed through a unique and equally historic bridge called Si-o-se-pol, or the bridge of 33 alcoves. The bricked alcoves in this bridge not only offer arched spaces and airy passages under the main upper structure itself but are also a fascinating spectacle to look at. In these open spaces, the Isfahanis picnic or pass their leisure time at *chaikhana*s where hookahs keep circulating amongst men discussing politics, religion, literature, or jobs. There are 11 bridges on Zayandeh Rud/River, each with its own history. The river begins in the Zagros Mountains, flowing eastwards through Isfahan and disappearing in Dasht-e-Kavir, the great desert. Further east of Isfahan are the provinces of Kerman and Sistan-Balochistan which border Pakistan, and towards the north-east direction is situated the famous province of Khorasan. The province is known for historic characters such as Rostam, Sohrab, and eminent littérateur like Firdausi, who sang of ancient Persian beauty, history, and majesty in his masterpiece, *Shahnameh*. This epic is the story of a proud Persia and celebrates the heroics of the famous wrestler-commanders, Rostam, and his son, Sohrab. The masterpiece has its own history as it was written during the reign of Mahmud of Ghazni, the Turkish conqueror from Afghanistan who had attacked India 17 times and annexed vast Persian areas within his empire. It was under his patronage that Firdausi wrote his *Shahnameh*, though stories abound that Mahmud did not properly compensate the classicist and presumably his ingratitude and miserable reward hastened the death of the famous poet.

Further south of Isfahan is the province of Fars or Faris that gave the names such as Persia and Persian, and it is here that the well-known city of Shiraz is located, which produced two of the most famous Persian classicists: Saadi and Hafiz. Both these lyricists lived just a few centuries after Firdausi but created such monumental, poetic, and prose works that even today they remain unsurpassed in their eloquence, depth, and impact. Saadi, also known as Sheikh Saadi, has become synonymous with wisdom and morality as his small fables of animals and human characters, both in prose and poetry, end on some moral. His *Gulistan*, which literally means garden, is a work in prose, while *Bostan*, again meaning garden, is a collection of poems of every genre varying from quadruplets to longer hymns and romantic compositions known as ghazals. Hafiz, like Saadi, is buried in Shiraz in the same garden, and thousands of people flock to their tombs in this city to enjoy its temperate climate, architectural beauty, and most of all, to pay homage to these literary classicists who are household names from China to Morocco. No wonder this language of Firdausi, Rumi, Saadi, Khayyam, Attar, Avicenna, Hafiz, and many other luminaries for centuries remained the lingua franca of people inhabiting so many distant places. India, China, Central Asia, and Turkey absorbed the Perso-Islamic culture which is evident in their heritage even today. Known South Asian writers such as Ghanimat Kunjahi (d. 1695), Mirza Abdul Qadir Bedil (d. 1720), Mirza Ghalib, and Muhammad Iqbal used Persian as the main literary expression for their poetical and philosophical works until English and the other national languages took over. Persian ruled the literary and official world in most of Muslim Asia and thus brought an exceptional degree of unity in Muslim intellectual activities. Universalization of Persian, compared to today's Iranian Persian or Afghanistan's Dari, appears more like a forgotten dream at a time when all these regions have evolved into nation-states from the debris of the erstwhile empires. Certainly territorial nationalism, along with other portents of modernity, sounded a death knell to Persianate.

Surrounded by beautiful gardens, canopied by magnificent trees, and facing a beautiful rectangular pool, stands the main structure of Chehel Sotoun, originally built as a recreational pavilion by Shah Abbas II that saw its completion in 1647. As the name denotes, the elevated pavilion, more like the nearby Ali Qapu Palace, has 20 pillars but their reflections in the pool certainly double their actual number. The frescoes on the ceilings, smaller rooms, and the larger hall adjacent to the pavilion represent a meticulous art work dating from the time when the city was experiencing art at its zenith. One of the contemporary paintings shows Mughal Emperor Humayun of India conferring with Shah Tahmasp, whereas another depicts the Amir of Turkestan accompanied by courtiers and dancing girls being received by Shah Abbas II. Other than ceramics and Safavid décor, several paintings display Shah Abbas feasting with his courtiers, while Shah Ismail is shown fighting the Ottomans and Uzbeks. Other than highlighting Persian heroics, these paintings reflect a strong tradition of celebrating human beauty and life, and have been allowed to be on display despite the Islamic Revolution of 1979. It was in a corner of the beautifully designed garden surrounding the palace that I had noticed the couple innocently exchanging amorous messages and vibes while the three elders minded their own business, and the radio alternated between sermons and songs. Unlike the pervasive views of Iran being a totally repressed society, one notices an impressive level of civility and tolerance at several levels. For instance, while having tea and some Persian sweets at Ghesaria café in Naqsh-e-Jahan Square, I chanced to speak to a couple sitting next to me. They were like several other youths enjoying a cooler evening at one of the city's informal social places and appeared to be quite close to each other. The café consisted of a few alcoves and an open space built over the northern entrance to the square and thus afforded a unique view of the historical monuments and of the brown mountains further to the south. Soon, I found myself talking to the young man who had come from Lorestan, the western province, whereas his friend was from Faris, deep in the south. Not only did their conversation reflect a natural ease about their own identities as post-1979 young Iranians, they equally felt no qualms in talking to a foreigner on a wide variety of subjects. They were curious about the West and Oxford in particular, though without any eagerness to leave the country. They sounded self-assured about their country and did not show any inherent anti-Americanism. As I noticed time and again during my travels in Iran, such encounters, often prompted by my own inquisitiveness, always resulted in friendly exchanges followed by a whiff of warm hospitality. Two days back, while flying from Tehran, a fellow passenger, returning from Texas on a short visit to his native Isfahan, had invited me to share a taxi ride and did not accept my share of the fare and made sure that I found my way to the historic Abbasi Hotel.

The Maidan, now known as Imam Khomeini Square, is the second biggest public square after the Tiananmen Square in Beijing. Though one cannot properly ascertain its size and grandeur unless one ventures into it and sees its beautifully maintained and dexterously designed landscaped sections with sprouting fountains and endless pathways built of slim yellow bricks. Its original name was Naqsh-e-Jahan (the symbol/charm of the world), which is still preferred by some of the old residents of Isfahan, and was completed in 1612. It is 600-metres-long with a width of 160-metres, and owes its majestic buildings and grand design to the determination of Abbas the Great. Towards the Maidan's southern end sits the grand Imam Mosque which symbolizes the city of Isfahan and, in a way, is a perfect specimen of Persian Islamic architecture. It is also one of the most beautiful mosques in the world; its blue dome is ornamented with golden floral designs and is guarded by two slim, tall, and majestic minarets. The arched entrance to the mosque is built to appear austere so as to reflect humbleness but once inside, the exquisiteness of each section moves even a stolid heart with its elegance, symmetry, and majesty. The entire structure of the mosque is divided into several sections; its entrance portal, despite its munificence, does not appear overpowering and on the contrary offers a greater sense of quiet, peace, and tranquillity. Though the 30-metre-high portal now provides an entrance into the mosque from the Maidan, it was originally built for decorative purposes as most of the worshippers come in from the Grand Bazaar using another corridor. The foundations of the walls of this majestic entrance are made of white marble, while the upper structure features elaborate floral motifs, impressive geometrical designs, and bold Quranic calligraphy, further canopied by the panels of stalactite mouldings in honeycomb patterns. These symmetrical arches and honeycombs remind one of the Muslim buildings in Spain symbolizing Moorish architecture which were further assimilated in Mudéjar traditions soon after the Inquisition and Expulsions. The work on this architectural classic began in 1611 and took 18 years to complete in 1629, coincidentally also the last year of the reign of Shah Abbas I. The earliest completed section of the Imam Mosque included the portal made of blue tiles with floral designs, whereas the alcoved corridors and arches leading to various sections and open prayer compound were built subsequently. The mosque, when compared to the oblong Maidan, sits slightly angled to the right so as to point correctly towards Makkah. The main portal, as mentioned above, leads one to several halls and corridors with high ceilings, all decorated meticulously and exuding a refreshing coolness until one reaches the courtyard where carpets are spread for prayers. There is an open water tank in the middle for ablution, surrounded on its four sides by *iwan*s which lead into adjacent sanctuaries. Here, once again, the walls surrounding the courtyard retain porches which are framed by floral designs of blue and yellow and, despite the passage of centuries and unobstructed usage by worshippers and visitors, they have not lost even an iota of their freshness. The main sanctuary houses the mihrab and mimbar and is topped by an ornate dome rising 51 metres above from the marble floor; it affords a unique view of the two minarets guarding over the portal and displaying the calligraphed names of Allah, the Prophet (PBUH), and Caliph Ali (RA). One can see the turquoise exterior of the main dome from within the two side sanctuaries which are used as madrassas. The dome changes its blue shades with the varying position of the sun. Like the other mosques in town and their older counterparts in Fes, Cairo, Timbuktu, Jerusalem, Iraq, Travnik, Konya, Khiva, Samarkand,

Bukhara, Herat, and South Asia, this is not an ordinary structure, given its history, size, and the collective efforts gone into its construction and maintenance. It reminds one of the Cordova Mosque that at one stage was the largest and one of the oldest of its type in the world. However, it now lies fiercely pierced by a cathedral in the middle and monitored by an army of minders to deter any potential Muslim worshipper. The Imam Mosque is open at all times and tourists mingle with the worshippers without any arrogant watchmen expelling anyone out.

Shah Abbas I used the Maidan or the Main Square as a royal mall which has three monuments including the Imam Mosque, Sheikh Lotfollah Mosque to its right, and the Ali Qapu Palace facing the latter. Both these magnificent mosques were built before the palace; the rows of the shops hemmed in within the scores of alcoves are rather recent additions. In other words, the original Maidan was bigger and broader than its present length and expanse, and was neighboured by the Grand Bazaar (Bazar-e-Bozorg) on one side and the Chehel Sotoun Palace further down towards the northwest while passing through another garden. Sheikh Lotfollah Mosque, facing the Ali Qapu Palace, is a smaller but equally impressive building dating back to the early Safavid era. Dedicated to the Lebanese father-in-law of Abbas I, it was built between 1602 and 1619 to serve as a mosque and a theological school, and was a memorial to the genius of the Sheikh who had himself supervised the construction of the Imam Mosque. This mosque, unlike the Imam Mosque, does not have a spacious courtyard but its portal exhibits some of the rarest mosaics in entire Iran. In shades such as blue and yellow, the floral designs emerging from vases offer a rich mixture of colours and patterns. The Lotfollah Mosque does not have a compound and, once inside the main entrance, a visitor reaches the main prayer hall through a splendidly built corridor which receives light from shifting angles. The sanctuary or the prayer hall presents a rare opportunity to study the intricate but immensely absorbing mosaics on the ceiling. Though simple in design, it still displays marvellous tile work and some unique calligraphy which also displays the year of its completion (1028 AH). The exterior of the dome, unlike its counterpart Imam Mosque, has a more visible yellow shade with blue, olive, and white floral patterns designed on it which gel quite naturally with the decorations and the tile work on the portal where a bluish background offers a fascinating contrast to yellow and orange. The interior of the dome of the Lotfollah Mosque has lemon-shaped mosaics which are delicately and superbly bordered by unglazed bricks, transmitting a unique evidence of Persian aesthetics. The Ali Qapu Palace had been built in the early seventeenth century and was actually meant to be a splendid gateway to the palaces beyond the Maidan and elsewhere by the Chahar Bagh Boulevard. Carrying the name of Hazrat Ali RA and built on an elevated terrace with 18 wooden slim pillars and consisting of seven levels, the 46-metre-high gateway was used as a public plaza where the kings met dignitaries. Given its location and height, it was a vantage point to oversee the beautiful gardens in the Maidan besides inspecting the special parades, races, and processions. Like the pillars in the Chehel Sotoun, its 18 pillars support a similar ornate ceiling for the royal court and family which are located higher than ground level and are accessible through narrow staircases. This viewing gallery is certainly expansive and its walls and ceilings, despite subsequent disfiguring, contain multicoloured floral decorations. Isfahan definitely benefited from Shah Abbas' munificence the way Agra, Delhi, Lahore, and Thatta were selected by Emperor Shah Jahan for his splendid artifices; a special exhibition at the British Museum in 2009 was certainly an overdue but befitting tribute to this Persian monarch.

A slightly open space right above the northern entrance to the Maidan housed the Ghesaria Tea Shop where tea, cakes, kebabs, naans, and hookah kept an unending stream of Iranians and tourists engaged. Located above ground level, the place afforded one of the best sights of the square and revealed the changing shades of the two mosques. By early evening, it appeared as if the entire city of Isfahan might have gathered at the Maidan. On the further end of the oblong Maidan, facing Imam Mosque to the north and behind Lotfollah Mosque on the western side sits the Grand Bazaar, Bazar-e-Bozorg. The bazaar, more like its counterpart in Istanbul, is a fully covered, well-maintained, elaborate structure which is always buzzing with social and commercial activities. The Grand Bazaar retains thousands of shops of every variety and nowhere does it show any structural decay or rot. A polite salaam and smile can go a long way in engaging artistes and artisans in small talk, even to the extent of receiving hospitality in the form of soft drinks or tea. Within the labyrinthine details of the bazaar, there are several alleyways with more mosques and seminaries and some of the oldest houses in this historic town. It is not merely a place to sell and buy but is equally a great social institution of immense cultural and political significance. Persian literature is full of stories and poems with the bazaar offering a locale where myths, news, and views were shared and the destiny of kingdoms was decided by merchants and their networks extending across the regions. Bazaars assembled artisans, craftsmen, authors, poets, storytellers, hakims, artists, clerics, travellers, musicians, Sufis, and politicians who informed public opinions and conjured up political alliances. It was in a bazaar like this in Tehran and elsewhere that the decision to overthrow the Shah was reached and clerics and communists joined the business class to bring about the February Revolution. The Grand Bazaar is certainly a grand city unto itself and one can wander here for hours without any fear of getting lost as the shoppers as well as the shopkeepers are the best guides and in most cases multilingual. Here one can see the traditional craftsmen at work knitting carpets, smithery, or such skills which involve delicate work on silk, wood, marble, metals, leather, and glass to produce some of the world's most unique pieces of art that Isfahan has been known for. Unlike some other places, the shopkeepers here do not haggle with visitors nor do women encounter any lewd remarks or jostling. Iran is certainly one of the fewer places on earth to have such an excellent level of civility and unobtrusiveness. People here may show an element of curiosity towards foreign visitors but always without any hostility or suspicion. They avoid staring at others nor do they crowd around women tourists. Their aloofness is out of respect for space and privacy and is devoid of jealousy or indifference. It is always fun to disappear into the side alleys to see craftsmen at work and to seek out small cafés to socialize with the locals. Many of these older neighbourhoods have shrines, mosques, and seminaries dating from pre-Safavid times when the city rivalled Baghdad, Merv, Samarkand, Herat, Cairo, Cordova, Damascus, Delhi, and Lahore. In fact, the oldest mosque in Isfahan dates back to the tenth century and is still in use. The Hakim Mosque's impressive portal was built during the Buyid era, and its expansive interior, central water tank, and sanctuaries on all the four sides had preceded Safavid architectural imprints. In a way, this mosque was apparently the role model for mosques and shrines subsequently built by the Safavids. Like the Mughals, Uzbeks, and Ottomans— their rival neighbours and contemporaries—the Safavids synthesized diverse patterns without compromising their own unique distinctness. Meandering through the winding lanes while glancing at several other historic relics, such as the older houses with carved wooden terraces and blue tile work, one suddenly comes face to face with the magnificent entrance to the Hakim Mosque which is located to the northwest of the bazaar. Here I met a father with his two young children who, with their endless smiles, practised some English on me and apparently were amused by my own lingual hybridity combining Persian, Urdu, and English.

While a detailed observation of the interiors of the magnificent and splendid Hakim Mosque had been spiritually and aesthetically reinvigorating, the Chelo kebabs at the Restoran-i-Saadi were gastronomically nourishing and offered a timely break. More than the food, it was the name of the restaurant with a friendly staff that caused several more visits in the days to come. My first encounter with the elaborate Shirazi salad, rice, and kebab was because I was famished, having been constantly on my feet for a very long time. Saadi, a true moralist and a Sufi to his core, always preferred simple food in the company of fellow Sufis and his meal sessions became proverbial for their congeniality and literary prowess. Confronted by any elaborate feast which many of his admirers liked to lay down during his visits, he usually pronounced some kind of nostalgic phrase about his native meal, *Daawat-i-Shiraz*. Emerging from the restaurant located in a basement, I headed back in the direction of the Madrassa-ye Nimurvand which lies in the north-eastern section of the bazaar and is certainly a hidden gem. It is a square structure with elegantly designed gardens and fountains in the courtyard embodying immaculate tile work on its multiple arches and veranda. It is a residential college, more like its Oxbridge counterparts or quadrangles at Aligarh and Bukhara, and is meant for male students who come from the various regions of the country to specialize in Islamic studies with an expected emphasis on Shia theology. Sitting out with these students over an endless supply of tea, one could certainly detect curiosity as well as self-sufficiency when talking of modernity and its Western imperatives. Remembering Saadi allowed appreciative wrinkles while Hafiz and Rumi caused some meaningful smiles. Some of the teachers were curious about Muhammad Iqbal and his poetry that they deeply appreciated due to its emphasis on self-awareness and powerful linkages with the Muslim past. Iqbal certainly added to my own status amongst these serious-minded scholars who happened to be more focused on Shia theology with a nationalist perspective on their Persianness. I was eager to know how the Iranian ulema had been able to create a synthesis between Persian nationalism and trans-territorial Shi'ism. The answer lies in these very madrassas and the Safavid way of creating their polity that allowed greater salience to Shia clergy while concurrently celebrating Persian exceptionalism. In fact, during the latter Safavid phase, especially under Shah Sultan Hussein (1694–1722), Shia theology became predominant with a legalist purview. In 1694, Shah Hussein appointed Muhammad Baqer Majlisi as his de facto minister and Mullah Bashi (the chief priest) who ensured implementation of the various rituals, such as mourning and chest-beating processions during the month of mourning (Muharram). Majlisi, the author of the noted work *Bihar al-Anwar*, encouraged Shia ulema to gain an upper hand in state structures and, amidst a grave intolerance towards Sunnis, Zoroastrians, and Jews, ensured their primacy. He also encouraged pilgrimages to the shrines of Imam Ali (RA) and Imam Hussain (RA) located in Najaf and Karbala respectively. Interestingly, this is the time when in northern India, the Nawabs of Awadh, with their capital in Lucknow, were implementing similar rituals during Muharram and were also encouraging pilgrimage to Najaf and Karbala. However, the latter did not allow an unchecked priestly primacy to Shia theologians and instead often encouraged literary activities in Urdu including elegies about Shia Imams.

Tall cypress trees beaming towards a sharp blue sky ensured scholarly solitude in Nimurvand from the humdrum of the bazaar, whereas the quad itself did not seem to be narrowing the space for learners quietly moving between their classrooms. Hiding my camera and confident of being away from the usual tourist haunts, I was trying hard to look like a lanky, mature student who was attempting his best to relive a medieval ethos right in one of the known seminaries of classical learning. The students were not to be left behind in their assessment of an intruder and were rather overjoyed to meet an academic from a distant neighbourhood. It took some time to explain the hyphenated identity on this end. After a brief session on curricula, texts, and future prospects for these seminary students, I could delineate commonalities with other similar Sunni seminaries over the centuries, though here the Shia tradition demanded greater immersion and exceptional brilliance. One wonders how such a rigorous training might reflect in the careers of these graduates, some of whom might be the future ayatollahs of the Shia theology. Qom was the cherished destination, whereas Najaf and Karbala came slightly lower down the hierarchical order.

After seeking a polite exit from the seminary as well as from the discussion on Islamic exegetes, I found myself amongst shoppers before walking towards the Mausoleum of Harun Vilayat, another graceful and elaborate shrine depicting unique Safavid architecture resplendent with the most attractive and rare frescoes. Here it is impossible to miss the grand minaret that had been affording me occasional glimpses of itself at various places across Isfahan but had somehow remained inaccessible. This immensely tall, bricked minaret, resembling Minar-e-Kalyan in Bukhara, had been etched on my mind as the historic symbol of this city and now I finally found myself standing underneath it. Known as the Minar-i-Ali Mosque, this impressively tall column of yellow bricks represents a combination of Mesopotamian and Central Asian architectural traditions that permeated Iran even before the Safavids. This 48-metre-high column embodies some elegant geometric designs and resembles Ziggurat and ancient Zoroastrian towers, and can be seen either from the neighbouring streets or by entering the mosque itself. It rises like a sentinel and, in many ways, looks like Delhi's Qutb Minar, though it lacks those elaborate circular galleries and calligraphic inscriptions which make the former slightly more ornamented. Moreover, the Qutb Minar is built of massive blocks of red stone found in the monuments built by the Delhi Sultans and the Great Mughals. It must be the nearest kin of Bukhara's Minar-e-Kalyan, predating and miraculously outliving the Mongol invasion which was once the tallest structure in entire Asia. Preservation of such monuments, despite the Iran-Iraq War and enduring global sanctions, is certainly owed to official policies but it is mainly the civil society which must be credited for looking after its heritage so assiduously. It is an even greater feat to accomplish this without any foreign consultants or financial injections in the name of some high-sounding global projects aimed at preserving rarities. Of course, Isfahan is a world heritage city but its splendid preservation is solely owed to its inhabitants. They ensure the longevity of the city through their devotion to its heritage and by keeping it impeccably clean and green. Like the paintings within the Chehel Sotoun Palace or cleanliness of the Maidan and the Rose Gardens, it is the commitment by the citizen groups that has ensured Isfahan's stature as *Nisf Jahan*. It can certainly provide an inspiring example to other historic cities in distress owing to their population, pollution, and political wrangles.

Not quite far from the Minar-i-Ali Mosque sits a historic monument that, other than combining several Islamic architectural traditions, happens to be one of the largest mosques in the world. The Jameh Mosque is the biggest mosque in Iran, covering 30,000 square metres. It incorporates Seljuk styles dating from the eleventh century and others all the way until the eighteenth century when the Qajars took over the reins of the country. The mosque's two domes top the northern and southern *iwan*s respectively and date back to the eleventh century, although a few of its sections were gutted down in the twelfth century by fire, necessitating the rebuilding of the mosque in 1121 AD. The Safavids devoted some attention to its exterior, though their priorities were their own buildings. During the Iraq-Iran War in the 1980s, a bomb damaged some portion of the mosque but it was quickly repaired. Like the main ablution fountain in the Kaaba and in Cordova Mosque, Isfahan's Jameh Mosque has an impressive fountain in the central courtyard which is bordered by two-storey porches built during the fifteenth century. The mosque's southern *iwan* has two minarets incorporating perfect geometrical designs originating from the Mongol era and some mosaics dating from the fifteenth century. The northern *iwan* retains some specimens of rare Kufic calligraphy of the Seljuk period and possesses a few impressive brick pillars in the sanctuary. The western *iwan* manifests elaborate geometric mosaics dating from the Safavid era, while a raised platform in the courtyard with a conical roof is used for adhan. In other words, the mosque has uniquely been a beneficiary of contributions both by the Sunni and Shia dynasties. Several rooms and halls inside the covered area of the Jameh Mosque have their own distinct features. For instance, Sultan Oljeitu's room dates from the fourteenth century, whereas the Timurid rulers built the winter hall in 1448. The two-domed rooms facing each other in the north and south date from the eleventh century and still exhibit their original Seljuk features.

The Jameh Mosque sits towards the northeast of the Chahar Bagh Abbasi Street, whereas the Maidan and Chehel Sutoun are located on the eastern side of the main thoroughfare. The Chahar Bagh itself is interspersed by a number of seminaries, gardens, and palaces all along this leafy boulevard. The impressive Chahar Bagh Madrassa is one of those known seminaries that dates from the eighteenth century, embodying quite a unique representation of Safavid architecture with its brick buildings, blue domes, floral patterns, and numerous arches with calligraphy. Featuring an open courtyard and a prayer hall with a splendid mihrab and topped by two Safavid minarets, this seminary was dedicated to a Queen Mother. It has two-storey porches that are decorated with some elaborate mosaics that lead one to the student accommodation, though the building is always in use both as a mosque and as a centre of traditional learning. The main function of the seminary is its residential instruction of Islamic disciplines besides offering facilities for daily worship. It is adjacent to the well-known Abbasi Hotel which is itself an excellent combination of old and new. The hotel's lawn is meticulously designed with manicured cypresses, rose bushes, and jasmine in neatly demarcated sections, all divided by minutely cropped hedges. The main dome of the Chahar Bagh Madrassa can be seen from the lawn of the hotel whose main lobby is itself like an art gallery with its traditional wood carvings, marble pillars, and impressive paintings dating from the early modern era. Across the hotel is a market devoted to books and magazines where one can see people of all age groups buying texts as well as other printed material. Most books are in Persian but English, Arabic, and French choices are also available. It appears that, given a wider public readership in Iran, all kinds of new titles get translated quickly into Persian without compromising the overall quality. Informal discussions with the owners and the number of buyers and browsers revealed that Iran was still an intact society of book lovers who like to celebrate poetry and appreciate literary finesse. The Iranians do not seem to shy away from learning European languages yet Persian continues to enjoy an unrivalled status at all levels and is a major medium of instruction. Not far from this triumvirate of the madrassa, hotel, and the book centre is situated the Hasht Behesht Palace (The Palace of Eight Heavens) which was completed in 1669 and closely resembles the Chehel Sutoun through its carved columns, raised terrace, elaborate gardens, and other similar integral features expected of a Safavid masterpiece. Inside the main building, one finds ornate ceilings in varying shapes, exquisitely beautiful mosaics, and stalactite mouldings which remind one of the Ali Qapu

Palace. By the main building, there remains a channel made of marble where water used to flow just like in the Mughal gardens in Lahore and Agra, and like other such gardens in the city, the area impressively looked free of rubbish and plastic bags.

The Zayandeh Rud, flowing in the south of Isfahan, divides the historic town and features 11 bridges, each displaying its own unique characteristics; five of them are old, whereas six were added in more recent times. Amongst the older ones, Si-o-se-pol (The Bridge of 33 Arches) is an impressive and unsurpassed piece of architecture consisting of two bricked storeys. The water flows through 33 channels built within the lower storey, whereas the cross ventilation adds a cooling effect and also some solitude over a cup of tea in its scenically located restaurant. This bridge is 160-metres-long and was completed in 1602, linking the upper and lower sections of the Chahar Bagh Abbasi Street. Further down towards the east and beyond the Firdausi Bridge is the Pole Choobi (The Wooden Bridge) which again is a spectacle of the traditional Iranian architecture and offers some quiet corners to catch up on reading while sipping coffee. This 150-metre-long bridge was built in 1665 by Shah Abbas II and was purported to divert some water for use in the royal palaces. About three kilometres from Si-o-se-pol and beyond the Chubi Bridge is located the Khaju Bridge, the most famous of all its rivals. Also built by Shah Abbas II, it is 132-metres-long and consists of two terraces and 23 arches; the bridge was completed in 1650 on an older counterpart dating from the time of Tamerlane. This bridge had a pavilion in the centre meant for the king's sightseeing; a few remains of the seats and traces of floral designs are still visible. Here, other than joining Isfahanis for small talk over tea, one may just sit and watch some of them trying to net fish. Three kilometres east of the Khaju Bridge lies the Shahrestan Bridge, the oldest of its kind, which was built in the twelfth century and sports 11 arched stone and brick structures. According to archaeological evidence, this bridge is built on the Sassanid site of an ancient counterpart. As mentioned earlier, the Chahar Bagh Abbasi Street eventually takes one to Zayandeh River, beyond which lie some of the most recent sections of Isfahan including Jolfa, the Armenian quarters, and the University of Isfahan. Here in the south, there are 13 churches and a cemetery, and the area remains predominantly Christian. The most famous church here is the Vank Cathedral (Kalisa-i-Vank), also known as the Church of Saintly Sisters, which was built between 1606 and 1655, and combines Islamic art with ornate Christian motifs. In the museum next door, there is a collection of some rare manuscripts, whereas its courtyard features a memorial to the Armenian massacre of 1915.

Isfahan lies in central Iran and is surrounded by the desert that melts into a bigger desert to the east until one reaches the vast lands of Balochistan and subsequently Sindh. On the way to Zahedan is the fabled city of Bam which was mercilessly destroyed by an earthquake in 2003. The old mud fort, a world heritage site, and the neighbouring houses were all flattened in the early hours of a winter morning. It appears that, like the thundering American neocons, the forces of nature had been equally out to test the Iranian resolve. Certainly, they are people of strong nerves as history has seen Greeks, Romans, Arabs, Mongols, Afghans, and Turks, all trying their prowess on them but in the end it will be Persia that will conquer their hearts and souls! Iran, a land of history, letters, architecture, and, most of all, cultured people, confident women, and friendly men is certainly an endowed society where religiosity and worldliness cohabit not always without tensions. It has been a closed society for the world outside especially since 1979 and it is always caricatured as a place of mad mullahs and oppressed black chador-clad women. But the real Iran, shorn of a tourist fantasy, is a land of pleasant surprises for any visitor. Here more than anywhere else in the region, one finds the largest number of women working in almost every field. Certainly, they have to dress in a specific way yet they prominently run immigration, banks, customs, universities, airlines, and hotels. Most of all, they reflect self-confidence. They look into the eyes of a man without any awe or rancour, and talking to an Iranian woman on any subject may be easier when compared to several other places. Secondly, Iran impresses a visitor with a high rate of literacy and keenness for books and magazines. It is not surprising to see kiosks and bookstores every few hundred yards where sometime one can see intellectuals engaged in lively discussion or poets reciting their favourite poems. Iranian men and women have a high rate of literacy reaching almost 80 per cent, whereas the quality of printing is equally astounding. It is not only a literate society, it is also an extremely polite society that follows clerics yet boisterously laughs over their follies and considers guests to be a blessing rather than a liability.

I wonder what the Isfahanis think about living in this city where history, beauty, arts, romance, and literature all coexist in a tolerant climate. The city of Isfahan, the half of the world or *Nisf Jahan*, receives people from all over whose appreciation of this jewel must send its inhabitants over the moon. Iran may not be too receptive to tourists, however, its friendly people miss them and befriend them in their usual courteous manner. Sadly, its culture, history, poetry, and architecture have once again become semi-obscure. All the way from the arid Zagros Mountain to the north and surrounded by deserts, the lovely oasis of Isfahan receives its life from the fresh air, Zayandeh Rud, and the warmth of its people whose own heritage must be invigorating them in their mundane worries.

Note

1. Aryanpur Kashani, *Odes to Hafiz*, trans. Abbas Aryanpur Kashani (Santa Ana: Mazda Publishers, 1974).

13

Cordova, Oh Cordova!

Love the wellspring of life; Love on which death has no claim.
Swiftly its tyrannous flood times' long current may roll:
Love itself is a tide stemming all opposite waves …
Love is Gabriel's breath, love is Mohamed's heart.
Love is the envoy of God, Love utterance of God …
Love is the plectrum that draws music from life's taut strings—
Love is the warmth of life.
Love's is the radiance of life.

Muhammad Iqbal, 'The Mosque of Cordova'[1]

They would occasionally call it mesquita but then to every visiting Muslim, the Cordovan security officials keep reiterating that it is not a mosque, instead it is a cathedral. Their posters, travel literature, and even books mention the Cordova Mosque as one of the earliest and biggest mosques. They earn millions of euros from an unending stream of tourists eager to absorb a glimpse of this 'mutilated' monument that once was the largest of its kind. Built in the early eighth century, less than a century after the Prophet (PBUH), the Cordova Mosque or Masjid-i-Qurtaba, for generations of millions of Muslims is certainly as much a sad reminder of their own plight as it is of its enduring bereavement. While Granada's Alhambra complex and Toledo's oldest mosque may equally transmit a greater sense of loss and grief, the poignancy calibrated by this otherwise mysterious yet immensely majestic structure in Cordova remains transcendent. Its antique walls, dark and gloomy interiors all overlaid by a hasty Christian memorabilia, the tampered calligraphic inscriptions over and above the red stone which has had its layers peeled off for centuries, and the intermittent chiming of bells in the tower where once a muezzin gave calls for prayer form an elegy of excruciating anguish for Muslims. The quietly opening gates of this square structure leading into a vast compound with rows of orange and palm trees and a few solitary cypresses have outlived its worshippers and now stand aloof, serenely watching endless rows of tourists sauntering into its colonnade labyrinths. Scores of elegant marble columns shoulder symmetrical horseshoe arches that embody faded red and white stripes. Once in a while, a few solitary Muslim visitors, visible by their complexion or attire, come in forcibly holding back their eagerness to seek a quick prayer in front of a deserted mihrab or behind the rows of slim columns, away from the piercing and prohibiting eyes of uniformed guards. Since 9/11 and the Madrid train blasts, Muslims are not allowed to pray or show any other sign of traditional solemnity in the mosque. The guards have become quite adept in recognizing Muslims from the hordes of tourists and follow them with prying eyes and, like their Inquisitional ancestors, never shirk from admonishing them by observing: 'You got to wear your shoes; it is not a mosque'. They do not realize that taking off shoes may be out of tradition and respect and is not meant to preamble a full prayer. This daily game of locating Muslims and chasing them, especially when they take off their shoes out of sacred norm occurs intermittently. It is well-rehearsed like these numerous annual fiestas across Spain where holy warriors fully buoyed up by maidens and carrying crosses defeat dark-skinned, turbaned Moors. It is quite curious to observe how here in this part of Europe, they forcibly urge you to wear your shoes, while further up north in France, head covering, burkini, or any show of religious symbolism at public places is illegal!

The Cordova Mosque is a powerful and unrelenting reminder of the Muslim past in a once plural and different kind of Spain. The intrusive superimposition of the cathedral subsequently built within only irks many of those who come here to see the faded Muslim glory underpinning Spanish Convivencia. More than history books, Spanish language, names of the cities and people, food items including oranges and olives, the irrigation system and music, the mosque, Alcázar, and Alhambra remain the most poignant and irascible symbols of an irretrievable era. As long as these few monuments survive—and surely they will as their beauty, majesty, and historicity guarantee stupendous revenue to Andalusia and other regions—Muslim Spain will never vanish from public memory. The cat and mouse game daily played in the mosque and the aggrieved Muslim faces from another era will keep on pleasing Samuel P. Huntington and Osama bin Laden in their resting places.

The enduring loneliness, permeating gloom, and ironical desertion of the Cordova Mosque deeply moved eminent poet-philosopher Muhammad Iqbal, who made a special journey to Andalusia and wrote his Urdu poem. Unlike present-day Spanish minders, the then Cordovan security guard allowed Iqbal to offer his prayer near the ornate mihrab. He might have been a lone visitor in centuries to the historic city in a poorer and rather exhausted Spain, and his venture might have even amused the guard, himself a small town apparatchik in a country that was slowly sliding into another agonizing phase of political instability. Certainly that Spain, unlike its reincarnation in the twenty-first century, was an impoverished land where religion remained crucial yet the economy and politics were piteous with the former possessions in Latin America offering no respite to the mother country. Iqbal subsequently travelled to Sicily and composed a similar, shorter, and even pithier poem where he remembered his literary mentor, Mirza Dagh, who had poured his heart out over the wanton British destruction of Delhi in 1858. Rampage at Delhi was no less sinister than that which befell Cordova or other cities and hamlets across Spain until history abruptly closed this chapter in 1492 with the Fall of Granada. The surrender by Boabdil in January outside the Alhambra was announced by the chiming of bells, followed by the expulsion and conversion of Muslims and Jews across the Iberian Peninsula. In addition, the resources acquired from them by Ferdinand and Isabella helped sponsor Columbus' campaign to discover a new route to the Indies. Columbus lived in Seville and is buried in this former Ashbiliyya but had been camped in Granada in 1491–2, waiting for the impending victory to seek a nod from the Conquerors.

In a sizzling Andalusian summer, Cordova might have looked as ordinary as an average version of a typical American Midwestern town or even a mohalla of historic Fes or Bukhara had it not been due to the mosque and its immediate environ where the late Syrian ambassador-poet and a preeminent Arabic scholar of his era, Nizar Kabbani (1923–98), would unconsciously start fumbling in his pockets looking for keys to his home back in Damascus. Belonging to a scholarly Damascene family, Kabbani had represented his country in Madrid and died in the closing years of the last century. His niece, Rana Kabbani, subsequently focused on the British literary figures of the nineteenth century in reference to Saidian's concept of Orientalism. An articulate and impressive writer, Rana had been shocked by a Cambridge don who would not believe that an Arab woman could have a fair complexion, brown eyes, and a piercing intellect. The English academic was used to foggy ideas of completely hidden Arab females who were supposedly least bothered to study English literature at Cambridge.

Of course, away from its modern boulevards and high-rise apartment complexes, the old town of Cordova consists of the mosque (cathedral, as the Spanish officials would insist!), the old palaces, and the waterworks on the River al-Kabir called Guadalquivir. The river fed the metropolis before meandering its way towards Seville and further down to the Atlantic. An old bridge on the river sits in line with the mihrab of the mosque, while the waterworks are adjacent to the Alcázar palace. Besieged by conifers, palms, and cypresses, Alcázar, like its counterpart in Seville, stands right across from the mosque and ironically is called Alcázar de los Reyes Cristianos (Castle of the Christian Kings). As the name itself suggests, the amirs and caliphs lived on these premises, whereas the biggest mosque in Muslim Spain, the central library, and other official buildings were situated in the neighbourhood within the walls of the Old City. In fact, Amir Abdur Rahman Al-Dakhil (lit: the Entrant, 731–88) had purchased this piece of land from Christian priests to build a mosque on the site which kept on increasing in size over subsequent centuries due to the growing population of this metropolitan city. Access to Cordova both from Seville or Granada is through an open but hilly terrain where miles and miles of orange and olive groves still exude a strong sense of history and sub-tropical climate. The present-day roads are built on old caravan routes and deserts have been tamed with irrigation schemes yet the villages and towns retain their Arab and Berber names and are also still located on vantage points with forts rising in the middle. Of course, all those mosques have been turned into cathedrals though a few traces of Quranic calligraphy or dome-like structures still exemplify their original contours. The white-painted Andalusian villages cling by the hillsides, and it is not uncommon to see isolated sentry posts and bunkers perched on the various peaks which were designed to provide security to trade routes as well as to ward off any sudden attack. Given the gradual decline of the caliphate from thirteenth century onwards, Spain's Muslims and

Jews gradually came to be confined to the little principality of Granada where the Nasrid Amirs maintained their hold through diplomacy, bribes, and by often even joining Christian kings against fellow Muslims.

Under the Umayyads, Cordova had 300 mosques and 100,000 houses and shops, making it one of the largest cities in Europe. The mosque, Cordova's winding narrow lanes, small squares characterized by lazily sprouting fountains, and certainly the ruins of Medina Azahara render this past metropolis into a unique experience in history, architecture, and a bygone pluralism. Built by Caliph Abdul Rahman III (889–961), the suburban city of Medina Azahara, like Emperor Akbar's Fatehpur Sikri, was a new metropolis with elaborate mosques, palaces, offices, cantonment, and private residences. Patterned like old Damascus, the new city soon ran out of water and was further devastated by invasions from the north. In subsequent centuries, vandals continued to loot the ruins until Madrid began to show some concern. Cordova was once not only a metropolitan city of mosques and churches, it was also a city of schools, seminaries, and libraries. The caliphal library had millions of books where philosophers and jurists debated on sacred and secular themes while poets composed romantic poetry idealizing the Arabian Desert, North African women, Spanish clime, and above all, the descending twilight that had already taken away Barcelona, Salamanca, Toledo, and many other towns and villages by pushing their citizens southward. The popularization of St. James' story of being buried in Asturias and the evolution of a Christian pilgrimage to match the Muslim hajj, within the context of the Crusades and a series of Papal bulls, had underwritten intermittent expulsions and conversions that would eventually make Spanish Muslims and Jews into 'American Indians' on their own soil. Cleansing, that once begun from the northeast, was to reach across the Mediterranean and the Atlantic, with millions of Africans and Native Americans subsequently falling victims to this aggressive onslaught. The world was ushering itself into a modern age!

One of the city's lanes has been named after one of the most illustrious Cordovan citizen, Ibn Rushd/Averroes. Known for his scholarship, this one-time judge had been an avid reader and keen traveller. His focus on reason without shunning faith was a pioneering effort to bring about a needed equilibrium between the two and, to a great extent, he resolved the age-old contestation between Mu'tazilah and Ash'ari. Ibn Tufail, a native Granadian, left his influence on Averroes and future generations of philosophers and novelists through his eminent works such as *Philosophus Autodidactus*, the story of an autodidact feral child brought up by a gazelle on an uninhabited island until he meets a castaway and begins his journey in disciplines like theology and philosophy. An allegorical novel known as *Hayye ibn Yaqzan* in its original Arabic was purported to respond to the Ash'ari issues raised by Islamic scholar, Imam Ghazali (1058–1111), in his *The Incoherence of Philosophers*. Ghazali had prioritized faith over the infallibility and invincibility of philosophy, with the former affording consensual responses to the numerous creedal queries. Ibn Tufail and Ibn Rushd, both practising Spanish Muslims and jurists, had raised issues with Ghazali's postulations and tried to create a needed balance between theology and philosophy. On the other end of Averroes Street by the restored home of Maimonides—the architect of Jewish renaissance—stands one of the oldest synagogues in European neighbourhood. Maimonides, like Averroes, enjoys an enduring influence on philosophical thought. He, during the autumn of the Cordovan caliphate, sought exile first in Morocco and then Saladin's Egypt. Founder of medieval Jewish renaissance in Andalusia, Maimonides, an intellectual, though not fond of poetry, first moved to Fes, a city favourite with Spanish exiles to assume a lecturing assignment at the Al-Karaouine University, founded by Fatima al-Fihri in 859. Being a family-oriented intellectual, he was deeply affected by the death of his brother, David, who was on his way to India. The news devastated him to the extent of confining him to his bed for a year in Egypt. A Sephardic Jew, Maimonides, unlike some contemporary opinions, never claimed to be a descendant of Prophet-King David.

Walking back towards the mosque just behind the humdrum of tourists with their bulging backpacks, we explored a clutch of souvenir shops in the rectangular structure of an old university which is guarded by the turbaned statue of Mohamed Al-Gaefqui, another famous twelfth century Cordovan luminary. Like Ibn Rushd and Maimonides, his recognition as a proud son of Cordova came into limelight only in recent decades when a more confident Spain gradually began to revisit its own past, stubbornly denied for centuries by countless generations of Spaniards. The Moors and Jews had been either routinely posited as outsiders or a mere temporary interregnum whose memory was to be exorcized through yearly fiestas.

My first visit to Cordova had been like that of a backpacker and I preferred to stay in a pension just across the mosque and in one of the oldest parts of the city. It was run by a Moroccan family. I soon came to realize that Mr Khan, a British Pakistani, owned this modest facility; his daughter had recently begun her studies in Middle Eastern history at St. Antony's. I had previously run into Mr Khan at Oxford but somehow our encounter here in Cordova, instead of being impromptu and a bit Pakistani style hullabaloo, turned out to be a hushed affair. Maybe he had several other things on his mind with diminished interest in meeting a fellow expatriate! Visits to the sun-kissed mosque and Alcázar during that early sojourn were interspersed by several forays into the university for meals—away from the usual tourist haunts. The evenings were surely joyous due to leisure walks over the ancient bridge. I had ventured out into the newer areas of this city but they did not impress me at all and I would soon get back to its older lanes where history seemed to have come to a standstill. The various kinds of olives, oranges, and melons and vegetables, certainly tasting more organic and original than their counterparts in supermarkets, had injected a new-found energy into my sinews. I must have clocked miles and miles of walks in the few days I spent in this historic city. I deeply admired the sense of history and cleanliness in the streets where flower baskets added to the colourfulness of low-lying houses. In my quest, I had also come across some old and new mosques including the one built by some Muslims from Norwich who had named themselves Murabitun—or returners. I did not fully grasp the meaning of this nostalgic term until I visited Morocco several years later where cities like Tangier, Rabat, and Casablanca still retain a sizeable number of people seeking their origins from Spain. The expulsions of Spanish Muslims and Jews led them to North Africa and Ottoman lands in the Balkans and that is how, other than Constantinople, cities such as Sarajevo became centres of Spanish Jews. In fact, Greece's second largest city, Thessaloniki, before 1925, had been the Jewish majority city in the world thanks to the Ottomans. Even today, the world's biggest Jewish cemetery is located on Mount Igman in Sarajevo which had been desecrated by the Serbs during their three-year-long siege of this Bosnian metropolis. After the Dayton Accords, the new government in Bosnia heroically restored the cemetery to its past incarnation—something that is worth celebrating, given a nauseating emphasis on clash of faiths.

That journey to Andalusia during the early 1990s had begun in Malaga and, other than Seville, had taken us to Cordova and Granada with an ample use of public transport, run-of-the-mill pensions, and a daily replenishment of fresh fruit and vegetables. Evening meals would always end up at some ethnic joint, preferably Spanish or North African, with intermittent coffee breaks. Andalusia had gone deeper into my veins since a long-time desire to visit this region—thanks to Iqbal and other such writers—had finally materialized. It was sheer coincidence or just good fortune that our stay in Cordova coincided with a full moon. The beauty of Alcázar with its sprouting fountains, sleepy lotus, and fragrant jasmine in the early evening left an indelible imprint on my memory. While walking on the bridge and looking at the mosque with a cathedral's belfry in the middle, we were filled with a deep sense of loss. The water drawing system sat on the left continuing with its centuries-old wait for its builders, though the reeds from the riverbed seemed to have reached quite high providing a kind of hijab to this medieval facility. Here in a small area of Cordova, the Roman, Muslim, and Christian past of this land appeared to neighbour one another in no less ironic proximity and, except for multitudes of tourists, Muslim seekers, and some historians, they seemed to have been mute witnesses of three bygone eras. In a world surrounded by modernist edifices and changed demographics, here the past belonged to a different kind of humanity, quite unreal or even surreal!

My second visit to Cordova, in the company of a probing Sidra, allowed me a bit of luxurious accommodation but still in the vicinity of the mosque. By then 9/11 had happened and the mosque's watchmen had become even more curious and intrusive towards 'Muslim-looking' visitors. They were keen on ensuring that the visitors would not take off their shoes and would rigorously abstain from offering quick prayers behind the medley of slim pillars. Our accommodation was next to the square that once housed Miguel de Cervantes (1547–1616), whose four hundred and sixtieth birth anniversary had already caused several special exhibits, seminars, and road shows. Our previous visit had been within the postscript of the fifth centenary of Columbian 'discovery' when Andalusia appeared even more melancholic than ever, though its guardians were less obtrusive. Sidra took off her slippers while entering the mosque and was soon confronted by two guards who insisted that she put them back on. She did not and left the mosque but then came back when she saw several other younger Muslims intent upon defiance. My senior years came in handy and the situation was saved, though my inner instinct was equally intent upon offering prayer near the mihrab; a kind of rebellious youthfulness seemed to have awoken but then sanity prevailed. The entire situation was a mockery of common sense but what can one do when the states begin to deny history to suit their own tunnel view of a rather complex past!

Professor Bilal Hashmi sadly passed away in Seattle soon after his visit to Andalusia. He had felt so energized and invigorated by his foray into Spain that he would not let anyone talk that evening at Oxford. To this socialist and liberal sociologist, it was not a mere impromptu visit to a balmy Andalusia; this was a soul-searching sojourn. He felt annoyed with himself for not having travelled to Spain earlier as an animated Bilal had spent hours in the Cordova Mosque and narrow lanes all around, often tiptoeing in Averroes Street. Of course, he was not a born-again Muslim yet he acknowledged his sense of anger, gloom, and even some spirituality. His wife, Margaret, when given a rare opportunity to converse, expressed her own surprise after seeing Bilal having clocked up dozens of visits to the mesquita from his pension. Bilal, the sociologist, went back to the United States laden not only with his happy memories but also as a convert to the historical pursuit along with a complimentary copy of my Pluto book. The avid reader was able to read it yet did not live to tell anyone what he thought of *Islam and Modernity*. I still plan to undertake a more detailed visit of Andalusia and eventually north to traverse a part, if not the entire, pilgrim trail to touch base with St. James, the Palestinian.

Note

1. V. G. Kiernan, *Poems from Iqbal* (Bombay, 1947), 37.

14

In the Land of Ibn Battuta
and Marabouts

Physically as well as spiritually man is a self-contained centre,
but he is not yet a complete individual.
The greater his distance from God, the less his individuality.
He who comes nearest to God is the complete person.
Not that he is fully absorbed in God.
On the contrary he absorbs God into himself.

Muhammad Iqbal[1]

Sitting near the Karaouine Mosque and looking over the minaret of
Moulay Idriss' *Zawiya* in Fes from a vantage point near Bab Guissa
while reading *Akhbar Majmu'a* certainly assumes a unique meaning and
context. It was here that the Berber, Arab, Andalusian, and Sub-Saharan
traditions and people met within an Islamic context and, joined by the
Jews, established unique plural states and societies which, following the
annexation of the Iberian Peninsula, flourished for several centuries.
Subsequent upon the Umayyad conquest of Andalusia of 711 CE,
as the Maghrebis and others called it, both North Africa and North
Mediterranean regions developed closer mutualities which were surely
not exempt from occasional acrimonies.[2] During the early phase, this
conquest allowed Muslims and Jews to migrate to the former regions and
during the subsequent civil wars and Reconquista, these processes were
reversed with their descendants and coreligionists being expelled from
Spain. Just like the Muslim and Jewish expulsions from Sicily and Bari,
these large Andalusian communities had to find shelters in Moroccan
cities such as Rabat, Sale, Fes, and further east in present-day Algeria,
Tunisia, Libya, and Egypt. Hundreds of thousands of Spanish Jews were

welcomed by the Ottomans and thus rescued from annihilation. Although many Muslims, following their forced conversion to Catholicism, were allowed to continue living in Spain, their presence was only acceptable within exclusive strictures. Their lifestyles and mobility had remained proscribed under the pale of suspicions until, due to large-scale violence by the mid-seventeenth century, their descendants were expelled once and for all and Spain became avowedly mono-creedal.

The Moroccan and, for that matter, Maghrebi outreach in Sicily, Spain, and Portugal, besides encounters with the French, offer a unique case in the study of Maghreb-Maghreb or South-North relations. These complex processes and their demographic fallout continued long after the Norman Conquest of southern Italy and the Crusades, followed by the Mongol invasions from the northeast which led to a huge squeeze on Muslim intellectual, political, and demographic persona for centuries to come. Fes is certainly the oldest and perhaps the biggest and most compact medieval city where Fes al-Bali and Fes al-Jadid provide undiminished connections with this trans-regional interface. In Karaouine, Ibn Rushd, Maimonides, and Ibn Khaldun taught at the world's oldest degree awarding university as it had been housed in one of the biggest mosques in the Muslim world, watched over by two minarets that were replicated in Marrakesh, Rabat, and Seville. The mosque and the madrassa were established by Fatima al-Fihiri in 859 CE, who herself was a refugee from Kairouan in present-day Tunisia. Her sister, Mariam, founded a mosque across the River Jawhar for displaced Andalusian Muslims, and in between these two historic institutions stands the Sidi Ahmed al-Tijani Madrassa founded for African Muslims. The narrow, winding, and often mind-boggling souks of the old Medina might be confusing for any first time visitor, yet they all ultimately reach one of the four main entrances to the Karaouine Mosque which is neighboured by some of the oldest seminaries. After Bou Inania Madrassa, Al-Attarine Madrassa is the most beautiful of the medieval colleges in Medina, Fes el-Bali—the oldest part of the city. In fact, Saffarin Madrassa, in metal workers street, has the credit of being the oldest and was meant to house students studying at the Karaouine Mosque. It was built in 1270, 80 years before the establishment of Madrassa Inania and 35 years before Madrassa Al-Attarine.

In Fes' old Medina, while there are about 360 mosques and that many *funduk*s (inns for travellers/traders), at least a million residents live in this comparatively small and compact area. In between, there are thousands of stalls and *riad*s (traditional homes) where artisans, like their ancestors, pursue crafts and manual skills to produce goods made of leather, wood, copper, cotton, and wool. Further to the west in Fes el-Jadid lies Mellah, the Jewish area in the neighbourhood of the old palace not far from Madrassa Inania. Here some of the oldest synagogues, double-storey buildings with wooden balconies and terraces in the vicinity of traditional gardens still remind a visitor of enduring mutuailties amongst these Abrahamic faiths. While Fes is closer to the Atlas Mountains and slightly away from the ocean, Rabat, the capital of Morocco, is strategically located on the Atlantic coast where River Bou Regreg allows a lagoon. The river provides an easy access to the historic city of Sale, though the latter ironically seems to be more associated with the Barbary Corsairs, many of whom happened to be Europeans. The Kasbah of Udayas in Rabat, founded by the Almohads in the twelfth century and strategically overlooking the river and the lagoon, is a fascinating specimen of early medieval architecture and, like Fes el-Bali, is truly a world heritage place. The entrance to the Kasbah is through a massive gate, Bab Oudaia, which to some observers remains the finest of its kind in the Muslim world. Religious differences apart, the multiple commonalities amongst the early Moroccans vetoed any communal hostilities, exactly like in Peshawar, Isfahan, Bukhara, Rawalpindi, Lahore, Agra, Lucknow, Delhi, Hyderabad, and Multan where traditional mores amongst Muslims, Hindus, Jews, Parsees, and Sikhs disallowed any friction until modernist politics and other chasms began to spawn suspicions.

It is certainly true that the historiography of the Mediterranean regions is yet to diversify and mature into a more comprehensive mould shorn of focus on the colonial and predominantly Eurocentric strands. The expansion of Muslims into Iberia was certainly more than a temporary military venture or just an imperial conquest. The eventual winding down of a pluralist culture is a development that took years and generations to occur, though not without sordid details which are now being recorded more copiously. After the Fall of Granada in 1492, either this erstwhile Andalusia became the 'other' or simply vanished from public discourses, except for triumphalism that one sees even today in scores of

Spain's annual fiestas. A hostile indifference towards Muslim (Moorish) Spain tried to wipe it out from texts, historical narratives, and literary outpourings as if the former was merely an abnormal blip that had been consigned to some forgotten bin of history. And if it ever existed in public consciousness, it was only through negative and immensely sordid images of barbaric, bloodthirsty *others* that these fiestas continue to permeate. For a long time, Catholic Spain and likewise an imperial Portugal did not want to confront that millennium which now historians are rediscovering as a cherished past with its recurrent cultural, literary, architectural, and artistic reverberations. The offloading of clichéd caricatures and discursive narratives on 'the Dark Ages' is generating a more pristine and holistic understanding of the medieval era. The study of Al-Andalusia inclusive of Portugal benefited from the works of Pascual de Gayangos y Arce (1809–97), Francisco Codera (1836–1917), Eduardo Saavedra (1829–1912), and Emilio Lafuente y Alcantara (1825–68) when several Arabic manuscripts were translated along with their historicized commentaries. *The Akhbar Majmu'a* was in fact one of scores of such manuscripts and artefacts which found their way from North Africa into France in the early modern period.[3] It was translated into modern Spanish by Alcantara in Madrid in 1867 but had not been translated into English until David James took the initiative. He compared its Spanish and French versions and, with an astute knowledge of Arabic, prefaced it with a detailed introduction that sheds light on one of the earliest sources of the Umayyad conquest of Iberia. Along with Ibn al-Qutiyya's *History*, it is housed in the Bibliothèque Nationale de France and is one of the 430 manuscripts acquired from the Arab world between 1671 and 1675. It does not identify the author(s) nor does it record the date of its earliest completion; it covers the events until 961 when Andalus had already become an Umayyad caliphate—distinct from its Abbasid counterpart in Baghdad.

Majmu'a traces the history of the conquest of Spain in 711 under Tariq ibn Ziyad and Musa ibn Nusayr for Caliph Al-Walid ibn Abd al-Malik back in Damascus and highlights various battles that continued until victorious generals met in Toledo. The former two were soon recalled by Sulayman ibn Abd al-Malik, the new caliph in Syria. It is basically a chronicle which provides extensive details on leading generals, members of the Umayyad family, Amir Abd al-Rahman's escapades all the way from Damascus to Cordova, and his singular victories over the Berber rebels and Abbasid rivals in Spain. The early Jewish support in the Muslim conquest, appointment of Jewish governors across Iberia, and correspondence between Caliph Abd al-Rahman III and his contemporaries offer interesting details on this early period. Tariq ibn Ziyad had landed on the Spanish coast in 711 CE with 1,700 Berbers to defeat the several times bigger army of Ludhriq (Roderic), the ruler of Hispania. The story moves all the way until the dramatic changes begin to take place in Syria. The Umayyad prince, Abd al-Rahman, flees from Syria via Iraq and Palestine, all the while being chased by the Abbasid opponents who have been killing most members of his family. While swimming across the Euphrates, he is shocked to see his brother being killed on the bank, since believing the promises of his pursuers, the latter had turned back midstream only to be executed by the Abbasid sleuths. Abd al-Rahman's coalition with the allies in North Africa and then in Andalusia is owed to his sagacity, courage, and fortune; it ensured the continuation of the Umayyad rule, though the focus in this treatise largely remains on battles and not much is written about the ordinary people in the Middle East, North Africa, and Spain. Other than the heroics of Abd al-Rahman I, the manuscript covers the 50 year reign of Abd al-Rahman III who had ascended the caliphate in 912 and ensured its cultural richness all the way until 962. In fact, he had provided financial support for the Karaouine Mosque and its extensive library and teaching facilities. But his lack of interest in military adventures and devotion to architectural and literary pursuits receive special attention in *Majmu'a*, which consists of 67 leaves of European papers, scribed by master calligrapher(s). Alcantara had published his translation with the original Arabic text and James has ensured a comparative textual criticism on both the versions. While Évariste Lévi-Provençal (1894–1956), the French specialist on Muslim Spain, was dismissive of *Majmu'a*'s historiographical significance, viewing it to be a lateral inscription from Valencia possibly dating around 1230s, Alcantara allocated it the due status as an early, primary, and valuable source. He had sought documentary evidence from the works on the same by the Dutch historian, Reinhart Dozy (1820–83), and Joseph Reinaud (1795–1865), the French Arabist who had notably acknowledged its historical authenticity. In more recent times, the manuscript received due academic attention from Sanches

Albornoz (1893–1984), the former education minister of Spain who subsequently sought exile in Argentina and divided the narrative into five distinct realms.

Majmu'a is certainly not a detailed history of the early Muslim Spain but, without being an exotica or a dull and dry chronicle of unending warfare and factionalism, it attempts an honest history where the author diligently avoids undue praise or sheer denigration. It offers some ethnographic data; provides details on various political groups in Syria and Spain; and in several cases, chronicles minute details on numerous events besides reproducing some contemporary royal correspondence. Caliph Abd al-Rahman's poetic samples are surely innovative, secular, and brimming with romantic love. For instance, while responding to a poem, the caliph notes:

> How would anyone who suffers
> the pain of love as I do
> expect an instant of rest
> or drink wine mixed with water?

> If a stone suffered my woes
> it would be as fragile as glass.
> As you well know, I had time for pleasure
> and was free of troubles.

> Now, absent from my beloved
> I feel the pains which are incurable.
> The rose increases my sadness
> and the lily makes me restless.

> My nights, so beautiful once
> are worse than the ugliest faces.
> Do not expect what you ask
> until the anxiety has gone from my mind.[4]

He was in fact responding to a poem by Ismail ibn Badr, who sought his permission to open the bottle of wine that the caliph had sent him on the eve of a victory over an opponent. It is no wonder that even centuries later, while sitting in Fes el-Bali, the mainspring of this magnificent culture immersed in history and traditions, one cannot afford to be irreverent of a bygone era.

This was the era that the world's Muslims remember as the Golden Period of Islam when sacred and secular existed in comparative harmony anchoring what Professor Mohammed Arkoun (1928–2010) calls Global Humanism.[5] Their political, intellectual, scientific, and cultural accomplishments ensured a greater sense of self-confidence and tolerance towards non-Muslims. The contemporary world of Islam had a sense of belonging to a dynamic global civilization despite its varying metropolitan centres such as the Abbasids in Baghdad, the Fatimids in North Africa and Sicily, the Arab-Berber-Spanish caliphate in Spain, Ismailis in Khorasan and north-western India, and the Seljuks in Asia Minor. Here the imperial pursuits converged with faith even if they might embody factionalism, yet entrepreneurship, literary, and artistic achievements, and openness towards the world at large underwrote their collective ethos. Philosophers like Ibn Sina, Ibn Rushd, and Shahabuddin Suhrawardi felt no qualms in borrowing from Greek, Zoroastrian, and Jewish traditions, nor did they exhibit any sense of Muslim exceptionalism. Morocco was not a mere extension of the Islamicate, with its core region being in the Arab Middle East or subsequently in Persian speaking urban centres, but instead it was a major bridgehead in a transcultural relationship which went beyond conquests or temporary mutualities. Both Morocco and Spain, even long after Sicily's unilateral integration in the Catholic world, were centres of vibrant debates and dynamic pluralities. While Spain eventually underwent a major change like Sicily, much at the expense of its plural heritage, Morocco proved to be an enduring bastion of tolerant traditions which persist even today. Surely it is the westernmost region in Islamic Maghreb but it has also been one of the earliest states in the world. According to some, it has been a state for 1,200 years—longer than several of its European counterparts, though Ceuta and Melilla, two of its northern towns on the Mediterranean coast, are still held by Spain. The Spaniards amidst Reconquista captured them when the tables were turned on the Muslims. Even to this day and before the Spanish conquest under the Hapsburgs, several Moroccans spoke Spanish besides of course Arabic and Berber languages. Now comprising 270,000 square miles inclusive of Western Sahara and a population of around 34 million, the land of *Moros* became part of Carthage (present-day Tunisia) under the Phoenicians until the Romans held these territories all the way till they reached the lower reaches of Mauritania and established a new capital, Volbilis, near Meknes and Fes. Islam spread here rather fast and without any large-scale warfare or forced conversions. The Arabs and Berbers worked together under the Umayyads; they captured Iberia and were only pushed back from Poitiers in 730 CE. Further east, the caliphate in the Middle East changed hands in 750 CE as the Abbasids, helped by the Persians, took over from the Umayyads, making Baghdad their capital. Finding themselves at the receiving end of the Abbasid wrath, princes like Abd al-Rahman sought refuge in Maghreb before moving into Spain; *Majmu'a* chronicles that story of flight and conquest, and a great deal of its space is devoted to the Arab Middle East during the tumultuous caliphal switchover.

The Shia had played a crucial part in bringing the Abbasids into power but, within a generation or two, they both parted company, and this deepening intra-Muslim gulf led to rival regimes and migrations. Some Arab Zaidi Shias, led by Moulay Idriss, came to present-day Tunisia and then moved into a rather secure valley, founding the city of Fes. According to some traditions, Idriss soon died of poison administered by pro-Baghdad elements. His son's rule proved quite beneficial for Fes until the Fatimids started to come this way during the ninth and tenth centuries when North Africa, like Spain, became autonomous of the caliphate in Baghdad and allowed Shia Fatimid influences to move westward from Cairo into Maghreb (north-western Africa) and then into Sicily. However, unlike Mesopotamia, the Sunni groups gradually came to dominate Maghreb, Sicily, and Spain, and the Shia elements almost disappeared from the region. In the same vein, the Ismaili presence in northern Iran and present-day Indus Valley gave way to Sunni Turkic and Afghan dynasties, though in northern Iran and parts of Syria, an Ismaili backlash persisted in the form of Assassins whose main fort, Alamut on Mount Alborz, continued to defy the weakened Abbasid caliphate until the Mongols destroyed it altogether as they did away with other Muslim power centres including Baghdad, Balkh, Bukhara, Merv, Isfahan, and Peshawar.

The Sunni domination in Morocco followed the Idrisid dynasty and was solidified under the Almoravids, Almohads, and the Merinids, whose own plural roots vacillated between Sufi and scripturalist strands of Islam. The Almoravids and Almohads kept Morocco and Spain integrated but a gradual squeeze in Spain had already begun to occur with Muslim taifa kings retreating before the encroachments from the north, now collectively called Reconquista. Their mutual dynastic and territorial squabbles and lack of any major systemic overhaul led to the fall of Toledo, Seville, Cordova, and the once Iberia-wide caliphate came to be confined to Nasrid Granada in the south-eastern corner of Andalusia. The Nasrid Emirate patronized arts and architecture generously in the twilight years of a plural era and survived by paying tributes and building alliances against a few remaining fellow Muslim potentates in Andalusia until history closed its chapter on them in 1492. By that time, Morocco had already become home away from home for Spanish Muslims and Jews, and Maghrebi coastal towns on the Mediterranean such as Tangier, Tetouan, Chefchaouen, Melilla, Oujda, Algiers, and Tripoli were now receiving wave after wave of displaced people from across Europe. Naturally, the Spanish and Portuguese conquests of some of these coastal places soon followed through and resistance often proved successful, besides taking the shape of piracy which found Algiers, Tangier, and Sale as its major operational centres and collectively came to be known as Barbary Corsairs.

Sale lies outside Rabat across the River Bou Regreg; though it is now an extended part of the Moroccan capital. In the early seventeenth century, it was an autonomous city-state run by Corsairs who included a sizeable number of European adventurers, converts, and refugees who had found a successful enterprise in privateering besides a form of revenge against the Venetians, Tuscans, Spaniards, English, Dutch, French, and the rest. Sale or Sallee is not a new city as it dates from the Roman era and was strategically located on the main route between Rabat and Fes, connecting the Atlantic coast with the interiors and across the valleys in Atlas Mountains. It is viewed as the oldest Moroccan city founded by the Phoenicians, though that particular site is now named Chellah, a historic necropolis situated between present-day Rabat and Sale. The Carthaginian accounts dating from the seventh century BCE mention Sale and later Roman chronicles, penned by Pliny the Elder, identify it as Sala Colonia, a city surrounded by deserts on three sides and infested with wild elephants. Those animals must have flourished in green habitations in the valleys and, perhaps with greater desertification and human migrations, they gradually vanished. Romans had controlled Sale from 40 CE until 250 CE when they left it to the local rulers. It was in the tenth century that Banu Ifran, a Berber tribe, settled on the current site and built the Great Mosque that holds a commanding place in this rather congested habitation. By 1146, the Almohad ruler, Abd al-Mu'min had turned Rabat into a secure fortress with fortified walls and watchtowers encircling the town. Literally meaning 'fort', Rabat was used by Mu'min to mount attacks on Spain and, with several victories to his credit, the city came to be called Rabat Al Fatah or the Victory Fort. The Almohads were strict Muslims who followed a literalist version of Islam and despite their Iberian victories, more like Almoravids, focused on this side of the straits. As a result, Morocco stayed together and was even strong, yet Spain reverted to the taifa kings and eventually fell before the invaders from the north who were deeply inspired by the crusading sentiments. The Almohad king, Abu Yusuf Yaqub al-Mansur, also known as Moulay Yaqub, moved his capital to Rabat and it was during his reign that the Kasbah of Udayas was built as a sentinel overlooking the mouth of Bou Regreg and the vast blue expanse of the Atlantic. The side of Rabat facing Sale saw the construction of Tour Hassan (Hassan Tower) next to an unfinished mosque and it is here where King Hassan II was buried in 1999. A few moments spent at this point bring back the strategic and historic significance of this area where two cities embody different parallel, imperial, and dynastic narratives. Due to the tower, the mosque and now the tomb, this area is quite exclusive and well looked after and, despite the new apartment blocks across the river in Sale and some recent housing developments in Rabat itself, the entire river valley, neighbouring the coast, Kasbah, and the environ still exude the ambience of a frontier region where Africa, Asia, and Europe seem reflecting in their own respective traditional ways. Perhaps it could be largely due to the perceptions about Sale, Corsairs, and the tough Moulay Yaqub and Moulay Ismail, the Bismarcks of early Morocco, that the country attained a historic continuity for over 12 centuries.

With the loss of the Almohad political power, Rabat lost its metropolitan status as it soon shifted to Fes, while Sale became more introverted until the seventeenth century when it became the Corsair Republic and Moulay Ismail (1672–1727) integrated it within his centralized polity based in Meknes. Present-day Sale has a population of 850,000 people and is essentially a commuter city within a metropolitan Rabat. With more focus on the new capital and due respect for its older Medina and Kasbah plus a more modern Hassan, the former appears a bit eclipsed. Nabil Matar has tried to offer a balanced view of piracy and its multiple forms involving almost every contemporary nation in and around the Mediterranean, though British historians such as Linda Colley try to paint a rather exclusive and fundamentalist portrait of Sale.[6] Her narrative of Elizabeth Marsh—whose captivity in Sale and then emancipation and voyages to Bengal during the eighteenth century— reconstruct an interesting interface across the three continents.[7] Giles Milton goes a step further while reconstructing the narratives of captives held by the Corsairs, and a more recent account by Adrian Tinniswood reflects the predominant European components of these Corsairs who mostly came from Holland and England.[8] Such authors may often conveniently forget that the pirates in most cases founded modern European empires, and sailors like De Gama, Raleigh, Hudson, Smith, Cook, Cortez, Diaz, Pizzaro, and several others were simply robbers in service of their crowns.

From the older parts of Rabat such as the Kasbah and Medina, Sale appears like a self-sufficient and distinct city on its own. While sitting by King Hassan's tomb on this side of the river and upon the plateau, Sale rises high above the hills with Chellah's necropolis in between. The former appears rather introverted though, with the new bridge and tram service along with the housing developments by the river and with the expansion of naval facilities, the two cities have turned into one. Sale is vital due to its Roman connection and its resettlement as a Berber town—unlike the Kasbah—and also because it was the capital of the Corsair state, the republic, until the tough Moulay Ismail annexed it before taking on the Spanish and Portuguese. The Sale Rovers were largely European émigrés with a large proportion of Moriscos who, after having been expelled from Spain, had turned to piracy and ran the Republic of Sale. They roamed to distant places such as North America, Iceland, Ireland, Pisa, Malta, Sardinia, and Southwestern England, bringing back wealth, goods, and human cargoes. Sometimes the native governments had to pay ransom for the release of these captives, while at others, they would become Muslim by turning native. In many cases, people like the Englishman, John Ward, the Dutch, Zymen Danseker, and the Spaniard, Sinan Reis, became the feared pirates of the seas, representing a very curious interchange between the ruling dynasts and privateers who shared the booty from piracy.

The access to Sale, the oldest Moroccan town in the Atlantic, through the Bou Regreg was not always easy, largely because of the silt, but those Corsairs were daring and expert navigators who posed serious challenges to the European states; the latter mounted frequent campaigns against them. For instance, in 1629, French Admiral Isaac de Reilly bombarded Sale along with destroying three Corsair ships. The British destroyed Tangier and then Algiers and Tripoli but eventually settled for entering into various treaties with the Barbary Corsairs. Daniel Defoe's character, Robinson Crusoe, had spent time in the captivity of the Sale Rovers and eventually sought liberty while sailing off from the mouth of Bou Regreg. The Alawites (Alaouites), ancestors of present-day rulers, finally annexed the republic in 1666, though occasional piracy campaigns went on for another two centuries. On one hand, Morocco was the first-ever country to recognize a newly independent United States during the revolution, while simultaneously, the first-ever naval campaign undertaken by the young United States was also against Morocco-based pirates. Under orders from President George Washington, *The Enterprise*, a special warship, was built to mount campaigns against Corsairs; it is now moored as a museum in Baltimore Harbor. President Monroe donated the building of the American centre in Tangier to Morocco, making it the earliest such US property in a foreign land. It is now used as a museum in the older parts of Ibn Battuta's native city. This was a long time before American writers such as Paul Bowls, Tennessee Williams, Truman Capote, Aaron Copland, Jack Kerouac, William Burroughs, Alan Ginsberg, and others started to camp in the bohemian parts of this northern city. Perhaps they were following the footsteps of early European artists such as Eugene Delacroix and Henri Matisse who were attracted to the culture and colours of Morocco during the nineteenth century. Delacroix had accompanied a delegation in 1832, whereas Matisse spent two years in Tangier and was deeply attached to the life to the extent that he famously exclaimed: 'Ah, Tangier, Tangier! I wish I had the courage to get the hell out'.[9] Those seedy bars and clubs providing easy contacts with the locals in a rather tolerant atmosphere of libertine rendezvous are long gone but the city certainly retains its cosmopolitan outlook and the most well-known Tangerine will be proud of its vitality and plurality. The town certainly suffered due to Iberian Conquistadores but the Riffans and their other compatriots, like Afghans, never surrendered before a series of European onslaughts. Morocco escaped a longer period of colonization, even though it was merely nine miles away from the European coast, and being such a strategic location, had its own hazards. The feuding European colonial powers haggled over Tangier and other coastal cities of Morocco for their own imperial and strategic reasons, and it was in 1912 that a superimposed arrangement was introduced whereby Tangier, more like Eastern China, was opened up to the European marauding powers along with the United States, whereas the Mediterranean coastal region was given to Spain. The rest of Morocco was grabbed by France that made Casablanca into its capital before developing newer satellite towns in Rabat, Marrakesh, and Fes which lie adjacent to older medinas and kasbahs. Ibn Battuta, who came from Tangier or from one of its suburbs, continued to amaze everyone with his diligence, observations, Sufi lifestyle, and most of all, his prodigious memory since he wrote his *Travels* after returning from his sojourns across three continents. He must have been blessed with a minute and enduring memory that ensured all the details about names, distances, rituals, languages, and landmarks, and as amply affirmed by Timothy Mackintosh-Smith, all that information remains authentic. The Bristolian author has been on the footsteps of the Tangerine checking on villages, temples, roads, towns, cemeteries, rivers, and the distances amongst them traversing the routes Ibn Battuta took and has found nothing remiss.[10]

Tangier was destroyed on and off by the European powers but they also sought it due to its strategic location. No wonder, like Jerusalem and Constantinople, it was both a city of 'world desire' and a tolerant place of plural attributes, something rare when uniformity often appeared in immensely aggressive forms and formulations. Despite its proximity with Spain and Europe for that matter, Tangier is essentially a Moroccan city that never lost its Arab-Berber cultural contours, with Islam playing a significant role. Moulay Idriss I, the founder of Fes and, for that matter, of the state of Morocco, first landed here in 788 CE; the place had been a busy habitation since the Phoenician and Roman times until Muslims, led by Tariq ibn Ziyad, sailed from here in 711 to begin their conquest of Iberia. Ziyad had landed on Gibraltar or Jabal Tariq (Tariq's Hill) with his mainly Berber army and some Arab soldiers. Following the unending streams of Muslim and Jewish refugees from Andalusia, Tangier became even more populous and cosmopolitan until in 1681 when the English moved into it. Three years later, they were defeated by Moulay Ismail, the founder of Meknes who is still popular amongst Moroccans. Lord Dartmouth, who was assisted by Samuel Pepys, detested the port where the English had begun to build some navigational facilities and had manoeuvred their withdrawal. Moulay Ismail had built Meknes as his new capital and designed a special division of Sub-Saharan troops who loyally fought for him. Through these African troops, he was able to quash tribal revolts and, like the Ottomans, he depended upon 'slave-soldiers'. It was in 1777 that the American ships were allowed to dock in Tangier and certainly the Moroccan goodwill and recognition of the young republic played a vital role in this mutuality. Spain, like other European powers, never lost interest in establishing a colonial presence in Tangier and other parts of northern Morocco, and often competed with other European powers over imperial avowals in Africa and beyond. Instead of fighting amongst themselves, these powers reached an agreement in 1912 in Fes which, like Shanghai, turned Tangier into an international zone; free to all. While Spain consolidated its control over most of the Mediterranean coastal Morocco, the rest, along with the Atlantic coast, went to France. This parcelling of Morocco was a microcosm of what had already happened in the rest of Africa and China until the Second World War augured the arrival of the American and British forces which landed in Casablanca in 1942. In the meantime, nationalist feelings grew very strong and the Alawites were exiled in 1953 until three years later when Morocco gained independence from France and Sultan Mohammed V was allowed to return as the monarch. Spain's territorial possessions both in the north and the Sahara took time to dwindle, though it still holds on to Ceuta and Melilla, the two enclaves that are administratively controlled from Malaga. Ceuta is right across from Gibraltar, while Melilla is further east. In the latter, Spanish remains the official language, though people are multilingual and there is a strong sense of Moroccan identity all along the Rif Coast.

King Mohammed V died in 1961 and was followed by the long reign of Hassan II who ruled the country until his death in 1999 and, like his father, is buried in Rabat next to Tour Hassan built by Yaqub al-Mansur, the Almohad. At the height of 164 feet, the Hassan Tower, like the adjacent mosque, remained incomplete due to Yaqub's death in 1199. Since 1999, Morocco has embarked upon a campaign to modernize its economic and administrative infrastructure. In this case, King Mohammed VI has played a central role despite the post-9/11 polarity within the Moroccan society and growing suspicions about Western powers, given their military campaigns in the Muslim world. The king released more than 10,000 political prisoners, relaxed censorship, and other such restrictions and quite significantly inducted a new penal code allowing more rights to women, including powers to seek divorce. Morocco is a Muslim country and certainly has its own vibes and tensions, and the bomb blasts in 2003 in Casablanca and again in 2009 in Marrakesh have been reminders of internal dissensions. Morocco's relations with its two neighbours, Algeria and Mauritania, have often been sour due to Morocco's claims and then the annexation of Western Sahara which Spain vacated in the early 1970s. Algeria had been helping leftist guerrillas, though turbulence within Algeria during the 1990s and other major changes in Maghreb have tempered down these interstate tensions. However, Morocco seems to be pursuing a cautious but steady policy of reforms and modernization, avoiding confrontational or status quoist politics. Since 9/11, it has been certainly a tough rope to walk but the dividends of peace are visible across the land, though protests in 2017 in the northern regions underlined several political and economic strains.

One can never have enough of places like Morocco, Iran, or Uzbekistan due to the way one is overawed by nature's grandeur when looking at Nanga Parbat, Rakaposhi, Lady's Finger, Shimshal Cones, or gliding over the live glacier of Passu in Upper Karakorams. Just behind Gilgit are hamlets looked over by steep hills embodying carved Buddhas who have watched over steep valleys and glacial streams for centuries. Created by monks on their way to Tibet and China through the South Asian stretches of the Silk Road, these Buddhas, like the monasteries in Swat and Taxila, were abuzz when Alexander came to Gandhara lands. Buddhism was partly revived by the great Emperor Ashoka, however, it was again absorbed by a reinvigorated Hinduism that had been the religion of powerful empires such as the Mauryas and Guptas. By the time Islam came into the Indus Valley, Hinduism had totally absorbed Buddhism, and a new phase in this intercultural hide-and-seek ensued with Islam finally becoming the mainstay in Indus regions. Generations of Muslims protected and respected these monasteries and carvings until the Taliban and Hindutva, the ultra-forms of religiosity, began to hold sway even in the valleys of the Hindu Kush, Himalayas, and Karakorams. Morocco has been a land of Islam for a very long time and its Atlas Mountains are uniquely beautiful in their own way and certainly its Sufi culture and music, along with a mosaic of ethnicities, bestow it a kind of plurality that one finds in Turkey and Pakistan. In fact, mountains and matters featured in a discussion that I was having in the modern Fes of boulevards, open air cafés, and shopping malls that otherwise I often strictly avoid. However, this time, I was at a café that was full of Moroccans and very few tourists, and the nearby tree-lined section of the boulevard was teeming with families out for a stroll and ice cream. Sitting right in the middle of this café and munching on some local sweets, we had started talking to a Moroccan couple. Rashid had served in the Moroccan embassy in Pakistan as a military attaché in the recent past and had chanced to explore the country's mountains which he definitely missed. He was now on the way to Tajikistan to see mountain ranges 'from the other side'. Rashid's wife, Zareen, had some fond memories of Pakistan which in many ways often reminded her of her own native roots near the Atlas Mountains. Our discussion attracted a few more neighbours who enjoyed my saying 'from Pakistan to *Englistan* and now in *Moroccistan*'. Such wayside experiences not only solidify one's own bonds with humanity at large, they may spring up some interesting surprises as well.

As mentioned above, Rabat got its name due to the fort that was built in one of its past incarnations. Given its location overlooking the ocean and across from Sale and a capital city since the French era, it offers a wonderful mix of old and new. Close to the train station and right across the parliament, we had simply walked into a hotel where the receptionist was duly enthusiastic to give us a more comfortable room when she heard that we were from Oxford. Her own son was coming to Oxford for an English language course and now she had visitors from the world-famous academic town who also happened to be from a fellow Muslim nation. The hotel's location, closer to the palace and other official buildings, allowed us to see the difference as well as continuity between the French and national phases in architecture. The post-independence buildings—other than those built in a hurry and often designed by Western architects—were certainly modern, but the more recent ones seemed to be making cultural statements by appropriating Morocco's own past, skills, and traditions. More than their façades, the interiors, tile work, arches, and woodwork all showed an authentic Maghrebi persona that one sees in their older 'Moorish' counterparts in Spain and also occasionally in California.

Of course, some of my cherished walks happened by the Bou Regreg River and then within the hilltop Kasbah of Udayas that overlooks the ocean and is a special gem in traditional architecture and a well-preserved 'mini Morocco'. The entrance to this village is through the grand gate that often reminded me of similar entrances to the historic seminaries and mosques in Bukhara, Samarkand, and Lahore. The books on Corsairs generally talk about open bazaars which were held right outside this gate on the way to Medina. Reportedly, here slaves and prisoners of war were paraded in the past besides other sociopolitical activities, including the preparations for resistance against foreign incursions that became too frequent in more recent centuries. Behind the gate, while passing through some beautiful gardens, one may seek a break at a café that overlooks the ocean and the river down below. It looks like a sheer drop from here and one can always see a few hardy bodies trying to splash around in the green, deep, and placid waters. Walking up the hill and discovering the Kasbah is a thrilling experience as it is a lived township and fully accustomed to visitors. Neighbourhood cafés, art galleries displaying quality arts, and certainly the fort commanding the highest vantage position on the hilltop can take one centuries back. Despite organized tour groups, the place does not seem to be crowded, nor is one accosted by hawkers and free guides, and the presence of local inhabitants allows a strong sense of authenticity and integrity to this splendid and exclusive hamlet. Its white walls, ornate ceilings, and blue doors and windows certainly resemble some of those Andalusian hilltop towns, though Kasbah retains its age-old Islamic heritage without turning into a bizarre showpiece for irreverent tourists.

Coming down from the Kasbah and after passing through the gate, one enters Medina, an expanse of lived neighbourhood which reminds one of Fes but with automobiles plying around and traders eager to sell their carpets and wares to groups of tourists. Compared to its counterpart in Fes, this is a smaller area but some specific gates open into the colonial-national areas of modern Rabat. For fresh fruit, authentic tagine dishes, and to hobnob with throngs of local people, Medina is the ideal place worth exploring, though my preference for visiting it were early mornings. The cafés and open spaces outside the modern hotels in Rabat are proper social points where locals meet over an unending supply of tea and a smoke. The atmosphere here feels quite Mediterranean with a visible presence of Moroccans of Iberian ancestry amongst the patrons. Unlike Medina, this is an area of affluence visited by politicians, bureaucrats, and other elite, since the palace and several ministry buildings are further up the hill. The royal palace certainly covers a huge area which is walled on all sides and is neighboured by an elegant mosque on its eastern side and the university to the west. My forays often took me to the university in the hope that I might run into Professor Fatima Mernissi (1940–2015), the eminent scholar and founder of Muslim feminism. I stood by the entrance to the building that once housed her office but came to know that she was not well and thus away from the campus. The professor passed away in November 2015 after a long illness but I keep meeting her students, followers, and colleagues in Alexandria, Dubai, Oxford, and London.

Notes

1. Muhammad Iqbal, *The Secrets of the Self* (*Asrar-e-Khudi*), trans. Reynold A. Nicholson (New York: Cosimo, Inc., 2010).

2. It is quite interesting to note that during the French colonial control of Maghreb, the Arabs were presented as the *others* who, with their invasions of presumably urban Berbers, had stalled their progress and self-governance. Some French writers, like the colonial British historians of India, tried to flag primacy of Western civilization by imputing dysfunctionality to the advent of Islam amongst Berber societies. Such premises not only underwrote the traditional divide-and-rule imperium but equally offered a moral and civilizational justification for colonial control. For an interesting review of the selective usage of Ibn Khaldun in French historiography, see Yves Lacoste, 'Ibn Khaldun and the Myth of "Arab Invasion",' *Verso*, June 23, 2017.

3. David James, trans., *A History of Early Al-Andalus: The Akhbar Majmu'a* (London: Routledge, 2012) reminds one of *Chach Nama*, a similar work written in India about the Arab conquest of Sindh in 711–2. Both these conquests and that of Central Asia happened during the Umayyad period and concurrently.

Chach Nama has also led to divergent historiographical interpretations where Arab armies could be seen both as deliverers and destroyers. For a recent study, see Manan A. Asif, *A Book of Conquest: The Chachnama and Muslim Origins in South Asia* (Cambridge: Harvard University Press, 2016).

4. Ibid.

5. Mohammed Arkoun, 'The Struggle for Humanism in Islamic Contexts,' *Journal of Levantine Studies*, no. 1 (Summer 2011): 156–9.

6. Nabil Matar, *Britain and Barbary 1589–1689* (Miami: University Press of Florida, 2006).

7. Linda Colley, *The Ordeal of Elizabeth Marsh: How a Remarkable Woman Crossed Seas and Empires to become part of World History* (London: Harper Perennial, 2008); *Captives: Britain, Empire and the World 1600–1850* (London: Pimlico, 2003).

8. Giles Milton, *White Gold: The Extraordinary Story of Thomas Pellow and North Africa's One Million European Slaves* (London: Hodder & Stoughton, 2005) and Adrian Tinniswood, *Pirates of Barbary: Corsairs, Conquests and Captivity in the 17th-Century Mediterranean* (London: Vintage, 2011).

9. Hilary Spurling, *Matisse the Master: A Life of Henri Matisse: The Conquest of Colour: 1909–1954* (New York: Knopf Doubleday Publishing Group, 2005), 102.

10. Tim Mckintosh-Smith, *The Travels of Ibn Battutah* (London: Picador, 2003).

15

Soaked in History: Discovering Fes

Life is a forward assimilative movement. Its essence is the continual creation of desires and ideas. For the purpose of its preservation and expansion, it had invented and developed, out of itself, certain instruments, e.g. sense, intellect etc., which help to assimilate obstructions. The greatest obstacle in the way of life is matter; yet nature is not evil since it enables the inner powers of life to unfold themselves. The Ego attains a freedom by the removal of all obstructions in its way. It is partly free, partly determined, and reaches fuller freedom by approaching the individual who is most free—God. In one word, life is an endeavour for freedom.

Muhammad Iqbal[1]

I did not get the entire Arabic message per se but figured out the intent: 'Where do we get the bus to Meknes, *Akhi?*' '*Anna ajnabbi, taasuff, akhi,*' I replied sheepishly, basically meaning that regrettably I was a stranger in town. He carried a little baby in his arms in this early overcast afternoon which was cooler for a usual September in Fes. A scarfed wife followed him as he moved away after bestowing a curious smile towards me. Did my funny shorts and rather wild hair (or rather what is left of it), further accentuated by my height, caused his curiosity or was it because I sounded too literary? I am sure this travelling Moroccan family must have received proper directions from some other wayfarer as we had happened to be at the main crossroads where all kinds of buses stopped but not without leaving me more doubtful about my Battuta pedigree. They mistook me for a Moroccan which was both a compliment and affirmation of my claim to have some family connection with surefooted

Moroccan world travellers of the fourteenth century. But that encounter equally deflated my own limitations as an Arabic speaker in Maghreb who had previously felt that with some basic knowledge of the great language, an exposure to a predominantly Arabic speaking culture, and equipped with a proper knowledge of Islamic salutations, I had sufficient enough reasons to assert my lingual and even pseudo native credentials.

Wait a minute: my great-great grandfather, the founder of our town in Potwar, might have been named after this historic city. Baba Faiz Bakhsh or Fes Bakhsh was the doyen of our clan as I had heard from my maternal grandparents and mother. In his time—the nineteenth century as that would be—he had limited interaction or possibly none with the British, though he had ongoing feuds with the ruling Sikhs. He helped the warriors fighting the Sikhs and then moved our clan to the present place, finding it strategically more secure right above an encircling nullah. The graves of some of those Sayyid warriors are situated on our ancestral lands and their occupants are respectfully called Shaheeds (martyrs). I remembered my great-great grandfather and those graves especially when I went up the hill to offer *fateha* at Marinid Tombs and the graves around them. In fact, some of the graves resembled my great-great grandfather's and a few around his in our ancestral cemetery. The medieval rulers of Fes and North Africa were Arabs and Berbers and, like the Mughals of India who came a few centuries later, the former pioneered some of the most enduring institutions in Morocco known for learning and architecture. That unique architecture not only survives in the gates, mosques, souks, and *riad*s in Fes, Rabat, Meknes, Marrakesh, and around but is also closely linked with similar, though often converted, edifices across the Straits in Spain.

Fez or Fes, the Fesians prefer the latter, is certainly an overwhelming place where, in its old Medina, time seems to have stopped long time ago, and where modernity sheepishly stands aloof as a curious observer and not like a hegemon. Except for electricity and mobile phones, it does not seem to have made any difference to this great medieval city. Like its other compatriots in Marrakesh, Rabat, Sale, and Meknes, Fes is a rare place on earth where one is pliantly transferred back into the Medieval Ages. At night, it is even more mysterious, majestic, and observant as if both time and history had come to an absolute stop. If one ignores the street bulbs, a few zealous shopkeepers, or some happily lost tourists with a sweaty pink glow, Fes is still catholically pre-modern and must stay so. I do feel privileged to live in Bath, the world's heritage town, but Fes is its more distinct, bigger, and austere counterpart where majesty, history, and humanity are blended together without the usual hullabaloo of tourism and expensive galore that one attributes to cities like Bath, Oxford, York, Paris, Rome, or Florence. It has its Sufi heart that one can see in its inhabitants, vendors, mosques, seminaries, inns, zawiyas, and certainly in its women, even if they are going about their daily chores of carrying water on steep hills or shooing mules laden with leather goods. They say that the Andalusian part of the old Medina has the most beautiful women in Maghreb, while the Karaouine side remains known for chivalrous men. What a combination! The next time I am here, I must quickly decide which side to live in.

Fes' mules and donkeys reminded me of my childhood when *Naanaji* and *Daada* (paternal grandfather)—the farmers in Northwest Punjab— talked about these beasts of burden while displaying naughty smiles. These animals, unlike camels and horses, were viewed as plain silly as the folklores went, yet they are sturdy and steady on hills, nullahs, and boulders even when these poor vegetarians are laden with heaps of goods further peaked by an urchin or two. Of course, Mullah Nasruddin's donkey was his closest associate and also his confidante and not a mere silly beast of burden! The Moroccan mules could be bigger or at least their loads make them look so but I did not see any stark difference between those and their Indus Valley counterparts. (Never mind, I envy their freedom in quaintly relieving themselves right in the middle of the souk or lane while still on the move and without soiling themselves or the passers-by. Carefree act with amazing alacrity!). These donkeys and mules are definitely gender friendly, but they must feel a bit embarrassed of soiling the majestic city's narrow, old, and busy lanes. However, they also keep the cars away and that is the illustrious distinction of this city that it stays automobile free. I know of another town, Hydra, in the Mediterranean, which has escaped cars and vehicles but that place is rather small and the hilly terrain of this Greek island makes it pertinent as well as possible to keep it car free. There, mules rule the souks and, unlike its Muslim past, it is the Albanian owners of these mules who ply the narrow, hilly lanes of Hydra while often swearing in their native tongue. Unlike the former Ottoman rulers of Hydra, these European Muslims keep their eyes low, not out of some apologia but largely because there are too many pink and coppery bodies around. I have special affinity with Hydra for two reasons: I lectured there and discovered it thoroughly on foot and on boat, and secondly, it is derived from my middle name which is both an Arabic and Turkish word for lion. I am afraid there no more lions back in Potwar and in Hydra but Fes is certainly an integral part of family history. No wonder that Moroccan mistook me for a native and asked for directions to his required bus stand!

By evening, Fes is purely medieval. Gone are the chatty shopkeepers, their haggling shoppers, odd tourists, freelance guides, and trains of mules traversing up and down. The mosques are locked up once again except when they open one last time for the late night (*Isha*) prayers, long after the carpet *wala*s have retired to their homes, having taken in gallons of sweet mint tea while delivering their crammed, multilingual presentations on their handicrafts from across the valleys, Rif and Sahara. Like the virtual power point presentation in a classroom, their lectures are real and illustrated with the assistants meticulously moving their samples with complete dexterity and at proper junctures during the oration by the boss. Losing way in old Medina, Fes el-Bali, by night is fun as the common sense of directions or someone's gesture following a salutation can steer the lost soul out of the warrens which otherwise account for maze after maze. During the day, Medina is certainly crowded and, being almost totally covered here, the temperature is not too hot, though voluntary and even intrusive guides, especially around the Karaouine Mosque and madrassas, abound. By night, like any old Muslim city, Maghreb's older towns revert to history except for tea stalls, a few bakeries, or some fruit vendors. From the outside at least, Madrassa Al-Attarine (the seminary of perfume sellers) is totally quiet except for some ruffling sound inside the al-Tijani Mosque where pupils might be getting ready to sleep after having completed the day's scholarship and other chores in the majestic mosque, still largely popular with the believers from the Sahara and further south.

During one such foray at night, I ran into the muezzin of the famous Karaouine Mosque outside one of the four gates of this great institution. He might have been out for his victuals or perhaps trying to seek some quiet corner for his cigarette, though I did not see one in his fingers. My salaam led to a short conversation where he explained the brief history of his mosque and the adjacent university established by Fatima al-Fihri in 859 when she moved here from Kairouan in Tunisia and felt the need for such a *maktab* (school), which turned out to be the oldest university in the world. It was a great link between the south and north and between the east and the west. Her mosque turned out to be the biggest in the Muslim world until, a few decades back, King Hassan II built another in Casablanca, surrounded by the sea on three sides. The Karaouine Mosque also houses the world's oldest degree awarding institution: Pope Sylvester II studied the Arabic language and jurisprudence here at a time when it had one of the world's largest collections of books and manuscripts— even more than the famed libraries in Baghdad and Cordova. Once this Maghreb used to reach out to another Maghreb right across the Mediterranean Straits where Tangier and Gibraltar sit as sentinels on two opposites sides—two opposite cultures and histories. Fes is the place that could rightly boast of some of the most eminent scholars on its faculty who belonged to different religious traditions as well as ethnicities but taught, debated, and researched right in the centre of an old medieval town now encircled by thousands of shops, tiny houses, ancient craft shops and of course a steady stream of worshippers at five times during the day.

Fes is divided into four major sections which correlate with the periodization of its history. The earliest two sections, Madinat Fas and Al-Aliya, now together are called Fes el-Bali, happen to be on both sides of the Jawhar River. To the west and adjacent to Fes el-Bali lies Fes el-Jadid that literally means 'new Fes', which is a misnomer, since this part of the city dates from the thirteenth century when a new section, including the palace, gardens, gates, Jewish quarters, inns, and many more madrassas, was built here by the Marinids. They definitely raised the political and architectural profile of this city that was destined to receive more refugees from across the Straits in the wake of Inquisitions and Expulsions which went on until the mid-seventeenth century when the 'last of the Moors' disappeared from Spain. The Iberian Muslims and Jews ended up in towns across Morocco, Tunisia, and Algeria. However, Fes' third city, Ville Nouvelle, dates from the colonial period when the French, like the British and Russians elsewhere, built their separate colonial offices, garrisons, and residences with broad boulevards leaving the older parts of the city to themselves. The urban developments during the post-independence era make the fourth section of this third largest Moroccan city which is a complete contrast to its medieval counterpart and thus, by all means, is a separate city unto itself. Here modernity has inducted a new phase in the history of this proud metropolis, though the country's capital, since the French era, happens to be Rabat. All through its history, despite the metropolis often being at Marrakesh, Meknes, and Rabat, Fes' own historical distinctness and a mystical uniqueness have never dimmed.

In the early years after its foundation in 789 by Moulay Idriss I of the Zaidi Shia Arab dynasty, the earliest Fes was called Madinat Fas and, as mentioned earlier, the southern side of the Jawhar was selected for it. Idriss I, a descendant of the Prophet (PBUH), had moved into this area after reaching present-day Tunisia and spread Islam to the Berbers (Imazighen) and the region's other tribes. His own life tenure proved quite short as he soon passed away but his pioneering work was taken over by his son, Moulay Idriss II, who, in 808, founded a new town across the river called Al-Aliya which became the capital of the Idrisid dynasty. It has been his spiritual influence that remains dominant even today with his shrine and attached madrassa located right in the middle of the Karaouine area with green pyramid-like roofs, a minaret, and a steady stream of male and female pilgrims. His stature as a Sufi mentor and the de facto founder of Fes has allocated him a guaranteed perpetuity. During 817, 8,800 Andalusian families, mainly of Berber origin displaced due to the Christian onslaught from northern Spain, sought refuge in Fes and its earliest section came to be known as Al-Andalus. They had also been affected by a revolt against the Umayyads of Spain which hastened their move across the Straits and then into Fes. In 824, 2,000 Arab families were banished from Kairouan following a rebellion; they found refuge in Fes, imprinting a dominant Arab character on the city. The Andalusians settled in Madinat Fas while the Tunisians moved into Al-Aliya and thus these two waves of immigrants gave their respective names to both the towns facing each other. Soon Al-Aliya came to be known as Adawat al Qairawaniyyin, while Madinat Fas acquired its name as Adwat al-Andalus. They mostly chose to settle in the Andalusian quarters and later in Fes el-Jadid which came into being under the Marinids, a mainly Berber dynasty like the Almoravids and Almohads. Both parts of the town, especially Al-Aliya, expanded around the Karaouine Mosque which was established in 859 and along with the madrassa became the biggest Muslim seminary of the time. The growing number of souks, *fundak*s, and madrassas, and a steady stream of immigrants from Africa, Middle East, and Iberia, kept increasing the population as well as the professional diversity of Fes.

Moulay Idriss is venerated as a patron saint and his shrine, Zawiya, is in Karaouine, not far from the mosque, though there is every possibility of losing the way in those countless souks and winding lanes. His tomb is canopied by a pyramid-like structure, which is visible only from the hilltops surrounding the old Medina, as the profusion of covered souks make it impossible to see the two minarets of the Karaouine Mosque and other such elevated structures from ground level. Medina, or Fes el-Bali, once had a robustly flowing Jawhar which has now shrunk into a shallow stream and across its eastern bank lies an old rival city. Mariam al-Fihri, the sister of Fatima, built her mosque and a seminary especially for the dwellers from Andalusia, and like the Karaouine Mosque, it is certainly a historic monument reflective of a graceful, enduring architecture. These sisters came from a rich Arab family and inherited wealth from their father and decided to open mosques and schools in Fes. Fatima was also called Umm al-Bannin, the mother of kids, given her penchant for education and for founding the first-ever degree awarding academic institution in human history. The souks in both parts of Medina are no less perplexing but they certainly transfer one to the olden times and cultures that one only reads about in books. Losing the way around both the famous mosques or by some bakery, smithery, or a teashop is not a major hazard as people happily guide you, sometimes even walk with you all the way to your intended destination. It is on these occasions that one feels humbled by the sublime virtues of traditional values and cultures that we all seem to have left behind in our haste to adopt an unbridled modernity.

The Fatimids, the empire builders in North Africa and Sicily during the ninth century and likewise the founders of Cairo, established themselves in Morocco in the early tenth century and expelled the Idrisids from the city in 927. This was exactly the time that the Muslim rule expanded into Sicily and the Fatimid influence remained quite visible there for a while. In 980, Fes became an important provincial city of the Andalusian caliphate and the Karaouine Mosque received special funds and imperial patronage for its refurbishment and expansion. The local governor, Amir Dunas Al-Maghrawi, tried to bring together rival townships by allowing more construction on both sides of the Jawhar while continuing to maintain their own respective walls. But it was the Almoravid king, Yusuf ibn Tashfin, who after his conquest of Fes in 1070, following a decade of battling, brought both the cities together by building bridges; he also organized an efficient water and sewerage system. He built a huge wall around Fes el-Bali with several impressive gates and ramparts, while the cemeteries remained perched on the surrounding hills, given the limited space within Medina itself. Many of those massive gates and portions of walls especially around Fes el-Bali date from Tashfin's era and stand sentinels to a bright chapter in Fesian history. It was under the Almoravids, a Berber dynasty, especially during 1134–43, that the Karaouine Mosque underwent its largest expansion, though the capital of the Almoravid Empire had been shifted to Marrakesh. Marrakesh was found more convenient to control regions as far as Senegal, yet Fes' reputation as the centre of intellectual and juridical developments remained undiminished, and Ibn Tashfin, with all his services to the city, is viewed as its second founder. In the meantime, steady streams of Andalusian Muslims had been moving into Fes and its city parameters kept expanding, however, those walls interspersed with massive gates continued to define Fes el-Bali, which meant smaller houses, narrower streets, and more population. By 1180, Fes had already become the world's second largest city after Merv, with more than 200,000 inhabitants living in a comparatively smaller and compact area, crisscrossed by warrens of narrow streets, souks, home-based factories, tanneries, inns, and certainly the mosques and madrassas. Merv, just on the eve of its total destruction by the Mongols in 1222, had half a million residents, and this Seljuk capital was viewed as one of the richest and most elegant cities in the world. Lying in southern Turkmenistan, the ruins of Merv extend over a wide area though its world-known tomb of Sultan Sanjar, built in 1157, still offers a glimpse of its long-gone glory.

The Almoravids had originated from amongst African tribes such as Berbers, Tuaregs, and others in the south, and had been inspired by a Sufi, Abdallah ibn Yasin, and in a Khaldunian way, combined their piety with austerity in an effort to bring about greater unity amongst Africa's north-western Muslims. During the 1050s, the Iberian caliphate acutely suffered due to indolent and schismatic rulers—taifa kings—when the Almoravids began to establish their rule over Ghana, Mauritania, and southern regions of present-day Morocco. Soon they turned into a formidable force and, after they had consolidated themselves in the northwest, invitations and emissaries began coming in from the Iberian Muslims to establish peace and unity in Spain in view of taxing factionalism and intermittent invasions from the north. Rome had already declared Spain another parallel arena of the Crusades that had to be cleansed of Muslims and Jews. Invitations to Almoravids from Spain began reaching their nadir in 1084, prompting Tashfin to prepare for a venture across the Straits. In larger cities like Marrakesh and Fes, Almoravid tribals covered their faces by turbans with only their eyes showing because of their tribal mores and climatic factors, given their Saharan origins. Marrakesh was the capital of this expansive kingdom allowing greater peace and prosperity, a fact not lost on Muslims and Jews in Spain. The Almoravids derived their name from *Al-Murabitun*, the people who brought people together, which fitted in very well as they co-opted and solidified diverse ethnic groups by offering an efficient administration. Ibn Tashfin went into Spain with fresh troops and energized vigour and defeated King Alfonso, who himself had been quite enthused by the papal bulls on Iberia and was being helped by a wide variety of European Christian volunteers and knights. Tashfin not only pushed the invaders back but also created a greater sense of unity amongst Spain's Muslims. He acknowledged the Abbasid caliph in Baghdad as the superordinate head, though subsequently he himself assumed the title of Amir al-Momineen—the leader of the faithful.

Ibn Tashfin's empire extended from Ghana and Senegal to Northern Spain including Mauritania (present-day Morocco) and parts of Portugal, and he is certainly remembered with respect and admiration. Even in far-away South Asia, one of the leading Urdu novelists wrote a novel about this conqueror introducing his readers to a Muslim hero in testing times. Sharif Hussain, aka Naseem Hijazi (1914–96) was a master storyteller and used historical characters in Muslim chronicles to reconstruct a bygone past where austere and dynamic heroes, despite all the odds, were able to protect and lead otherwise beleaguered Muslim communities. His novels, *Shaheen*, *Kaleesa aur Aag*, *Yusaf bin Tashfin*, and *Andhairi Raat ka Musafir* are specifically about Spanish Reconquista and Inquisition, whereas *Moazzam Ali* and *Aur Talwar Toot Gai* focus on Muslim resistance to the British in Bengal and Mysore, and *Khaak aur Khoon* is about Pakistan's independence. His historical fiction warned Muslims in general, but of India in particular, of a major debacle in case they did not take stock of their precarious situation. To a great extent, his fiction helped M. A. Jinnah (1876–1948) and the Muslim League in popularizing the idea of Pakistan amongst literate people besides relinking them with the Muslim past elsewhere. I often remembered Hijazi in Cordova, Granada, Seville, and surely in Rabat and Fes, given the fact that a Muslim writer from the hinterlands of British India, with obvious limitations in resources and no opportunity to travel to Spain, Maghreb, or even Bengal, still had a grasp of historical events thousands of miles away in Iberia and elsewhere. More than anybody else in the subcontinent, he alerted Muslim middle classes to more Andalusias, if by any chance they ever failed in protecting their communal existence. Some liberals may find issues with Hijazi's premises, but since my childhood, his fiction has stayed with me and it is not entirely doom and gloom, as without sermonizing, he was able to convey his poignant message. His fiction allowed his numerous readers to relive a utopian era that could still be brought back despite all the disincentives.

Following pitched battles and some fractious wars—amongst the Berber dynasties and rulers of Maghreb and Spain and as a posthumous to Almoravids and Almohads—came the Al-Marinids who, following their conquest of Morocco, built more mosques, palaces, and seminaries including the famous Madrassa Bou Inania in Fes. The Marinids extended Fes further towards the west and called it Fes el-Jadid. Bab Bou Jeloud, which is often used as the main entrance to Jadid, allows proximity to the palaces, Inania Madrassa, and the Jewish neighbourhood. Like el-Bali, Jadid was built mainly as a residential facility but it included palaces, gardens, seminaries, and Jewish quarters, the last being called Mellah. The new rulers wanted to make their part of Fes unique and a magnificent improvement on the older one which would remind a visitor of Shah Jahan's Delhi, which the Mughal emperor visualized as a place of architectural splendour. Historically, every empire tried to outlive itself through architectural edifices and that is where the Marinids were no exception and equally sought to build mosques and madrassas as atonement for their otherwise worldly exploits.

The Marinid Tombs are located to the north of Bab el-Guissa on the hills facing Fes el-Bali and, other than their intricate architecture, their location at a vantage point offers a panoramic view of a pear-like Medina including glimpses of el-Jadid. The Marinid rule began in 1248 and is seen as the golden era in Fasian history. It was followed by the Saadians until the Alawites took over at a time when the Ottomans were trying to establish their suzerainty over Africa's Mediterranean coast. The Saadians were always weary of Fasian defiance and hence they built Borj Nord during the sixteenth century to the north of el-Jadid and parallel to the Marinid Tombs. It stands as a sentinel over the Medina since the ruling dynasty wanted it to operate as an observation tower. The Ottomans reached quite close to Fes in 1554 after their conquest of Oujda when the Wattasid Dynasty took control of Fes with Ottoman assistance. The Hapsburgs of Spain and the Portuguese monarchs had been able to capture some coastal towns of Morocco, though these conquests remained untenable and often challenged by the Ottomans. Spain took hold of the northern coastal areas, whereas the Portuguese focused on the Atlantic coast further south, and towns like El-Jadida (Mogador) became their strongholds. Tangier, due to its location right across from Gibraltar and control of Mediterranean traffic, remained a bone of contention amongst several European rivals until it was designated as an international protectorate in 1923, just a decade after the French took control of most of Morocco, including Fes, Rabat, and Marrakesh. Morocco gained independence from France in 1956, though the Alawites as the ruling dynasty had been only holding nominal authority. Spain vacated the southern regions bordering Morocco and Mauritania in 1975, and since then this Saharan region has been a bone of contention between Morocco, Mauritania, and Algeria. However, more than anyone else, Morocco seems to have more influence over this disputed territory.

Off and on, the Moroccans fought back the Portuguese, Spanish, Dutch, and the Italian invaders at a time when privateering had already become a way of life. These pirates or privateers belonged to a wide variety of nations in Europe and North Africa, and impacted trade and mobility across the Mediterranean and the Atlantic. The Barbary Corsairs have received immense literary and historical attention to the extent of becoming notoriously synonymous with universal piracy, yet the fact remains that pirates pioneered all the modern European colonial empires and were patronized and even sponsored by their respective monarchies. Such reciprocal arrangements suited the mercantilist imperatives of the time, allowing commerce, colonialism, and Christianity to flourish in non-European regions where the West gained its multiple dominance, often in collaboration with the local influentials. Western salience brought more confidence and prestige to the colonizers, however, psychologically and ideologically, it left severe legacies which even after several decades have not been rectified. Other than territorial warfare and divided ethnicities, the psychological imprints of this uneven relationship have refused to wither away on all sides.

In the early seventeenth century, Fes once again changed hands and came under the control of the Saadi Dynasty who had shifted their capital to Marrakesh. After the fall of this dynasty in 1649, Fes assumed an increased commercial significance and continued to produce tarboosh (the red, tasselled hat also known as Fes). This hat soon became the symbol of Ottoman troops and an important symbol of the elite in the caliphate until Ataturk banned it in the 1920s. In fact, other than pioneering the home-based industries of these hats, Fes was known for producing the special type of dye extracted from a specific kind of berry grown outside the city which gave the velvety red colour to the exterior of these hats. Tanneries in Fes kept themselves busy by producing leather goods in order to meet for its significant demand both from Europe and North Africa.

Fes itself remained the Moroccan capital until 1912 when the French established their hold over Atlantic cities like Casablanca and Rabat along with Marrakesh, Fes, and Meknes. They opted for Rabat as their capital and, while ignoring the older kasbahs and medinas, they built colonial settlements characterized by wide boulevards, bungalows, and cantonments with modem civic facilities. These new towns, like the British imperial cantonments, were built in grid-styles with ample spaces for parks, hotels, offices, and mansions and are called Ville Nouvelle. Since independence in 1953, Fes, like the rest of Morocco, has been witnessing a steady increase in urban population besides newer suburbia with residential and commercial buildings accounting for the most recent additions to urban sprawls. King Hassan II took a lead in such urban development, whereas his son and successor since 1999, King Muhammad VI, has been dexterously preserving old cities besides expanding a modern service and tourist industry. Thus, Morocco and all its cities, towns, and rural and tribal settlements present a unique mixture of old and new. Of course, modern Fes has all the amenities for a visitor but it is the old medinas in Fes, Marrakesh, and Rabat or cities like Sale, Meknes, and Tangier that leave lasting imprints on one's memory. Even in a very modern sprawling city like Casablanca, the financial capital of Morocco, which is quite modern like Tangier, the old neighbourhoods and traditional lifestyles persist, though they appear vulnerable to an encroaching modernity. Fes and the old Medina of Rabat, along with its Kasbah of Udayas, have largely remained traditional and their elevation as world heritage cities allows quite a degree of optimism, though tourism, mobility, and greater access to consumerist modernity pose serious threats to this unique heritage.

Note

1. Muhammad Iqbal, *The Secrets of the Self (Asrar-e-Khudi)*, trans. Reynold A. Nicholson (New York: Cosimo, Inc., 2010).

16

Encountering Italy:
Leaning and Learning in Pisa

I was collected from the airport by a young Italian man who had been flagging my correctly spelt name on a paper, and in the same manner, a few days later, I was dropped back by a smartly dressed and equally courteous hotel official. Like Pisa itself, the exterior of the Pisa Airport, named after Galileo, its most famous son, displayed a colourful façade. It was more post-modern in tune instead of being classical or neo-Gothic—attributes that one attaches to this famed town in Tuscany. Over a few days, I had a heartfelt glimpse of Pisa, though I was determined to come back to explore more of its medieval ambience and also to comb the Tuscan hills. On my way back to the airport, I once again felt envious of the cyclists but not too enamoured of their Lycra outfits. The terminal building was abuzz with the usual noises as mothers ran after their edgy toddlers who were more intent on buying teddy bears than sitting quietly amongst an ever-increasing throng of passengers. Toddlers are alike wherever one goes, especially at airports. There they discover their anarchic autonomy and make full use of the open space and their parents cannot rebuke them so sternly and the younger crowd exploits their superimposed calmness to the hilt.

The passengers at this small yet busy airport definitely looked fresh. They seemed to cling to their seats as the lounge inside featured only a few, which were constantly being stared over by a wall of wine bottles. Rows of Tuscan Chianti were absorbing searching glares from the passengers besides cushioning the clinking noises from a small cafeteria tucked behind in a corner. It was aromatic and slightly atmospheric like an Italian piazza where everybody is usually talking to everybody else. Just watching these people without looking too curious could be a good way of spending some extra time before the departure, especially after many of them have already measured up a tall South Asian passenger (or possibly an Arab or North African) amongst them. The fragrant Italian coffee was equally seductive, allowing one's imagination to wander off in the direction of a long queue of cakes and pastries sitting expectantly by the coffee machine that one encounters everywhere. It was not that everybody here at the Pisa airport on that mid-November day in 2007 was on a holiday, it just happened to be a Sunday instead; perhaps being small was after all not so bad, and the lounge appeared more like a homely social club!

I knew that my flight would be comfortable, short, and on time but how could I forget the first time I was in this country on an extended family visit way back in the early 1990s. Afghanistan was restive but 9/11 had not yet happened, though Bosnia was bleeding profusely, and within the EU, some groups had begun to talk of an impending invasion by immigrant hordes waiting outside the Fortress Europe. Despite the fact that the furore over Salman Rushdie's *The Satanic Verses* had died down and Saddam Hussein had been confined to his palaces, a new phase in Islamophobia had been ushered in all over the continent and North Atlantic regions. Communism had been quickly replaced by Islam as the new bogeyman, with some fundamentalist Muslims offering helping hands. After a joyous sojourn in Rome, Florence, and Venice, and fresh with fond experiences of a unique country, we had been in the transit lounge waiting for our flight back to London. We had reached the Rome Airport a couple of hours ahead of our flight and all four of us were rather overwhelmed after absorbing so much of art, history, and of course, the sun and the Mediterranean food. A couple of Carabinieri appeared out of somewhere and started asking us questions in Italian. They certainly did not speak English nor did we know much of Italian, though I could make out from their gestures that they wanted to see our 'documents'. We showed them the passports, which they leafed through for some time while giving us thorough stares to ensure our authenticity. Both Sidra and Farooq—quite young at that time—viewed it as a routine while for us parents it was a non-event since the officials departed after returning our passports. Within half an hour, another group of policemen repeated the same exercise and then left us on our own, though the third visitation luckily happened just before the embarkation so we tried to 'sleep on it'.

Certainly, Italy was not welcoming to non-white passengers, including those in the transit lounge, which is supposed to be an international space. At least their French counterparts had after all allowed Ali, the Iranian asylum seeker, to live in such a lounge for years until Hollywood discovered him and Steven Spielberg turned the story into *The Terminal*. But, in spite of clocking so many years and fame, Ali preferred to live on in a limbo, as the outside world appeared to him as either too ambiguous or simply hostile.

After the third police visit, I wanted to raise my voice but prudence would not allow that. I knew that we were being singled out for this special attention due to our green passports even though it carried required stamps of our residency in Britain. Our complexion and certainly the Pakistani passports were attracting the Italian police like wasps in a summer garden. We surely did not want to go through this exercise incessantly and looked at the wall clocks yearningly. I definitely wanted to tell these probing officials about Uncle Aziz who lies buried in southern Italy after having been killed in 1943 while soldiering on the Sicilian soil. He, like hundreds of thousands of many other South Asians and Africans, had fought for the 'Mother Country' and were daringly engaged in the liberation of this country. The sceptic in me was never comfortable of these countless young men dying for a fuzzy cause which in no way seemed to be their concern. Maybe such Indians and Africans were the heroes of a different type and of a distant era, giving their lives in the rugged hills of Afghanistan, marshy jungles of Burma and Malaya, on the scorching deserts of the Middle East and North Africa, in the damp trenches of Normandy, and the volcanic crevices of southern Italy. Uncle Aziz's vivacious and undaunted lifestyle, as recounted by my mother in her grief-stricken moments of remembering a lost brother, would conjure the image of an immensely dashing and debonair young man who had often been involved in love affairs, parties, and other romantic heroics until he was bundled off to the British Indian Army. Perhaps it was one more mantel taken up for the clan's honour for my maternal grandfather or a sheer case of economic necessity! My mother's 'most handsome' brother died fighting on the front line of a country equally known as a land of romance and heroes—a land which for so long had been closing its doors on people of Aziz's complexion. Aziz had been valorously soldiering since the troops landed in Sicily until his body disappeared in the thick plume of smoke and dust. His two daughters and a son would never see their father again and grew on their own while being looked after by the extended family. What a coincidence that my cousin, Saeed, had passed away only a few months before my visit to Pisa in 2007. On my second evening in my hotel, while looking at the fuming waves, I had been remembering Uncle Aziz and Saeed as if the lashing winds strewing the picnic tables around palm trees across the lawn were waging a war underneath an overcast Tuscan sky!

Saeed was very much alive when the four of us had hunkered down in the corner of Rome's transit in 1993, and were being interrogated by the police but Pisa spared me from such an encounter as I presented my British passport at the counter which is meant for the world's select few, who are righteously defined as EU citizens. My other memory of Italy was of flying from the US on a PanAm flight into Rome in 1979. The moment the Jumbo aircraft touched the runway, scores of Italian-Americans had begun to clap their hands amidst resounding nostalgic songs. Many of them were second or third generation Americans who had boarded the flight from New York and had certainly been a lively crowd all across the Atlantic. After Rome, while flying into Tehran on the same flight, it had turned out to be a different experience. The quiet was broken with a couple of cleaners coming in to whisper their questions into my ears: 'We love our Imam Khomeini. What do you think of him?' Naturally, I would not go against the common grain of the contemporary mood and besides I had often protested against the Shah's dictatorship over the preceding years but still it was too early to form a decisive opinion on the Islamic Revolution.

My Pisan visit in 2007 had occurred due to an invitation from Scuola Superiore Sant'Anna that had been commissioned by the European Union to train a large group of election observers soon to depart for Pakistan to monitor the national polls. President Musharraf, after playing havoc with the higher judiciary, constitution, and media, and then through the imposition of emergency in 2007—often known in the contemporary parlance as the second military coup by the General-President—had decided to hold elections on 8 January 2008. The EU countries had nominated about 70 observers to tour Pakistan along with some representation from non-EU nations. Almost totally white with no black or brown person in the group, the monitors appeared well-informed and certainly good-intentioned who, in several cases, had been on similar missions before and took this assignment as one more engagement with all its financial and professional benefits. They had been lectured by a few other experts, whereas my sessions dealt with the cultural dos and don'ts along with the political and economic realities of the country. On the last day of the training workshop, I aimed at responding to several queries about personal safety, status of women, Islam, and such other themes. Earlier that morning, the group had been escorted to some special defence facilities where mock kidnappings and rescue missions were staged to ensure their initiation into security risks and possible retrieval through a steadfast resolution and common sense.

The evening meal in Livorno's Old Castle was certainly an appropriate finale after week-long groundings in tribal politics, national hazards, and religious complexities of a vital state like Pakistan. Passing through a labyrinth of steamers, surrounded by twisting railway lines, and the usual industrial clusters, we had reached the interiors of this medieval castle which had not only defended Tuscany for centuries but which was also used to send off hordes of Crusaders to the distant Holy Land. One of its smaller halls was reserved for our candlelit dinner, though the bare walls, familiar pasta, a fish menu, and Tuscan wines somehow robbed the expected medieval ambience that one usually attributes to such places. The live music tried to divert our attention from our ambivalence between old and new, although it was neither the usual Italian operatic rendition nor a pure rock and roll outpouring, even though the artists certainly appeared dexterous in their performance. One of the course participants at our table hailed from Budapest and had studied in Moscow during the Soviet era and was visibly allergic to seafood. Despite our incessant solicitations to the bearers, she had to wait for almost an hour to get her vegetarian dish which was not out of any tardiness but only signified the usual Italian approach to eating where a meal is quite a relaxed activity and service could be equally laid back.

While we were stepping out of the refectory at the castle, the sudden sight of a full moon on a rather clear horizon was a noble surprise, especially after the preceding two days of squally rain and howling wind; on a chilly November night, one certainly felt short of being moonstruck. The cool sea breeze hastened us to file into our coaches that raced back to the hotel which was a busy place during the holiday season. The hotel, however, appeared a far cry from the older buildings that one usually attributes to Italy. Surrounded by palm trees, this concrete structure fitted in well with several such buildings in the neighbourhoods, which again appeared distant from the usual images of an otherworldly Pisa. My dispositional defiance led me to leave the hotel early next morning to explore the town of Tirrenia itself, as it lay across the road and not too close to the beaches. Here, wandering in the quiet streets, I relished the tree-lined houses, retreat-style cottages, and even detected some residents peering down from their French bay windows. This must be one of the residential suburbs of Pisa and, except for a small shopping area near the main road, it was quiet and looked both detached and thoughtful. I was glad that I got away from the hotel and the familiar hustle and bustle that one comes across in the lobbies where conferences happen one after the other, with throngs of people moving around holding folders. With most of the participants gone, the few remaining conferees, while waiting for their flights, begin to feel estranged in these lobbies and turn into observers until the drivers come in to announce: 'Sir, your ride to the airport is ready'. One more hotel, one more venue, and one more 'has been'; maybe many people enjoy being on the move all the time. Solitude and the sameness of the place and routine certainly are not to everyone's liking.

The access to Pisa from Tirrenia is through a suburban road that snakes through the countryside of various old and new villages often separated by farms, while the pines and poplars lining the road occasionally afford several glimpses of the sea and its inlets interspersed with marinas. Pisa itself is perched on this side of the mountains and is crossed by the river, Fume Arno, where, like in Rome, several bridges allow its two parts to connect with each other. On both sides stand some of the older buildings, often painted in diverse colours yet affording symmetrical and even enchanting views. The narrow lanes and streets are always full of pedestrians and vendors, while cyclists of all age groups snake their way through the familiar hordes of tourists, students, and onlookers. The town receives millions of tourists but does not seem to be overwhelmed as its stone buildings, numerous cafés, and bars appear to have the capacity of absorbing armies of people. The aromatic air never leaves one alone nor does the marble that has been quarried from the neighbouring hills for centuries and remains the best of its kind. Italy is certainly a grand museum if one looks at its towns, plazas, cathedrals, historical monuments, and galleries sporting some of the most splendid paintings and sculptures. Its tropical climate, its waterways, friendly and often sociable people, and its joyous cuisine have always attracted a constant presence of admirers varying from poets to fortune seekers. Its city-states such as Venice, Piedmont, Lombardy, Tuscany, Sardinia, Sicily, and Rome operated as full-fledged kingdoms patronizing arts and battles, and the land of the Romans eventually became the centre of Roman Catholicism. Otherwise fun-loving and vivacious, the Italians by majority are quite committed Catholics and the Popes have always played a vanguard role in their collective lives. Following the schisms with the Greek Orthodox and then the fall of Constantinople in 1453, Rome became even more significant as the home of papacy. The Holy Roman Empire was itself a hand wagon of the Pope whose extraterritorial role might have been anathema to regional monarchs, but they avoided seeking confrontation with the Holy See. In 1095, the Pope assumed even more powers by declaring the First Crusade that led to many French, Italians, Germans, and other Europeans joining armies and navies to reach the Holy Land so as to wrest it from Muslim control. On the way to Palestine, these knights and their followers killed Jews and rival Christian groups, marauding cities and towns all the way to Jerusalem. The Muslims such as the Seljuk Turks, Kurds, and Arabs confronted them in what proved to be an extended confrontation between the Cross and the Crescent for more than two hundred years until the Muslims finally regained control. The Crusades had their own heroes and rivals such as the Knights Templar, Saladin, and King Richard, but along with the genocidal sprees in Al-Aqsa and other places, they came to symbolize an early clash of cultures which continues to reverberate even today, especially after 9/11.

The Popes would often arbitrate between the warring European kings, delineate their possessions in the colonies, and motivate Counter-Reformation, Inquisition, and Expulsions in the early modern era where Europe would mount its annihilative religious and territorial conquests. Slavery was allowed while emotions were instigated to fight the Turks and North Africans until, amidst an expansive Europeanization of the world, Christianity found new and vast homes in the Western Hemisphere, Africa, Asia, and Australia. Culture, commerce, Christianity, conquest, and capitalism underwrote this domination of Europe over the rest, though like Muslims, Hindus, and Buddhists, new Christian communities were also divided amongst the Protestants, Catholics, and Orthodox, whereas the Copts and Armenians usually remained confined to their traditional heartlands. Italian nationalists during the nineteenth century, including well-known names such as Count Cavour (1810–61), Giuseppe Mazzini (1805–72), and Giuseppe Garibaldi (1807–82), were aware of an immense papal influence and, like ruling princes, viewed it as a major impediment towards a commonly desired unification. Other than princely rivalries and Pope's overriding influence, the nationalists felt thwarted by France, which for a long time had been acting as a Big Brother by exploiting disunity. Italy's unification came about in 1870, following the amalgamation of most of the states into a single territorial entity besides a crushing Prussian defeat of France where the nationalists had joined hands with Otto von Bismarck (1815–98) to extricate themselves from the extraterritorial French and Austrian influences. The unification of Italy would not be complete until the redefinition of the papal authority which took several more efforts and decades until the Vatican, Rome's sprawling neighbourhood in the vicinity of St. Peter's, was designated as the proverbial 'City upon Hill'. Here the Pope carried on with his eclectic and mundane pursuits with his own religious and worldly bureaucracy, enjoying the status of a state within the state but virtually confined to a smaller territory and a less obtrusive role, but surely a growing flock. The Pope's presence and the Vatican's pre-eminence as the headquarters for the world's Catholics allow Italy a greater global role besides a happy populace which can easily move between its sacred and secular pursuits.

There was a time when a state like Venice would assume a global role as the centre of trade with Venetians plying ships and running trade caravans as far afield as China besides fighting wars with the Genoans, Turks, and others. The Silk Road connected Europe with the proverbial East and Marco Polo's travelogue remained a bestseller for several centuries. Marco Polo (1254–1324), who had spent two decades at the imperial Mongol court of Emperor Kublai Khan in China, brought back silk and other riches of the East; most importantly noodles, which soon authenticated themselves into Italian pasta. The Polos also introduced China to Christianity and thus trade and religion—the age-old Italian professions—reached East Asia. It is a different thing that Marco Polo somehow failed to mention the Great Wall of China, foot binding, and tea from his narratives of China. Such discrepancies and several other small anomalies led to serious academic scepticism about the authenticity of his account. Some historians even hinted towards a possible ghost writing, as to them Marco Polo had never gone beyond the Bosporus and in fact had spent quite some time in a Genoan jail where he had been under 'house arrest' with another prisoner. Such a view would have not made some ripples in the papers and academia if not for Frances Wood, a known Sinologist and the head of the Chinese Department at the British Library. Her book, *Did Marco Polo Go to China?*, came out just before the internet made its entry and certainly received wide comments but failed to shake up the long-held public belief in the authenticity of Polo's travel accounts.[1] The head of world-known Dunhuang Project that consists of thousands of rare artefacts from caves in Western China attributed to Buddhist monks, she was perplexed over Polo's absence from the local Venetian or even contemporary papal archives.

Interestingly, Marco Polo's narrative defines Buddhists and other Chinese as 'idol worshippers', and his usage of other similar terms reveal a greater dependence upon contemporary Muslim Persian sources. Undoubtedly, the Venetian traders had a monopoly over commerce with the Middle East and the regions adjoining the Silk Road, and like the Pope, they never forgave the Turks for their conquest of Constantinople. In fact, Muslims had captured Central Asia in 711, the year when the Umayyad caliphate also conquered Spain and the Indus Valley, hurting the erstwhile Venetian monopoly over international trade. Columbus was a Genoan who lived in Seville and had been successful in persuading King Ferdinand and Queen Isabella to sponsor his campaign to locate a new route to India. The Spanish couple had been able to complete the Reconquest and, after acquiring riches belonging to the Muslim and Jewish Spaniards, were able to finance such a campaign. John Cabot, like Marco Polo, was a Venetian and a contemporary of Columbus who undertook similar exploratory visits to North America, whereas the Italian mapmaker, Amerigo Vespucci (1454–1512), gave name to the two continents. Cabot or Giovanni Cabot (1450–98), a Italian settled in England, sailed from Bristol in 1497 on his ship, *The Matthew*, and like his more known fellow Italian, believed in going East via West. He reached Canada, which he mistook for Asia. A tower, located near the university of Bristol, surrounded by elegant Georgian houses eternalizes the memory of this famous Venetian, besides of course, a local cab company with the same name. What a travesty! However, many Bristolian enthusiasts worked for years to reconstruct a replica of *The Matthew* which, since its launch in 1997—commemorating the five-hundredth anniversary of Cabot's voyage to Newfoundland—is moored in Bristol harbour, open to visitors and special private functions.

The Venetians remained persistent in trying to remove Turks from the Balkans and Constantinople, and trained saboteurs to kill the caliphs and other Ottoman notables. For instance, just as in the case of Sultan Suleiman the Magnificent, the Venetians sponsored 14 attempts on his life but the former escaped each time. During the subsequent period, the Russian, British, French, and Venetian embassies in the Ottoman capital often financed, trained, and patronized elements to serve their interests. The Popes also provided shelter and support to several royal contenders from the Ottoman households, and the hostility towards Islam and the Ottomans converged where Muslims came be known as 'terrible' Turks.[2] The conversion of European Christians to Islam was called 'going Turk' and such individuals came to be known as Renegades—Spanish term dating from the Reconquest. Such hostility to Islam had its roots in religious, economic, and political factors, and no single European society was exempt from viewing Muslims (Moors) as enemies. Colonialism did not just create powerful discourses such as Orientalism, it further compounded and substantiated them. In the same vein, as many studies reveal, the specific American views of Muslims have had their roots in the traditional unfriendly European attitudes towards Islam. Captain John Smith (1580–1631), a mercenary soldier fighting for the Dutch, French, and Austrians, had been fighting the Turks in the Balkans and sported a unique body shield with three Turks' heads engraved on it since he was reputed to have killed three Turks. However, he was arrested by the Ottomans and sent off to Crimea. The life of this former pirate, a founder of Jamestown and coiner of the term, New England, had been saved by a Turkish woman. When he ventured into North America, he named northern Massachusetts as Tragabigzanda after her but the area was subsequently renamed Cape Ann. As is recorded in his *The True Travels*, Captain Smith also named the three coastal islands as the 'Three Turks' and tried to revive the fledgling colony of Virginia.[3]

Italy's location in Europe and proximity to Africa and the Near East, along with its pivotal role in Catholicism as well as in Renaissance, allowed it to have a unique relationship with the world of Islam. Its geography, despite the country's comparative smaller size, has been crucial in its domestic and regional developments. The country has a visible north-south divide which is reflected in lifestyles, economies, and politics, and has been historically crucial in determining the country's relationship with its neighbours. The region of Piedmont borders Switzerland and France, and lying in Southern Alps consists of hills and valleys fed by the River Po and its tributaries. More akin to its neighbours, this region features industry and agriculture. Also, its major city, Turin, was the capital of the Savoy. Neighbouring this region is Lombardy, an area equally known for its industries and commerce, and its famous city of Milan remains one of the fashion capitals of the world. To the east lies another prosperous region called Trentino with its capital in Trento, known for agriculture, wine production, ski resorts, and software industry. Further to the southeast reaching all the way to the Adriatic lies the region of Venetia, known for the city of Venice. Venice remained a metropolis of trade, arts, and religions, and its traders, other than outdoing their Genoan rivals, tried to monopolize commerce with the East. The fall of Constantinople was a major blow for the Venetians and, in collaboration with other Italians and some Balkan followers, they often tried to destabilize the Ottomans. Built out in the sea and criss-crossed by canals and gondolas, the city is itself a microcosm of a romantic land like Italy. The Church of St. Marks, reached through numerous otherworldly lanes or on gondolas, symbolized the religiosity as well as the opulence of the Venetians; Italy's famous son Marco Polo was a native Venetian. The murals on the walls of this famous church and on several other historic buildings reveal age-old Venetian connections with the Muslim regions around the Silk Road.

Located slightly to the south of Liguria and the west of Emilia-Romagna lies Tuscany, which again is certainly the microcosm of Italy in every aspect. Its climate, terrain, arts, mountains, sunny coast, and certainly a fair number of splendid architectural specimens ensure Tuscan exceptionalism. The historic cities of Florence, Pisa, Livorno, Lucca, and Siena are almost unrivalled amongst their own urban counterparts and that is largely owing to their arts. Florence's churches such as the

Duomo and galleries including the Uffizi embody some of the unique Renaissance specimens of painting and sculpture with works by Leonardo de Vinci, Michelangelo, Botticelli, Raphael, and Titian deserving more than a short tourist spell. Florence, the home to Dante Alighieri (1265–1321), flourished under the enlightened rule of the Medicis who, like the Mughals in India and Safavids in Persia, patronized arts and learning and had advisors such as Niccolò Machiavelli (1469–1527), who is viewed as the architect of realpolitik. The combination of arts, politics, trade, learning, and religion, all turned Florence into a vanguard city of Italian Renaissance. The Chianti region in southern Tuscany is known for its specialty—wine—while further south lies Latium, which was the place of origin for the Romans, as is explained by Virgil in his classic, *Aneid*. Here the city of Rome sits as one of the historic metropolises in human history, besides also hosting the Vatican. Towards the Adriatic coast and across the mountainous spine are located the regions of Marches, Abruzzi, and Apulia, while going deeper south from Rome, one passes through Campania, Pompeii, Basilicata, and Calabria. Sicily is just across Calabria on the other side of the Ionian Sea and not too far from the tip of the southern shoe. Sardinia lies out in the Mediterranean, though France controls its northern neighbour, the island of Corsica.

Pisa's Roman past is preserved through an ancient parameter wall and some restored baths, whereas its medieval embodiment certainly overshadows both the ancient and modern counterparts. It is a town which houses perhaps the most famous tower in the world besides some other unique monuments yet, unlike Florence, Rome, Naples, or Venice, it is still a town that luckily escaped the awesomeness that usually comes with a city status. Pisa was an important port and a city-state in the tenth century, and rivalled Genoa and Venice in trade and politics. The Pisans were often engaged in wars against Muslims and played a crucial role in expelling Arabs from Sicily, Sardinia, and other neighbouring Mediterranean islands. These campaigns were motivated by commercial, religious, and political factors and coalesced with the series and centuries of the Crusades. Countless Pisans responded to the papal call for the First Crusade in 1096 and undertook journeys to the Near East and Palestine. Joining Germans, Franks, and other European Christians, they played a vanguard role in the destruction of cities and cathedrals belonging to the Orthodox and Armenian Christians, and exhibited a harrowing degree of anti-Semitism. Long before the Turks would capture Constantinople and the Balkans, the Crusaders had laid waste to the regions belonging to the Byzantine Empire also known as the Eastern Roman Empire. The Catholic fanatics engaged in killings and arson sprees in areas such as Anatolia which, according to Muslims, are interestingly still identified as Rum or Roman. The Crusades allowed more mobility and energy besides access to newer goods and markets. Many returning Crusaders brought soil from the Holy Land and deposited it near the cathedral, and the special cemetery, Camp Santo, was built around the site.

The Pisans reached their zenith during the twelfth and thirteenth centuries and began building universities, churches, and other worldly institutions. During their heyday in the early medieval era, the Pisans initiated religious architecture in their city-state along with similar edifices in Corsica and Sardinia which had been under their control. The unlimited supply of marble from the neighbouring hills, an accentuated religious devotion, increased material resourcefulness, and skills enjoyed by some families of traditional architects augured the golden period in Pisan architecture. Known for its elegant and sober style, Pisan architecture was pioneered by Niccolò Pisano, an architect-sculptor who combined realism with ancient traditions. He died in 1260 CE after building pulpits in the Pisan Baptistery, a section of the Cathedral in Siena, the Tomb of St. Dominic in Bologna, and the famed fountain in Perugia. His son, Giovanni (1250–1331), carried on his father's tradition and added special sections in the Cathedral of Pisa that exhibit more pronounced emphasis on passion and dramatization. Another known Pisan architect, Andrea Pisano (1270–1348), accomplished most of his work in Florence, whereas his son, Nino (d. 1365), specialized in sculpture, which one can see displayed in museums and galleries across Pisa. However, the most famous Pisan was certainly Galileo (1564–1642), the known physicist and astronomer who used Pisa's Cathedral and the Tower to study the movement of the pendulum besides assessing the law of gravity. The Leaning Tower helped him establish the acceleration of falling bodies owing to their weight. His theory of the rotation of the earth around the sun was too radical to be accepted by the ecclesiasts who viewed the former to be the centre of the universe. Due to a harrowing Inquisition, he was reprimanded for holding 'heretical' views and was made to appear before the papal authorities. According to one tradition, the Italian scientist while responding to the litany by the Inquisitioners, still found courage to whisper in despair: 'nevertheless it [earth] does turn'. Despite several demands, Pope Zinger, like his predecessors, refused to recant on papal inquisition of Galileo and instead often spoke of his own brand of Christianity as being the only true creed. A leading university in Rome refused to invite the Pope for a special lecture in early 2008 since the latter had refused to tender his apology on what had been done to the leading scientist many centuries back. While one can accredit the Italian academics for standing up for their long-gone colleague, it is certainly surprising that the British print and visual media almost hushed the news. One wonders whether the news would have made it to banner headlines followed by endless comments if the subject in question was a Muslim in place of the Pope. Freedom of expression, gender politics, and religious self-righteousness are inveighed only in reference to Muslims, while all other faith-based establishments are somehow usually not viewed that newsworthy and a kind of self-imposed censorship remains enforced.

Following the pedestrian way from the southern end towards Piazza Del Duomo in Pisa, one certainly comes across several graceful buildings, narrow lanes, and multitudes of tourists. The bookshops, expensive jewellery outlets, fashion showrooms, and several eateries seem to be anchoring multistorey buildings which, like the historic section in Barcelona, stand mute and majestic overlooking visitors, students, and artists. The Arno River that criss-crosses the town makes a semicircle through the heart of the town and, like Venice and Rome, has some majestic buildings, both sacred and secular, guarding its banks. Piazza Garibaldi is in a way the entry point to the oldest parts of the town and in the square stands the statue of a bearded Garibaldi whose head is always crowned by a couple of pigeons. A few hundred yards to the left of the statue, neighboured by a long queue of similar buildings, stands a palatial house which was once home to Lord Byron (1788–1824), the romantic poet of the Victorian era. No. 37 was a palace where the English poet completed his *Don Juan*. Byron—known for his multiple love affairs and an erratic lifestyle which met its finale in Greece while he was planning to fight the Turks—is one of the greatest English poets and has become synonymous with romanticism, courage, and buoyant lifestyles. A tormented and unstable soul, the poet saw the Arno from his windows above the Luggarno Pacinotti, which also afforded him a generous view of the Tuscany hills. (Certainly, Byron would not have been flattered by a small fashion shop in his neighbourhood in 2007 advertising itself as 'Dickhead Fashion Store'.)

Garibaldi's statue is kept company not only by obese pigeons but also neighboured by cafés and shops which are always abuzz with a miscellany of languages. The statue evokes varied sentiments, and across the Comune Di Pisa was displayed a life-size poster of Aung San Suu Kyi, the then popular and now disputatious Burmese leader, showing that the Pisans were not just self-obsessed Tuscans who did not care about human rights issues. Further deep into the recesses of the older parts of the town, passing by old bookshops and vendors selling items varying from Africana to Pisan sketches, one comes across the Scuola Superiore Sant'Anna, which is a part of the university and specializes in conflict management and other such contemporary subjects. Looking like a castle, the building appeared forbidding as all the entry points seemed to be shut and, despite my curiosity to see the premises of my host institution, I could not enter the academy and decided to move on to the Roman baths just on this side of the old City Wall. Of course, these structures are at home on their native soil, though they do not appear very different from their counterparts elsewhere outside Italy. A kind of historicity, quiet, and awe characterizes their ambience. At a short distance from them is located the Piazza Del Duomo, which houses the four Pisan masterpieces and has brought an everlasting fame to Galileo's city. They include the Cathedral, the Baptistery, the Leaning Tower, and the Cemetery. Entering from the east, one sees the Cathedral and its adjoining tower right away. Surrounded by grassy lawns and shimmering in the sun, these white structures date from the early medieval era and feature all the splendid characteristics of complex, devotional, and creative arts. Built in the Pisan Romanesque style (1068–1118), the cathedral is made of marble of varying colours. Its original architect was Buscheto, whose own tomb is located on the left as one enters the main hall through the western entrance. Characterized by several blind arches and 54 marble columns arranged in four tiers, the Cathedral's front is graceful and features friezes carved with animals. The doors and the side panels depict the life of Christ by some of the known early Italian artists. The hall is quite impressive and elaborate. It has a high ceiling which displays numerous scenes from Christian beliefs in Creation which are certainly impressive without being overwhelming, though one definitely becomes aware of one's littleness in such a huge yet graceful edifice. The nave, pulpit, gigantic pillars, scores of tall columns, and coffered ceiling majestically transmit amazement and appreciation. Across the Cathedral sits the Baptistery (Battistero), which is again all made of marble. Here the work began in 1153 and took three centuries to complete. Mainly built in Romanesque, it is a circular building which has a domed roof of an unusual appearance. The main entrance dates from the thirteenth century and is framed between columns decorated by carvings depicting the life of St. John the Baptist and other apostles. The dome is certainly quite gigantic with a splendid echoing effect. Niccolò Pisano designed the pulpit in 1260; his creation depicts the Nativity scene, Crucifixion, and the Last Judgement.

Again built in the Romanesque style, the Leaning Tower originated as a belfry built of Pisan marble, with its construction beginning in 1174 under the supervision of Via Bonanno Pisano and reaching completion in 1350. It began to lean a long time back due to defective foundations laid in the subsoil, though some may attribute its unique posture to the architect's desire to prove his adept skill. While climbing up the 269 steps, especially on the leaning side, one cannot escape the feeling of being gravitated towards the earth. The Tower took several decades to complete as the work was often stopped for long intervals as debate went on between those who wanted to demolish it altogether and those who felt that its unique embodiment should be allowed to survive by ensuring proper support mechanisms. From a distance, the multistorey and cylindrical structure appears to be made of a single marble slab with circular rows of carved arches. Surely it is the history, artistic rigour, and its leaning position which have together bestowed it with a unique distinction amongst all its counterparts. Without being huge or gigantic, the Tower exudes elegance and, other than its shape, the dexterity gone into its construction evokes spontaneous admiration. Religion and art seem to have converged here to create a splendid monument which stands so comfortably and confidently along with its other three illustrious neighbours. All four of them, having been built of an almost transparent marble, emanate a deep sense of quiet majesty and aesthetics, and owe their creation to an innate human desire for immortality through arts besides, of course, a heightened wave of religiosity during the Crusades which underlay these and similar other impressive monuments. Human devotion to religion and even aversion often ushers itself through the arts where a mortal being tries to wonder at, as well as celebrate, the solemnity of some superior divinity, though people have often used religion for annihilative purposes as well. Unlike religion, the arts have mostly inspired love, aesthetics, affection, appreciation, and respect, yet some forms and manifestations of art could also be vulnerable to clandestine motives.

The Cemetery or Camp Santo, located to the right of the Cathedral and Baptistery, has been held in high esteem for centuries. It is an oblong structure of various ossuaries and galleries surrounding an open grassy lawn. The soil for this sacred burial place was brought all the way from the Hill of Calvary by the Crusaders and, other than the Italian zeal for a sustained campaign to wrest the Holy Land from the Muslims, it equally affirms the primacy of religion in a region that has been the centre of one of the largest Christian denominations. The Cemetery was founded in the thirteenth century and has more than six hundred tombstones in those galleries that surround the four sides of the sacred site. Its eastern section features a domed chapel whereupon the various frescoes on the walls have benefited from an ongoing restoration work. In all these galleries, the graves of famous Italians, early Pisans, and other Tuscan notables are identifiable only by their small tombstones, otherwise they are all underneath the floor. Mostly people walk over the resting places, unless one can tread a narrow pathway without stepping on the graves underneath. The frescoes on the walls and in the gallery beyond the Chapel date from the fourteenth century and depict various long-held Christian beliefs and rites. For instance, the frescoes in the western gallery depict the Story of Esther (1591) and the Story of Judith (1607), while in the centre lie the chains from the old port of Pisa. The walls in the northern gallery retain 23 depictions from the Old Testament painted during 1468–84 by the Florentine artist, Benozzo Gozzoli. After passing through this particular gallery, one enters a room with 'The Triumph of Death', a celebrated fresco completed by Bonamico Buffalmacco, another known Florentine artist of the early fourteenth century. This painting shows the mortality of life and the superficiality of worldly pleasures. Facing it are 'The Last Judgment' and 'Hell', again focusing on the triviality of worldly existence. Many of the wall sketches in the Cemetery were wiped out with the passage of time, whereas the Chapel's dome and some galleries also suffered from aerial bombings in 1944. Behind the western boundary wall of Camp Santo is a square, grassy lawn, and towards its further end lies the walled Jewish cemetery. Its walls are astoundingly high with two giant gates permanently locked, and it is only through some minor openings between the wooden beams of the massive doors that one gets a glimpse of rows of graves, otherwise the site is not even signposted nor is there any other way of getting into it. Located just 30 or so feet behind Camp Santo in the north-western corner of a site that receives millions of visitors every year, the Jewish graveyard is symbolic of a complex experience in a Christian heartland.

Pisa's winding alleys take a visitor to the National Museum which is housed in a monastery where rooms are built around the cloisters which themselves date from the fifteenth century and display paintings as well as Pisan sculptures. The room devoted to Giovanni Pisano is astounding with its rare collection, whereas the adjacent hall holds Andrea Pisano's wooden statue of the Virgin of the Annunciation. Pisa's traditional architecture is certainly found all over the old town, though a good place for browsing could be Piazza dei Cavalieri, which is named after a military order known as the Knights of St. Stephens who earned fame by fighting Muslims. Here the Church and Campanile were designed by Vasari to be completed in 1569. Vasari designed the left side of the Church in 1562 in addition to designing the Palazzo Gherardesca, which stands on a former prison site. In 1288, Ugolino della Gherardesca, his sons, and grandsons were condemned to death by starvation in that prison, which Dante has narrated in his Divine Comedy. There are several more churches in Pisa dating from the early times, housing some rare paintings and sculptures. For example, St. Paul on the Arno is built in Romanesque-Gothic style, while St. Catherine's Church (Santa Caterina) features a Gothic façade and houses delicate statues sculpted by Nino Pisano.

While Italy itself is a living human and natural museum, Tuscany is its regional microcosm, whereas Florence and Pisa might be viewed both as its compact and certainly splendid representations. A few miles outside Pisa, while heading towards Livorno, one passes through Tirrenia, which is known for its beaches, film studios, and the pine forest. It was here in the hotel's bar that I heard two families engaged in a heated discussion. According to a steward, this was an unending contestation between the

Pisans and Livornans on determining who excelled the opposite side in various spheres of life. It reminded me of the guard posted at the Cemetery who, on my query about Galileo's grave, had nonchalantly observed: 'The Florentines took him away from us and entombed him in Florence to lay claim over our most famous Pisan'. Remembering these words, which allowed a rather wry smile, I headed towards my plane and it felt as if a lively and boisterous Italy had been left light years behind.

Notes

1. Frances Wood, *Did Marco Polo Go to China?* (London: Perseus, 1997).
2. For an interesting study of intrigues against the Ottomans, see Philip Mansel, *Constantinople: City of the World's Desire, 1453–1926* (London: John Murray, 2006).
3. John Smith, *The True Travels, Adventures and Observations of Captain John Smith, Vol. VI: In Europe, Asia, Africa and America, 1593–1629* (London: Kessinger Publishing, 2010).

17

Contemplating in Tuscany, Lost in Sicily

Is there no cause beyond the common claim,
endear'd to all childhood's very name?
Ah! Sure some stronger impulse vibrates here,
which whispers, friendship will be doubly dear.
To one who thus for kindred hearts must roam,
and seek abroad, the love denied at home.
Those hearts, dear Ida, I found in thee,
a home, a world, a paradise to me.

Byron[1]

After my first visit of November 2007 to Tuscany, I returned to Pisa in February 2008 to train more European monitors for impending elections in Pakistan—the second course of such type organized by the Scuola Superiore Sant'Anna of the university and the EU. Altogether I had lectured more than 120 monitors from several nations along with some Russians, Canadians, and Ukrainians, though on both these occasions, I never came across any non-white individual. Perhaps I was the only non-white by virtue of my Pakistani connection and also because of my research on the country. I did not see any Turks, North Africans, Sub-Saharan Africans, Asians, or even Bosnians amongst these groups, which included many 'veterans' from such other well-paid assignments across the developing world and who were regularly nominated by their respective governments. This was my third experience of this type besides interaction with similar groups and institutes in Brussels over the decades. They were interesting groups of people, exhibiting immense keenness to a total indifference to their assigned country, yet were quite sociable and friendly especially over meals and drinks. Smugness was more apparent in the old-timers than amongst the younger participants who appeared eager as well as energetic. The second session had a young Pakistani man who was to advise on security, given the fact that he was part of some local security outfit and, like these EU observers, must have had good connections with the higher-ups in Islamabad. Despite the undiminished hullabaloo on immigration and Europe being swamped by plural groups, it was not so strange—albeit ironic—that the EU still was a unilinear club of white men and women when it came to power. To many Europeans and the people in the developing world, Europe certainly means a powerful club of white clusters where even the second and third generation non-whites either remain invisible or at the most move shadow-like on the margins. One way of entering this restrictive club, as heralded by Bishop Michael Nazir-Ali and his ilk of cheerleaders, might be by converting Muslims and others to Christianity, which is not so strange, especially when the EU's draft constitution written by the committee headed by Valery Giscard D'Estaing (secular France's former president) had even suggested to define EU as a 'Christian' community. At the most, they could have included Jews by virtue of their predominantly white complexion and certainly the influence that the community commands, aided by a sense of Europe's guilt over the mistreatment of Jews for countless centuries.

The flight into Pisa this time had taken longer as I had to change the plane in Milan that incurred extra two hours due to a delay in the incoming flight. After leaving my luggage at the Pisan hotel which was located not too far from the older parts of the town, I moved to its bar to eat a quick pizza before embarking on my nocturnal journey to the Piazza Del Duomo. A deserted bar and a rather dry pizza had not dampened my determination to see the Leaning Tower, Cathedral, Baptistery, and Camp Santo by night, especially when it appeared to be a full moon and the weather did not feel cold at all. It was well past midnight when I began traversing Via Bonanno Pisano which, passing by the old and new churches and some old university buildings and the hospital, finally took me to Piazza Manin that sits as a sentinel to the monuments. The lanes around the Piazza, which are otherwise thronged by tourists and vendors during the daytime, were now totally deserted, and the Christian and Jewish cemeteries to my left were locked and quiet as ever. Soon I was hearing my own footsteps, the resounding sound of which was joined by a rhythmic clip-clap from the other side of the road. Facing the Baptistery and me was a semi-clad woman saying something suggestive to me. Naturally, with the divine forces at rest, late-night human enticements had taken over the holy zone, though I tended not to notice the calls. Instead, I concentrated on the white shimmering sheen of the Cathedral, Baptistery, and certainly the Leaning Tower. Both of us kept walking on two opposite pavements while exchanging curious glances but our paths remained parallel, though I felt bad for not having exchanged some pleasantries with the working lady. At least, at a human level, I could have held an exchange without being a customer or a patronizing moralist. I guess, I still feel guilty over my prevarication or sheer timidity. A clear sky with a full moon right in the middle allowed these marble masterpieces to exude a different kind of majesty, quietude, and ambience that one does not encounter during the day when the site is full of visitors and hawkers. By the Tower, I noticed a police car and some security guards busy in their own small talk, ignoring a wayfarer who might be one of the insomniacs who visit Pisa at odd hours as if to absorb its grace and historical munificence to its fullest. Such solitary souls must be feeling elevated with all the divine and human creativity at their sole disposal at such a quiet and sublime hour. It was almost early morning when, after several rounds of the site and aiming at the moon and constellations from across the monuments by alternating my own observation places, I had a heart full of Pisa's heartland. After bidding goodnight to Galileo and the bishops deep in their sleep on the soil brought in from the Holy Land during the Crusades, I traced my careful steps back to my own mundane abode.

The entire city of Pisa is certainly embedded in history and, like Italy itself, is a museum displaying the best of human creativity. Its location, climate, resourcefulness in timber and marble, and acumen for trade combined with religious fervour allowed it to attain this uniqueness, which certainly multiplied with the Leaning Tower and Galileo. Located in Tuscany, it often rivalled Florence—a bigger Tuscan metropolis to the east—and Genoa to the west. Globally, it led the campaigns against the Muslims and eventually controlled the Mediterranean trade, while during the Crusades, it pursued a preeminent role as a significant port of departure and return for holy warriors and hence the soil from Palestine. Some Muslim Corsairs also tried to get at Pisa and this part of Italy in later centuries, though we need more historical research in this realm, which again largely remains focused on Sicily and Malta. Pisa, like Florence, pioneered the Italian renaissance and then, during the nineteenth century, gave birth to Risorgimento, the intellectual and political movement that ushered a united, modern Italy. Historically, it is held that the ancient Etruscans established their first settlement by the Arno in the vicinity of Piazza Garibaldi, and the town remained a major Roman port until Christianity overtook its culture, with the Pisans becoming the vanguard warriors and publicists for Catholicism. Religion also provided a significant impetus and expression for the visual arts and unique architecture, which were derived from competition with the Florentine counterparts. Certainly both architecture and sculpting benefited from the natural scenery and an abundant supply of quality marble. Owing to its location in the quality vineyards and by virtue of its port facilities, Pisa housed earlier wineries and guilds in the area now lying between the Arno and the Duomo. In fact, the Royal Victoria Hotel, one of the landmarks in history and hospitality, is located about a hundred yards to the right of Garibaldi's statue and still cherishes a tower where once the earliest Pisan wine guild had existed. Another old building dating from the same period housed the earliest university building in town.

While going further left from Garibaldi's statue and staying on Lungarno Mediceo, one reaches a graceful square building hoisting the EU flag next to a Union Jack. It is here at number 37 that Lord Byron, the eminent romantic English poet, lived during 1821–2 while pursuing his second phase of Mediterranean travels. He composed some of the Cantos for his *Don Juan* in Pisa before moving on to Genoa, in addition to carrying on with his amorous liaisons. Byron had been impressed by Sufi Islam and acknowledged that Persian and Ottoman historical traditions influenced his own thought processes and poetry; he noted: 'With these countries, and events connected with them, all my really poetical feelings begin and end'.[2] With a disturbed childhood but good education at Harrow and Cambridge, Byron, during the Napoleonic era, took off on foreign visits which involved all kinds of heroics and sexual escapades. His visits took him to Greece, Turkey, and Albania where he developed an interest in the regional history besides focusing on the Armenian language. In the meantime, publication of his romantic poems back home had already made him into a kind of a cult figure. With more personal frustrations, including failed marital relations, Byron, an heir to a grand estate and aristocratic title, left England in 1816 for the last time and stayed in Italy before moving on to Greece to help the Greeks fight the Ottomans. He spent some personal fortune to build up a Greek naval contingent and planned to fight the Turks at Lepanto in Corinth Bay. But before his actual participation in the warfare, he fell ill and followed some kind of traditional treatment involving blood extraction. In the process, his health worsened and he passed away in Greece, much to the mourning of his Greek allies and readers back home. His sexual escapades with men and women, including accusations of incestuous affairs, did not let Westminster Abbey or St. Paul's Cathedral allow a memorial to this hero of the Greek war of independence, though this recognition came belatedly about a century and a half after his death.

I had visited Byron's place during my last visit and had even ventured into Dickhead Fashion Store situated next to it, but wanted to explore another English icon this time—the Royal Victoria Hotel.

Ayyub Malik (d. 2007), my late architect-friend, was a frequent visitor of Pisa and always stayed at the Royal Victoria Hotel whenever he had to inspect and order special marble designs for his buildings in Britain. He was fascinated by its history and architecture, and was a bit surprised that during my first visit in November 2007, my accommodation was at a new hotel in Tirrenia, located halfway between Pisa and Locarno. I had enjoyed that stay and had wandered off in the woods and cypresses in and around my hotel along with a visit to the Locarno castle, another major fortification associated with the Crusades. However, I was determined to visit the Victoria Hotel during my second visit. In fact, Ayyub had passed away just a few weeks after my first visit, which further added to my determination to visit one of his favourite Tuscan haunts. He had been living in Brentford Docks, a place in West London by River Thames on one side and the Grand Union Canal on the other. The 135-mile-long Grand Union Canal virtually merged into Thames right behind his house that offered a unique view of the river and the Kew Gardens. It was here at Brentford that Julius Caesar had crossed the river to reach inner London, and once upon a time, there stood a fort near the High Street where the eighth century Mercia ruler from England's Northwest, King Offa, was interned. King Offa is known to have a special fascination for Muslims as his gold coins carried both the cross and the crescent on them along with the *Kalima*, the Muslim statement on the unity of Allah and the Prophethood of Muhammad (PBUH). The various sections of Ayyub Malik's neighbourhood had Roman names such as Julius, Augustus, Cornelius, Claudius, and so on, but ironically an ultra-modern housing scheme and the neighbouring Hounslow neighbourhoods did not harbour any Roman antecedents at all.

However, the Victoria in Pisa is certainly both English and Italian in its contours and characteristics, especially when one looks at its evolution as an accommodation facility in the nineteenth century. It set the trend for an entire new hotel and the hospitality industry in Italy. Pisa had a pivotal role not only because it was home to Italian nationalism in the form of Risorgimento, but because its location at an international crossroads also allowed it to become the earliest hub of the hotel industry in Italy in pre-unification era. Certainly trade, climate, and most of all, its unique architecture bestowed by cherished Tuscan marble did not diminish a steady arrival of foreign visitors. The Victoria, the favourite abode of Ayyub Malik, is located in the oldest part of Pisa which was destined to dominate the Mediterranean trade during the medieval period. It was during the tenth century that Tuscany's Winemakers' Guild built their headquarters and a tower on the present site of the hotel. This structure soon became part of the university and was named as Collegio Vittoriano. During the sixteenth century, following Florence's suzerainty over Pisa, the tavern dating from the days of the early winemakers came to be known as Locanda della Vittoria or the Inn of the Victory. In 1837, Pasquale Piegaja, a native of the Duchy of Lucca, purchased the tower and other neighbouring places including the tavern and renamed them as Hotel Royal de la Vittoria; that certainly coincided with the contemporary reign of Queen Victoria. Following Byron's example and prodding by Romantic poets such as the Shelleys, S. T. Coleridge, and John Keats often venturing into Italy, numerous English tourists began to arrive in large numbers and the Pisan hotel came to be known as the Royal Victoria Hotel, though it lacked central heating and running water. Piegaja, during his youth, had been a student at the University of London for some years, and through his contacts in Britain turned towards organizing tours and holiday villas for his British visitors. Given the arrival of the railways in the historic town and its fame due to the Leaning Tower and the university, Piegaja was right in developing this hotel at a time when nationalists had started to congregate in Pisa for their efforts to unify disparate Italian city-states. Pisa and its university were soon to germinate the Risorgimento that was to augur unity, nationalism, and democracy in Italy. Giuseppe Mazzini, Garibaldi, and Cavour, and their followers had based themselves in Pisa since 1839 when the First Conference of Italian Scientists took place in the town, auguring a revolutionary revivalism in this romantic city.

The Royal Victoria Hotel is still owned by the descendants of the Piegaja family and is listed as a historic building inclusive of the tenth century tower, plaza from the fourteenth century, and three other towers dating from the early medieval era. It has a Duomo, the medieval church, and two residential buildings which had been erected during the eighteenth century, though some of these buildings had been damaged during the Second World War and were rebuilt. The war was not the only bad news for Pisa, as other natural disasters such as the floods in 1966 also played havoc within the town, though its resilience ensured proper restoration of most of its landmarks in a few years. My visit to the hotel coincided with an elaborate restoration plan that manifested itself through a complete scaffolding of the entire structure, both from within and the outside. Timidly, I strolled in to familiarize myself with its lobby and mezzanine floor until a uniformed waiter came up to me speaking immaculate English: 'May I help you, Sir? We are closed because of some extended repair work but you can still come in,' he said. 'My friend used to stay at your hotel and he passed away only a few weeks back and I just wanted to see his favourite hotel in Pisa,' I replied. 'Please, do come in and have a seat in that section of our lounge. You are most welcome to move around,' he added. And then with a polite pause, he observed, 'Though we are closed for business, I can still get you tea if you plan to spend some time here.'

I was still lost in the pictures on the walls when the waiter brought me tea, which certainly included a wide variety of tea sachets along with an assortment of biscuits and cookies. The entire tray included a whole array of cutlery and ceramics as if the order was meant for a whole family. I got so absorbed in my tea indulgence and a book that I almost forgot about the time and did not pay much attention even to some noise coming from a group of visitors who fluctuated between English and Italian. I thought of Ayyub in the lobby with its mixture of English and

Italian décor, where he must have sipped on his evening drink and given his romantic disposition, I could see him in appropriate company at the meal. A hard working man, Ayyub did not allow any personal frivolities to bother his routine until 6pm when he was ready for his stiff whiskey shot, but never before that. Soon Ayyub was at his best, especially when he had a female companion with some shared interest in arts and music. I could well imagine Ayyub moving the discussion away from architecture to literature and slowly to mystical music but without any nostalgia for his homeland, unless the companion happened to be a close friend. Ayyub's Anglicization did not allow him to get too personal about his own past. To him, the East, Islam, and India were all collective identities which overtook his own persona. I could imagine Ayyub talking all along over his meal without letting any monotony thwart the congenial atmosphere that he was so good in creating, especially when it came to smaller groups.

Pisa allowed visits to Florence, Siena, and Lucca, with each city exhibiting its own unique immersion in history and arts. This was our second visit to Florence since our first visit had happened in the early 1990s when more youthful sinews had allowed us to visit all the major galleries and cathedrals that held the Renaissance's master artistes. A short stroll into Duomo was followed by ventures into older, narrower lanes in search of Dante's home. The great medieval classicist, fond of Arabo-Persian literary traditions but not enamoured with Islam and the Prophet (PBUH) as such, Dante Alighieri wrote most of his works in Latin yet also popularized Italian through his *The Divine Comedy*. Dante had been an active participant and affectee of contemporary monarchical and papal conflicts and as a consequence had to suffer exile. It was during his exile that he penned this masterpiece in Tuscan dialect which brought him lateral fame, especially during the Romantic Age in the nineteenth century. Dante had been in love with Beatrice and it is she and Virgil, the great Roman poet, who guide him through his tripartite journey through hell, purgatory, and paradise. A kind of spiritual and humanist celebration, this poem is deeply influenced by Christian theology where a journey through hell—*Inferno*—is quite the familiar scene and purgatory is created through most powerful poetics, while paradise once again relocates Christian symbolism until the famous verse, when the poet meets God: *All'alta fantasia qui mancò possa* (At this high moment, ability failed my capacity to describe). I visited Dante's home, which is now a museum and faces the small community church where once the eminent poet used to worship. His tomb is located in Ravenna where it was rebuilt in 1780, while the cenotaph is located in the Basilica of Santa Croce in Florence. In fact, a sculpture of robed Dante stands at Piazza di Santa Croce welcoming visitors. Most of these churches and piazzas, given their histories, collections of paintings, and sculptures besides their unique architectural designs, make Florence what it is. Of course, this city of Medicis, Machiavelli, Da Vinci, Raphael, and Michelangelo was the heart of the Renaissance and thus a trendsetter for the modern era. However, it did suffer from a wide variety of conflicts and rivalries but never forsook its knack for the arts and philosophy. Florentines even appropriated Pisan Galileo, for which Pisans will never forgive their fellow Tuscan metropolis. Reflecting inside the Uffizi is always rewarding, though coming back from Florence without trying some local ice cream will be considered heretical. I, however, prefer watching street artistes making pen portraits of passers-by while the latter wait; should I have asked them to make one for me during my first visit in 1992? Looking back at it now, it could have been fun with all the hair over a bit agile physique.

Making Pisa as the focal point for ventures across Tuscany and even beyond to Venice or Rome on public transport is not a bad idea. Our next journey took us to Siena, once known for its bankers and now visited by throngs of visitors to see the old churches, palatial houses, and nunneries, all often decorated by the sculptures of wolves, *lupus*, a Roman symbol and also the evidence of this town's global outreach. It is always a mother wolf with her cubs, which again is a plausible sign that refused to disappear even before a diehard Christianization of this peninsula. The old town is slightly away from the train station and its modern neighbourhood, and could be a good walk or cycle ride to roam about leisurely. All lanes and pathways eventually lead to Palazzo Pubblico, whose appendicular form is surrounded by some of the oldest houses and churches with eateries now overshadowing the place, looked over by quite a tall medieval tower, Torre del Mangia, featuring a unique belfry. Other than museums, cathedrals, and art galleries, there are narrow lanes going all around the older parts of the town where one could disappear for a quick snack or drink amongst locals or could even follow a smiling nun to a hermitage not too far from Palazzo but a totally different world of peace and tranquillity. The Basilica of San Domenico, or Basilica Cateriniana, is nicely and peaceably tucked away at a convenient distance from the Palazzo and is accessible through several winding lanes and smaller intersections. Built in the early thirteenth century, this Gothic gem has been a place of worship plus a nunnery where, in addition to sublime sculpture, one's aesthetics are definitely subdued by some of the most enchanting paintings near the altar. After our due share of immersion at this holy place, we sought out a side alley where a former medieval home had been converted into a restaurant. Despite the building's graceful antiquity, its current incarnation as a bar was not overbearing at all, and the soup and salad were both divine, allowing us to think that St. Catherine must have been pleased with our frugal choice. Most buildings in Siena and even the banks, once owned by the Lombards, are made of red bricks which is rather unique, given the profusion of marble and Tuscan stone. After walking through the warrens of alleyways and peering at medieval worship places while passing through hungry tourists, tired legs lead one to the open space at Palazzo Pubblico, where they can sit on the floor to enjoy a bout with some steaming coffee and Italian pastries.

By the evening, when the tourists are gone to Florence, Pisa, or Rome, Siena looks more placid with some of those alleys now looking deserted, however, the image of it being one of the richest medieval cities in the world never leaves one alone. In its heyday, it must have rivalled Venice in money, though not in size or imperial outreach. However, my favourite Tuscan town after Pisa is certainly Lucca which is about 20 miles to the northwest and not exactly on the coast. The short bus ride let us have glimpses of smaller villages, vineyards, and open fields all the way to this town where time seemed to have stalled somewhere in its medieval phase. The walled town with plazas, churches, shops, and neighbourhood cafés is certainly a major tourist attraction but its medieval ambience is a persistent accompaniment. Despite the fact that the city had a tumultuous history interspersed with republican, imperial, papal, and feudal phases, it is perhaps the only place in this part of Italy where the ancient town is still safeguarded by its medieval parameter wall which remains intact; though many modern sections have sprung up outside the wall, the gardens, foliage, and proper preservation efforts have helped retain the originality of the place. Inside the older town, there are amply broad squares, wide streets lined by very tall and majestic trees, and neighbourhoods featuring graceful homes, often in the proximity of some of the most elegant Renaissance churches in Tuscany. Eighty-five thousand people live in and around Lucca but there is a rural subtleness in the place with its inhabitants using bicycles, enjoying mid-day lunches in the sun, or having coffee with the local confectionaries. The presence of elderly people and their ease in moving around does not let a visitor get away with the feeling that this is inherently a favourite tourist destination. The river has replenished its gardens, whereas the Guinigi Tower guards the old town. Built in the early thirteenth century, this Tower is uniquely topped by a garden featuring Holm Oaks—symbolizing life—and was bequeathed by the Guinigi family to the town. It is said that such towers were very much in fashion in the medieval period as the rich families built them in competition with one another as status symbols. A visit to Lucca is incomplete without visiting its bookstalls, handicraft shops, and certainly without trying its coffee and cake. From the famous varieties of Tuscan wine, I decided on a bottle of white along with the necessary assortment of local cheese and bread. To my amazement, this wine cost me only two euros, less than what I would pay for a decent coffee in Oxford or Bath. We sat in an open air café in a square with tall sentinel-like trees and tried to hold a conversation with an elderly lady sitting next to us whose English was certainly better than our Italian. She loved her town and its history, and was not bothered at the profusion of tourists at all. While cycling away to her local grocery shop, she advised us to visit the Lucca Cathedral of San Martino, a beautiful cathedral built of Tuscan marble which resembled its counterparts in Florence, Pisa, and Siena. In size and design, I found it akin to English cathedrals in Wells, Exeter, and Salisbury but slightly different from the Abbey in Bath. While wandering around in Lucca, given the majesty and historicity of this town, I was imagining every Luccan to be an artist or a writer. A dreaming writer in me even cajoled with the idea of living in Lucca at some stage to write a historical novel that my friends keep suggesting since, to them, it is a terrain worth trying after all those historical tomes that nobody reads!

***

After visiting Rome, Venice, and Florence with several sojourns of Pisa and around, how could I ignore Italy's South! Sure, I still need to visit the east coast and Naples but Sicily had been with me for quite some time. Like Spain, I always felt some personal nearness with Sicily partly because it has been a historical and cultural crossroads where three continents and several faiths cohered, though not often peacefully. Equally, it retained a strong Muslim past via North Africa and is still on the route to Europe for hundreds of thousands of refugees running away from famished and war weary places in search of their Sienas and Luccas. A major proportion of them routinely drowns in a cruel Mediterranean; several are killed between international borders, while others keep on rotting in prisons after having lost their meagre belongings and hopes to smugglers, middle men, and functionaries. Muhammad Iqbal, after his sojourn in Cordova, had visited Palermo and wrote another moving poem remembering Delhi after 1857, symbolizing it as the decline of Muslims all over the world. Here he went to the city's cathedral, which once used to be the Juma Mosque, and like Cordova's Mesquita, he offered his prayers here. Though not too well-known as a religious practitioner, Iqbal's pilgrimage was meant to seek out deeper meanings in historical phases and a personal immersion in a bygone past. But perhaps the most persuasive reason for me to visit Sicily was to remember my long-departed uncle who, like many others soldiers of the Raj, lost his youthful life here in 1943. Malik Aziz Khan was an ebullient soldier from a peasant background who, like his senior brothers, had been recruited first to fight in Al-Alamein and then was the vanguard that attacked Sicily. I never met him as his life ended a few years before my birth, but the stories of his romances and heroics as narrated by my mother and his proud sister have stayed with me.

While there is a growing interest in the Muslim phase in the historical accounts of Italy in regions such as Sicily and Bari, one feels as if comparatively more attention has been devoted to the Norman Conquest and the Crusades rather than what preceded them. Sicily is often stereotyped as a land of mafia and crimes, and these families evolved as a defence mechanism to protect the near ones at a time when the law and order situation could have been chaotic. The Muslim conquest of Sicily happened in the tenth century and various Arab and Berber dynasties held power for almost two centuries. The Jews here, like in

Spain, flourished due to Muslim internationalism, though when they finally lost to the Normans in the late eleventh century, both became the main casualties. Their properties were taken over by the old and new Christian Sicilians who busied themselves by building newer churches besides converting mosques and synagogues into cathedrals. The Muslims, for a while, remained confined to Bari and other places until the expulsions, conversions, and even sheer cleansing changed the demographics of southern Italy. Of course, Muhammad al-Idrisi (1100–65), the famous geographer, was a Sicilian who had moved to North Africa but was recalled by Roger II (1095–1154) to draw maps and help build academic centres. The king, who spoke fluent Arabic and often wore 'Muslim costumes', had allowed some Muslims to carry on living in Sicily to run irrigation schemes as to not upset the agriculture with a large-scale outflow.[3] However, historical tides were unstoppable and the only few remnants of that Muslim past can be seen in the cathedral, whose architecture plus frescoes are still a powerful evidence of North African imprints. A few hundred metres to the east, a palatial place with its arched windows and corridors is still in use, whereas some mosques near the Spanish sections and by the old harbour, though changed into churches centuries back, can surprise a keen observer of that forgotten past. Today's Muslims are mostly refugees who have been able to make it beyond Lampedusa and are waiting for their status to be determined by the officials. Trapani has a sizeable Muslim presence, followed by smaller communities of Muslim immigrants in Ragusa and Agrigento, whereas further west across the sea, Sardinia, Corsica, and Malta do reveal some Muslim architectural imprints in their hidden corners.

Notes

1. Baron George Gordon Byron, *Life, Letters, and Journals of Lord Byron: Complete in One Volume* (London: John Murray, 1976), 22.
2. Byron Blackstone, 'Byron and Islam: the triple Eros,' *Journal of European Studies* 4, no. 4 (December 1974): 325–63; *Byron's Letters and Journals, Volume V: 'So late into the night', 1816*–1817, ed. Leslie Marchand (London: John Murray, 1976), 45.
3. For a study based on some early archives, see Alex Metcalfe, *The Muslims of Medieval Italy* (Edinburgh: Edinburgh University Press, 2009).

III
NESTLING IN THE WEST

18

The Book of Curiosities at Oxford's Bodleian Library

The total number of special collections, rare manuscripts, unique paintings, maps, photographs, private papers, and official reports at Oxford's Bodleian Library could be anybody's guess. However, the books, journals, dissertations, and such other recent publications might themselves run into millions, making it the world's largest non-lending library. Located in the heart of medieval Oxford, it mainly comprises four buildings: Old and Weston, History Faculty Library, and the Radcliffe Camera, all adjacent to one another, whereas the specialized libraries of 35 colleges, several departments, and numerous faculties are also part of this college-based university system. In addition, the world's oldest Ashmolean Museum, Pitt Rivers Natural History Museum, the Museum of the History of Science, the Oriental Institute, faculties, and the newly-founded Rothermere Institute of American Studies, inclusive of the Rhodes House with their collections, are the arteries of a complex library system. This structure is certainly baffling to any visitor who is used to a centralized, 24-hour 'modern' single-building complex. It is equally an undiscovered world for those who spend their academic session here, confined to the laboratories or some specialized library corner. The reading halls, rare wall paintings, winding tunnels, and the individual appearances of the various Bodleian buildings have their own mystifying stories going back centuries, whereas their respective architectural designs offer several variations of Gothic, Baroque, Edwardian, and even modern traditions. The Old Bodleian is itself a unique representation of the late medieval style, topped up with spires, whereas its interior boasts of two unique buildings, one over the other. Like the courtyard of this main complex, the Divinity School is always full of visitors and tourists, while the most fascinating building remains the Duke Humfrey's Library, located above the school and accessible only to the ticket holders. It is a complete wooden structure with ornate ceilings and semi-lit alcoves, surrounded by old leather-bound volumes, all exuding a mysterious quiet within an overall dark brown surrounding. Only members can venture into this section where furniture, ambience, dark-panelled walls, sombre shelves, and creaking wooden floors all represent a bygone age instead of being a mere repository of the mass of postgraduate monographs. Next door, the Radcliffe Camera—a part of the Old Bodleian and housing History Faculty Library now— symbolizes the heart of medieval Oxford with its unique architecture that one only comes across in Rome and some other Italian cities. Stacked with books and journals, it is a labyrinthine of alcoves watched over by books in countless shelves and connected with the Old Bod through an underground tunnel. Its exterior is cylindrical with a canopy-like roof supported by intricate pillars, windows, and ventilators that allow enough supply of light, whereas the brown stone building itself is located in a square featuring world-famous cobblestones. Earlier, the history collection used to be housed in the Indian Institute building that faces the Old Bod and Weston. It was constructed in the nineteenth century to train the Raj's civil servants, besides a whole army of Indologists and Orientalists in order to bring closer 'the Aryas of India and England'.

Around the main courtyard in the Old Bod, which is accessible through two small corridors and one main entrance, there are several halls for the specialist staff, highlighting their titles in Latin. One such section, *Schola Naturalis Philosophiae*, was, until recently, reserved for exhibitions on special and rare themes. In 2015, with the conversion of New Bodleian into Weston Library, and after the sad dispersal of Indian Institute Library, such exhibits take place in Weston, which also sports a café and resembles the British Library in London. However, it was in the Old Quad that a rare copy of an eleventh century Arabic manuscript had been on display during the summer of 2004. Acquired through grants from Aramco and the Heritage Lottery Fund, *Kitab-I- Ghraib al Funoon wah Malahal Ayoon* or simply *The Book of Curiosities of the Science and Marvels for the Eyes* was composed in Egypt during 1020–50 AD. Consisting of 48 folios or 96 pages, the rare manuscript is rather incomplete and is a copy composed around 1200 AD—150 years after the original treatise was prepared—that went on display in Oxford. Consisting of two major thematic sections, the early part of this historic manuscript deals with heavenly themes, the Cosmos, whereas the second is devoted to the earthly sphere. The library did not put all the folios on exhibit; it displayed only a few samples, along with some other rare Islamic and European manuscripts and the English renditions of the maps and contents.

The title page of *The Book of Curiosities* displays its full Arabic caption along with the seals of the owner(s) over the successive centuries. The leather binding, dating from a subsequent era, sat next to a golden seal, an old reed pen, and an ornate case that held pens and an inkpot. The historicity of the manuscript and its beautiful calligraphy takes the viewer back to a time when Muslim cultures and learning exhibited unparalleled confidence and creativity. Its author possessed near-perfect knowledge of the five rivers and major oceans falling within and around Asia, Europe, and Africa, and highlighted the location of several cities and states on three continents. The source of the River Nile is attributed to a Mountain of Moon shown through a canopy-like dark brown figure, whereas all the rivers are in a greenish blue shade. As a matter of fact, the source of the Nile remained contentious amongst the European explorers and colonialists until the latter half of the nineteenth century. Victorians such as Richard Burton, John Hanning Speke, Samuel Baker, David Livingstone, and Henry Morton Stanley pursued their quest for the source during the 1860s and 1870s, and in the process discovered Lake Tanganyika, Victoria Falls, and the heart of the Congo Basin. Burton (1821–90), a British official in India (commanding mastery of several languages including Sindhi, Persian, and Arabic), was the first non-Muslim European to venture into Kaaba posing as a Sindhi Muslim, whereas Scottish David Livingstone (1813–73) had been one of the most notable Victorian missionary-doctors working in Africa, equally known for his explorations. He inspired several other young Oxbridge graduates to volunteer for evangelical work in Africa and when no news was heard about his adventurous campaigns for quite some time, another Briton, Henry Morton Stanley (1841–1904), took to Africa. Originally a Welsh, Stanley, known to be a shady character, had fought in the American Civil War on both sides before working as a journalist for the *New York Herald*. It was this newspaper that sponsored his visit to Africa in search of Dr Livingstone who, in his latest pursuit, had lost contact with the outside world. Finally, after trekking through the interiors for hundreds of miles and mapping the Congo region, they both met in November 1871 in present-day Tanzania with Stanley uttering his oft-quoted phrase: 'Dr Livingstone, I presume?'[1] Quite sexist and racist in his opinions and notorious for his mistreatment of African porters, Stanley offered his services and knowledge of Africa to a moronic Leopold II, the King of Belgium, who appropriated entire Congo for himself and, applying all kinds of unfair practices, ensured the ignoble plunder of Central Africa. Speke (1827–64) had been killed in a shooting incident outside Bath on September 15, 1864, a day before one of the historic debates on the Nile was to take place in the Georgian City between him and Burton. Speke, a Devonian like Burton, had served in India before undertaking exploratory visits to Somalia and neighbouring parts of East Africa. Sponsored by the Royal Geographical Society, a promoter of such explorations in Africa and Central Asia, he was the first European to comb the interiors of Uganda; he had reached Lake Victoria in the company of Burton. Initially, both agreed on Lake Victoria as being the source of the Nile but then diverged, and the mentioned debate was in fact meant to highlight their distinct views which equally emanated from their mutual bickering. A self-conscious Burton looked down upon Speke for his unfamiliarity with many Asian and African languages, though both spoke Hindustani with ease.

On a folio in *The Book of Curiosities* depicting the map of the Indian Ocean, the Indus is shown emerging from the Himalayas and then being joined by a number of its tributaries, while the Land of *Hind* itself begins from the city of Qanuj, quite east of the mighty river. However, it is shown combined with the Ganges and Brahmaputra into one river system, which may be partially true due to the Himalayan origins of the three main South Asian rivers. Further down, two itineraries suggest that the Muslims in the early eleventh century used the land route from India into China. The Oxus, Euphrates, and the Tigris are shown winding their ways across different terrains, especially the last one with all the major cities and towns elaborately shown on both its banks. The river is joined by the Euphrates, which appears rather like a junior partner.

An elaborate circular map in *The Book of Curiosities* affirms the fact that the Muslims knew that the earth was not only round but also that its outer sphere was surrounded by water. This map is similar to the one that the famous Sicilian Arab geographer, Al-Idrisi, had prepared in 1154 for Roger II, the Norman King of Sicily. Muslims had ruled Sicily for quite some time before the Normans captured it, yet the latter tolerated Islam for a while and benefited from Muslim learning and their acumen in sciences and agriculture. Though the Crusades did not begin until 1096 AD, the Muslim control of Iberia, Cyprus, Upper Volga Valley, and other regions in Asia Minor allowed them multiple engagements with Europe. The mentioned map even shows Britain in one corner, making it one of the oldest maps of the British Isles. However, this exhaustive map establishes the fact that contemporary Muslims had a fair knowledge of the various regions and their geography even long before Al-Idrisi pioneered some of his unique cartographical creations which, after Ptolemy, allocated him the most prestigious place in the world of cartography. The rectangular map in *The Book of Curiosities* is a complex and comprehensive graph which is a rather holistic effort, showing rivers, mountains, oceans, cities, and the various kingdoms. The detailed map of the Indian Ocean depicts it combined with the South China Sea, the Bay of Bengal, and the waters off the coast of East Africa. The section on the African coast gives the names of several islands, inlets, and ports, since Muslim navigators and traders had detailed knowledge of the Afro-Asian regions especially on the eastern seaboard.

Another green-shaded and oval-shaped map is focused on the Mediterranean Ocean, which is crammed with 120 islands in addition to 121 anchorages all around its coast. The information on routes, landmarks, itineraries, and winds offer rich details on the eastern Mediterranean but is not as exhaustive on Muslim Spain and Portugal. However, the maps of medieval cities of Tinnis, Al-Mahdiyah, and of the islands of Cyprus and Sicily are exceptionally comprehensive. Al-Mahdiyah, as depicted in a separate map in the manuscript, was a thriving Fatimid metropolis in the Maghreb and its colourful, multistorey buildings with arched windows, round minarets, and ornate balconies reveal its grandeur as a political, cultural, and commercial metropolis. Founded in 921 as the first Fatimid capital, its depiction reveals a fascinating mix of blue, red, light blue, green, and yellow, individually embodied by nicely-laid brick walls, square windows, semicircular arches, and half-dome tops. The wooden doors have their own distinct panelled structures, even showing handles and locks coloured in darker shades. Tinnis was another bustling city built on an island in the Nile delta, and presumably the author of *The Book of Curiosities* belonged to this Egyptian city, which was completely destroyed during the Crusades in 1227. The map of Sicily offers unique details of the island, its geographical contours, towns, and inlets, long before the Norman invasion. Palermo, lava-spewing Mount Etna, more than a dozen ports, and several settlements feature in this map with accompanying names and relevant information inscribed in Arabic. In the same vein, the diagrammatic map of Cyprus, the earliest of its type, affirms both the significance of this Mediterranean crossroads and the prevalent knowledge about the Muslim-Byzantine trade. The map documents the island's 27 harbours providing several channels for bilateral trade. The diagram of 'Bays of Byzantium' (Khaleej), as the manuscript reveals, stood for the Aegean Sea with its 27 ports and, more like the Mediterranean, abuzz with commercial and cultural enterprises. Beginning near the Turkish-controlled Rhodes Island, the Aegean is shown linked with Bahaira-i-Rum (Mediterranean Ocean).

The Book of Curiosities, in reference to heavenly subjects, focuses on comets, planets, zodiac signs, stars, solar system, and other cosmological bodies. The categorization of stars and constellations had been devised in Arabia and Greater Persia under the Muslims; the former had used smaller star systems to define 'lunar mansions'. The risings and settings of these mansions, 28 altogether, were considered helpful in predicting rain and other meteorological phenomena. The stars were believed to be located in a hollow sphere above the earth and rotating around it. As discussed in greater details in two chapters in the manuscript, comets were considered to be of the utmost significance and their movements and shapes meant both positive and dire consequences for humans and the cosmos.

Historically, dexterous map-making skills are owed to the ancient Greeks in Alexandria, sharing a pervasive belief that the earth was spherical and its one-fourth was covered by a landmass. Ptolemy, in his monumental *Geography* which was completed in 150 AD, devised ways to present the earth on the map as it was; his maps were not preserved, though his volume was available in Arabic. The early Arabs must have possessed some knowledge of these maps and, with their own seafaring and mobility especially after the rise of Islam, they pioneered some of the most detailed maps including those now preserved in *The Book of Curiosities*. In some cases, they even accepted the myths and legends from preceding civilizations including the story of Gog and Magog, immensely feared as the enemies of civilization. The legend of Gog and Magog (*Ya'ajooj Ma'ajooj*) attributed to Alexander—also identified as Dhul-Qarnayn—is a myth where the great conqueror is shown building a barrier to stop their encroachment. Dhul-Qarnayn would literally mean the wearer of a hat with two horns, whereas the barrier could also symbolize the China Wall that the ancient Chinese built to deter the intermittent Mongol invasions from the north. Perhaps two different past episodes got enmeshed in each other! Also worth noticing is the contemporary legend of the *Waqwaq* tree, which was supposed to bear humanoid fruit and its sketch in the manuscript shows miniature humans peering from the branches. One wonders about the origin of the terms such as 'family tree' or *shajra-i-nasb*!

With Greek maps non-existent, Muslims pioneered the entire discipline of geography, map-making, and navigation, which was further helped by the invention of astrolabe in Guadalajara in Muslim Spain in 1081. It proved to be the most valuable instrument for Muslims and Europeans, and equipped with geometry, astronomy, and algebra, Muslims certainly led the way in explorations. The ninth century Muslim texts on algebra became compulsory readings in Europe the way works by Avicenna, Al-Khwarizmi, Al-Razi, and Averroes ushered a neo-classicism. Chaucer's *Treatise on the Astrolabe*, completed in the fourteenth century, reaffirms Muslim influence on European learning. Since the early centuries, several schools of cartographers existed in contemporary Muslim kingdoms, though the most famous amongst them was called the Balkhi School, which was based in the Afghan city of Balkh. A map of Syria, designed by the Balkhi cartographer, shows rivers, cities, and surrounding territories of the old Syria, with south and west located at the top and north and east shown towards the lower end. The map is a combination of semi and full circles and long arrow-shaped geometrical diagrams symbolizing oceans. Another map depicts the Caspian Sea and its surroundings by highlighting Khwarazm and the Khazarite kingdom, which were eventually trampled by the Mongols. The maps and the treatises on cosmos were a favourite research pursuit with the early Muslim scholars. For instance, *The Book of Constellations of the Fixed Stars*, composed by Abd al-Rahman al-Sufi (d. 986), was one of the earliest surviving works on the subject. Al-Sufi was a court astronomer in Isfahan, another eminent centre of learning in early Muslim Persia, and his work reveals two drawings of each of the 48 classical constellations. The folio on display next to its counterparts from *The Book of Curiosities* shows the well-known constellation of Orion through two turbaned human figures and illustrated sketches. In another case, one could see an open folio from *Kitabul Hind* (The Book of India) by Al-Biruni, an eminent Bukharan scholar who came to India during the tenth century AD and completed his magnus opus in the Salt Range of present-day Pakistan. Like *The Book of Curiosities*, Al-Biruni was well-versed with contemporary geographical knowledge and, while based in Nandna near River Jhelum, he measured the circumference of the earth. By the thirteenth century, European cartographers had also begun to sketch regional maps. For instance, Matthew Paris (d. 1259) drew a map of Palestine at England's St. Alban's Abbey, while Pietro Vesconte drew a map of the Middle East around 1320. Like Muslims focusing on Makkah, the Christian mapmakers tried to posit Jerusalem as the centrepiece of their cartographic efforts. For Muslims, Makkah not only symbolized the birthplace of the Prophet (PBUH) but it was also the focal point for the correct orientation as the qiblah. The exhibition at the Bodleian focusing on *The Book of Curiosities*, along with representations from the works of Al-Sufi, Al-Biruni, and Pietro Vesconte, and the Turkish navigational maps by Piri Reis, reveal a unique sharing of various scholarly and cosmological traditions by all concerned. It is no surprise that Columbus, in his search for a new route to India in 1492, took an Arabic-speaking Spanish Jew on board with him. And it was a Muslim sailor who, just six years after the Columbian campaign, guided Vasco de Gama to Southwestern India while the latter had been endlessly lost around the shores of Southern Africa, and depending upon one's own understanding of the Chinese archives and their interpretation by Colin Menzies in *1421: When China Discovered the World*, Zheng He, the Muslim Chinese admiral, is claimed to have heralded his great naval campaign 71 years before Columbus' arrival in the West Indies.

Note

1. Clare Pettitt, *Dr Livingstone I Presume: Missionaries, Journalists, Explorers and Empire* (London: Profile Books, 2013).

19

'Encounters' at Victoria and Albert Museum

The first time I landed in London on that late August day in 1983, I had settled for a room in a small hotel near Russell Square so that I could be in the Bloomsbury heart of London. I was on my way to New York's Columbia University and wanted to explore the historic and academic dimensions of Britain that I had been reading and hearing about since my childhood. I had been to the United States earlier for higher education during the 1970s and had returned to Pakistan to resume teaching at the Islamabad University, brimming with idealism and energy. However, Pakistan had changed from a truncated democracy to militarist authoritarianism and the 'Bhutto-ist' jargonistic Islamic socialism had long evaporated before a lasting and lashing Islamist martial law of General Ziaul Haq (1924–88). Numerous Pakistanis were being daily strapped on to this surreal wooden structure called *Tiktiki*, as the subdued spectators saw their impoverished fellow countrymen being lashed for possessing a few ounces of cocaine, a bottle of vodka, or for other petty crimes. Imprisoned Pakistanis, given a choice out of the triple legal medley of martial law, Islamic law (Hudood), and Western (modern) law, were overwhelmingly opting for the last one, given the vagaries and severities of the other two. The generation that had idealized a 'Jinnah-ist' vision of this country often fell victim to intermittent and self-justifying military takeovers concurrent with consolidated feudalism and monopolistic bureaucracy enjoying primacy. Ordinary Pakistanis had unendingly and stoically suffered from the trauma of unnecessary wars, brutal martial law regulations, dehumanization of the eastern part of their country, and the charade of a 'new Pakistan'. The generals struck at the middle of the night while an adrift Zulfikar Ali Bhutto

(1928–79) endlessly evaded reconciliation with his opponents and, mired in sycophancy, obliviously sang the American national anthem on the fourth of July at the US Embassy in 1977.

At the apex of this familiar khaki pyramid of coercive power sat a moustachioed and devious General Zia, who had been selected by an indolent Bhutto as the least politicized of his corps commanders. Zia turned out to be the most ruthless dictator of this troubled nation by ensuring the co-option of mullahs from the so-called Sunni majority. The Soviet invasion of Afghanistan in 1979, very much like 9/11 for General Pervez Musharraf, catapulted Zia into the role of a close ally for Washington. It was Brezhnev's Christmas gift for Zia, who had overnight become the most allied ally of the Cold Warriors. Invariably and callously, Jinnah's Pakistan was handed over to the jihadi zealots armed by the Central Intelligence Agency (CIA), funded by the Saudis, and trained by the Pakistani ISI (Inter-Services Intelligence). What happened to Pakistan's civic and democratic imperatives was nobody's business as has been the case again after 9/11 when Washington and London preferred General Musharraf over and above the country's constitutional probity. History never tires of repeating itself, especially in the wake of double standards! Thus, after 1979, it was jihad against 'the evil empire' that preceded everything else, and the Afghans were not only the valiant fighters—the Mujahedeen—but also 'the moral equivalent of the Founding Fathers', as was decreed by Reagan. Enthusiasm shaken, if not shattered, amidst a daily scroll of coercion and corruption all around, I needed to reenergize my sinews after four grilling years on the periphery of a metropolis that carried the name of Islam yet impassively behaved every other way.

I had a few appointments in London before absorbing myself into the archives at the India Office Records by the Blackfriars Bridge. Firstly, I had to visit the British Museum to brood in its reading room where Karl Marx had wrestled with philosophy and history to steer the world out of oppression, and where Sir Syed Ahmed Khan (1817–98) had rigorously worked on his biography of the Prophet PBHU during the height of colonial obduracy and Orientalist denigration of everything Eastern. Moreover, I wanted to see the Egyptian Mummies to my fill, though I had seen quite a few of them in Chicago and New York in the 1970s; here they had Ramses II and one in particular of a shepherd that had been on display without the usual wrapping and casing. Secondly, I wanted to visit the Victoria & Albert (V&A), followed by forays into the Imperial College, and the Natural History Museum. For too long, I had harboured the desire to see Tipu Sultan's musical organ—Tippoo's Tiger—that symbolized the valiant fight by the Sultan of Mysore (1750–99) against the English East India Company. It was kept here at V&A in a very elaborate section on South Asia, close to galleries devoted to Islamic arts and handicrafts. My visits to all these eminent institutions since 1983 have been thrilling as I never felt any sense of saturation with these massive Victorian structures and their immensely diverse, valuable, and enriching collections. I always felt envious but equally consoled that at least the colonial 'loot' was being properly looked after instead of being hurled into obscurity by the corrupt and inept scions of the developing world. Although I was not fully certain of this latter justification as it too smacked of derision of those 'developing' societies. These art collections generated both a sense of empowerment and helplessness that overtook me during those early days when, at a comparatively autumny youth, I was still vulnerable to sporadic bouts of zeal and passion, and perhaps simplistically attuned to seeing the world in white and black without being fully cognisant of its multiple grey layers.

After a research tenure at Columbia and Berkeley, I had returned to Pakistan again with renewed vigour, which would last me another decade until God Almighty recalled Zia and his coterie of generals in 1988, and we were all fired up by another sought-after opportunity of democratization. For a moment, like other *Midnight's Children*, I rediscovered my youth but the dream turned out to be another blimp as a new pack of avaricious scavengers began to gnaw at the shrunk skeleton of a nation that had aged overnight. The sudden and traumatic greying of a young Pakistan happened through a rude denial of youth to it. An 'old' England finally opened its arms to a forlorn soul in a yet undefeated body and the quest for a home away from home ensued in Oxford. After Oxford, Russell Square with its colleges, libraries, and of course, the Bloomsbury proved to be a favourite hideout while visits to V&A became more frequent. But Tippoo's Tiger had been removed due to worries about its wooden structure and like others I had to content myself with miniature reproductions of it in the museum's shop. Once an elderly sales clerk had confided in me that the post cards, pens, and other such small souvenirs depicting Tipu's stripy tiger holding down a Redcoat were popular items amongst the visitors. The long, silky, and embroidered robes (*jama*), sashes, and turban jewels of the Mughal emperors, rare carpets, ornamented swords, protruding muskets, decorative motifs, splendid miniatures, elaborate court edicts, exceptional specimens of jewellery, and several other artefacts adorned an endlessly enticing Indian section. In 1999, the V&A celebrated the third centenary of the foundation of Sikh Khalsa by Guru Govind Singh, where Sikh costumes, swords, and miniature paintings bearing ornate Persian calligraphy were displayed representing synthesized Sufi and Bhagat traditions. In particular, it was fascinating to see the throne of Maharaja Ranjit Singh (1780–1839), which had been built in 1818 by Hafiz Muhammad, a Muslim artist from Multan. It was not a typically high or huge pedestal with elaborate canopies and jewelled arm rests for the royal limbs but a rather simple wooden structure encased in gold leaf with some tassels and a few diamonds. The Maharaja loved to sit on the takht in a typical Indian yogi style with legs folded under the torso as it suited his native taste. That exhibition also included portraits of the Gurus attributed to the Pahari School of Punjab. The portrait of a youthful Duleep Singh (1838–93) attired in all the Five Ks was certainly quite impressive. He was the only surviving son of the late Maharaja who as a young child was brought to London after Punjab's annexation in 1849 and then lived most of his life in Britain. Initially, he had converted to Christianity and married a local woman, however, some lateral reports suggest of his reconversion to Sikhism in the closing years of a tumultuous life. His estate in Thetford in East Anglia is still visited by many British Sikhs, and in 1997, Prince Charles ceremoniously unveiled a statute of a young and turbaned Duleep Singh riding a stallion. His eldest daughter, Princess Bamba (1869–1957), had been to Lahore a few times where her former husband, David Sutherland (d. 1939), headed the King Edward Medical College. Subsequently, she married a Pakistani, Pir Karim Bakhsh, and following her death, a private family funeral was held for this granddaughter of Maharaja Ranjit Singh. Princess Bamba's extensive art collection of several paintings and photographs was sold to Pakistan and is on display at the historic Lahore Fort which, having been built by the Mughal Emperor Akbar, used to be the capital of her grandfather in the early nineteenth century.

Another memorable exhibition held in 1997–8 at V&A was devoted to the traditional and recent textiles of the north-western subcontinent and was named as 'The Colours of the Indus'. Mainly consisting of contemporary Pakistani artists and designers, the exhibit presented a fascinating mix of old and new and coincided with the fiftieth anniversary of the country's independence. Three years later, it was followed by a multidimensional effort at the Brunei Gallery, which represented both the antiquity as well as diversity of the Pakistani culture and arts. The Mughal style miniatures and figurative portraits of Abdullah Chughtai, the doyen of neo-classicism, had captivated visitors to 'Pakistan: Another Vision', held in April–June 2000. Himself a representative of traditional Mughal culture and aesthetics, Chughtai, a self-taught artist with his Fes cap, towering figure, and genteel personality, was a memorable mentor in Lahore. Sadequain's unparalleled calligraphy and specimens from Guljee's versatility were also on display next to the superb creations of Zubeida Agha, Shakir Ali, Ghulam Rasool, Anwar Ijaz, and several other recent painters from Lahore's National College of Arts (NCA). The late Shakir Ali, a former principal at NCA, had laudably dedicated his own home and arts to the nation as freely accessible premises, whereas Chughtai's gallery, being looked after by his family, is not too far from Ali's home-cum-gallery in Lahore. I never met Sadequain, the preeminent calligrapher and portrait maker, though I saw him from afar, whereas with Gulgee, I had quite an interesting encounter in Oxford when I received him at the train station to drive him to Dr Abdus Salam's residence in Summertown where the latter stayed homebound due to Parkinson's. The famous scientist received us warmly and soon Gulgee set to his work by first taking pictures of this Nobel Laureate physicist, who had been a former Ravian; in fact, I had stayed in the same hostel room where the illustrious scholar from Jhang had lived during the 1940s. Gulgee refused my offer for a proper lunch because he skipped eating during his work and instead mostly lived on fluids of all types. Visiting that exhibition at the Brunei Gallery evidenced the courage of our artists who, despite martial laws and intelligence agencies ruling the roost often in cahoots with the obscurants, had not compromised on their creative efforts. Here at School of Oriental and African Studies (SOAS), the ensemble reflected a vibrant persona of a society that is often reduced to unending stories of violence and fundamentalism. In a powerful way, they celebrated the humanity of the ordinary inhabitants of the Indus lands. The exhibit of the rare Mughal monument, *Hamzanama*, in 2003 was again another memorable event at V&A, highlighting the unprecedented skills of calligraphy and miniature art as the splendid features of the Indo-Muslim civilization.

During the autumn of 2004, V&A mounted its well-publicized exhibition, 'Encounters', covering the East-West relationship during 1500–1800. Divided into three sections, 'Discoveries', 'Encounters', and 'Exchanges', it focused on the early Portuguese expansion across the Indian and Pacific Oceans which gradually gave way to the Dutch and finally to the British supremacy. The 'West' in the exhibit largely symbolized Portugal and England, whereas the East included India, the East Indies, China, and Japan. An appropriate terminal point for this multimedia effort was 1800, since it was around this time that a steadily declining Mughal Empire had left a power vacuum; the East India Company had defeated the French and the death of Tipu Sultan in 1799 had sealed the fate of India's sporadic resistance to an encroaching foreign control. The Dutch had gradually moved on to the East Indies, whereas the Portuguese were confined to Goa, Macao, and some other islands across the Pacific. After defeating the Spanish Armada with Ottoman help in 1588, the British controlled seafaring, trade, and vast lands across Asia. The early esteem for the East was soon replaced by colonial arrogance—a hegemonic sense of moral and cultural superiority with 'the Asiatics' needing control—coercion, and a total reorientation. Concurrently, by the early nineteenth century, missionary enterprise had already come of age and the Europeanization of the world was in its full swing, despite some moral baggage added by utilitarian and other Quaker-like moral objectors of slavery. While Asia in this early East-West relationship evoked respect, Africa on the contrary was deemed free for all. Since 1453, when the Portuguese initiated a modern form of slave trade, Africa, over the next three centuries, lost around 16–18 million able-bodied men and women to run the plantations and dredge the prairies across the Western Hemisphere. The end of the slave trade in the early nineteenth century did not stop the British from dispatching millions of Indians to the other colonial possessions in the West Indies, Africa, and Southeast Asia. Owing to this 'coolie trade', East met East, yet such sardonic themes were somehow absent from this otherwise refreshing effort to reassess this early modern past.

Divided into three separate halls, 'Encounters' offered a broad sweep by displaying terracotta, ceramics, textiles, armoury, miniatures, wall hangings, furniture, coins, gunnery, sacraments, ornaments, and other such artefacts. They overwhelmingly represented a confident yet 'traditional' East, though a few contemporary paintings by Western artists and the replication of Eastern luxuries also offered a Western window on these vast regions. The Ottoman conquest of Constantinople in 1453 had blocked the age-old East-West trade, and a post-Renaissance energized Western Europe, now under ambitious political authorities continued its search for new routes to the East. It was in 1488 that Bartolomeu Dias reached the Cape of Good Hope, whereas a decade later, Vasco de Gama, guided by an Indian Muslim sailor, made it to the Malabar Coast. Even before the establishment of the Mughal dynasty in India, the Portuguese had captured Goa and Hormuz controlled Malacca and, by 1513, were importing spices from China. The next few years saw them establish factories across South East Asia and on the Japanese coast. Lisbon, as shown in one of the contemporary portraits, soon emerged as a thriving global metropolis. As depicted in Abu'l Fazal's *Akbarnama*, the Portuguese Jesuits were fully engaged in interfaith debates during the 1580s at Fatehpur Sikri under the tutelage of Emperor Akbar, though his advisors had returned the prized European present. His nine leading advisors—*Naurattan*—feared that the printing press brought in by the Portuguese would destroy the age-old calligraphic skills. One wonders whether Asia missed out on a great contemporary invention by adopting a rather non-scientific attitude! The Chinese, Javanese, Ottomans, Safavids, and the Japanese responded in similar fashion to other newer technologies and knowledge capital by assuming a false sense of self-sufficiency.

It was in 1600 that the English East India Company was established in Threadneedle Street to conduct trade with the Indies and soon made its presence felt by founding Fort St. George at Madras and Fort William in Bengal by the Hooghly River, whereas the Dutch shifted east to Batavia. By this time, Japan's Shoguns had begun to expel the Portuguese missionaries as contemporary Portugal itself, like the neighbouring Spain, showed signs of exhaustion by overstretching its imperial possessions. In 1644, the Mings—the Manchus—founded their dynastic rule in

China but, more like introverted Mughals and Shoguns, opted to ignore European explorations. Eighteen years later, Portugal ceded Bombay to King Charles II of England as a part of Catherine of Braganza's dowry, while France joined the competition in 1664 by establishing the French East India Company. Nadir Shah's destruction of Delhi and the remnants of the Mughal Empire in 1739, the defeat of the Bengali armies at Plassey by Robert Clive in 1757, and the subsequent English ascendancy over their French rivals led to the evolution of the Company's Raj. While the Indian nabobs and rajas either fought amongst themselves or simply kowtowed to the Company, it was left only to Mysore's Sultan Hyder Ali and his son, Tipu Sultan, to defy the new emerging power in the subcontinent. Amongst several items on display at the exhibition, a Japanese screen from the 1630s depicted the arrival of a Portuguese ship in ink, colours, and gold leaf, in which an arrogant-looking captain is shown sitting under a canopy. In continuation of this pictorial history by some contemporary Japanese artist, the goods are being taken ashore where a bazaar occurs with its usual hustle and bustle but strictly in a dignified way. The Japanese shops are well-stocked, and towards the lower corner, one notices a barber giving a dexterous cut to a hairy Dutch sailor. It could be a scene from any part of rural Africa or Asia even today, where barbers with their weather-beaten leathery chairs assume a greater sense of authority over their weary clients.

A showcase in the second section held vases, cups, ewers, spoons, and caskets from India, Sri Lanka, China, and Japan, brought over by the early Europeans, while an impressive chair-like seat represented a rare gift from Queen Catherine of Austria to Emperor Maximilian II. This stool was in fact made of the bones of an elephant which the queen had gifted to the Holy Roman Emperor in 1552; following its death two years later, the bones were used to build a commemorative seat. The exhibit also included a folio from the world-famous Persian manuscript, *Padshahnama*, which had been commissioned by the Mughal Emperor, Shah Jahan (1592–1666) and had taken several years to complete. The original manuscript, along with a uniquely ornamented calligraphic narrative of Mughal history, contains some of the most beautiful miniatures based on the prose itself. *Padshahnama* has been in the possession of the British Queen, who also owns several similar rare manuscripts and artefacts in her collections at the Windsor and

Buckingham Palaces. The Nawab of Awadh, who presented it to King George III in 1797 through the Company's officials, had earlier acquired this Mughal masterpiece. On the eve of the inauguration of the Queen's Gallery during the 1990s, the Queen had allowed the first-ever public viewing of this manuscript, which certainly attracted long queues of viewers, both in London and Washington. These individuals paid huge sums not only to see the *Padshahnama* in its entirety but also bought its accompanying voluminous catalogue.[1] The miniature included in 'Encounters' showed Shah Jahan receiving his sons, courtiers, and the emissaries of the East India Company. As in all other miniatures, a halo encircled the royal head, whereas the Europeans were depicted in a corner of the Durbar, revealing a contemporary hierarchical order.

The Europeans, in pursuit of profit and missionary zeal, had used firepower to impose their terms on the people of coastal India and the Indonesian archipelago, however, the early Mughals and Mings dictated encounters with the West on Asian terms. The Asians were certainly impressed by European technology in areas of weaponry, glassware, and medicine. The former tried to acquire European muskets and even attempted to reproduce them in the local armouries. Moreover, the contemporary European gadgets, medicines, and lenses fascinated them. The lenses soon became an immensely popular trade commodity since the Asians used them for spectacles and telescopes. Concurrently, contemporary Europeans adored Asian clothes, spices, tea, furnishings, silk, muslin, and such other items which were bought either in barter trade or by paying in silver. Gradually, the Europeans ran out of a steady supply of silver, which led to all kinds of unsavoury practices. For instance, the British began exporting Indian opium to China in exchange for Chinese commodities and, in the process, millions of Chinese got hooked to opium, eventually leading to the Opium Wars. The Europeans, unable to import expensive Indian cloth and furnishing, tried to produce their local replicas, which also found an ample representation in 'Encounters'.

Next to the miniatures from *Padshahnama*, a human-size painting showed a powerful combination of East and West during the closing years of this early dialogue. This was an elaborate portrait of Muhammad Darvish Khan, a general in Sultan Tipu's army who had been sent to France to seek official help against the British. The portrait of this turbaned and bearded general was completed in Paris in 1787 by

Elisabeth Vigee-Lebrun (1755–1842) and is titled 'Darvich Khan Saeb', deputed by 'Padshah' Tipu. Khan's full white, embroidered silk dress (*khalat*) with a matching turban (*pattka*) reveal the style popular with the Mughal nobility and is complete with a sword. Needless to say, the mission did not succeed as France soon underwent its revolution in 1789 and it took Napoleon another decade to embark on his historic expedition to Egypt and by that time Tipu Sultan had already laid down his life in Seringapatam. Another similar and contemporary portrait is Tilly Kettle's Muhammad Ali Wallajah (1770), which shows the bearded Nawab of Arcot in his muslin robe, jewelled turban, and sashes, holding a long sword. The other artefacts in 'Encounters' included the portrait of Michael Alphonsius Shen Fu Tsung, an important and early Chinese · Christian who had undertaken well-publicized visits to Britain, France, and Italy before his death on the Continent in 1691. In Oxford, he had helped catalogue Chinese texts at the Bodleian Library and sat for a commissioned portrait by the royal painter, Sir Godfrey Kneller. The influence of Christianity in China was also evident in a variety of ivory and wooden items bearing engraved crosses. The priests offered all types of material temptations to Asians for conversion purposes which certainly led to frequent backlash. It was quite interesting to see a Japanese edict on a wooden plank (1682) issued by the Shogunate banning Christianity and ordering Japanese converts to renounce it. The inked edict, reflective of a Japanese Inquisition, offered rewards to those who would inform about their fellow citizens secretly practising Christianity.

A fascinating section of the exhibition dwelt on the Europeans turning 'native' by donning Asian clothes, marrying local women, and by immersing in Asian pastimes. Johann Zoffany's three well-known portraits focusing on the British in India during the last quarter of the eighteenth century featured those themes; one also encounters the same themes in William Dalrymple's *The White Mughals*.[2] As described by Dalrymple in his chapter in the 400-page-long catalogue accompanying 'Encounters', several of Zoffany's subjects in the portraits were real individuals, such as General Palmer, who had married Faiz Baksh, a Muslim lady, and sired several children from her. 'The Palmer Family' (1785) was a commissioned work, like the other portraits by Zoffany which showcased an entire family seated together, not only exhibiting European and Indian costumes but also a myriad of several other subtleties within a bicultural setting. Baksh, who survived Palmer, was a dynamic and independent woman who did not succumb to any racial or gender subordination and, unlike Khair-un-Nissa, the tragedy struck Mrs Kirkpatrick in *The White Mughals*, was endowed with longer life. Zoffany's proverbial depiction of the early Indo-European sporting mutualities is reflected through 'Colonel Mordaunt's Cock Match', where a mixed crowd of nobility and laity is jostling over a cockfight. It is a scene from Awadh with Indians and Europeans betting as well as egging their roosters. The colour depiction is a charming mix of the Mughal and European traditions, though the impressive feature of the work is its lack of any satire or moral uprighteousness. It shows both cultures at par with each other—a tradition that was soon to give way to a policy of conquest, control, and communal segregation at the behest of the Marquis of Wellesley and the future British regimes in India and elsewhere. 'Captain John Foote' (1765) by Sir Joshua Reynolds shows a British military official wearing flowery *jama*, *pattka*, and a waist shawl. Another portrait on paper in opaque watercolours depicts the procession of Muslim Ashura—Muharram mourning—where an orderly and serene crowd is passing through a built-in area. The domes, banners, horses, elephants, and the *rouza* featured in this portrait are by some Indian artist commissioned by George Farrington (1752–88) who shared a keen interest in the portrayal of religious customs. The locale of this work is Murshidabad and interestingly not Lucknow. Another portrait made by Dip Chand in the 1760s was of William Fullerton, a senior Company official in Murshidabad, the capital of Bengal, where he is shown seated on a terrace in the company of his favourite hookah. A contemporary portrait is of a rather authoritative-looking Mutabbey, the Bibi of William Fullerton, who is shown confidently seated on a chair, busy with her hookah. With the death of Tipu Sultan, not only did India lose its autonomy, its communal interface between the Indians and Europeans also breathed its last. A few more contemporary portraits showing greater interface—by the Asian and European artists—revealed mutual borrowings of themes, locales, and techniques. A portrait shows a seated Sir David Ochterlony in an Indian costume with a hookah, watching a *nautch* (dance) by girls, who could have been his 13 Indian concubines. Some Japanese and Chinese wall hangings interestingly caricatured Europeans as barbarians and uncouth individuals. The latter appear big, unkempt, wild-looking, and only seeking profit and quick sex. A rather explicit Japanese painting showed a Maruyama courtesan in a sexual intercourse with a burly, bearded Dutchman whom she is exhorting to 'perform' with more vigour, as if his drunkenness had already bereft him of virility. Her satirical exhortations are inscribed in Japanese next to her quizzical expressions, symbolizing a unique sense of ridicule.

Certainly such portraits hold a reservoir of information for any historian seeking cultural, economic, technical, and political antecedents in these primary documents. For instance, Thomas Daniell's 'A Composition of Indian Architecture' (1799) is a neat and detailed oil depiction on canvas of the Taj Mahal besides a Hindu temple and a *trishul* (trident) in the vicinity of a few Indian worshippers and two elephants. The brown and light green in the portrait harmoniously mingle with the rising Himalayas silhouetted in the background. It was painted for the Indian Drawing Room of Thomas Hope's celebrated Duchess Street mansion, showing both Muslim and Hindu monuments. 'Sake Dean Mahomed' by Thomas Baynes dates from 1820, when the Indian Muslim had already become a celebrity in England after spending several years in Cork, prior to his arrival in England. Before reaching Ireland in 1782, he had served in the Bengal Army and, in 1793, published *Travels of Dean Mahomed*, which earned him the cherished designation of the first-ever Indian writer in English. He and his Irish wife moved to London and pioneered South Asian cuisine there. Opened in 1810, the Hindoostanee Coffee House was the earliest Indian restaurant in England, followed by an Indian therapeutic facility in Brighton where several herbal and traditional oil massages were offered to treat muscle-related ailments. In the portrait, he looks sharp, smartly dressed, and self-confident with a receding hairline owed to an eventful life. Dean Mahomed had treated the Prince of Wales and a Russian Czar at his Brighton's Mahomed's Baths, and a few years back, this portrait at Christy's had led to an editorial comment in the *Guardian*, eulogizing this early British Muslim who had been at ease with his plural identities.

Depending upon one's own judgment, 'Tippoo's Tiger' could be held as the ultimate emblem of 'Encounters', as this wooden music instrument not only reflected the recreational dimension of contemporary Indian/ Asian life but also equally symbolized cultural tensions and political dissent. Professor Samuel P. Huntington could have certainly used it as an apt dust cover for his noted work, *The Clash of Civilizations*.[3] Made under the orders from the Sultan of Mysore whose sword, turban, and embroidered robes sit in the South Asian section at V&A, this music piece consists of two main items and was reputedly manufactured by a French artisan residing in India. Its lower wooden half is basically the body of a Redcoat fully dressed in the Company's uniform, while the upper half is a full-length Bengal tiger holding the neck of the former in its jaws. Inside the tiger's stomach is a harmonium with eight white knobs operable through a comfortable hollow section. A metallic handle was applied to wind up the instrument, which would then release a rendition of shouts and whizzes while the tiger would gradually tighten its grip. The tiger certainly represented Tipu Sultan himself who had grabbed the *Ferningee* (lit: foreigner) in his jaws while mounting his body, and the music was supposed to be the latter's plea for life. For quite some time, 'Tippoo's Tiger' had been stored in a safe house away from public glare out of fear for its life, but it was included in this exhibition. 'Encounters' was surely purported to celebrate cultural and artistic commonalities away from the subsequent hegemonic attitudes, as featured through Orientalism, Neo-racism, and politico-economic subjugation. The exhibit not only offered a pertinent perspective on the early and formative stage in this West-East encounter but also accounted for a conscious effort to highlight interdependence in an age notorious for its preoccupation with proclivities. However, the final word goes to a young British girl who on that Sunday wondered at the display while simultaneously listening to an audio commentary through her earphones: 'Dad,' she said rather loudly, 'why were those Christians trying to convert these people by offering them jewels?' Her father was so moved by her spontaneity that he lifted her up saying: 'A very good point, indeed! We'll discuss that at home. But I'm proud of you for asking this!'

Notes

1. Amin Jaffer and Anna Jackson, eds., *Encounters: The Meeting of Asia and Europe, 1500–1800* (London: V & A Publications, 2004).

2. William Dalrymple, *The White Mughals: Love and Betrayal in Eighteenth-century India* (London: Harper Perennial, 2004).
3. Samuel P. Huntington, *The Clash of Civilizations and the Remaking of World Order* (London: Simon & Schuster, 2002).

20

A Tatar Amongst Finnish Tatars

Ancient Greece begat Rome, Rome begat Christian Europe, Christian
Europe begat the Renaissance, the Renaissance the Enlightenment, the
Enlightenment political democracy and the industrial revolution. Industry
crossed with democracy and in turn yielded the United States, embodying
the rights to life, liberty and the pursuit of happiness

Eric Wolf[1]

'Am just coming back from Amman via Istanbul. I'm Saul, a Finnish
surgeon, and work for the Red Cross.' This senior man extended his hand,
sporting a kind smile on his countenance, while a pair of thick, totally
grey, and visibly protruding eyebrows joined in, reaffirming his warm and
passionate humanity. Following my reciprocity, Saul mentioned his visits
to Peshawar and Kohat where, during the 1980s, he had treated Afghan
patients besides training Pakistani surgeons. Retirement from his teaching
job four decades back had allowed him to work for Finland's Red Cross,
often amongst people displaced by wars and conflicts. Still there was no
sign of exhaustion or arrogance on his face that seemed to have absorbed
a generous dose of the Jordanian sun. Despite a long journey, including
the transfer time in Istanbul, this Nordic soul looked fully energized
and eager to talk during our shared taxi ride from the Helsinki Airport.
It had been an uneventful flight that followed a rather early morning
coach journey from Oxford to Heathrow where a warm neighbourhood
in the waiting lounge with some vocal Lebanese couples had enlivened
it slightly. Their flight for Beirut had been delayed, allowing them more
complaints amidst laughter, interspersed with frequent incantations of
Insha'Allah. They were Maronites with shiny crosses around some senior
women's necks. My intermittent smiles over unending cups of coffee and

munching had allowed them to go beyond a few generations in nostalgia to when their cosmopolitan city was Asia's Beirut and before those rustic cousins from the Gulf began to build their obnoxious concrete castles across the sands.

The Nordic airhostesses, flaring generous blonde canopies yet eager to charge for canapés, had been smiling all through the flight which was steadily heading towards the northeast and that too in the month of February. In my capacity of an Erasmus teacher, scheduled to offer lectures on history and theology, I had already flown over Erasmus's native land, and following our route over Denmark, we were soon checking on the Swedes below the ever-grey Scandinavian clouds. Clouds over Europe and North Atlantic are unfailing companions, as if like their regimes, they are eager to veil those societies from any intruders or unwanted immigrants. France, Belgium, and some others have already banned veils but the veils and burkinis above their horizons never seem to part company and it is only when one comes back closer to the European soil, interspersed with opulent green foliage and numerous lakes, that Mother Nature's purdah finally rises. Compared to some other busy airports, Helsinki's appears rather more relaxed with its own sprinkling of plurality, though it is not unfair to suggest that most airports, like their passengers, look alike and so does their ambience. A shared taxi ride to one's destination may be a rather quiet affair, with passengers orientating themselves and strategizing to brave an impending jetlag, yet some exceptions get re-energized who, like Saul, find themselves on native soil following the completion of another mission. Adrenalin in such people rushes up. I could have asked the noble surgeon for a night cap had it been a routine homecoming but I was slightly preoccupied about my own engagements at a totally new place, which that Sunday evening in 2015 was already covered with layers of white ice.

The university accommodation happens to be at a short distance away from the main campus itself, which sits in the historic district in the capital city and neighbours museums, official blocks, shopping centres while facing the harbour which links Finland with Russia and other Baltic states besides ensuring its cultural and commercial mutualities with Scandinavia. Area wise, it is the fifth largest country within the European Union and equals Pakistan's Balochistan in its size and population; its affinities with its other Scandinavian neighbours are quite visible. Still given the pulls from its east and having been under the strong thumb of a big brother—Russia—there is a strong sense of Finnish distinctness from everyone else. After Sweden and Russia, it is the Baltic states, not too distant in the south, which share several ethno-religious similarities with this avowedly Lutheran nation that retains a very small presence of Greek Orthodox and Muslims amongst its five million inhabitants. The passenger next to me on the flight, with dark jet black hair and a rather petite built, surprisingly proved to be receptive to small talk since travel, like visits to hospitals and cemeteries, can amazingly mellow us down. She was an Estonian who lived in Italy and was returning from a week-long visit to San Francisco. Italians, especially in the north, may sometimes resemble their Swiss and Austrian neighbours but they usually have Mediterranean features and their hair colour often tends to be dark. Lula could be passed for an Italian if not for her transparently white complexion, which her dark hair made even more pronounced. She had enjoyed the comparatively liberal lifestyle of San Francisco and had been to several 'interesting' places in Castro Street, though she felt bad for not having visited Berkeley.

'Why don't you take a ferry to Tallinn? It's not too far from Helsinki,' she had inquired. 'I would love to but I have got only one week with academic sessions happening every day including a day's visit to Turku in-between. The next time round!' I noticed a small MSU ring on her index finger and told her about my own Spartan background. In fact, her mother had been to Michigan State University in East Lansing to earn an MA and it was her ring that Lula sported on her finger. I thought of my old alma mater covered in February's all-white layers, as did the city of Helsinki below that itself came into existence as a fishing and maritime village in 1550 on the northern shores of the Gulf of Finland. It became a capital only in the early nineteenth century when the Russians took control, signalling the end of a 700-year-long Swedish rule which had held its court at Turku.

I knew that I was only an hour away from St. Petersburg and perhaps that could be an even more possible option in case I happened to come back to *her* Baltic region, though she herself lives by the Aegean and did not miss the ice and sleet except for the fact that her parents lived back home. One wonders how the integration of Europe and North America, that we all tend to call the West, has brought together diverse people so close, which could not have been possible even two generations back, as they were engaged in horrible wars and ethnic cleansings, not only on this continent but elsewhere as well. Still, Europe in general never forgot its bible and churches, and European control of the world proved to be the power engine for Christianity. Saints Paul, Peter, Augustine, Andrews, Aquinas, Jerome, James, Antony, Patrick, Barnabas, and a whole list of Popes would be smiling all the way in their next abodes, given their men on horsebacks holding on to sword and epistle in their unending civilizing missions of the heathens! The mission continues with the same intensity when it comes to Muslims now whose 'savagery' and 'terror' have to be dissected and even decimated, whereas in the meantime, Western Muslims have to rise to newer occasions and horizons to justify their total acculturation. Their communities, mosques, younger groups, and student societies on campuses have to be monitored as their movements across the lands, since these 'Turks' are the 'old' and 'new' trouble makers. The Russians under Putin and capitalist-communist Chinese might be major irritants for an altruist West but the real spoiler at geopolitical levels is Islam that refuses to assume a subterranean and even toothless existence.

Lula and Saul were my pleasant orientation to this part of Northern Europe since, in common parlance on Islam-West or East-West tensions, the Baltic regions and Scandinavia have often tended to be overshadowed by the 'bigger' brothers to the west and east. As I landed in Finland, the contemporary British Conservative Defence Secretary seemed to be alerting his audience on Putin's alleged designs on the Baltic regions in the latter's expansive efforts to recreate another Soviet Union. One might notice people concerned in Finland, and other Baltic states, a bit unnerved with the ongoing instability in eastern Ukraine. However, some would even venture to suggest that a hasty expansion of the North Atlantic Treaty Organization (NATO) and EU could have led to the renewal of these older rivalries. The economic sanctions were hurting Russians but they also caused economic and some political worries for Finland and the Baltic states which still retain extensive commercial ties with Moscow. Located in the eastern and northern most region of Scandinavia, Finland, like Greenland and Iceland, is a gigantic territorial expanse, though during the Second World War, some of its eastern territories were taken over by the USSR along with a stupendous war indemnity which Helsinki had to pay to Moscow; at one stage, the latter accounted for almost half of its GDP. But owing to these war reparations and then Russia being such an insatiable market, Finland was able to diversify its economy and became an exporting industrial state, which certainly underpinned its own development. Located in a testing region, the Finns were able to cash in on their extensive resourcefulness in timber, fisheries, ship building, and paper products, and certainly Nokia and other media technologies have allowed them to claim a major share in the world market. *Finlandization* during the Cold War was a testing phase for being locked between the former communist bloc and an ever-vigilant NATO; however, the dissolution of the Soviet Union and hazy days of Yeltsin allowed Finland a significant integration within the EU.

Known for vast icy expanses, polar bears, numerous lakes, unbound wood resources, and people often portrayed as well-fed and more attuned to peace, Scandinavia is viewed as a very homogenous and prosperous region that somehow escaped the drudgeries of the rest. A closer study of its past shows this region as not being so isolated; instead we find it integrated with the rest of the world in several areas. Given its location near the North Pole, the ice age receded here later than elsewhere, agriculture was introduced centuries after it had already become the mainstay in other regions. The land of the midnight sun and Northern Lights remained rural and agrarian for a long period. Even today, Finland's forests claim 2.2 billion square metres, accounting for 86 per cent of its landmass, as does the Danish Jutland which is again quite a rich, fertile arable farmland. Southern Sweden and Norway also feature fertile land, though mountains, forests, and longer winter months equally impact agrarian cycles. The early inhabitants of the region were food gatherers who owned tame dogs and used bows and arrows. The Samis are often seen as the Aborigines of Scandinavia while some may take them as originating from Siberia. Even in the nineteenth century, scholars such as M. A. Castren believed that the Finns, like the Hungarians, had originated from Outer Mongolia, though recent research reveals migrations from the Baltic regions into Scandinavia during the fifth century CE. Like Finns, there are numerous hypotheses about the origins of today's Danes, Swedes, and Norwegians, though there is no doubt about their being proficient ship builders who mostly lived on fish and hunted boar and deer. By the early Greco-Roman period, there was scarcity of information on Northern Europe where people were believed to live like 'barbarians'. Tacitus (CE 56–CE 117) was the first ever Gaelic-Roman historian to write about the political and cultural achievements of the Suiones or Upper Swedes who had their own kings, were well-off, and built big ships. Roman emperors, Augustus and Nero, sent campaigns into Scandinavia to gather more information about these ancient North Europeans and, as a consequence, such cross-cultural incursions might have possibly resulted in a distinct Scandinavian alphabet.

It was during the early medieval period that Scandinavians turned a new page in their history when, known as Vikings, they began a series of encroachments upon neighbouring European countries and beyond, all the way to North America and North Africa. The Vikings vanquished the native Anglo-Saxons in England, beginning with their first invasion of Dorset in 789, followed by several more in the years to come. Holding on to their pagan beliefs and imbued with eagerness to capture wealth, they did not spare monasteries and churches. The Vikings found their equal in Charlemagne, who fought against them like he did against the Muslims and in the process angered these Danes even more. During the ninth century, the Vikings engaged in invading Gibraltar and Algeciras, followed by the enslavement of several men in Morocco in order to sell them off in Ireland. Led by Hastein, these Vikings laid siege to Pisa after having sacked Lisbon, Cadiz, and Seville during the 850s. These must have been the earliest contacts between the Scandinavians and Muslims that preceded the expansion of Christianity in Scandinavia. Such forays had allowed Scandinavians to interact with the Christian population, though Roman Catholicism came into the region from Northern Europe, and missionaries from Ireland and England took the lead in evangelical efforts. In fact, Hastein desired to be buried in Rome, though he ended up in Luna. In his contempt, he destroyed it, followed by a similar fate for Alexandria. The Viking era in Britain, France, and Germany came to an end in the eleventh century following separate monarchies in Norway, Sweden, and Denmark. By this time, Christianity had been able to gain a stronghold in all these countries, as one finds evidence of sizeable Norwegian contingents engaged in the Crusades.

In the meantime, one learns of the Swedish campaign around the Caspian region right in the heart of Asia, while they busied themselves in active Silk Road trade with their eyes on Constantinople, which was then viewed as the richest city, partly because of its location and also because it was the capital of the Byzantine Empire. A contemporary Arab traveller and diplomat in Eurasia, Ahmad ibn Fadlan (b. CE 822), found these Swedes physically quite towering, often with blond hair and ruddy faces; they were not too abashed about sexual encounters with slave girls in the open. In 921, the Abbasid caliph sent Ibn Fadlan into the interiors of Eurasia as an emissary who, during his extensive travels through Central Asia and further northwest, encountered the Bulgars, Khazars, Russians, and Norsemen. He met a group of Vikings in Upper Volga and left his impression on the people from the north. Another Spanish Arab traveller, Abu Bakr Muhammad at-Turtushi (1059–1126), visited Hedeby during the eleventh century and found most of the natives preferring fish to beef, along with a curious interest in facial make-up; tattoos were popular with both men and women. Hedeby, a personal fiefdom of the Danish royals, is close to German borders and was a major city in the disputed region of Schleswig-Holstein that caused several wars between the Germans and the Danes. It is also a major archaeological site in the southern part of Denmark's Jutland. At-Turtushi, like Ibn Fadlan, had been sent as an emissary to these north European regions by the Spanish Muslim caliph and left his travel accounts. The Swedes maintained commercial relations with the Muslims as affirmed by the old coins with Arabic scripts found at several archaeological sites. The Swedish influences reached the Balkans and Russia and, like the Vikings, they too practised polygamy and still followed their own pagan creeds. Muhammad al-Idrisi, the well-known Sicilian geographer from Ceuta, in his cartographic work, *Tabula Rogeriana*, mentioned Finland as an imperial nation with its capital at the busy seaport of Turku. The Norman King, Roger II, had invited Idrisi to Sicily to undertake some cartographic work in Palermo.

At the beginning of the twelfth century, Sweden, led by Erik I, annexed Finland, which remained under its control until the Russians took over in the nineteenth century, following Napoleon's defeat. Earlier, the Black Death had visited these regions during the mid-fourteenth century, claiming numerous lives. Norway lost half of its population due to the epidemic. Reformation came to this part of Europe in the second quarter of the sixteenth century and Scandinavia overwhelmingly became Lutheran. The dynastic wars between Denmark and Sweden continued to claim many more lives, whereas Sweden held on to Finland as a province, and Denmark annexed Norway in 1536. The Congress of Vienna's settlement of 1815 had also joined Sweden and Norway but allowed Czar Alexander to lay claims on his western neighbour. The Russian troops included a fair number of Muslim Tatars who settled down in Finland with frequent ventures back home to marry; went on pilgrimage to the Hejaz and kept following Islam in their northern abode. They also developed a close relationship with the Muslims in Poland and Lithuania, though eventually they all were called Tatars. Over generations, there were some conversions and marriages between Tatars and Finnish women, which made this community quite distinct by virtue of its indigenization as well as retention of religion and lingual plurality. The Tatars, irrespective of their origins from Mongolia or Siberia, are Central Asian people who moved further west and south and established their communities in regions around the Caspian until the thirteenth century, when they faced the Mongol invasions. They survived the havoc only with some instinctive prowess and cultural fortitude, and soon the city of Kazan became the centre of Western Tatars, while many others moved towards South Asia and Anatolia. This Turkic infusion of fresh blood and energy allowed a new leash of life to Muslim empires such as the Mughals, Safavids, and the Ottomans—the land-based kingdoms. In the meantime, Russian Czars began their expansionist campaigns, which were anchored on Russification of the conquered people besides their conversion to Orthodox Church. The Kazan Khanate—the main Tatar political entity since the invasions by the Mongols and their subsequent conversion to Islam—was captured by the Russians in 1552 and a strenuous struggle for survival against odds from the west began.

Back in Finland, Turku was the long-time capital under the Swedes, whereas the Russians preferred Helsinki and ensured construction of many beautiful buildings around the Senate Square including Orthodox churches, official blocks, and university premises which were mostly designed by a leading German architect, Carl Ludwig Engel, who also built several magnificent buildings in St. Petersburg. It was during the nineteenth century that a romantic form of nationalism took its roots in Scandinavia amidst vast migrations to the United States known as the Great Exodus, which had been triggered by a population explosion. One-fourth of Swedes and a similar ratio of people from Denmark,

Norway, and Finland migrated to North America. Some of the known Scandinavians such as Carl Linnaeus, Alfred Nobel, Hans Christian Andersen, Soren Kierkegaard, and Henrik Ibsen offered a greater sense of pride to North Europeans and became role models in their own areas including sciences, literature, philosophy, and music. Finland was under Russian control for more than a century and became independent in 1917, following the October Revolution due to Moscow's own preoccupation; the former soon became a theatre of a civil war between the Whites and the Reds. The earlier persuasion by the Germans and nods from the British helped the Finns proclaim their independence, though the civil war left its own scars of revenge killings and concentration camps, which have often been preened from historical accounts. General Baron Gustaf Mannerheim, a former White Russian cavalry officer, led Swedish volunteers and about 12,000 German mercenaries to fight against 30,000 Finnish Red Guards who, after seizing Helsinki, had declared a Socialist Workers' Republic which only lasted for four months. Lenin had in fact encouraged the local communists to take over the country but, given Russia's own internal issues, the Finns, helped by external volunteers, were able to defeat the socialists and then began their spree of revenge.

The civil war caused about 24,000 casualties and almost an equal number of Red sympathizers were subsequently executed or left to die in the camps. Some of these vigilante perpetrations were inspired by ultra religio-nationalist sentiment and were called Lapua Pietists, who went on a rampage that resembled ethnic cleansing. They not only killed many communists but also banished quite a few of them to Russia besides forcing their newly-formed government to ban communism altogether. The Tatar-Finns were definitely put right in the middle of this volatile ideological divide, yet the community survived and so did its creed. To a great extent, their multilingualism and acculturation within the mainstream Finnish culture allowed them space that was certainly helped by democratization of the country. The Pietists were only stopped by the army which saw its patience reach an ultimate limit. The Finn nationalists had initially thought of installing one of German Kaiser William's sons as their monarch, partly owing to the German support in their civil war, but the German defeat in the Great War allowed the path towards an independent republic. Kaarlo Juho Stahlberg, the professor of law, was chosen as the founding president of the republic and soon a treaty with the Soviet Union guaranteed the autonomy of this newly-formed state. The longest road in Finland making the main artery in Helsinki is named after General Mannerheim, who once again came back to lead the Finns during the Second World War despite his senior age. Following the German retreat from Stalingrad, the Soviets had once again encroached upon Finland and withdrew only after holding on to some Finnish territories in the east besides a pledge for war reparations, which accounted for almost half of the Finnish GDP. The twentieth century, especially the developments since 1917, imprinted a serious strain on Finnish Tatars, leading to a total disconnect with the ancestral land back in Russia and further south.

Finlandization was a common political term that was often used with reference to the country's neutral status by virtue of its being lodged between the West and the East; however, it guaranteed its autonomy during the hot and cold phases of the Cold War. The Russian Czars, during their heyday in the nineteenth century, allowed some religious and cultural leeway to the Finns and in fact wanted to showcase their high levels of tolerance and civility to Western Europe through an accommodative policy in Finland. They built graceful buildings in Helsinki, Turku, and other urban centres, held balls in bigger cities and, despite building grand Orthodox churches, strictly avoided a total Russification of Finland. As noted earlier, the Russian armies during the Napoleonic era came in with a sizeable number of Muslim Tatar soldiers whose descendants live in Finland and, despite all kinds of ideological and violent changes all around them, seem to have preserved their Muslim identity. Some of them engaged in trade and construction businesses such as in Bomarsund, which has an early Muslim cemetery. Other than these early Tatar soldiers and builders, some more families moved into Finland in the 1870s from Upper Volga and it is their descendants who are mostly concentrated in Helsinki. However, some communities became part of the Soviet Union in 1940 when a few Finnish territories were ceded to Moscow. Making one of the earliest and perhaps the oldest Muslim community in Scandinavia, the early Tatars used to travel back and forth until the October Revolution, but grievously suffered under Stalin with his purges which kept non-Russian communities being churned around so as to create a Soviet melting pot of all these uprooted people. The survival of Tatar Muslims, like their cousins in Crimea, despite their delinking with the other Muslim communities a few generations back, is no less extraordinary and smacks of the view of the Muslims being vanquished like their Andalusian coreligionists either through ghettoization or owing to forced conversions due to an evangelical and powerful majoritarianism. Their own resilience and adaptation within Russia and Finland, besides seeking vitality within the community's own multilingual dynamics, helped Tatars survive at both the places. The Finnish Tatars established their Finlandiay Islam Cemaati (Finland's Islamic Association) soon after the Finnish civil war, which was finally recognized by the regime in 1925. In that sense, this was a pioneer Muslim organization in Northern Europe to be officially recognized, which offered educational, lingual, literary, and religious services to Finnish Tatars. For a long time, instruction in Tatar language, belonging to the family of Altai-Turkic languages, was organized by the association and was helped by the government in Helsinki. The poetry recitals, private lessons, and a greater usage of Tatar at home and in the mosques ensured the persistence of this language though, like the community itself, it has been suffering from a steady diminution. The sister communities in Poland, Lithuania, and Estonia are smaller and not enough is known about these Muslims, given the internecine warfare, the Cold War, and an accentuation on exclusive nationalisms. Inclusion of these states in the EU has allowed greater mobility and access to other such smaller Muslim groups whose own documentary and oral evidence may help scholars add to our scanty knowledge of Islam in north-eastern Europe. The arrival of Muslim immigrants, their travels within the EU, and academic openness are already allowing newer opportunities for scholarly and cultural insights on a hitherto unknown Islamic presence in Northern Europe whose survival against odds, like the Jews, is surely astounding.

Stalin's purges and banishments of Muslim communities across eastern regions including Siberia and Finland's overwhelming Lutheranism have been acute challenges for Tatars on both sides, yet their survival against odds is certainly unprecedented. Long before Stalin, Ivan the Terrible (1530–84) perpetrated heinous crimes against Muslims including destruction of mosques, forced conversions, and prohibition of religious rituals. Ivan was following the footsteps of the Mongol invaders whose ire also fell on Tatars, Bishkirs, and other Muslims. It was only after some rejuvenating efforts that the Khanate of Kazan had evolved as a reinvigorated Muslim kingdom until the Czar annexed it, following the annihilating venture directed against non-Russian and non-Orthodox population groups. Such campaigns were taken in the spirit of a forced Russification as the erstwhile Muscovite state aggressively and exponentially expanded in all directions. Catherine the Great (1729–96) did allow some remission to Tatars and other Muslims but soon an exclusive emphasis on nationalism and orthodoxy gained major momentum under Czar Nicholas II (1868–1918), which focused on communities like Muslims across Russia. Joseph Stalin (1878–1953), in that sense, was pursuing his demographic engineering under a communist praxis, however, ironically his purges and repressive conformism fell in line with the early coercive assimilation by the Czars. At present, Russia's Tatar republic remains an economic success story due to natural gas reserves, developed manufacturing, and high-tech industry and that too when demographically this smaller region underwent major changes with the settlement of several Russians on its soil. There is a small sprinkling of Russians in Finland today, especially those who have mixed marriages or have been the descendants of such marriages in the past, but it is only through buildings, some historical accounts, and mixed views of Finland's Russian past and interaction with the Soviets that Russia emerges as a factor. Of course, it is a giant next door whose most historic city, St. Petersburg, is not too far from Helsinki and a portion of Finland itself is part of Russia.

In the Senate Square, right in the heart of the historic district and facing the town hall which is a symbol of old Helsinki and is more like its Trafalgar Square, stands the only but no less grand piece of sculpture. Surrounded by peasants, courtiers, and holy men, a relaxed but regal Czar Alexander I stands high on the podium over and above everyone else. His back is towards the all-white town hall, which is built in Greek Orthodox style with typical rising circular columns on all its sides and its location on higher ground allows it a unique prominence as well as elegance. A city of less than a million people but with broad boulevards, new high-rises, and being criss-crossed by trams, buses, and lakes, this part of Helsinki is perhaps the most splendid section embodying its imperial past. The Senate Square is surrounded by buildings of Neo-Gothic-Georgian styles, often featuring rising Greco-Roman columns that one usually finds in the older and especially Western parts of the Continent, while

Helsinki's streets are straight, broad, and often paved with bricks or cobble stones. The maroon Finnish lime often provides the lower base for many nineteenth century buildings so as to protect their foundations against arctic elements. Buildings like those housing the parliament, national library, university's rectory, bookshops, and academies devoted to Finnish and Swedish literature, along with several majestic houses owned by barons and knights, surround the Senate Square on all its four sides. Through its graceful streets one can head further south, and just a few hundred yards away is the harbour, which has been the hub of mobility in the Baltic region, plus it is neighboured by some uniquely graceful buildings. The Finnish presidency is based in a building that once housed the Russian administration, while next door sits the Swedish Embassy that for a long time symbolized Swedish control of this section of their empire, though both the Finns and the Swedes often avoid using the term 'colonial' for this relationship which was spread over 12 centuries. Perhaps blood is thicker than water, or a kind of pragmatic approach with a greater sense of history disallows any dissensions. The special sentries guarding the presidency face the harbour and their grey woollen uniforms, especially their fur hats resemble their Russian military counterparts. The difference is only in colour but not in style and texture. Around the corner and across a small bridge stands the Greek Orthodox Church, crowning a red hill. It is made of red stones with its canopies and onion domes and crosses in complete Kremlin style. Along with the town hall on the north-eastern side, this church appears more beautiful but its solitariness and struggle against mist coming in from the sea beckon a visitor to a long-gone past. Some momentary wanderings help one understand *Finlandization* quite effectively, where two powerful historic influences, both from the east and the west, are synthesized with a stronger sense of self-reliance but definitely interspersed with immense restraint. In the case of Sweden and Lutheran-cum-Nordic mutualities, the relationship is more relaxed, though the Swedish elite and their institutions have often been the Finnish Brahmins, yet only 5 per cent Finns speak Swedish. It is a unique form of relationship where strong bonds disallow any modicum of dire hostility while still allowing some infrequent humour about a sustained exceptional status enjoyed by the Swedish legacies and legatees. Russian, on the other hand, did not become a pervasive reality even during the nineteenth century and is now a selective academic pursuit that has been further affected with the thinning of Russian visitors, owing to sanctions and other restrictions. The rich Russians may still opt for London, Paris, or Vienna and choose to not settle too close to St. Petersburg. A land of the 'great game' in the last several centuries, Finland is still a far cry from Afghanistan in every sense of the word, though their unique roles as 'buffers' or even front line states may harbour some unique commonalities.

The University of Helsinki, like the rest of Finland, is a well-endowed and faculty-based institution whose academic community, in many cases, includes its own former graduates whose research has often allowed them to travel across Western Europe, especially Britain. English is almost the second language in the country and people are eager to use it, but more so in the university where it is the medium of instruction. It is not only a *cause celebre* to gain access to a larger and envied scholarship in English but is also meant to attract international students. There is a growing number of international students largely because the university education is free, though subsistence in the cities in the south is understandably expensive. The universities in Helsinki and Turku pursue more linkages with the world's known universities, but graduate students have to juggle with growingly stringent immigration laws of their country. Finland, partly because of the smaller number of its population and also because of its location and recent integration within the EU, is less multicultural compared to Sweden or Holland but has a small presence of Africans and Turks. African Christians and Muslim Somalis account for visible population groups amongst the new Finns, whereas one notices a steady presence of tourists from China, South Korea, and Japan. The number of South Asians in the country is quite meagre, though some bilingual Bangladeshis run restaurants such as Mr Don's and Bhangra Club, while one may also notice some Nepalese restaurants in Helsinki, though their menus are typical Indian or uniquely Bangladeshi. Amongst Muslims, Tatars are the oldest Finns, followed by Turks, some Bosnians, Kosovars, and now Somalis, though one may not be completely sure about the presence of refugees from Iraq and Syria, as like Afghan refugees, they have often ended up in their neighbouring countries.

My early lectures in 2015 dealt with Islam and politics in Pakistan and Turkey where history and post-9/11 issues were highlighted, allowing younger students a greater chance to absorb long-terms strands in multiple identities. On another day, I spoke to a larger group of students where other than a female majority, I noticed a fair number of mature students, some completing their doctoral degrees. The Faculty of Theology is world-known with long-term interests in diverse religious traditions, philosophical strands, and now in Islam itself; my lecture tried to cover South Asian history of parallel identities in more recent centuries. In February 2015, I ventured into Helsinki's Juma Mosque for namaz and was guided upstairs into a tastefully decorated hall by two ladies. Soon, I was able to understand portions of the speech by the imam as it was interspersed with many familiar Turkish, Persian, Arabic, and Urdu words, and I felt no sense of unease and strangeness. I met the energetic imam, a doctoral student at the University of Helsinki, and was introduced to his family and other Finnish Tatars who had history, courage, humility written large on their smiling faces. I was left to reflect on how even in a distant India, Muslims were identified as Tatars by their European colonizers. Following the Rebellion of 1857, in a revenge spree, the victors exiled the last Mughal Emperor to Burma on a bullock cart. Before his ignominious departure, the 80-year-old monarch-poet was presented the severed heads of his two sons by Colonel Hodson, an East India Company official who was soon to convey to London the following message: 'In 24 hours I disposed of the principal members of the house of Timur the Tartar. I am not cruel, but I confess I did enjoy the opportunity of ridding the earth of these wretches'. A few years later, when the exiled king, Bahadur Shah Zafar, passed away in Rangoon, another colonial official communicated to London: 'At 4pm on a hazy November afternoon in Rangoon, 1862, a shrouded corpse was escorted by a small group of British soldiers to an anonymous grave in a prison enclosure. As the British Commissioner in charge insisted, "No vestige should remain to distinguish where the last of the Great Moghuls rests"'.[2] That day, the Tatar imam introduced me to his spouse and two sons by observing: 'Professor, I want to send my two sons to Oxford to learn Oxonian English'. With a mischievous smile, I responded: 'Sure. That is quite possible, but before that, please do accept salaam and regards from a fellow South Asian Tatar'. And they all laughed, given their awareness of Asian Muslims having been often identified as Turks and Tatars.

The following day that February, I journeyed to Turku, which took two hours on a quiet, fast, and equally comfortable train that reminded me of Canadian double-deck trains. This is the southern heartland of industry, education, research, and also of shipping, which provide the country with all its demographic and scientific depth. The train sailed through numerous towns, all covered in snow. The countryside looked even more picturesque, reminding me of Michigan, except that here it was hillier, densely wooded, and sparsely populated. Sometimes, there were large expanses of open spaces completely covered in layers of powdery snow with pine trees, wooden houses, and some brooding horses; my eyes kept searching for reindeers. Women walking dogs, men skiing, and cars often journeying across the thin lines of treated roads appeared as exceptions and not the norm on this landscape all the way until Turku. There were surely factories and shopping centres with public transport plying around to show that even in this northern most part of Europe, prosperity, ingenuity, and vigour coexisted with the well-known utilitarian model of public welfare.

Europe may be a small continent—both population and area wise—but its impact across the continents remains ascendant since a very long time, even if one goes beyond a Eurocentric view of world history. Europe's salience increased and even multiplied with the so-called age of discoveries that brought it vast territories, unlimited resources, and unbound energies. More than that, it allowed Europe to transfer its huge population to those places where European cultures based on vigorous Christianity, trade, multiple forms of control, and certainly a greater sense of racial and cultural superiority, all germinated the modern era. Europe retained its own traditions, however, with industrial and political might, it positioned itself as the power engine of modernization, which is certainly a manifestation of Westernization. Of course, intellectual and knowledge-based prowess has been a crucial part of it. However, this European globalism cost non-Europeans major setbacks including the massive disappearance of indigenous peoples, enslavement of millions of Africans, and the regimentation of an inferiority complex amongst all the 'vanquished' communities. While Europe and Christianity gained—both engineering a rather curious and interdependent relationship—the imprints of European globalism created newer hierarchies and an acute unevenness over the world. In the wake of these momentous changes characterized by unprecedented mobility, Europe itself changed in every aspect. Though assuming Europe as one monolithic entity is not the premise here, but certainly the continent has often shown sameness, which since the Second World War reflects an amazing amount of harmonious unity, especially in the EU regions.

Turku has its share of historic buildings, though most of them disappeared due to the devastating fire of 1827. However, the Cathedral is the landmark building in the historic district and, other than its magnitude, it evidences the arrival of Christianity in this part of Scandinavia. A number of early priests are buried here and, though its bell tower and several interior regions were refurbished and repaired in subsequent centuries, its own status within the community at large as the sentinel of Catholicism before Lutheranism allocate it a special status. On its eastern side lies the university with some listed and newer buildings, whereas heading towards the city centre, one crosses the bridge over River Aurajoki that meanders through the town. Following my lecture at the university and a discussion with three scarf-clad Muslim students, my host took me on a walking tour of the city and we ended up at a restaurant near the impressive library located on the western side of the river. Here, Czar Alexander used to hold balls to show his immersion in Europe's high culture and also to make a statement on Russia being its integral part and not an 'Asiatic' nation, as many West Europeans condescendingly thought of Russians.

My second week-long visit to Finland happened a year later in 2016, and with a home-like familiarity. I was able to move around quite comfortably and I included a longer session with the Tatar imam and some senior members of his congregation. To my happy surprise, two of them had been to various Pakistani cities in the 1980s to buy carpets and shared their fond memories of their visits with me. They even remembered some Urdu words and Punjabi jokes, especially about General Ziaul Haq, the military dictator, and affirmed their own affinity with the Sufi traditions in South Asia. My narratives of visits to Uzbekistan and especially the resting place of Bahauddin Naqshband elicited special interest from both ladies and men. At the end of my session, Imam Kamil Belyaef underlined the special status of the Iranian restaurant housed in the building, known for its halal dishes, which was run by a multilingual Iranian. I was faithfully advised to try its kebab and pulao dishes. I did turn up that evening at the restaurant and was not disappointed by the quality of food and service, and the Iranian host was quite quick in recognizing me. Imam Kamil was a kind reference as, the very next day, he especially came to my public lecture on Political Islam at the university which, other than a fair number of students, was attended by some community members as well.

A busy teaching schedule at Helsinki, though interspersed with visits to the Engel Café and walks by the marina, did not deter me from going back to Mr Don's Café, run by a Bangladeshi with several screens showing football matches. He recognized me right away and, other than offering his speciality pizza, shared knowledge of the local Muslim community with me. He appreciated the quality of life and standard of tolerance in Finland, yet missed East London more than his own native Bangladesh. Café Engel was the right place for soups and cakes amidst chatty Finns and faculty members and, given my frequent visits, a Nepali hostess began to offer special salaam and namaskar. She had recently finished her degree at the university and was working here to make some extra money so as to continue her higher degree in Britain or the US. Sita's recommendations on trying a variety of Finnish cakes would be mostly complied by me, though a few times I did try to explore major bookstores for lunches or tea breaks where crowds reminded me of their counterparts at Waterstones and Blackwells in Oxford. Another café, not too far from where the Strategic Arms Limitation Talks (SALT) agreements had been signed in the 1970s, attracted me due to its exterior, plus a fair number of African customers who appeared to be political exiles, symbolizing the place as kind of an Afro-Asian joint. For a couple of evenings, I tried seafood at restaurants in my own neighbourhood, which seemed to be a favourite with the locals. Though in that area, I did not notice any takeaways, which could partly be the reason for these people not being obese. In addition, I would often see people of all age groups, including seniors and minors, treading over snow and some even riding their special road bikes attuned to Arctic winters. Finland, even in its capital, did not give any sign of being overpopulous or of people rushing around, as one may encounter in London and New York. The pace definitely seemed to be slower with fewer propensities for being hectic. Of course, there are not many watering holes, though some squares in the newer neighbourhoods featured some bars, but here again a quiet ambience prevailed. A greater sense of security and prosperity prevails in this country as in the rest of Scandinavia, with people enjoying longevity and excellent health. I always hoped for a visit to the north to the Sami people but that will have to wait for another day.

Notes

1. Eric Wolf, *Europe and the People without History* (Berkeley: University of California Press, 1982), 5, quoted in Peter Frankopan, *The Silk Roads: A New History of the World* (London: Bloomsbury, 2015), xviii.
2. Quoted in William Dalrymple, *The Last Mughal: The Fall of Delhi, 1857* (London: Bloomsbury, 2007).

21

Switzerland:
The Land of Honey But Whose Money?

In their mellow moments, many ideologues from the developing world grieve over the inability of regions like Kashmir, Afghanistan, Tibet, Nepal, Uganda, Pakistan, Argentina, Chechnya, Syria, Palestine, and several others on having the potential yet not the fortune to turn into the 'Switzerland' of their respective regions. Violence, poverty, exploitation, and insecurity reign supreme in most of the developing world where even nature occasionally seems to lose interest in the people and places. Civil wars, border issues, volatile ethnicities, poverty, population explosions, droughts, floods, earthquakes, the scorching sun, billions of flies and other insects, scarce water (that too contaminated), and unfulfilled basic needs are the sad realities of these numerous candidates for the Swiss model, whose unending supply of tyrants and rhetoricians takes a toll on the forsaken lands and dashed hopes. The World Bank, International Monetary Fund (IMF), United States Agency for International Development (USAID), Department for International Development (DFID), the Ford Foundation, Oxfam, and several other such foundations are the pedigreed gods whose bounties refuse to leave the voluptuous files, though statistically, the crusade on poverty, AIDS, hunger, debts, and pollution remains ascendant. For instance, in 2004, 25,000 American farmers were annually receiving four billion dollars in subsidy to keep their cotton prices low, as opposed to the grim livelihood of 10 million West African growers. Each English cow was receiving two pounds a day from the EU in subsidies, while its Japanese counterpart cost Tokyo seven pounds. Contrasted with these 'holy cows', the average income of 70 per cent of the world population was not even two dollars a day. No wonder many of us become so otherworldly, dreaming of our 'Switzerland' in the world hereafter!

Switzerland has been informally neutral for three centuries but it formalized its neutrality even more effectively following the Napoleonic wars. Being an integral part of Europe while managing to evade its internecine wars and such other enterprises is no minor feat if one looks at human history where, as the records reveal, there has been one year of peace for every 13 years of violence and warfare. The Swiss Confederation's long-standing neutral status has underpinned a unique political stability and lasting peace, helping it become one of the world's most prosperous countries where the per capita income is around $80,000 (compared to $1,700 in a nuclearized South Asia and, according to some surveys, even lesser than that in Sub-Saharan Africa). The second most important and rather unprecedented feature of Swiss history is the countrywide recognition and celebration of an inherent pluralism. It is a unique European cultural and linguistic crossroad, with about two-thirds of its total population of 7.1 million speaking German, nearly one-fifth speaking French, and about 7 per cent Italian. Rumantsch, the country's fourth national language, is spoken by less than 1 per cent of the population. In addition, several other languages such as English, Arabic, Turkish, and Chinese are heard in this landlocked and exceptionally scenic country. It does not mean that everyone is welcome here, since the immigration and naturalization laws involve complicated and long-drawn procedures to the extent of impossibility. It is only money that moves easily as well as secretly through a labyrinthine network of banks and investment institutions. No wonder Switzerland has become synonymous with money, luxury, and natural bounties, all orchestrated through very strict timekeeping.

The third major feature of Swiss uniqueness is the devolution of powers within the cantons or prefectures where most decisions are made locally through periodic referenda on issues including naturalization, foreign policy, constitutional amendments, and politico-economic integration with the rest of Europe. In 1992, the Swiss, by a clear majority, rejected their economic integration into the European community and subsequently voted down the membership of the EU itself, although it continued maintaining special relations with their European partners and that too in a beneficial way. It was only in 2001 that Switzerland became a regular member of the United Nations though, curiously, the erstwhile League of Nations, International Court of Justice, International Crimes Court, and several UN institutions have been located in Geneva. Continued peace, respect for equal citizenship, separation of the sacred from the secular and the spiritual from the mundane, and an unrivalled secrecy over personal investments and savings have endowed the country with that unique fame that every other nation in the world may only dream of. Even while Germans, French, and the Italians were fighting internecine religious and imperial wars, Switzerland, despite a hodge-podge of all three nationality groups, pursued neutrality and peace. However, it did not shy away from simultaneously selling its goods and fuel to all these contenders. Even Protestant reformers such as John Calvin (1509–64) and Ulrich Zwingli (1484–1531) found the Swiss 'ready to do business' with the God's army. Calvin urged them to pursue a Protestant ethic of hard work and missionary motivation that subsequently led Max Weber and R. H. Tawney to conceptualize the Protestant virtues of capitalism.

Standing next to St. Pierre's Cathedral on a hilltop in the centre of medieval Geneva and surrounded by magnificent old buildings, one momentarily forgets that this is the heart of a modern capitalist economy where billions stashed away in millions of accounts are churning out more billions each passing week. During the inter-War decades, Switzerland attracted enormous deposits from the Nazis and Jews. Most of these depositors were either killed or forgotten, while the Swiss vaults bulged with their savings. It is only in the last few years that persistent Jewish groups were able to unearth hidden records of massive savings left by Holocaust victims. Following the untiring efforts by Jewish groups, the records of ill-gotten money and other treasures obtained through shadowy and offshore facilities under fictitious names have become common knowledge.

While we were strolling through the historic district in old Geneva in 2005, our Swiss friend enlightened us on the ancient roots of her favourite city and with a wink observed that the Swiss Calvinism still permeated the national life, at least in its architecture—straight and upward. Her secular upbringing had never made her irreverent to her Calvinist heritage. Even the old tavern next-door, named after the founder of Puritanism who had preached in this cathedral five centuries back, was proudly selling beer. Located all around are the canton buildings where important civic decisions are made behind massive wooden doors and gigantic stone walls. One of these tall buildings housed the foundational meeting of the Red Cross. 'I wish we could have been more honest and transparent in our ideals of global peace and welfare,' my friend moaned. 'We formed the Red Cross, stayed out of violent conflicts, and created high-quality life standards; yet are notorious for secretly hoarding people's money which, in most cases, is tainted. Here I feel doubly guilty as I myself work for a similar consultancy for overseas investors.' I wondered whether it was Calvinism, Calvin Beer, or just a split moment of truth because of which an honest confession poured out so spontaneously!

Of course, the case of a promising Pakistani politician came up in our conversation at a time when the tavern and its open area were surrounded by a group of musicians donning traditional costumes and playing on their harps and bagpipes. My friend felt that the politician had let the Pakistani people down; everyone in Pakistan and the West had felt that this charismatic and well-educated individual would lead Pakistan out of the economic and social quagmire it was in, but unfortunately, that was not to be. 'What a travesty!' She said so unequivocally, which is again uncharacteristic of the typical West European reserve. 'Most of us are in [the] service industry and stay in touch with the latest in the world. Our reputation as the tourist destination or our fame for watches and military knives are the useful smokescreens. My company handles global finance as does every other second concern in Geneva and we are abreast of all the developments related to our clients,' she added. 'I enjoy living in this old Geneva and will not give it away for anything in the world but sometimes I wonder how come people like Marcos, Mobotu, Khashoggi, Saudi royals, and others of their ilk keep on robbing their own helpless people. I seek relief in assuming that more like the Biblical treasury as narrated by Jesus Christ, these bandits may never be able to relish their plunder in the first place!' But in the meantime, the Swiss have their gala days or rather centuries.

Even the paucity of very good bookstores, other than Payot, bothers one in Switzerland as one notices an overpowering abundance of cafés, hotels, stores, and banks. The second-hand English bookshop selling locally acquired interesting collections and steamy tea is not a bad place if one is not claustrophobic and does not feel too nostalgic for Oxbridge stiff upper lip when encountered with an American salesmanship. It is the politeness, tolerance, child friendliness, love for dogs, safety, and, most of all, an efficient transport system that make Switzerland so adorable. The civic cleanliness and respect for pluralism are no minor traits when one compares Swiss cities with several other Western counterparts, though several walls have graffiti sprayed on. The Swiss are, by temperament and tradition, peace loving people and their criticism of Anglo-American attacks on Afghanistan and Iraq may have gone unnoticed in the global media. A Swiss academic confided: 'It may be owing to our smaller size, otherwise peace movement in Switzerland has been at its strongest, like in Scandinavia'. Even several years later, many windows displayed the peace flags of rainbow colours, whereas in private meetings, one notices an uneasy emphasis on the increasing 'otherness' of Britain and the United States. Tony Blair's third way was seen as plainly ridiculous, whereas an irresponsible Bush was perceived as being egged on by ambitious zealots. Our Chinese diplomat-friend was less restrained in his views on the Anglo-American efforts of 'reverting to the UN after creating the mess in West Asia'. He was glad that both London and Washington were no more routinely critical of his country as had been the case before. 'China is a power and reality to be reckoned with. North Korea is not a forsaken global backyard like Afghanistan; it is our neighbour. They have to go through us and that too politely. Not the cowboy style!'

We saw an ingenious pluralism at its best in a Genevan hotel where we were initially attracted by the loud Arabian/Maghrebi music, but to our happy surprise, discovered a Bar Mitzvah party in progress. The Hebrew and Arabic lyrics accompanied the ceremonies of robed men and women with the rabbi authoritatively donning his full attire. Both orthodox and reformed groups of European and African origins, along with their families, sauntered around in posh lobbies. A few heavy-set, bearded, all-black rabbis munched on koshered food as several teenagers wearing Kippahs over braided hair and glitzy black jackets kept running around. Nearby, an all-male party of some rich Arab Sheikhs went along unencumbered by their noisy neighbours. Our Italian waiter, while offering us our beverages and performing his little bow, whispered: 'Wish they could do the same back-home in the Middle East'. A few feet away, a well-groomed Asian diplomat was ensconced with an American colleague in some serious parleys while sipping honey-mixed tea. We could see two Marks & Spencer bags marking their presence in their hands as the diplomats finally made it to the elevator, meandering their way through the Jewish dancers.

The mixture of old and new is equally prominent in Lausanne where affluence, history, religion, and politics neighbour one another in the oldest and comparatively elevated part of the city. While walking across the well-lined streets of endowed designer shops, expensive hotels, and cafés, we noted the old cathedral that stands out as an eternal sentinel, well-blended in its environment of a castle, gymnasium, city museum, and the seats of the local prefecture. This part of the city is not just old, it is ancient. One would like these official cars to be banished once and for all from its cobbled streets. It was somewhere in the vicinity that the Treaty of Lausanne was finalized in 1923, granting statehood to modern Turkey; the kebab shops never let one forget the presence of Turks and Kurds in this country. Despite the understandable trepidation that a foreigner goes through while exploring some 'official' cafeteria, I ventured into a very old, low-ceiling, and semi-lit coffee shop which was basically meant for students and lecturers; however, senior ladies did not hesitate for a moment in offering me a steamy cup of coffee. It was lunchtime and soon they were munching on something meaty with red wineglasses stoutly guarding the plates. Employees drinking during their short break was a rather amusing encounter!

The city's main museum duly launches a visitor into the Swiss past with some searchlight on local history, yet its most impressive feature was a special exhibition on knowledge. The pens from the earliest reeds to their more recent incarnations such as Parker's, Mont Blanc, and Cartier's were encased to show the human journey on the road to modernity. The early handwritten documents—all in Western scripts—were on display. One wondered about the human march from caves to space while looking at the feather pens and inkpots of all hues and sizes. The curator was standing not too far as the teacher within me took over the proceedings:

'Don't mind my saying this, but this is the key to human civilization and no wonder even more than fourteen hundreds years back, God almighty, in the inaugural message to an unschooled Arab, reminded him of His adoration of knowledge and pen'. She knew I was referring to the Prophet Muhammad (PBUH) and the first revelation celebrating knowledge and pen, which many of his followers seem to have forsaken a long time back. No wonder other than some visiting rich Arabs and Maghrebi and Turkish blue-collar workers, the Muslim factor in a panoramic Switzerland is present only through hush-hush money, stacked in the coffers of numerous private and tight-lipped banks, vigilantly watched over by hordes of financial consultants. I encountered a few fluttering banners by the Rhone in Geneva announcing a special exhibition of 'Islam and Orientalism' which, however, turned out to be a small shop and not a museum. Its Arabo-Persian and Indian artefacts and antiques were refreshing and definitely expensive, displaying the personal interest of the owner of Baghery's. A bookshop in the business district selling books on Islam was another refreshing experience, though the grand carpet emporium, 'Persia', neighbouring a Moorish synagogue, had changed hands a few generations back. No wonder the land of beauty and bounty still remains a cherished utopia for so many and the destination for their money!

***

Zurich is certainly as beautiful as any other Swiss region, endowed with natural beauty and impressive buildings which have remained untouched by numerous European troubles, reflecting a high degree of urban affluence and an unmissable sense of self-sufficiency. This predominantly German speaking city is the largest of all its counterparts, including Geneva, Lausanne, Bern, and Basel, and is certainly very different from rural Switzerland, yet it remains comfortably ambivalent about the proverbial neutrality. Venturing into this part of Switzerland, especially during an autumny interregnum when rain as well as wind factor were both absent, offered a unique opportunity to explore some ancient alleys in this city which sit on both sides of the river, just before it empties itself into Lake Zurich. The 2006 conference on Islam and Orientalism at the university, convened by academics and journalists, was still a day away, and the early evening found us following Andreas to a traditional Swiss restaurant through the labyrinths of small lanes traversing what were once low-lying hills that now house the older parts of the city. Andreas was a world apart from the proverbial German efficiency and discipline, though he did not lack in efforts to try it in his own otherworldly way. He smiled more than he talked but it did not mean that even a minute matter missed his acute observation. As we were soon to discover, even while he shepherded us back from coffee and lunch breaks during the conference, his polite smile never left him, nor did an element of warm resignation over an unending academic penchant for parleys. He had put in more than a year in convening this event, which had brought delegates from all over and had ensured the open participation by the university community. He was duly helped by a meticulous Michaela, the doctoral student at the university, with a personality as unobtrusive as his.

Andreas was a journalist who worked hard to organize this biannual conference, '1001 Newsflashes: Western and Eastern Images' by bringing in academia and media together to brood over the issues of Islam and the West. In addition, over the preceding two years, an unassuming Andreas had tried to raise funds to finance it. Several colleagues at the university behind our hotel, right on the hilltop and its counterpart—the federally funded Technical University—had helped him. Both universities seemed to be competing with each other in grandeur and are visible from afar, though Zurich itself expands well behind them into villages and valleys of traditional chalets, nestling the ski resorts of the surrounding Alps. From the hotel, one could climb up the stairs to reach the university as do most students, or one has the option of taking the trolley which connects such high altitude areas with the city centre located by the river and visible from our hotel. Other than trolleys, trains, trams, and certainly the pleasure boats on the lake, ply people around, though proportionately, numerous cars equally seem to be vying for space. Andreas held this conference to coincide with the eightieth birthday of Arnold Hottinger, who had been a pre-eminent correspondent for *Neuen Zürcher Zeitung* (*NZZ*) on the Muslim world for many decades and was then living in Lausanne. Needless to say, *NZZ* happened to be a widely read and equally influential Swiss newspaper, and Hottinger's successor at the newspaper seemed well-ensconced in his job, though he often displayed some deference to his predecessor. Hottinger, like William Dalrymple and many more European writers, is fascinated, amongst others, by the Mughals. He published a book from Munich on Emperor Akbar in 1998. His inspiration came from the Mughal architecture and miniature art which he saw across South Asia during his long tenure as a journalist. In one of our lunch breaks, we happened to cross Straus Hottinger, which leads to a suburban village with the same name and, as modestly explained by Arnold, had nothing to do with him but with a medieval tribe sharing the name who had settled on this side of the Swiss Alps. Hottinger had not lost his alertness nor did his German exactness wither away by any chance, which became evident with several interventions that the veteran journalist made on various occasions. His ease with the three main European languages and a lifetime exposure to the historical and contemporary intricacies of Asian politics had added to a whiff of kindly authoritarianism in him, since even his witty remarks failed to cause an accompanying smile on his face. Hottinger often walked down the stairs and pavements while leaning on his partner, however, he was seen getting into a taxi when an Italian lunch seemed to linger on slightly longer, despite some more fidgety movements from Andreas. Hottinger had to chair the next session at the university but, other than the time factor, the steep ascent, especially after a hearty lunch in a quiet corner of the town, appeared unusually formidable.

Our hotel, like our host, was also quite unassuming to the extent of being basic. Despite the fact that it was located in two separate and small buildings and not perched on a high hill, it still surprisingly afforded a pleasant early morning view of stunningly white Alps covered in powdery snow that had fallen during the night. Drawing the curtain in the morning had unexpectedly unveiled this spectacle where the contrast with autumn colours, well over and above the grey buildings, led one's eyes straight to the slopes and low-lying woods. I remembered some Swiss participants complaining about the unusually mild weather at a time when it was meant to be cold and snowy, and thus a whiff of timely snowfall must have cheered up skiers that one associates with those who are vacationing in Switzerland, who also seem to be a permanent feature of crowds in the shopping areas or at the train stations. The year 2006, being the warmest in recorded European history, raised concerns about global warming that were already turning into serious worries. Some environmentalists were even predicting the disappearance of snow in the next 45 years, fearing that the grandchildren of present-day skiers would only see snowy Alps in pictures of the past. Until then, hope springs eternal in the human breast especially of those with a bulging pocket and strong lungs.

Switzerland's proverbial neutrality and wealth have allowed various cultural imprints from other Western societies, but when it comes to laws governing immigration and naturalization, the local communities and cantons show an extreme form of conservatism, often bordering on open resistance. Switzerland, like elsewhere in Western Europe, needs younger bodies and fresher blood, but it is not so accommodative when it comes to allowing full citizenship rights to such people. It is true that the German and French speaking citizens operate white-collar positions and also dominate the countryside, but it is the Italians who mainly run the cuisine from a number of outlets. One comes across several North Africans and some Asians in the service sector but most of them happen to be in the country by virtue of their EU citizenship and, despite living in the country and paying full taxes, might still not be eligible for the Swiss passport. Like Germany earlier on, it is in Switzerland that the term 'foreigners' is used so openly and unreservedly even by those people who might be otherwise expected to be more sensitive on lexicon. Of course, France and Britain have their vocal sections of critical groups who see integration only as a one-way process where minorities/immigrants or their locally born descendants are expected to take all the acculturative initiatives, however, they would still think twice before 'othering' settled minorities as foreigners. Similarly, at Swiss airports, the customs and passport clearance is always quicker for the EU citizens, North Americans, Japanese, and Australians, and it is not unusual to see an African or Asian being detained for closer scrutiny or even baggage check. One can see other travellers subtly avoiding queues where some 'foreigner' is facing a battery of questions from the immigration officials. Certainly, in recent years, even Westerners with Muslim names or brown and black complexions are increasingly being observed, which sometimes even may involve disembarkation from the plane just for reading a book on Syria or Daesh. Beard and brown complexion with a backpack could certainly raise heckles if not eyebrows of the security personnel.

In one of the sessions at the Zurich conference, while analyzing the tensions between Muslims and the majority population groups, a Swiss citizen of Dutch origin confided her own inability in getting a Swiss passport even though she had been living in the country for more than 12 years. She herself felt uneasy over the terms used for plural, non-white communities and expressed her unease with an unwieldy decentralized system in the country that bogs down all initiatives on simplifying processes for naturalization. Like countless other EU citizens, she enjoyed living in Switzerland with its immensely high standard of living and a secure life without the Swiss passport at all, but the process certainly confounded her. To a few other frank Swiss academics, notable factors such as religion, militarism, economy, and neutrality, all had been deeply intertwined in the nation's policies. However, their ambivalence allowed greater leeway to the country in gaining prestige, prosperity, and political cohesion without immersing itself in political and militarist quagmires elsewhere. Such self-critical elements would instead frown upon the high cost of a military budget, which involved universal conscription, greater preparedness, and a well-regimented celebration of a martial type of patriotism that might also define the country's own distinct identity, away from any possible irredentism from across the borders. One may have reasons to feel that such critical remarks, often uttered in private meetings, not only express dismay over a regimented and even romanticized insularity but are also meant to ventilate disenchantment that chattering classes share in some private moments. The rather self-indulgent lifestyles and an immense level of self-sufficiency certainly veto such isolated rebukes by a few sensitive Swiss citizens who otherwise have the best of all the worlds without really getting involved in global agonies. It is only in this country where the United Nations, like its predecessor—the League of Nations—has maintained its vast establishment, even if the host country never bothered to attain the membership of the world body until only a few years back. In the same vein, the European Union may guarantee a safer and prosperous Europe for everyone's benefit yet why bother to join it when any Swiss citizen can still bask in its multiple benefits!

Some European citizens, especially in the United Kingdom, besmirch Swiss neutrality, Scandinavian pacifism, and German economic preponderance while they rush to derive benefits after the former have already sweated it out. Some West European and American societies do not lack in critical opinion groups who feel that 'the Old Europe' hedonistically and rather obsessively shirks from taking on challenging responsibilities. To such sections, Europeans are too self-indulgent in the name of pacifism and liberalism, and are habitually evading a more proactive and even participatory role which may even stipulate a strong-arm policy. But their pacifism does not preclude them from reaping the benefits after some others have already borne the cost.

During the Cold War, the US was the guarantor of peace and security for Western Europe and Japan, but since its dissolution and following the Balkan imbroglio, an increasing number of Americans feel exasperated with what they deem as an opportunistic passivity. Some Americans critique what they call an indifferent and indolent Europe, and aim at prodding the latter and the Japanese to involve themselves more in global geopolitics. However, this American paternalism is simultaneously envious of European integration and its steady political and economic benefits, though the dividends owe themselves to an exceptional form of sustained post-War peace where regionalization had been able to considerably tone down statist nationalisms until recent times. Many Americans might be ambivalent about the tensions within the EU owing to the historical and economic factors, and could be aghast at Europe not becoming 'United States of Europe'. It is not a superficial premise, given the powerful Europeanization of the world over the past several centuries, where non-Europeans have genuine reasons to see this predominantly white and Christian continent as a monolith. However, as seen in the case of Brexit and the growth of populist forces all over Europe focusing on immigration and Islam, along with the past conflicts and divergent political setups, a European nation-state system remains quite vocal and entrenched without any possibility of a single homogenous statehood. The Americans and Europeans might need each other more in the coming decades due to newer challenges from Russia, China, and India, which are evolving in competitive areas including trade, energy, market control, technology, and science. China's sustained economic growth amazes all observers, whereas India is already the third largest investor in Britain, while Russia controls the vital oil and gas pipelines into Europe and is often willing to cause some confrontational challenges. An unstable Muslim West Asia and North African regions, thanks to hasty and unilateral military interventionism and surrogate and capricious leadership, pose serious challenges for Europe as well as the emerging trio of China, India, and Russia, especially at a time when the EU has taken a back seat and the United States is both adrift and exhausted. It is a time when multilateral alliances like the UN, EU, and the Organization of Islamic Cooperation (OIC) sit marginalized, thanks to an ideological vacuum and a harrowing absence of substantive post-Cold War policies. Afghanistan, Iraq, Libya, Syria, Chechnya, and Palestine are the microcosm of this wider institutional malaise that requires more sensible and proactive leadership and ideas.

However, apart from such intra-European criticism, one wonders how the globalization of Europe since the early modern era has often relayed itself through diverse trajectories. Europeans, in several cases, exacerbated collective human agonies in several other regions but simultaneously never presented the spectre of an exhausted continent. It will be unfair to suggest that Europe's rise to prosperity and global hegemony is solely owed to the human and natural resources of the non-European world, and even if so, the ability to sustain this primacy itself is not a minor achievement. Despite a persuasive critique of capitalism, colonialism, and even an evangelical Christianity often juxtaposed with racism and intellectual denigration of the non-Europeans, the prosperity of countries like Switzerland cannot be explained only in reference to these paradigms. Calvin and Zwingli might have spawned Protestant ethics here for their own country and the rest of Western Europe, but the sectarian division of post-Reformation Europe was an immensely painful and enduring process until the EU evolved as an enduring mechanism, guaranteeing peace within a unified as well as diverse Europe. Switzerland, like in the early Protestant era, led the break from the Catholic past, but still achieved a decentralized system, itself fortified by a broad consensus on peace and capitalist ethics; this is how this country stood centuries ahead of its neighbours including those who boasted of greater empires and celebrated Enlightenment. The newcomers into the EU are more emphatic about their newly-redefined European-ness and no wonder many of them, soon after entering the NATO and the EU, earnestly joined in the ongoing US-led military campaigns. One could attribute this to a more-loyal-than-the-king attitude to that traditional subservience that once obligingly bonded these new entrants with the former Soviet Union. At least here Switzerland could deserve a few kudos for not seeking quicker certification for its loyalty to this discretionary concept of Westernism, which itself is fanning the clash across the communities.

Europe's welcome to 'foreigners' is through the army of its consulates and visa offices where high sounding benevolence gives way to a sordid rejection or even reluctance, quite in league with the closed borders. Here, the EU leads the US because, unlike the latter, it does not pride itself as a land of immigrants. Even if it talks of migrations, the discourse is only in reference to early historical phases and emphatically defines itself as an intra-European affair. On the other hand, the emigrations to other continents, and more recently to the Mediterranean from Northern countries, remain absent from this one-dimensional debate. Until the 1970s, the United States, at least theoretically and textually, defined and prided itself as a land of immigrants, though even then naturalization was a selective and tedious process, whereas borders remained closed. With the end of the Cold War, the celebratory pronouncements on immigration have evaporated altogether. It is only in private meetings that one hears about mixed parents from 'the Old World' and here again, the choice is often frequently for European and occasionally native ancestry. Africa and Asia might come in rarely but not so vocally. Thus, Switzerland has rather preceded the US and the EU by a few decades, with its borders always closed and its cantons simply consensual on retaining the Swiss exclusivity with its unpronounced yet pervasive racialized contours. Following the crisis in Syria and the instability in Libya, Europe, North America, and Australia have been adamantly resistant in accepting refugees. Germany was an exception and here demographic realities have played a crucial role, though all these 'western' countries never pursued open-door policies and, in recent years, juxtaposing immigration with Islam and terror has only intensified Islamophobia besides underpinning nationalist resurgence. Brexit, in case of Britain, and strict Muslim-specific laws in almost every Western country, along with some of the intolerant parties already in coalition or vying for power, are crucially damaging regionalization and democracy.

It was during our conference in Zurich that the British press carried stories of singer James Blunt moving into a Swiss Alpine village so as to avoid taxes in his native Britain. The former tank commander with his 11 times platinum album, 'Back to Bedlam', had decided to settle in the resort village of Vertier by finding company with international jet set such as Michael Schumacher, 'Elvis', Johnny Halliday, Phil Collins, Tina Turner, Boris Becker, and several others. According to some contemporary press reports, Switzerland was a tax haven to 3,700 foreign millionaires including many from the developing world. One of the richest residents was Ingvar Kamprad, the founder of the Ikea chain and himself above 80, who had sought to retire in Switzerland. Many EU politicians would like to challenge cantons in Switzerland so as to end this tax banditry but the federal government remains quite protective about it and even offers attractive incentives to the Irish, French, Russian, Asian, and Italian millionaires to deposit their wealth in this republic. Some Swiss defend their country by highlighting the higher tax rates for their own citizens including Roger Federer whose contributions are proportionately higher than those of the other émigrés. The Swiss model of attracting the rich and the wealthy of the world is being used by many governments including Britain, where several incentives have been on hand for investments in London as a secure and profitable financial centre. On the contrary, the elite from the developing nations, as per Panama Leaks, hasten to transfer their assets abroad, either to be deposited in the banks or to be spent on buying property through third parties. Before the emergence of Dubai as a financial hub and centre for unfettered recreation, Western Europe received stupendous financial injections from the Afro-Asian regions. As documented by Craig Unger, affluent Saudis, especially the royal family, had hundreds of billions of dollars stacked in the United States, whereas similar offshore accounts by Arab and South Asian individuals remain undocumented.[1] During the 1980s, the Bank of Commerce and Credit International (BCCI) was known to have been noxiously engaged in such illegal transfers through fictitious accounts and it was also issuing loans without having enough backup deposits in its own coffers. Despite initial goodwill and prospects, its executive managers followed daredevil pursuits until the day of reckoning. Some of its supporters, including its management, tried to call foul but to no avail. Dillydallying with some seamy crowds and irreverence towards transparency caught up with them, though some of them took to Dubai and such other places, while its founder, Hasan Abedi, rediscovered Pakistan as his home and soon passed away in ignominy and ill health. This ludicrous effort to replicate the canny Swiss model was destined to meet disaster and that is where several small-time account holders turned out to be the main losers. There was no succour in complaining of double standards and arguing about a feeble transparency regime being an inherent component of banking, and soon BCCI became a forgotten chapter in global money transfers even though the late Sheikh Zayd bin Sultan of Abu Dhabi was rumoured to have tried to salvage it. The banking scandals of 2008–9 caused a major economic slow-down and dwarfed even what BCCI executives had been accused of, but as seen further down the years, these banks and their executives often went on without being reprimanded.

The spectrum of failing states or the presumed apprehensions about the institutions run by the developing world, due to some uneven playing fields, still do not bear out the rationale for running them recklessly. Of course, the big fish would devour the little ones, yet the latter have mostly survived by sharpening their own survival strategies, though predatory humans equipped with all the modern equipment may pose a tougher challenge now. After all, Switzerland is a story of human engineering where odd couples are able to form a successful extended family, which enjoys a rather lasting peace and enviable prosperity. While the bigger fish of Europe fought endlessly, the Swiss watched for their bounties to spill over across into their borders to be looked after pitiably and professionally. Peace did have its dividends and one cannot deny the ingeniousness of the Swiss. While Muslim societies, eager to modernize, may be worried about losing some tradition in the wake, they must not forget the fact that peace within and without, along with a substantial institutionalization, can certainly take them further along the road to cherished destinations. It will be hypocritical to suggest that no other community or country, including Muslims, would like to live like the Swiss; then why not face the reality and be a bit more mundane and realistic! One wonders about such parallels while sipping tea just underneath the majestic cathedral where Zwingli preached Protestantism. Like Calvin in Geneva, Zwingli's Zurich found no qualms in keeping God and Mammon together. It is more like St. Paul's Cathedral looking over and even guarding the City in London—the richest square mile on earth, inhabited by powerful companies and international financial concerns with the East India Company's former nest right in its heart.

Note

1. Craig Unger, *House of Bush, House of Saud: The Secret Relationship Between the World's Two Most Powerful Dynasties* (New York: Simon & Schuster, 2004).

22

Back to the Pavilion:
India and the Indus Journey

On a clear day, flying back from Delhi, I could see the vast green plains of Punjab melting into their counterparts across the Indo-Pakistan border. The green squares in late March were in fact wheat and mustard fields which extended for miles—all the way to the Salt Range and even beyond. In-between hair-like metalled roads and some brownish hamlets jutted out as dotted human encroachments, otherwise the west of Delhi and beyond was all in bloom. Assuming that we might have been flying over Pakistan, I began to look for the Indus, which back in 2011 had unleashed such unprecedented havoc by dislocating 20 million people, all the way from Swat to lower Sindh. Many of those people had already gone back to their devastated villages to harvest a rather bumper crop, while several still stayed encamped in schools and other make-shift centres extending from the lower reaches of Kohistan to the Indus Delta. River Sindh had fumed in rage like it has often done, though its recent upsurge was a rebuke to human infraction that it has borne for at least three generations. Since the canalization during the Raj and the construction of dams and barrages, Sindh and its tributaries have been 'tamed' but now many more millions depend on them and the old Sindhu of Rig Veda knows this quite well and not with much mirth. It took revenge on the descendants of the ancient Indus Valley people with the toll of miseries even surpassing two tsunamis and two earthquakes put together. However, the rest of the world moved on indifferently as if misery after misery was destined for Sindhu people. Their own 'Sattar Edhis' and a whole array of do-gooders had to make amends within their own means, however meagre they might be. The mighty Western nations—having already spent more than a trillion dollars on a phony war on terror featuring unaccounted collective human fatalities and degradation of Southwestern ecology—were not really interested in reaching out as their preoccupation remained focused on pursuing the phantom enemies from amongst the Pashtuns and Arab stragglers ensconced in these 'bad lands'.

I had made it to India on my British passport and persistence had been successful despite all the usual vacillations, while the conference had also been a successful encounter on 'all' sides, including a major section of students and faculty at the Jamia Millia Islamia. I had insisted on a visa on my British passport, not that I prevaricate in using my green passport, but simply because the latter, while traveling to India, puts me through grinding procedures one after the other. Initially, separate forms for Pakistanis require all kinds of biographical details of our several past generations, besides an accompanying clutch of documents which routinely end up with some 'Bhai Sahib' in one of those buildings in New Delhi. Preened through a whole host of functionaries and minutely studied by sleuths with suspicious eyes and magnifying glasses, the verdict finally depends upon the state of the Indo-Pakistan relationship at that particular moment, which is often unpredictable like between two siblings or, better to say, is more temperamental like an obsequious Mir's beloved.[1] People are curiously shocked when I tell them about my late father having taken my late mother to Aurangabad for their honeymoon all the way from his hamlet in the balmy Potwar Plateau where his house neighboured *Joharan di Marri*. Well, it was long before 1947— one of those several painful sevens in our history—and his regiment was based somewhere near Emperor Aurangzeb Alamgir's tomb. After offering *fateha*, my parents had a picnic there in the bagh; my mother as a shy damsel—the youngest in the family—sporting marigold and jasmine flowers in her hair, while her ears and nose were laden with those traditional jewels that our Indus Valley ancestors had prided themselves on millennia ago.

Following the issuance of a visa—if you are lucky and the 'Delhi *Babus*' have been happy on the day and you were not deemed as a security threat or a member of Lashkar-e-Taiba—you look for a separate queue where another bunch of forms await before you are ushered into the labyrinths of an impressive Indira Gandhi International Airport. In my previous visits, it resembled its ramshackle counterpart in Islamabad, both sharing their unique dinginess. Islamabad's posh and powerful dwellers often derided their airport as Chaklala, reminding one of Rawalpindi as the traditional abode of Lalas and Bhapas.[2] Pakistanis holding green passport are certainly accorded a distinct treatment at the airport—in currency long before the Mumbai atrocities of 2008—and are meant to report and register at a police station within the first 24 hours as their visa is valid for specific towns and not for the country as such. Finding the proper thana by yourself on a rickshaw or with your friends from across the Wagah border is surely a 'Farhadian' strife. Nonetheless, the ride allows you to be scouted around the newer and older parts of Delhi, and amidst unending traffic jams, one forgets about being on the 'other' side of the border. If it were not for the well-fed, autonomous cows sometimes dozing in the middle of the street or salubrious monkeys aiming at ripe bananas, one may detect familiar faces and voices that they would encounter in either Rawalpindi's Raja Bazaar, Lahore's Anarkali, or inside one of those 13 gates of the Old City.

India, for a Pakistani, irrespective of his green or red passport, is both a familiar and a foreign land. Its familiarity is borne out by lingual commonality, food habits, popular vocality, urban chaos, and casual attitudes towards several mundane pursuits often interspersed with the muezzin's calls or shooed down by capricious policemen seeking their own little fee for otherwise basic human rigmarole. Like the older clubs where ripe black plums fall on your shirts or vendors hawk their spicy morsels, both Pakistan and India sport a whole generation of retired civil and military officials, often sharing a mantra of peace which is both genuine and nostalgic. Conferences on both sides are mostly social gatherings where exchanging cards over generous food portions supersede the serious scholarly deliberations behind the walls. Hierarchical relations between the 'seniors' and younger folks, in the name of civility and tradition, are too visible to be discarded and here South Asia comes alive with Shiris, Sahibs, and Sahibas. Pakistani after-dinner montage could allow some forbidden liquids, whereas in India, there are no such restrictions unless you are polite enough not to offend any senior soul intent upon recounting some nostalgic discourse. The travails of visa acquisition and police registration—painstakingly similar for Indians on the Pakistani side—soon dissolve in thin or thick air and one staggers to a waiting rickshaw late at night, brooding over the absurdities of this schismatic relationship between two neighbours sharing at least the same ecology and temperament.

While thinking of our region where nukes, ballistic missiles, and blue navies raise emotions as well as hair, I soon realized that our aircraft was already flying over the tribal Pashtun regions, grievously called 'the bad lands'. In South Asia, in case of any irresponsible showdown, we will only be left with losers and no winners. Of course, I could not see any American drones—rather predators—that routinely fly over this 1500-mile-long territory caught between the proverbial devil and the deep sea. These machines, operated through push buttons on play stations far away in Florida and Kentucky, swoop on turbaned, bearded fellows whose ancestors were similarly hunted down by the Greeks, Mongols, Persians, Mughals, Russians, and now 38 plus nations intent upon delivering civilization and women's emancipation on the back of B-52s and Apaches. Led by the US, these nations have been pursuing the longest war in their respective histories and that too in one of the poorest countries on earth which has already turned into a nation of widows, refugees, and orphans. Macedonian Alexander read Herodotus by night during his forays into Afghanistan and Swat, and though the Greek pioneering historian had never been beyond Anatolia, yet he had warned his readers of the fierce, handsome tribals, whom he identified as 'Aapridis'. Afridis had caused reversals amongst the Greeks who ended up in upper Chitral—the Kalasha Valley—and marched through Swat until their battle with Raja Porus took place by the Jhelum, 80-miles from my hometown, 60 miles from Khushwant Singh's Hadali up in the Salt Range, and 55 miles from Manmohan Singh's native Gah.

Soon our flight was hastening over Bamyan in central Afghanistan, surrounded by the snow-peaked Hindu Kush merging into the lofty Pamirs to the north and Suleiman to the south. Certainly we had left Parachinar, Tora Bora, Khost, and Kabul far behind—some of the areas I had tried to hike around in 1983, but here from above 32,000 feet, I was absorbing the most glorious spectacle on earth for the umpteenth time. The mountains and the valleys down below were all white due to snow and the peaks resembled burqa/burkini-clad women standing together, each beaming her own individuality. I was glad they were not in France, otherwise they would be reprimanded for being fully covered! I remembered, back in France, Sarkozy had been intent upon banning burqas, worn by 2,000 women—some out of convention and some out of protestation—but here these vast peaceful valleys offered an altogether different view of a turbulent Afghanistan. Leaving a publicity seeking Sarkozy aside and his glamorous wife, Carla Bruni, I reveried about Firdausi and Hafiz, the romantic poets whose Persian ghazals and verses still reawaken my otherwise weather-beaten sinews. It is owing to them and to Roudaki, Rumi, Khayyam, and a whole generation of those sages, that I keep rediscovering a unique kind of aesthetics in a body otherwise worn down by memories and travesties of history. Certainly the best time to see Afghanistan is at sunrise when planes from the West reach South Asian horizons; with men having gone out to the fields after their morning prayers and women sharing the latest with their neighbours over mud walls. Of course, one cannot see humans from such a height but being able to peer through an unpolluted atmosphere for miles and miles is no less heart-warming. Surely from such a stupendous altitude, one cannot detect the Bamyan Buddhas that Emperor Ashoka had built, which were venomously destroyed in 2001 by obscurants. These were bombed by some Taliban, and Afghan and Japanese archaeologists have been busy restoring them. For centuries, the ancestors of these perpetrators had protected these monuments, which once heralded a traveller's entry into the lands of Sindhu and Siddhartha. In my visits to Gilgit and Hunza in Upper Karakorams, I had seen several such Buddha carvings on rock faces and often requested local villagers to protect this shared heritage. I hope some of these fellow Pakistanis do not turn against our Gandhara Buddha for all those atrocities that some Burmese monks have been committing against Rohingya Muslims.

Slightly north-west of the Hazara region lies Balkh, the heart of Bactria, once a landmark on the Silk Road that connected Persia and India with Central Asia and beyond. It was the meeting ground of Gandhara and Sogdiana, as these regions were known to our past ancestors. Balkh's old parameters of the city wall, castle, some debilitated houses, and a few tiled mosques remind one of its past glory. Mazar-e-Sharif is better known largely because of its Uzbek population which may share ethnicity with neighbours to the north, yet remain fatefully bound with fellow Afghan Pashtuns, Hazaras, and Tajiks. Even the connection with neighbouring Turkmenistan remains quite limited, and under the warlord, Rashid Dostum, Mazar-e-Sharif has been a loser in trade, visitors, and a positive reputation. Further south is another historic Afghan city, Herat, which was once the Timurid capital, flourishing because of the beneficence of Queen Gawhar Shad Begum and her son, Ulugh Beg, who ensured a profusion of madrassas and mosques here. In fact, like Fatima al-Fihri's first-ever university established in 859 CE in Fes, Gawhar Shad pioneered women's education in this part of Khorasan, which often changed hands between Persia and India/Afghanistan until in the mid-eighteenth century when it became an integral part of Afghanistan. Gawhar Shad was happily married to Shah Rukh, Tamerlane's son and heir who, after shifting his capital from Samarkand to Herat, ensured complete Persianization of his kingdom. It is pleasing to know that in 2003, a women's university in Kabul was named after this illustrious queen. After Balkh, Herat was the entry point for the Silk Road to Persia for traders, pilgrims, fortune seekers, and conquerors, since it was on the way to Mashhad and Rey, and not too far from Merv. While Mashhad has continued to receive waves of pilgrims from Shia communities all over the world, Rey lies in ruins or has been simply overtaken by Tehran.

***

In the recent past, there has been a renewed interest in the medieval cities that lost their glory to Mongol fury, and here Merv tops the list. While Bukhara, Samarkand, and to some extent Balkh and Herat, were rebuilt by the Timurids and Shaybanis, Nishapur, on the contrary, went into oblivion, whereas Merv (present-day Turkmenistan) is a living elegy of one of the greatest and oldest cities in the world. In 1200, with a population of half a million, it was the largest city in the world which had been established in the sixth century BCE and remained a major trading post on the Silk Road. Connected with Bukhara, Balkh to the northeast, and Nishapur and Rey in the Southeast, this must have been an urban centre of immense significance which further flourished under the Seljuks as their cherished capital. One of the longest serving kings, Sultan Sanjar, was buried in a grand mausoleum in Merv and that is the only relic—bruised no less—which still remains intact and visible from afar otherwise, as noted by George Curzon, it is a huge jumble of 'crumbling brick and clay, the spectacle of walls, towers, ramparts, and domes, stretching in bewildering confusion to the horizon'.[3] The future viceroy of India, notorious for his imperial arrogance, yet with keen interest in archaeological sites, stood aghast at the miles of rubble, dust, and the ghost-like broken structures made of brown mud bricks. Sultan Sanjar's mausoleum, patterned on Samanid Mausoleum in Bukhara, only taller, grander, and with a more elaborate exterior, was one of the central features of this once-beautiful town that was crisscrossed by a number of canals drawing water from the Murghab River flowing in from Afghanistan. Its turquoise dome was so intensely blue that according to Yaqut al-Hamawi, the Arab geographer who visited Merv in the thirteenth century, it 'could be seen from a day's journey away'.[4]

Ten thousand workmen operated Merv's water system, and its serais accommodated traders and visitors from all over the Silk Road regions, besides a major share of intellectuals such as Khayyam and Fariduddin Attar. Du Huan, a Chinese soldier who had been incarcerated in Merv as a prisoner of war for a decade in the eighth century, wrote appreciatively about the fertility of this oasis surrounded by Karakum Desert and noted: 'A big river ... flows into its territory, where it divides into several hundred canals irrigating the whole area. Villages and fences touch each other and everywhere there are trees'.[5] The tenth century Persian traveller and geographer, Al-Istakhri noted: 'For its cleanliness, its good streets, the divisions of its buildings and quarters amongst the rivers ... their city [Merv] is superior to the rest of the cities of Khurasan'. 'Of all the countries of Iran,'' Al-Istakhri wrote of Merv, 'these people were noted for their talents and education.' The tenth century Arab traveller, Ibn Hawqal recorded: 'The fruits of Merv are finer than those of any other place ... and in no other city are to be seen such palaces and groves, and gardens and streams'. Al-Hamawi, a primary source on the city's glory just before the Mongol invasion, counted at least 10 significant libraries in the city, including one attached to a major mosque that contained 12,000 volumes. He was forced to flee the libraries of Merv as the armies of Genghis Khan's son, Tolui Khan, attacked Merv. 'Verily, but for the Mongols I would have stayed and lived and died there, and hardly could I tear myself away,' he noted. In 1221, Merv was totally decimated with reportedly 700,000 of its inhabitants put to death by Tolui Khan. And it never recovered. Idrisi, the famous Sicilian cartographer was appreciative of textiles made in Merv and was fully aware of its imperial and commercial eminence, whereas Arab historian

Ibn al-Athir has offered further details on the Mongol genocide of Merv's inhabitants and the total destruction of the city's buildings, followed by arson that went on for days.[6]

In a few hours, I had left the stans behind, and after we had flown over the Caucasus, the sun and the earth were folded over by thick clouds and mist. Bavaria allowed a few glimpses of green fields and orderly habitations, typifying the German punctiliousness; however, Southwest Asia had receded far behind in distance, though not in musings and memories.

Notes

1. Mir Taqi Mir (1722–1810) was one of the pioneering Urdu poets whose romantic verses talk about an apparently unattainable beloved, and the love smitten poet sings in her praise while complaining about her irreverence to his devotion. Mir was also a witness to the destruction of Delhi by Nadir Shah in 1739 and wrote elegiac poems on large-scale massacres and devastation of this once grand Mughal capital.
2. Colloquial terms, meaning fellow brothers, often used for salutations in Rawalpindi and around.
3. George N. Curzon, *Russia in Central Asia in 1889 and the Anglo-Russian Question* (London: Longmans, Green, and Co., 1889), 135.
4. For details, see Kanishk Tharoor, 'The lost city of Merv' and 'How the magnificent city of Merv was razed—and never recovered,' *The Guardian*, August 12, 2016.
5. Ibid.
6. Ibid.

Index